"These essays continue Neil Elliott's usual wide-ranging and comprehensively critical analysis and discussion of Paul's gospel in the controlling political-economic context of the ancient Roman empire. Again and again Elliott offers insights into the implications of Paul's counter-imperial letters for struggles against the empire of global capitalism and its neoliberal ideology by secular Marxist philosophers as well as by theologians and churches. This collection of articles exposes the problems with standard misunderstandings of Paul and provides additional indications that Elliott is this generation's most profound and challenging interpreter of Paul."

—RICHARD HORSLEY
Distinguished Professor of Liberal Arts and the Study of Religion, University of
Massachusetts Boston , emeritus

"Neil Elliott's collection of essays and lectures, composed over the past thirty years, consistently confronts readers with startling and provocative questions, exposing the ideological assumptions that constrain contemporary interpretations of Paul's epistles. Based upon deep knowledge of the socioeconomic realities of the Greco-Roman world, Elliott deploys Postcolonial and Marxist strategies of reading to disclose previously occluded dimensions of Paul's thought."

—L. L. WELBORN
Professor of New Testament, Fordham University

"In his most recent collection of essays, Neil Elliott offers highly valuable insights from a wide range of scholarly approaches to Pauline studies from Marxist and Postcolonial readings to the Paul within Judaism perspective. The essays are beautifully tied together by the idea that our interpretation of Paul has much to do with how we understand our own history and responsibilities today, making it intensely relevant to a broad audience, not only one interested in Paul."

—KARIN HEDNER ZETTERHOLM
Associate Professor of Jewish Studies, Lund University

"*Currents in the Interpretation of Paul* is an important collection in its own right, but it is further so for showcasing the innovative work of Neil Elliott as among the most important in Pauline studies over the past fifty years. With learning deep and wide, Elliott goes beyond the parochialism of Pauline scholarship and engages with questions of philosophy, theory, religion, race, class, and colonialism—to name a few—and shows how significant Marxism is for the study of Christian origins and early Judaism. The advantage for those sympathetic to Elliott's readings is that they have an advocate whose work cannot be ignored."

—JAMES CROSSLEY
Professor of Bible, politics, and society, MF Oslo

"Modern New Testament scholarship features a diverse and expansive array of interpretive strategies and conversations about how Pauline texts and traditions ought to be read and understood in the contemporary world. Discussion of how and for whom such methods came to be and what work we make the Pauline corpus do with their help is less common. This welcome and timely collection of Neil Elliott's essays provides readers with a freshly textured map to navigate dense Pauline terrain, helping us understand the landscape in new and empathetic ways."

—DAVINA C. LOPEZ
Professor of religious studies, Eckerd College

Currents in the Interpretation of Paul

Currents in the Interpretation of Paul

Collected Essays

NEIL ELLIOTT

CASCADE *Books* · Eugene, Oregon

CURRENTS IN THE INTERPRETATION OF PAUL

Collected Essays

Cascade Books
An Imprint of Wipf and Stock Publishers
199 W. 8th Ave., Suite 3
Eugene, OR 97401

www.wipfandstock.com

PAPERBACK ISBN: 978–1-6667–5270–0
HARDCOVER ISBN: 978–1-6667–5271–7
EBOOK ISBN: 978–1-6667–5272–4

Cataloging-in-Publication data:

Names: Elliott, Neil, 1956–, author.
Title: Currents in the interpretation of Paul : collected essays / Neil Elliott
Description: Eugene, OR: Cascade Books, 2024. | Includes bibliographical references and index.
Identifiers: ISBN: 978–1-6667–5270–0 (PAPERBACK). | ISBN: 978–1-6667–5271–7 (HARDCOVER). | ISBN: 978–1-6667–5272–4 (EBOOK).
Subjects: LCSH: Paul, the Apostle, Saint. | Bible.—Epistles of Paul—Criticism, interpretation, etc.
Classification: BS2650.2 E45 2024 (print). | BS2650.2 (epub).

Contents

Figures

Acknowledgments

Any scholar's work depends upon a host of connections, older and newer, with friends and critics alike (often the same people). In gathering this collection of essays I have been happily reminded of conversations, many of them ongoing over the years, with Roland Boer, William S. Campbell, W. Royce Clark, Kathy Ehrensperger, Pamela Eisenbaum, Paula Fredriksen, Richard A. Horsley, Richard Hughes, Brigitte Kahl, Davina Lopez, Mark Nanos, Steve Newcom, Todd Penner, Grant Stevenson, Diana Swancutt, Larry Welborn, Vincent Wimbush, Karin Hedner Zetterholm, and Magnus Zetterholm, among many others. Of course, none of them bears responsibility for judgments expressed in the following pages.

I am particularly grateful for the interest and persistence of K. C. Hanson, longtime friend and worthy colleague in academic publishing and scholarship alike, in bringing this volume to life. Thanks also to Jeremy Funk and Ian Creeger for their meticulous work on these pages.

Chapter 1 first appeared in *Foundations & Facets Forum* 9.3–4 (1993) 237–56.

Chapter 2 was a lecture given at the University of Copenhagen in 2010. I am grateful to Troels Engberg-Pedersen, Karin Hedner Zetterholm, and Magnus Zetterholm for their kind invitations to give that and adjacent lectures, and to Karin and Magnus for their warm hospitality.

Chapter 3 first appeared in *Hidden Transcripts and the Arts of Resistance: Applying the Work of James C. Scott to Jesus and Paul*, edited by Richard A. Horsley; *Semeia* 48 (Atlanta: Scholars, 2004). Reprinted with kind permission of the Society of Biblical Literature.

Chapter 4 first appeared in *Biblical Interpretation* 13 (2005) 239–49, a special issue edited by Mark D. Nanos. I thank Mark for the invitation to participate in the volume.

Chapter 5 appeared in *The Colonized Apostle: Paul through Postcolonial Eyes*, edited by Christopher D. Stanley; Paul in Critical Contexts

(Minneapolis: Fortress, 2011); published here with kind permission of Fortress Press.

Chapter 6 appeared in the online, open-access journal *Bible and Critical Theory* 8.2 (2012) 1–12. I thank Roland Boer for the kind invitation to write for the journal.

Chapter 7 represents a lecture offered to a conference on Paul and the Philosophers at the University of British Columbia; I thank Douglas Harink for his kind invitation. It first appeared in *Paul, Philosophy, and the Theopolitical*, edited by Douglas Harink; Theopolitical Visions (Eugene, OR: Cascade Books, 2010), reprinted with kind permission of Wipf and Stock Publishers.

Chapter 8 appeared in *Paul in the Grip of the Philosophers: The Apostle and Contemporary Continental Philosophy*, edited by Peter Frick; Paul in Critical Contexts (Minneapolis: Fortress, 2013); reprinted with kind permission of Fortress Press.

Chapter 9 appeared in *Bridges in New Testament Interpretation*, which I coedited with Werner Kelber (Lanham, MD: Lexington Books/Fortress Academic, 2018). Reprinted with kind permission of Lexington Books/Fortress Academic.

Chapter 10 appeared in *Paul and Economics: A Handbook*, edited by Tom Blanton and Raymond Pickett (Minneapolis: Fortress, 2017); reprinted with kind permission of Fortress Press.

Chapter 11 began as a presentation submitted remotely to an online conference hosted by Comenius University, Bratislava, in 2022; I thank Prof. Msgr. František Ábel for his kind invitation to participate, and his kind adaptation to my circumstances. The essay appears in *Receptions of Paul in the First Two Centuries: Exploration of the Jewish Exploration of Early Christianity*, edited by František Ábel (Lanham, MD: Lexington Books/Fortress Academic, 2023). Reprinted by kind permission of Lexington Books/Fortress Academic.

Abbreviations

BibInt	*Biblical Interpretation*
BibInt	Biblical Interpretation Series
CBQ	*Catholic Biblical Quarterly*
JBL	*Journal of Biblical Literature*
JSNT	*Journal for the Study of the New Testament*
JSNTSup	Journal for the Study of the New Testament Supplements
LCL	Loeb Classical Library
NTS	*New Testament Studies*
SNTW	Studies in the New Testament and Its World
TDNT	*Theological Dictionary of the New Testament.* 10 vols. Edited by Gerhard Kittel and Gerhard Friedrich. Translated by Geoffrey W. Bromiley. Grand Rapids: Eerdmans, 1964–1976
WUNT	Wissenschaftliche Untersuchungen zum Neuen Testament

Introduction

Reading Paul in Interesting Times

"MAY YOU LIVE IN interesting times," runs the notorious blessing—or is it a curse?

No one would dispute that the phrase is an apt—if understated—characterization of the last half century, which has seen, among other dramatic developments, the collapse of the Soviet Union and the Eastern Bloc in Europe, the spread of neoliberal capitalism globally, the widening gap between a rich fraction of the population and the growing masses of the immiserated, the expansion of perpetual militarism in a global "war on terror," movements of protest and resistance, and an accelerating and irreversible degradation of the planet's climate.

"Interesting times": The phrase applies as well to biblical scholarship. This is just what we should expect. After all, academic disciplines are also expressions of cultural values and are shaped by trends and events around them, no less than any other aspect of society. The contrary notions, that theology and its auxiliary disciplines somehow float above the ephemera of worldly crisis and the sweep of history, and that theologians calmly derive sublime truths from the unchanging self-disclosure of God alone, have long seemed to me a peculiar fantasy. The related notion that these truths are divinely entrusted to one privileged segment of humanity—the church, and more particularly, to its devout biblical and theological scholars—has long struck me as rather arrogant as well.[1]

So, too, with scholarship on the apostle Paul. The serious reexaminations of Paul's relationship to Judaism that have appeared in the last fifty years arose in the terrible shadow of the Shoah. "Political" readings of the

---

1. This will seem anti-theological only to those unfamiliar with the world of analogical and metaphorical theological method, to which I was introduced already in college. Particular signposts include Baum, *Man Becoming*; Kaufman, *Essay on Theological Method*; Kaufman *In Face of Mystery*; and Keller, *Cloud of the Impossible*.

apostle proliferated as a consequence of the civil rights, Black Power, anti-war, and anti-apartheid movements. Feminism and the global decolonization movement generated their own distinct approaches, perspectives, and methodologies, not least the "hermeneutic of suspicion"; the theologies of liberation urged us to practice a "preferential option for the poor"; LGBTQ+ rights, the study of sexuality and gender, and Queer theology have challenged the cis-heterosexism that claims the Bible for its own. And so on.

To be sure, these important currents have not constituted a single mighty stream of progress toward a new interpretive future. Decades ago, Bent Noack published an essay proposing to distinguish "current and back-water in the epistle to the Romans,"[2] and the metaphor invites reuse. Which currents of interpretation pull us forward; which divert us into comfortably familiar backwaters? For every essay or movement raising questions or pointing out historical or theological or moral problems in established interpretations of Paul, there have been others offering the conventional answers—or dismissing the relevance of the questions, or suggesting the impertinence of the questioner. Some scholars decry the new approach as inappropriate; perhaps as often, others simply ignore it and continue their own course on the placid waters of Protestant theology.[3] I doubt there is another field of biblical studies where feelings run stronger regarding the goal of interpretation: is it to pass on, intact, what was delivered as a sacred trust, or to challenge hallowed convention in solidarity with those who have suffered most because of the apostle's legacy?

In this volume I do not attempt a comprehensive survey of all the important controversies in Pauline scholarship today. Rather, I have more modestly gathered essays from recent decades in which I have engaged several important questions in the field. In this effort, the book joins two other volumes of essays, one focused on the entangled questions of "Paul within Judaism" and "Paul and Empire"; the other, on the interpretation of the letter to the Romans.[4] This Introduction will describe some of the particular contexts in which the questions addressed in these pages arose.

---

2. Noack, "Current and Backwater."

3. So, feminist scholarship merits a single paragraph in Wright's survey, *Paul in Fresh Perspective*; it is not mentioned, and Marxist and postcolonial interpretation are dismissed as fads, by Hurtado, "Fashions, Fallacies, and Future Prospects."

4. See Elliott, *Paul the Jew under Roman Rule*, forthoming; Elliott, *Paul against the Nations*.

PAUL AND VIOLENCE

Early in my teaching career, colleagues at a neighboring university invited me to a conference of the newly organized Colloquium on Violence and Religion (COV&R), dedicated to applying René Girard's theorization of mimetic violence to religion and theology. I was already familiar with Girard as a theorist of religion, having read him in graduate courses at Princeton University and discussed him in the world religions courses I taught at Rutgers. As important, I had been involved since my early days at Princeton Seminary in efforts to describe and resist the systemic violence imposed by U.S. economic and political interference in Central American and Caribbean nations. The campus Plowshares group also coordinated with the area Coalition for Nuclear Disarmament, and I prepared presentations based on the memories of atomic bombings that *hibakusha,* Japanese survivors of the atomic bombings in Hiroshima and Nagasaki, had committed to paper in drawings and paintings.[5] As well, my dissertation research had immersed me in ancient and modern rhetorical theory, which routinely set persuasion over against the application of force and violence, including torture.

Now, I was thrilled by the prospect of a theoretical engagement with violence among politically engaged peers. No one had mentioned specific signal manifestations of violence, such as those at the Río Sumpul or El Mozote, for example; nor did I hear anything similar to Noam Chomsky's analysis of the distinction of "worthy" from "unworthy victims" in a functioning propaganda system, an analysis to which I was already attuned.[6] Still, the conference seemed a promising start.

That first meeting didn't go as I'd hoped. I was invited to join a panel review of Robert Hamerton-Kelly's Girardian interpretation of Paul.[7] I criticized the work for relying on unhistorical stereotypes of Judaism as a fundamentally violent religion, a theme already current among some in the COV&R set (see Chapter 1). One of my New Testament colleagues rallied to my side, but the ensuing discussion made clear that we were out of step with the COV&R program at that time. We were told that "exegetes" like the two of us—the term was meant derogatorily—"simply cannot understand theology."[8]

---

5. See Japanese Broadcasting Corporation, *Unforgettable Fire.*

6. Danner, *Massacre at El Mozote*; Chomsky and Herman, *Manufacturing Consent.* Danner's subsequent *Torture and Truth* echoed current scholarship on the conception of torture as productive of truth in ancient Greek and Roman writings, beginning with Aristotle. None of this discussion entered the COV&R orbit at the time.

7. Hamerton-Kelly, *Sacred Violence.*

8. Later that year, or the next, I attended a panel review of Hamerton-Kelly's book

In following years, I would continue to address the topic of violence, but squarely in the frame of *structural* violence within society, as articulated by Brazilian bishop and theologian Dom Hélder Câmara (see Chapter 2). I'd been turned on to his discussion of "the spiral of violence" by Richard A. Horsley's path-breaking *Jesus and the Spiral of Violence,*[9] and was impressed by a New Testament scholar relying on contemporary theoretical models from outside biblical studies to understand ancient contexts—and doing this so effectively.

Another such model to which Horsley made resort was anthropologist James C. Scott's theorization of "voice under domination," based on his studies of contemporary sites of socioeconomic exploitation. In conversation with scholars Horsley assembled in the 1990s, I attempted to apply Scott's theory to *past* communities, Paul's assemblies (see Chapter 3). Our efforts helped to launch what would in subsequent years become a sustained discussion of "hidden transcripts" in the Pauline letters.

RELIGIOUS AND NATIONAL INNOCENCE

Horsley also urged me to join with him and others in launching the "Paul and Politics" consultation, now Group, at the SBL. One of the consultation's remits, we agreed, would be the "politics" of contemporary interpretation. I'd been impressed by how quickly some circles of Pauline interpreters had responded to the challenges posed by E. P. Sanders's *Paul and Palestinian Judaism* by embracing one proposed solution, that of James D. G. Dunn's "New Perspective." This meant in various ways championing a putative early Jewish "universalism," represented (solely, it seemed) by Paul and Pauline Christianity, over against its antithesis, a predominant ancient Jewish "ethnocentrism."

Some interpreters made explicit the parallel they saw between that contrast and the opposition of modern liberal democracy to forms of ethnic or religious identitarian politics, as in Samuel P. Huntington's thesis concerning a contemporary "clash of civilizations." But I already understood that Huntington's deeply flawed work had become influential by reinforcing a dominant narrative of self-congratulation in the democratic West.[10]

---

at the SBL Annual Meeting. Daniel Boyarin's devastating critique of the book was profoundly moving and humane; Hamerton-Kelly's attempted ripostes seemed to me both cynical and shallow.

9. Horsley, *Jesus and the Spiral of Violence.*

10. Huntington, "Clash of Civilizations"; Huntington, *Clash of Civilizations*; in rebuttal, Achcar, *Clash of Barbarisms.*

I welcomed the opportunity presented by Mark D. Nanos's invitation to contribute to a special issue of *Biblical Interpretation*, to ask how much the "new perspective on Paul" owed its success to a similar congeniality with the self-congratulatory representation of cultural innocence in the West (see Chapter 4). I'd been impressed by Mark's first monograph on Romans, and our early conversations launched a long friendship. I was also pleased in that essay to be able to rely on the recent publication of Richard Hughes's *Myths America Lives By*, not least because Hughes had been one of the most influential of my religious studies professors in college and had provoked a lively interest in American civil religion.[11]

My essay now strikes me as rather dated, perhaps inevitably, though the myth of American innocence that I discussed is proving to be as consequential as ever.

The astonishing brutality of Hamas's murderous assault on Israel on October 7, 2023, retains all its shattering and heartbreaking force as I write these words, months later. Terrorists savagely killed more than one thousand Israelis and kidnapped more than 240, evoking an immediate declaration of "war" from the embattled right-wing Israeli government of Benjamin Netanyahu. That government promptly launched weeks of retaliatory bombardment and a ground invasion of Gaza, in a few weeks killing more than twelve thousand Palestinian civilians, displacing three quarters of Gaza's population, and provoking international outrage by closing off food, medical, and fuel supplies, repeatedly shutting off power and communications throughout the Strip, and targeting ostensibly civilian sites (hospitals, schools, churches) that Israel claimed Hamas was using as "shields." The onslaught continues as I write.

Those dread events have provoked a tangled firestorm of protests around the world. The vast majority of protests have called for a ceasefire, as well as for an end to Israel's long-standing occupation of Gaza and the West Bank, even as many protesters have acknowledged the horrific savagery of the Hamas attack.[12] But in the United States, some American Leftists initially expressed nothing but enthusiasm for Hamas, relying on slogans and chants that were readily heard and read by others as calling

11. Hughes, *Myths America Lives By.* I had long wanted to develop a course on American civil religion at Metropolitan State University, but could not find an adequate textbook; the available resources were an assortment of topical essays like Bellah's "American Civil Religion." After Hughes published his book—decades after he had introduced me to the topic—he informed me that he and Bellah had been co-participants in a seminar on civil religion in the 1970s. *Myths* was a rousing classroom success.

12. The rape, sexual mutilation, and torture of Israeli women by Hamas forces were not only frequent but were organized in advance: Williamson, "Israel, Gaza: Hamas Raped and Mutilated Women."

for the end of the Israeli state ("from the river to the sea . . ."). Other self-styled Leftists even offered praise for the "Al Aqsa Flood" (Hamas's name for their long-planned, murderous assault) as justified "resistance" to Israel's decades-long occupation. These seemed to me, and to others, callous as well as self-defeating moves that scandalized people of conscience. They were also senseless; romanticizing Hamas's brutality as a liberationist struggle ignored the cynical calculation of its leaders that the predictable deaths of tens of thousands of innocent Palestinians could be accounted as "martyrdoms" in pursuit of their own goals.[13]

A founding member of Democratic Socialists of America (DSA) resigned in protest of the heedless sloganeering of some DSA chapters.[14] Some Leftist faculty who championed the Hamas action as "energizing" or "exhilarating" were placed on leave or lost their academic positions. The sole Palestinian American member of Congress was censured for having invoked the slogan "from the river to the sea" at a pro-Palestine march and quickly became a target of the right-wing pro-Israel lobby AIPAC. Of course, others observed that the slogan also described a long-standing agenda *on the Israeli Right*,[15] but exploring that detail was apparently less important than enforcing solid and unflinching official support for the State of Israel.

Meanwhile, opportunists on the Right wasted no time tarring the Left in general, and criticism of Israel in particular, as anti-Semitic—*even when it came from Jews*.[16] As historian Masha Gessen observes, equating

---

13. One Gazan political scientist observed that most Palestinians "had a lot to lose" in any conflict, but Hamas members regarded civilian deaths for "a just cause" as worthy (Rasgon and Kirkpatrick, "What Was Hamas Thinking?"). Hamas gained a measure of political power at the cost of thousands of Palestinian lives (Hubbard, "While Gazans Suffer").

14. Isserman, "Why I Just Quit DSA." The DSA's national web page published a statement on October 7 declaring the Hamas attack to be "the direct result of Israel's apartheid regime"; while it went on to stipulate that "we unequivocally condemn the killing of all civilians," Hamas's assault was not specifically condemned, but rather seemed implicitly to be justified: "this was not unprovoked." In contrast, the Episcopal caucus of the DSA (of which I am a member) issued much more profound statements of grief, condolence, and protest, including links to a variety of Episcopal Church resources.

15. Historian Omer Bartov was interviewed on *DemocracyNow.com* on November 10, 2023 (Bartov, "From the River to the Sea"). Similarly, Rashid Khalidi observed that "Far from being a mere slogan, the phrase captures both the longtime ambitions of the Israeli right and the reality Israel has imposed on Palestine since 1967" (Khalidi, "It's Time"). The Likud Party platform of 1977 declared, "The right of the Jewish people to the land of Israel is eternal and indisputable . . . therefore, Judea and Samaria will not be handed to any foreign administration; *between the Sea and the Jordan* there will only be Israeli sovereignty" (emphasis added).

16. Lee, "Anti-Defamation League Maps Jewish Peace Rallies." Naomi Klein pointed

criticism of Israeli state policies with anti-Semitism has opened important doors—in the U.S. and Europe alike—for the hard Right to vilify, harass, and prosecute Left-leaning Jews and Muslims. It bears reflection that the same White House occupant who celebrated "fine people on both sides" in Charlottesville, Virginia—including the khaki-clad racists chanting "Jews will not replace us!"—enthusiastically signed an executive order to withhold federal funding from colleges where students were not "protected" from listening to criticism of Israel's occupation. In the politically polarized United States, it seems, "anti-Semitism" is often in the eye of the beholder.[17]

Another reflex on the Left was to protest Israel's "settler colonialism," a shorthand that also provoked criticism.[18] Scholars like Israeli historian Ilan Pappé nevertheless have had no trouble describing Mandatory Palestine as a colonial enterprise.[19] It seems to me that a more precise designation of the broad historical phenomenon would be "settler colonialism by proxy," since many of the effective decisions regarding settling European Jews in British-Mandate Palestine were made by Great Britain and the United States, and the international organs they dominated, in their pursuit of the region's resources. But somehow, acknowledging those facts seems to detract from the romantic picture, popular after 1967, of Israel as a scrappy, independent little nation of brave, self-made pioneers. Israel's continuing dependence on U.S. support and cover, not least at the UN, extends an older story.

Other protesters have called for an end to Israel's "genocide," prompting more critiques of an out-of-touch Left. One counterargument was, in effect, that (until the current catastrophe) Israel's forces have managed to kill only a few thousand Palestinians at a time, surely not rising to the level of "genocide."[20] The point was awkwardly made, but undeniable. More precise language appeared earlier in the UN Human Rights Council's Goldstone Report (2009), which described Israel's conduct of Operation Cast

---

out, one week into Israel's bombardment of Gaza, that the Jewish Voice for Peace protest in the U.S. Capitol rotunda was the largest such event ever; such Jewish demonstrations (including in Israel) only grew in size and number over following weeks. Sirota, "Naomi Klein and Omar Baddar Discuss."

17. Gessen, "In the Shadow of the Holocaust."

18. In the pages of the *Atlantic*, Simon Sebag Montefiore protested that "The Decolonization Narrative Is Dangerous and False"; he meant that European refugees couldn't be considered "colonizers," and besides, other settler-colonial enterprises were both more successful and more deadly. At the November 2023 SBL Annual Meeting, Mark Leuchter critiqued a number of facile protests of Israeli "colonialism" and pled for sound academic reasoning even in wrenching circumstances ("Leveraging the Academy against Itself").

19. Pappé, *History of Modern Palestine*, ch. 3.

20. Montefiore, "Decolonization Narrative."

Lead (2008–9) as a "deliberate policy" of "disproportionate destruction and violence against civilians" in Gaza, "a deliberately disproportionate attack designed to *punish, humiliate, and terrorize* a civilian population." The operation constituted "massive war crimes and possible crimes against humanity"—as did Hamas's barbarity, though the Report stipulated that the vast difference in scale was significant. The Israeli campaign seemed designed so that "the civilian population would find life so intolerable that they would leave (if that were possible) or turn Hamas out of office."[21] The latter alternative—if actually imagined by any Israeli officials—was fanciful; Hamas's grip on Gaza hardly afforded the population any meaningful political agency.[22] But the current displacement of some 1.8 million Palestinians (out of a total population of 2.1 million) seems to confirm the lively anticipation by at least some Israeli officials of the first alternative, the forced depopulation of Gaza, giving weight to the charge of "ethnic cleansing" (which historian Pappé finds an appropriate description for the intentions and actions of prominent Israelis already in the beginnings of the state).[23] Months into its war in Gaza, members of Netanyahu's government expressly called for the depopulation of the Strip and denied the possibility that any of its residents should be held harmless.[24] Meanwhile, in the U.S., the son-in-law of one presidential nominee—and his former "senior foreign policy advisor" in the Middle East—has publicly urged the forced removal of Gaza's population into the Negev in order to facilitate the development of the splendid potential of Gaza as waterfront property.[25]

If what other observers have described as an apartheid regime has continued over decades, despite the collective will of the vast majority of the UN's member states and a majority of Israelis themselves for a two-state solution, it is in part because the longest-lasting administration in Israel's history has found it convenient to perpetuate unstable rivalries in the Occupied Territories, even by "propping up" Hamas, to avoid precisely such

---

21. United Nations, Human Rights Council, *Report*; see Finkelstein, *Method and Madness*.

22. Rasgan and Kirkpatrick, "What Was Hamas Thinking?"

23. Pappé, *History of Palestine*, ch. 4. Moshe Dayan was clear enough in his boasts to a university audience in 1969: "We came here to a country that was populated by Arabs, and we are building here a Hebrew, Jewish state. Instead of Arab villages, Jewish villages were established. You do not even know the names of these villages . . . all the [Arab] villages do not exist . . . There is not a single Jewish settlement not established in the place of a former Arab village." Awad and Levin, "Roots of the Nakba," 20, quoting from Shoenman, *Hidden History*, 41.

24. Tharoor, "Israeli Right"; Ha'aretz, "'100–200,000, not Two Million.'"

25. Wintour, "Jared Kushner says."

a possibility;[26] and in part because the United States has long exerted its tremendous political, economic, and military power to protect Israel from accountability to international law. So, while in the White House, Donald Trump abandoned the two-state framework, approved Israel's annexation of the Golan and the West Bank, green-lighting accelerated Israeli settlement of the Occupied Territories, and moved the U.S. embassy from Tel Aviv to Jerusalem.

President Joe Biden has not reversed those moves. In these latest awful and tumultuous weeks, he has offered unflagging political support and cover to Israel, rebuffing calls for a ceasefire, even vetoing an urgent call for the same at the United Nations, and, in end-runs around U.S. law and State Department policy, providing unprecedented military support on a massive scale—five times the usual annual appropriation to Israel, which was already almost half of all U.S. military appropriations worldwide. Those apparent breaches of U.S. and international law have provoked the resignations of a State Department official responsible for monitoring foreign arms appropriations and an official of the UN Relief and Works Agency, and the protests of numerous administration advisers who feared the U.S. risked being made complicit in war crimes.[27] The Biden administration continues to declare itself committed to a two-state solution, and opposed to the forcible displacement of Palestinians from Gaza, or any effort to reoccupy, blockade, or besiege Gaza or reduce its territory.[28] But a leaked report from Israeli intelligence floats precisely the emptying of Gaza as the optimal endgame for the current campaign, in line with the most extremist elements in Netanyahu's governing coalition.[29] None of this seems to have caused a moment of hesitation in wholehearted practical U.S. support for the destruction of Gaza.

It is hard to see that the state of Israel will face any consequences for flouting the wistfully expressed preferences of its unstinting benefactor. For that reason, it is as hard to imagine that the world will soon unlearn what

26. Schneider, "For years, Netanyahu propped up Hamas"; earlier, Finkelstein, *Method and Madness*.

27. A. Goodman, "State Department Official Resigns"; Pilkington, "Top UN official." NBC reported on November 2, 2023, that "[a]dministration officials [were] worried that the president's quick support for Israel after Hamas' attack could backfire" (Lee and Kube, "Biden Officials Voice New Concerns"). According to CNN, advisers warned Israel that it had "limited time" to continue its relentless assault on Gaza "before uproar over the humanitarian suffering and civilian casualties—and calls for a ceasefire—reaches a tipping point" (Liptak et al., "U.S. Warns Israel," Nov. 3).

28. Goals stated by Secretary of State Anthony Blinken and NSC spokesperson John Kirby: Lee, "Blinken Will Return."

29. A. Goodman, "Another Nakba?"

journalist Nesrine Malik has called an "intense lesson in Western hypocrisy." She attributed what she described as an increasingly prevalent "sense of losing your mind" to the fact that "western powers are unable to credibly pretend that there is some global system of rules that they uphold. They seem simply to say: there are exceptions, and that's just the way it is," at least until Israeli authorities decide otherwise.

None of this should minimize the execrable violence of Hamas. But it is self-evident to very many of us, Malik writes, that the truly "horrific events of 7 October cannot be erased by even more horror." We are being asked nevertheless to accept as noble the calculation that they can. "The lesson," she writes, "is brutal and short: human rights are not universal and international law is arbitrarily applied."[30] Nevertheless, U.S. policy continues to be cloaked in solemn professions of our constant "friendship" with Israel, which redounds on our nation as proof of its righteous exceptionalism and its innocence.[31]

I invoke these realities to describe some of the vertiginous context in which the study of Paul is carried out today. Efforts to understand Paul "within Judaism" have been dismissed, on one side, by scholars convinced that his Judaism may have consisted in loyalty to his ethnic group, a Jewishness *kata sarka,* but nothing more—and that efforts to understand him *theologically* "within Judaism" are the results of misty-eyed post-Holocaust sentimentality.[32] Meanwhile, in other circles, dedicated precisely to placing Paul—along with the rest of the New Testament—"within Judaism," some participants seem committed to exonerating all of Christianity's founding documents from any complicity with the long history of supersessionism or anti-Judaism.[33] The Messianic Jewish movement has been invoked in some "within Judaism" and "post-supersessionist" discussions as a remarkable, even miraculous contemporary continuation of Paul's very Jewish gospel. Other scholars have worried, however, that a more generalized celebration of Messianic Judaism risks an overlap with Christian Zionism, with its fantasies of contemporary "Judea and Samaria" (Israel and occupied Palestine) as a site of eschatological fulfillment—and a corresponding enthusiasm for the settler movement in Palestine.[34] The rush to proclaim Jewish-Christian harmony before the Jews, Christians, and Muslims of Palestine are safe from annihilation seems premature.

30. Malik, "War in Gaza."

31. See also Ackerman, "What the Rules Allow."

32. Wright, *Paul and the Faithfulness of God,* 1413.

33. Consider the agenda of the Society for Post-Supersessionist Theology.

34. DuToit, "Radical New Perspective."

I invoke the ongoing catastrophe in Israel and Palestine, not only out of a profound sense of solidarity with the powerless, but in order to press home the need for clear thinking and an appreciation of the gravity of history, not least as we engage in biblical interpretation. Myths of innocence—whether national, religious, or academic—are as dangerous today as they are abundant and influential.

PAUL AND MARXIST THOUGHT

My interest in the politics of interpretation has extended to other areas as well. More than a decade ago, I heard scholars in several different conference sessions refer to "implicit Marxism" in biblical scholarship—apparently meaning the occasional bursts of interest in questions of class or the material basis of history. I was more impressed at the time by the resistance that any reference to Marx could occasion, outside of narrowly drawn circles. "Social-scientific" scholarship seemed studiously to avoid Marxist categories, when not deliberately flouting them, and even ostensibly respectful references often relayed misapprehensions of Marxist categories. Two essays on the matter appear here as Chapters 5 and 6.

I have read Marx and Marxists, and have been impressed with (a) the candor of Marxists about the limitations of Marx's own thought and its predictive value; (b) Marxists' unrelenting interest in the conditions of the exploited classes—unusual enough in an age where even the use of the term "exploitation" can invite sneers from pundits and elected officials alike; and (c) Marxists' genuine sympathetic interest in religion as a social phenomenon. I have been surprised, and in equal measures amused and discomfited, when I have been invited to write an essay or respond academically to others on the basis of my acquaintance with the Marxist tradition. I have taken such invitations as an indicator, not of my own erudition, but of the fact that genuine interest in that tradition, such as mine, is still a remarkable rarity among biblical scholars and theologians.

The obvious exception to that statement is the explosion of interest over the last few decades in Marxist or "post-Marxist" thinkers who have made appeal to the apostle Paul. Sometimes grouped together as "the Continental philosophers," figures including Benjamin, Althusser, Deleuze and Guattari, Taubes, Badiou, Agamben, and Žižek have inspired important philosophical and political discussions. The interest these cultured nonbelievers have shown in the apostle has strangely warmed the hearts of many of the faithful in the guild of New Testament studies. It is easy to regard this enthusiasm with some skepticism. If we are not pious antiquarians after all, then, but chic, avant-garde, *relevant* to our universities, has this relevance been purchased at the cost, yet again, of throwing Judaism under the theological bus? And was the resort to a figure from the distant past an entertaining way for "new Leftists" to distract ourselves from the complexity of contemporary struggles for socialism? Many of the discussions among Paul scholars have not concerned questions of class struggle or historical agency. It seems that the philosophers have given Pauline studies an important, but possibly transitory relevance in the university curriculum, more than they have reoriented the field around dialectical-material concerns. Two of my essays here address those questions (see Chapters 7 and 8). I am grateful to Douglas Harink for his invitation to a conference at the University of British Columbia, and to Peter Frick for his invitation to contribute to a volume of essays on these concerns.

PAUL AND ECONOMIC REALITIES

New questions about the "politics" of Paul's world and of contemporary interpretation alike have gone hand in hand with questions about economics—a subject, remarkably, that some acclaimed "social-science" interpreters have flatly, though unconvincingly, declared irrelevant to the ancient world.[35] Important work by Stephen Friesen, Justin Meggitt, and Peter Oakes, among others, has awakened new awareness of the presence and salience of poverty in Pauline studies.[36] My own experiences in and around Haiti—including participation in a human rights investigation in 1995 and work on the U.S. staff of a Haitian NGO in 2000 and 2001—brought home to me the depth of material realities involved in proper political interpretation.[37] Chapter 9 addresses the relevance of economic realities for aspects of New Testament studies more broadly; Chapter 10 is more focused on the interpretation of Paul's exhortations regarding the Lord's Supper in Corinth.

PAUL'S CONTESTED LEGACY

The final essay in this volume concerns the afterlife of the Pauline legacy. It resulted from an invitation by Msgr. Prof. František Ábel to participate

35. See e.g. Malina and Pilch, *Social-Science Commentary on the Letters of Paul.*

36. I rely here on critiques in Friesen, "Poverty in Pauline Studies"; Friesen, "Blessings of Hegemony"; Meggitt, *Paul, Poverty and Survival*; Oakes, *Reading Romans in Pompeii.*

37. Advocates for Human Rights, *Another Violence against Women.* I served for a year as development director and then assistant director of the Lambi Fund of Haiti.

in a conference in Bratislava concerned with the representation of Paul's Judaism in the post-Pauline literature. (I was unable to travel, but Professor Ábel allowed me to submit a video presentation, and I give him my warm thanks for his generosity.) My first purpose was to discuss the historical and theoretical work of Willie James Jennings, whose *The Christian Imagination*[38] launched an important agenda for investigating the Christian theological origins of the Western legacy of dispossession. I defend his work against a particular criticism that I find off target. But I also offer a friendly amendment: what Jennings finds as a Pauline foundation for the theology of dispossession is, I argue, rooted rather in the pseudo-Pauline Ephesians. It is a theology, I have argued elsewhere as well as here, that Paul sought to resist in his own letter to the Romans. That the apostle may have failed in his effort—a failure that coincides substantially with the reception of Ephesians as a "quintessential" summary of the Pauline gospel—only reinforces my sense that how we understand Paul has much to do with how we understand our own history and our responsibilities today.

I am aware of some overlap and repetition across these essays, which is perhaps inevitable; I hope it is not too distracting. I have not edited the essays beyond bringing them into some stylistic conformity, especially regarding citations.

The reader may observe some terminological variation over the years in which these essays were written. I have translated the Greek *Ioudaioi* as "Jews" but also, in more recent essays, as "Judeans," meaning with the latter word to indicate the geographic and ethnic sense of the term but without restricting it to those meanings. (The effort of some interpreters to render *Ioudaioi* as a merely geographic term used by "Israelites" elsewhere, e.g., in Galilee, seems to me transparently to serve theological or apologetic Christian interests, and I find it unconvincing.) Although I used the term "Gentile" or "Gentile-Christian" in earlier essays, it has always troubled me: the Roman world knew no ethnic identification of "Gentiles," and Paul's use of the plural *ethnē* fairly clearly continues the Septuagintal use that is almost always rendered "nations," i.e. "the nations other than Israel." Finally, I do not now think the term "Christian" is appropriate for Paul's time, and try various alternatives in one or another essay, none to my own complete satisfaction.

---

38. Jennings, *Christian Imagination*.

Finally, the breadth of subjects addressed over the years represented in these essays impresses me that we continue to live in tumultuous times, when what the *Book of Common Prayer* calls the "evil forces that corrupt and destroy the creatures of God" remain as powerful—and, as theologians like William Stringfellow encourage us to add, as cunning—as ever. Resisting those forces, and respecting "the dignity of every human being," are commitments in my church's Baptismal Covenant. They continue to inform my work, however imperfectly. May they haunt the reception of these essays.[39]

39. Episcopal Church, *Book of Common Prayer 1979*, 304–5.

1

Paul and the Lethality of the Law

IN HIS REMARKABLE NEW book *Sacred Violence: Paul's Hermeneutic of the Cross,* Robert G. Hamerton-Kelly applies René Girard's theory of mimetic rivalry to the interpretation of Paul. The book makes three arguments: (a) that Girard's theory allows us to "decode texts," Paul's letters serving as the test case (39); that Paul's letters themselves constitute an application—by Paul—of a "hermeneutic of the Cross," a sort of proto-Girardian deconstruction in which the violence in his own religion and culture was disclosed (63); and (c) that Paul's writings are therefore an appropriate basis for "rethinking Christianity" along the lines of a cultural renunciation of violence (60). The last argument depends upon the second argument holding up to critical scrutiny, and it is to such scrutiny that most of this essay is devoted.

First, however, one suspects that Hamerton-Kelly has not selected Paul's letters as a test application of Girard's theory at random. There is a great deal at stake in this project, and it is here I wish to begin.

WHAT IS AT STAKE?

René Girard has set forward a comprehensive theory revealing the origins of human culture in the mystification of mimetic violence. Sacrifice, law, religious ritual, all of culture are constituted from a tremendous redirection of violence toward appropriate victims, and the consequent misapprehension of that redirection through myth and ritual. The theory suggests, Girard observes, that "human culture is predisposed to the permanent concealment of its origins in collective violence." Yet Girard also claims to reveal what culture conceals, and thus confronts us with a dilemma. Either he is wrong, or there is some vantage-point within human culture that allows him—and us—to escape the "ethnocentrism" of our own culture and reveal, and possibly disarm, the mechanisms of sacred violence at its heart.[1]

How is this possible? How can Girard (or any of us) in fact escape this deadly ethnocentric self-deception? Girard identifies his vantage-point unequivocally: the Christian Bible provides the "force of revelation" that militates constantly against the dynamics of mimetic violence.[2]

Suddenly, the issue seems to have shifted from anthropology to theology. If Girard is right, the revelation claimed at the heart of Christian religion not only is true, but is the only hope for the survival of our species.

This possibility is the horizon of Hamerton-Kelly's project. He writes, "Girard points us to a possible restatement of biblical faith that places it at the center of the struggle for a culture beyond violence. This possibility demands to be taken seriously, for the sake of the Bible and the culture." Hamerton-Kelly focuses on the writings of Paul, one segment of the biblical deposit that "reveals the founding mechanisms with extraordinary frankness and so speaks a clear word of criticism and hope to our time of limitless violence. I call this application of the theory of sacred violence a hermeneutic of the Cross" (59–60).

Girard finds the scapegoat mechanism exposed in the Bible, and declares that this exposure reaches a "climax" in the Gospels, especially in the accounts of the Passion, which are clearly written from the perspective of the Victim. He is aware of suggestions in recent scholarship that the Gospels also conceal a victimage mechanism or perpetuate victimage themselves, specifically by exonerating Rome for the crucifixion and shifting blame for Jesus' death onto the Jews of Jerusalem; but these suggestions he dismisses as modern "sentimentalism," the view of those baser souls who "would explain everything in the New Testament in the most ignoble light"; pursuit of these suggestions is "a waste of time," among "the most foolish undertakings of mankind."[3]

Although Hamerton-Kelly seems more willing to admit—in theory— that the Gospels themselves may include a *mixture* of concealment and

---

1. Girard, *Scapegoat,* 100. Girard's theory is worked out in a number of books, including Girard, *Violence and the Sacred*; Girard, *Things Hidden since the Foundation of the World* (with Jean-Michel Oughourlian and Guy Lefort); and Hamerton-Kelly, *Violent Origins.*

2. Girard, *Scapegoat,* 100; Girard, *Things Hidden,* 138.

3. Hamerton-Kelly, *Violent Origins,* 143; Girard, *Scapegoat,* 106, 109.

revelation,[4] he follows Girard in insisting that even if subsequent genera-
tions of Christians have misinterpreted the Gospels, Christianity is, *at its
origins,* innocent of sacred violence (11). That is a theological statement at
variance with recent Gospel criticism.[5]

Already D. F. Strauss had proposed (1835) that the Gospels represent
mythic projections of the self-consciousness of early Christians; in the
1920s, Rudolf Bultmann's form-criticism directed attention decisively to
early Christian *communities.* Rosemary Radford Ruether (1974) provoked
a lively debate that continues today, whether these mythifications of community self-consciousness were inherently and inextricably anti-Jewish. To
be precise, the question concerns whether the Passion narratives have purchased the demonstration of Jesus' messianic identity at the cost of exonerating the Roman governor and shifting the blame for Jesus' death onto the
Jewish population of Jerusalem. Note that this assessment exactly resembles
Hamerton-Kelly's own description of persecution texts, which "accuse their
victims of incredible crimes"—the murder of the Son of God, in this case;
"although the texts accept those accusations as true, we know them to be
false. We also know the victims and their sufferings to be real. Thus we have
an instance of the founding mechanism working before our eyes" (38).

Do the Gospels expose the victimage mechanism, or do they perpetuate it? The question is, in part, a matter of historical-critical inquiry. To any
who give credence to the profile of Pilate's rule in Judea sketched in the history of Flavius Josephus, the Gospel accounts will appear "scarcely credible
as history."[6]

Literary criticism of the Gospels, with an eye to determining their
propaganda purposes, is also involved. The case for generative violence in
the "deep structure" of these narratives is easiest to make in the Gospel of
Matthew, where Jesus actually pronounces his Pharisaic opponents guilty

4. Noting that feminist biblical scholars routinely distinguish elements of a "tradition of liberation" in the Bible from evidence of "a deceiving patriarchal tradition" per-
vading the Bible, Hamerton-Kelly suggests that Girard also reads the Bible as "texts in
travail between myth and the gospel—that is, between the concealment of violence and
victimage, on the one hand, and their disclosure, on the other" (55–56). But his citation
of Girard does not support this reading. Girard locates *us* "between myth and gospel"
(see Hamerton-Kelly, *Violent Origins,* 145); he nowhere admits, and in fact denies the
presence of (scapegoating) myth in the Gospels themselves.

5. See especially Mack, "Innocent Transgressor."

6. This is Paula Fredriksen's sustained argument throughout *From Jesus to Christ,*
chapter 7. Although she does not discuss Girard's work, her interpretation of the development of christology and of the composition of the Gospels is remarkably comple-
mentary to Girard's theory (but applied to the Gospels themselves: see below).

of "all the innocent blood shed on earth"[7] from the foundation of the world
(23:35), and pronounces God's punishment on the Jewish population of Jerusalem (23:36–39; cf. 21:33–34; 22:1–10); and where, a few chapters later,
the Jewish people accept the curse: "his blood be on our heads and the heads
of our children" (27:25). Matthew's reader recognizes the allusion immediately: despite forty intervening years of increasing violence, the reader is to
understand that the destruction of Jerusalem in 70 CE *was caused by* Jesus'
murder *by the Jews of Jerusalem.*

I think it would be hard to find a clearer example of a persecution
text, or of Girard's concept of mimetic rivalry. Matthew's community, affirming the crucified Messiah's lordship over human history, is plunged
into mimetic rivalry as lordship over human history becomes the apparent
prerogative *of the Roman legions.* Rather than risk annihilation in the direct
(albeit symbolic) confrontation of its God with Rome, the Matthean myth
deflects mimetic violence onto the available victims—the tens of thousands
of Jews who died in the Roman suppression of Judea. The result of this sacred violence (God's own vengeance for the murder of his beloved son) is
peace, namely, harmony with Rome (expressed mythically in Pilate's excul-
pation of Jesus).

The scapegoat mechanism is perhaps clearest in Matthew, but it has
been detected in the other Gospels as well, through historical and literary-
critical arguments that (unlike Hamerton-Kelly) I find compelling, but will
not attempt to defend here.[8] Rather than argue the relative complicity of
each Gospel, I wish to return to the question of vantage-point: How is it
possible for modern biblical scholars to discover a scapegoat mechanism
that has lain concealed in plain view in the Gospel for twenty centuries?

To judge from the absence of explicit citation, it is not because these
biblical scholars have read Girard. Neither is their insight *simply* the result of
rigorous application of the appropriate historical or literary-critical methods (the methods have been employed previously without reaching these
results). Rather, the insight into the victimage mechanism in the Gospels
is usually linked to a particular historical context in which we are increasingly aware of the Christian victimization of Jews, namely, the aftermath
of the Nazi attempt to annihilate Jews and Judaism and the perception of
Christian complicity in that attempt. We recognize victimage in the Gospels
because we have been confronted with the horror of the Holocaust. Yet even
here we have not necessarily transcended the limits of ethnocentrism in

7. Translations of biblical quotations are mine unless otherwise specified.

8. On the Gospels in general, see the survey in Fredriksen, *From Jesus to Christ,* ch.
8; on Mark in particular, see Mack, *Myth of Innocence.*

the American theological context, since the victims of the Holocaust are not usually perceived by Americans as "our" victims; in fact the Holocaust has become paradigmatic for Christian theology during the same time that Reinhold Niebuhr's dialectic of love and justice has provided a theological legitimation for *Realpolitik*. The theological and moral lessons of the Second World War are often perceived selectively: we speak more often of "post-Holocaust" theology, not "post-Hiroshima" or "post-Dresden" theology.[9]

These admittedly provocative theses are meant to express a pervasive doubt that we can escape the delusions of ethnocentrism simply by virtue of our participation in the Christian theological tradition, since that tradition derives from founding narratives that function precisely as myths of sacred violence. We must take a different vantage-point, from which the biblical (and theological and liturgical) traditions themselves may be criticized and, possibly, reformulated. I also suspect that mere possession of Girard's theory as a hermeneutical tool will not provide that vantage-point.[10]

What is called for is a moral conversion in which we recognize *our own* complicity in violence by coming to identify with *our own* victims and take their part.

But this brings us to Hamerton-Kelly's discussion of Paul.

THE SIGNIFICANCE OF
A GIRARDIAN READING OF PAUL

There are several reasons *prima facie* why one might hope to find in Paul what (in my view) the Gospels cannot provide, namely, a genuinely Christian hermeneutic innocent of mimetic rivalry. First, Paul carried out his apostolate *before* the Judean War that (on the theory sketched above) so determined the shape of the Gospels, and (arguably) before the Jewish "rejection" of the Christian message had become a historical *fait accompli*. The possibility arises that Paul's thinking and practice may be innocent of the anti-Jewish scapegoating mechanisms endemic to the next Christian generation.

Second, since the 1970s, Pauline studies have been convulsed by questions raised in the "post-Holocaust situation." That decade saw the

9. Note a significant exception in Hamerton-Kelly's question, how we might understand the theological task "in the light of the burning children of Auschwitz and Hiroshima" (*Sacred Violence*, 15).

10. I dissent here from Hamerton-Kelly's comments about "biblical enlightenment," because of which "we can no longer ritualize or rationalize our violence" (*Sacred Violence*, 39), and from his apologetic defense of the innocence of Christian theology (*Sacred Violence*, 48–54).

publication of Ruether's indictment of Paul as a mythologizer of early Christian anti-Judaism (1974); E. P. Sanders's demonstration that Paul's "attack" on Jewish works-righteousness was historically unsupportable from extant Jewish literature, and his corollary hypothesis that Paul's (anti-Jewish) theology was fundamentally illogical (1977, 1983); and Krister Stendahl's plea (1976) for a thoroughly historical-critical reading of Paul free from the theological agendas of Western, "introspective" Christianity (the legacy of Augustine and, more specifically, Luther: original essay, 1963). If Gospel studies have proceeded to chart the "anti-Judaic left hand" of the Gospel narratives, Pauline studies have been plunged into a fierce debate over whether Paul *has* an anti-Judaic left hand. The only point of wide agreement—constituting "the New Perspective on Paul"[11]—seems to be that the "Lutheran" reading of Paul (as an opponent of Jewish works-righteousness) is untenable.

Third, an important stream of modern Protestant scholarship has emphasized the centrality of the Cross of Christ in Paul's thought, and has also sharply distinguished Paul's interpretation of the Cross from the "sacrificial" interpretation of Jesus' death current among other sectors of the early church. Rudolf Bultmann, for example, wrote that in Paul's thinking about the Cross, "the categories of cultic-juristic thinking are broken through: *Christ's death* is not merely a sacrifice which cancels the guilt of sin (i.e., the punishment contracted by sinning), but is also *the means of release from the powers of this age: Law, Sin, and Death.*"[12] The same contrast is at the center of the more recent "apocalyptic" interpretation of Paul.[13]

At the same time, grave doubts about Paul's insight into mimetic violence emerge from a different quarter. It is a commonplace in current literature that Paul's ethical teachings reflect a marked social conservatism, a "love patriachalism" that leaves unjust social structures intact while promoting an ameliorative ethos of camaraderie within the Christian congregation.[14]

This conservatism is often attributed to Paul's "missionary" or "pastoral" concern that his congregations escape public criticism by conforming to prevailing standards of decorum. Given that in several of his letters Paul seems to oppose a more conservative policy to more egalitarian implications that some Christians have drawn from his proclamation for their common life, it is reasonable to suggest that the mechanisms of mimetic rivalry may

11. See Dunn, "New Perspective on Paul."

12. Bultmann, *Theology of the New Testament*, 1:297–98 (emphasis in original).

13. Beker, *Paul the Apostle*; Käsemann, *Commentary on Romans*.

14. Troeltsch, *Social Teaching of the Christian Churches*; Theissen, *Social Setting of Pauline Christianity*.

play a significant role in Paul's thought after all—directed, however, toward socially stratified congregations in the cities of the Empire.[15] A related issue is Paul's apparent endorsement of the coercive violence of the Roman state in Romans 13. Hamerton-Kelly argues that Paul encourages a "rational curb on rivalry by the responsible acceptance of the differentiated functions of an ordered society" (151), and "defends the state's monopoly on vindication" (155). Whether he successfully exonerates Paul from being an advocate for the *Roman* system of sacred violence is debatable.

But these issues would take us far afield from the focus of this essay. In what follows I turn to issues of interpretation regarding Paul and the Torah.

QUESTIONS ABOUT
THE ARGUMENT IN *SACRED VIOLENCE*

It would be hard to exaggerate the significance of the work before us. Hamerton-Kelly has proposed and worked out a comprehensive alternative to the major interpretations of Paul in the Western tradition, and in so doing proposes to resolve some of the most controverted issues in recent Pauline interpretation. With Martin Luther, he understands Paul's thought to center in a hermeneutic of the Cross (5); yet against Luther (and, following him, Bultmann), he doubts that that hermeneutic centers in Paul's opposition to Jewish legalism, "works-righteousness," or the "legal demand of obedience" (7). Hamerton-Kelly relies here on E. P. Sanders, who has demonstrated in his 1977 book that the sort of Jewish works-righteousness long assumed to be the object of Paul's attack in fact never predominated in ancient Judaism.

Yet Hamerton-Kelly dissents from Sanders's corollary argument that *since* the Jewish legalism Paul appears to attack did not in fact exist, that attack does not proceed from any negative experience of Judaism on Paul's part. Sanders describes Paul as a convert whose enthusiasm for a new allegiance exceeds his ability or interest in rational argument, and declares that "In short, *this is what Paul finds wrong in Judaism: it is not Christianity.*"[16]

Hamerton-Kelly agrees that Paul has changed allegiances, but believes (against Sanders) that this change is occasioned by a profound insight into "the sacred violence in his ancestral religion"; in a paraphrase of Sanders, he writes that for Paul "the problem with Judaism was . . . that it was a sacrificial structure of sacred violence" (6–7). This insight is won through

---

15. See discussions in Schüssler Fiorenza, *In Memory of Her*; and more recently in Wire, *Corinthian Women Prophets*.

16. Sanders, *Paul and Palestinian Judaism*, 552 (emphasis in original).

the crucifixion of Jesus, which becomes in Paul's thinking "not a sacrificial mechanism but the deconstruction of sacrifice" (60).

Hamerton-Kelly expects such provocative remarks to spark instant reactions in the current discussion of Paul and Judaism; thus he declares in a Preface that he has "tried to nuance" his interpretations so as not to give offense, although he could not "remove the 'offense' that is plainly there, that Paul rejected his ancestral religion because of the violence he perceived in it. So be it" (xiii). Readers are challenged to approach the historical question honestly, not cringing from uncomfortable facts; to "take seriously Paul's attack on Judaism, and Judaism's attack on Paul" (64).

Taking Paul's attitude toward Judaism seriously is at once the most urgent and the most controversial task in Pauline studies today. It is therefore imperative to use language carefully, not only to avoid "unnecessary offense" but also in order to lay any claim to historical precision. When historical interpretation is our concern, and it is Hamerton-Kelly's (4), confirmation or disconfirmation of hypotheses must outweigh the "elegance" of theories (3); some of the most elegant theories in Pauline studies now stand abandoned, and for good reason. I believe Paul's "hermeneutic of the Cross" can indeed serve the purposes the book envisions, but I also consider several of the book's hypotheses concerning Paul's "repudiation of his ancestral religion" to be misrepresentations of Paul that may serve to *deflect* from that goal.

Which "Judaism" Is in View?

At the beginning of chapter 3 we find the declaration that Paul's understanding of Judaism as a structure of sacred violence "emerged from within Paul's own experience and should therefore not be generalized to all the Judaism of that time" (63). If the Cross is for Paul "an epiphany of the violence of the primitive Sacred in Judaism," this does not mean that "all Judaism at that time was violent in this way, nor that it was without its own antidotes to sacred violence, but only that the Cross and the experience of Paul are authentic disclosures of the sacred violence that was indeed present" (65). These are, I think, essential qualifications, but they are not carried through consistently. Instead the word "Judaism" is used in at least three senses, without discrimination: (a) to refer to *Judaism in general* in Paul's day; (b) to refer to *Judaism as Paul had experienced it,* however representative or unrepresentative this might have been of Judaism in general; and (c) to refer to *the object of Paul's remarks,* whatever their relation to his own experience *of Judaism.*

If the issue is—as Hamerton-Kelly's comments suggest (64)—the sort of "Jewish collaboration with the Roman power" that Josephus allows us to locate in the ruling priestly aristocracy in Jerusalem, it would be preferable to use *that* (admittedly cumbersome) phrase—and then to go on to describe the range of Jewish opposition to such collaboration; that is, to set Paul's reaction within the range of sacred violence *and antidotes to sacred violence* within Judaism. Curiously, Hamerton-Kelly refuses to separate the temple priesthood, "a sordid establishment of collaborators and quislings, quite capable of feeding victims to the Roman terror" (11), from Judaism as such. In fact, he labels the suggestion that the Jerusalem priesthood was less than "truly Jewish" a "desperate expedient" (64), without noticing that just that "desperate expedient" informed a wide range of Jewish perceptions in the Second Temple period (the Dead Sea Scrolls come readily to mind).

If the issue is "zealous Jewish persecution of those who did not observe the Mosaic Law according to the interpretation they favored," then such language might well be used consistently instead of writing simply "Judaism."

And if, as Hamerton-Kelly insists, we are to rely on "the firsthand evidence of the Jew Saul of Tarsus" for a "violent and xenophobic" Judaism (64, see 7n.13), then we should give more attention to numerous voices that insist today that Paul's experience and views were uncharacteristic of the wealth of Jewish thought in the period. Curiously, Hyam Maccoby's flamboyant essay is the only such voice heard from here, only to be dismissed as "preposterous" (64).

Finally, when one reads much later in the book that the prohibition of "lust" (ἐπιθυμία) was a standard summary of the Torah for both Hellenistic Judaism (147n.16) and the rabbis (158), *as it is for Paul*, one must doubt whether Paul's insight into the prohibition of lust as the "true meaning of the Torah" was possible *only* in light of the Cross of Jesus, and whether that insight must therefore have constituted a repudiation of "Judaism."

What Is the Nature of Paul's "Attack on Judaism"?

According to Hamerton-Kelly, the "hermeneutic of the Cross" operates in Paul's thinking at three distinct levels. At a personal level, "the Cross showed Paul that he had been the servant of sacred violence. At the next horizon it exposed the Judaism that Paul served as an expression of sacred violence. Along the widest horizon it exposed the generative role of the primitive Sacred in all religion and culture" (183).

At the first (personal) level, Hamerton-Kelly's exposition of the reversal in Paul's conduct is compelling. Paul clearly understood the Judaism *of his own past,* the Judaism in which he "excelled" and "surpassed" his fellow Jews (Gal 1:14), to be a sacred order resting on appropriate violence; and clearly his "discovery" of this violence *and withdrawal from it* was occasioned by his confrontation with the crucified as God's Son (Gal 1:16). Any future discussions of Paul's "conversion" that leave out this integral dynamic should be judged inadequate.

It is proper, furthermore, to situate Paul in a violent strain within Judaism; but that strain must be articulated precisely. I have in mind Paula Fredriksen's careful arguments tying both the death of Jesus, and Paul's persecution of his followers after his death, to the (often violently coercive) religio-political establishment in Jerusalem. It is surprising in this regard that although Hamerton-Kelly mentions "Jewish collaboration with Rome" (62), the phenomenon plays no significant role in his discussion. Fredriksen looks to the delicate balance of power maintained by Jews in the Roman world in arguing that to a Jew like Paul, the *political* volatility of "the enthusiastic proclamation of a messiah executed very recently as a political insurrectionist—*a crucified messiah*—combined with a vision of the approaching End *preached also to Gentiles*" was justification enough for persecuting the early Christian communities.[17]

Approaching this line of interpretation from a Girardian perspective, we might discover that Paul's confrontation with the crucified Messiah exposed *his* complicity in a system of violence (i.e., Rome's client state in Judea). Against Hamerton-Kelly's position, such a discovery would not necessarily generalize—for *either* Paul *or* the modern interpreter—to Judaism *as such* as a system of violence.

For Hamerton-Kelly, however, the structure of Paul's thought consists in a "double realization that the Law had been responsible for the death of Christ, and that the sharp distinction between Jews and gentiles expressed the same violence as had killed Christ" (68); his own pre-Christian persecution of the church was "of a piece with the violence that killed Jesus and scapegoated the gentiles" (10). The historian's potential objection that Jesus was *not* "killed by the Law" but by Roman imperialism he dismisses as irrelevant, since "we are concerned with Paul's perceptions of that history and not the perceptions of modern historiography" (63).

But what of modern historiography's reconstruction of Paul's perceptions? *Did* Paul blame the Jews, Judaism, and the Mosaic Torah for the death of Christ? We move here to the second "horizon" of the hermeneutics of the Cross, in Hamerton-Kelly's view: its exposure of the violence *inherent in*

---

17. Fredriksen, *From Jesus to Christ*, 154 (emphasis in original).

Judaism. The following observations suggest that his case rests on historically improbable suppositions.

Did Judaism Kill Jesus, according to Paul?

Hamerton-Kelly argues that in Paul's view Jesus was killed *by the Jews.* He
adduces 1 Thess 2:15–16, which refers to "the Jews, who killed both the
Lord Jesus and the prophets, and drove us out, and displease God and oppose all people by hindering us from speaking to the Gentiles" and declares
that "God's wrath has come upon them at last." Precisely because Paul
nowhere else identifies *"the Jews"* as those responsible for Jesus' death—in
1 Cor 2:8, for example, there is no suggestion that "the powers of this age"
have anything to do with Jews *or* Judeans (the two possible translations of
'Ιουδαῖοι)—and because the finality of the reference to "God's wrath" and its
restriction to "the Jews" (rather than to all humanity as in Rom 1:17–18)
suggests a (Gentile-) Christian view of the destruction of Jerusalem in 70
CE (six years after Paul's death)—many scholars view the passage as an interpolation.[18] Hamerton-Kelly cites K. P. Donfried's defense of the passage's
authenticity, but does not himself address the objections just cited.[19]

Whatever the merits of the case *in 1 Thessalonians,* I see no reason to
allow those verses to dominate the interpretation of the other letters, as "the
key" to Romans 1–3, for example (100–101).

Is "Exclusion of Gentiles" the Same as "Sacred Violence"?

A second argument linking Paul's conversion as the impact of the Cross
("level 1") with the exposure of sacred violence in Judaism ("level 2") focuses on the apparent proximity of these issues in Galatians: "the most
revealing indications we have of what it was in the Law that disenchanted
[Paul] come from the debate with Peter and the Judaizers in Antioch" (67).
Here again the argument relies on assumptions that (despite their popular-
ity since F. C. Baur and the Tübingen school) are seriously in doubt today.
These assumptions bear scrutiny:

1. that Jews eating with Gentiles must have abandoned the observance
   of "the ritual laws," namely, circumcision, sabbath, and kosher laws
   (67). To the contrary, Jews ate with Gentiles fairly regularly, either

18. See the arguments advanced in Pearson, "1 Thessalonians 2:13–16."
19. Hamerton-Kelly, *Sacred Violence,* 82n.40, 100–101n.23; Donfried, "Paul and
Judaism."

by observing the sorts of instructions later codified in the Mishnah[20] or by adopting a policy of not taking offense when idolatry was not explicit.[21]

2. that Paul, as a Pharisee, would have traveled throughout Roman Syria to discipline Jews who ate at table with Gentiles. This appears reasonable to modern readers only because of the stereotypic characterization of the Pharisees in the Gospels; but there, and in discussions of Paul's Pharisaic past, the stereotype should be rejected as caricature.[22]

3. that the Jewish Christians in Antioch had in fact abandoned Torah observance, and this *because of* their faith in Jesus; and that this is the policy both Peter and Paul had adopted from the first, conversion to Christ being tantamount to repudiating the Torah and leaving the Jewish community (67–68). But this interpretation is not necessary: Paul does not say that "one can be justified only by giving up the works of the Law," but that "one is not justified by the works of the Law" (Gal 2:15). Neither is Hamerton-Kelly's interpretation likely: there is no conclusive evidence that Paul, Peter, or any other Jewish Christian group gave up Torah observance as a result of coming to faith in Jesus.[23] Furthermore, the assumption they did so makes nonsense (or deceit) of Paul's explicit statement that Peter, James, and John *endorsed* Paul's Law-free mission to the Gentiles (Gal 2:7–9).

4. that Paul recounts the Antioch incident because Peter there represents the same "Judaizing" position that now threatens the Galatians and which Paul is now so concerned to oppose. This equation is F. C. Baur's enduring legacy, despite Johannes Munck's demonstration that the problem in Galatia consists in *Gentile* interest in Judaizing,[24] and

20. Hare, *Jewish Persecution of Christians*, 8–9.

21. Sanders, *Jewish Law from Jesus to the Mishnah*, 277–82.

22. See Fredriksen, *From Jesus to Christ,* 106 (on the Gospel caricature), 152 (on activities within the early Hellenistic congregations).

23. See Davies's remarks on "the significant fact that throughout his life Paul was a practicing Jew who never ceased to insist that his gospel was first to the Jews, who also expected Jewish Christians to persist in their loyalty to the Torah of Judaism" (*Paul and Rabbinic Judaism*, 321). On Paul's ethical teaching as consistent with halakah, Tomson, *Paul and the Jewish Law*; on the absence of any evidence that early Jewish Christians abandoned Torah observance, Fredriksen, *From Jesus to Christ,* 146.

24. Munck, *Paul and the Salvation of Mankind*, 87–134. This insight, never refuted by scholars who nevertheless continue to interpret Paul's theology against the backdrop of *Judaism,* has become a premise in some more recent works including Gaston, *Paul and the Torah*; Tomson, *Paul and the Jewish Law*; and Campbell, *Paul's Gospel in an Intercultural Context.*

despite Sanders's demonstration that the argument in Galatians 2–3 "is against Christian missionaries, not against Judaism," and that in fact "the quality and character of Judaism are not in view."[25]

5. Perhaps most remarkably: that Jewish observance of the kosher laws in Torah can reasonably be equated with "exclusion of Gentiles," and thereby with "violence." The impression that keeping kosher is a form of "violence" is sustained through harsh language: Gentiles excluded are "afflicted"; the Law is a "wall of separation," imposing "rituals of exclusion." The equation (which is evacuated of meaning if in fact Galatians involves *Gentiles* seeking circumcision) leads, perhaps inevitably, to the conclusion that in Paul's thinking, Christ's death made it "clearly unnecessary and undesirable for the gentiles, or any Jew, ever to adopt that way of life [i.e., Torah observance] again" (76).

Against these assumptions, a coherent alternative explanation of Galatians 2–3 can be proposed: Jews in the Antioch church ate with Gentiles on the basis of a common understanding that is represented, for example, in the "Apostolic Decree" (Acts 15: blood and idol meat are not to be consumed). The "Antioch incident" occurs when Peter makes personal concessions to the stricter scruples of visiting Jews. (Neither his table fellowship with Gentiles nor his withdrawal from the same constitutes an abrogation of Torah.) Paul brings the incident up in Galatians *only* because it may be commonly recognized as a precedent, and one potentially damaging to his case: it could be taken, that is, as evidence that Peter personally preferred a stricter observance of kashrut than that to which the Antiochene Gentiles were accustomed. The speech Paul reports is for the sake of *Galatian* ears; it does *not* represent a fundamental disagreement existing between Paul and Torah-observant Jews.

Is Judaism the Target in Romans?

In chapter 4, Hamerton-Kelly assembles a sequence of passages from Romans from which he reconstructs the Law's function in generating "sacred violence and original sin." These passages, that is, are taken together as Paul's more or less reflective articulation of the "hermeneutic of the Cross" at the second level, the exposure of the violence inherent in Judaism as Paul "reads back" the violence of the Cross into Adam's encounter with the commandment (91). Hamerton-Kelly's exposition of Genesis 2–3 and Romans 1–3 in terms of mimetic rivalry against God is ingenious; so is his insight that

---

25. Sanders, *Paul, the Law, and the Jewish People*, 19.

for Paul "the true meaning of Torah [is] the prohibition of mimetic rivalry" (112 and passim). Yet no attention is given to *the argumentative contexts* of these passages, and as a result the role of Judaism in Paul's argument is fundamentally misunderstood, as the following observations may illustrate.

a. Following the dominant tradition of Protestant interpretation, Hamerton-Kelly finds in Rom 1:18—3:20 an indictment of human sinfulness (or an exposure of mimetic rivalry with God) aimed primarily at the Jew (101). Against this interpretation, however, careful attention to how the diatribal elements function in these chapters reveals that "the Jew" is not in view before the explicit address in 2:17. Before that, "it is anachronistic and completely unwarranted to think that Paul has only the Jew in mind . . . or that he characterizes the typical Jew."[26]

   After that point, Paul's rhetoric serves to distinguish correct submission to the Law's demand from boasting in the Law as a false claim of privilege, without presuming that "the Jew" automatically belongs on one side or the other of that distinction; the flow of diatribal back-and-forth in chapters 2 and 3 suggests that "the Jew" is a partner, not an adversary, in conversation.[27]

b. Despite the awareness that Adam's disastrous encounter with the divine prohibition is submerged in Romans 7, and that Paul is concerned to declare the Law "holy, just, and good" (107), Hamerton-Kelly finds in this chapter a "severe indictment of Judaism." This is possible because he identifies the exegetically notorious "I" who speaks here with Paul himself, and by generalization "the representative Jewish self" (108). But then it becomes impossible to decipher what it can mean for the Jew to have been "once alive apart from the Law" (Rom 7:9);[28] at any rate, Paul states clearly enough in 7:5 that the poisonous action of the Law described in 7:7–25 is the experience of his audience—and these, if we may trust the immediate context (6:1–21), are Gentiles.

c. With regard to Rom 5:12–21, Hamerton-Kelly must supply the crucial key that Paul reads the Adam story with *Jewish* violence in mind (91), despite Paul's clear statement that the Jewish Law arrives too late to determine the basic dynamics of mimetic rivalry and death (5:20).

26. Stowers, *Diatribe and Paul's Letter to the Romans*, 112.

27. Stowers, *Diatribe*; I have argued this case at greater length in Elliott, *Rhetoric of Romans*.

28. This is one of Kümmel's arguments against reading the chapter autobiographically in *Römer 7 und die Bekehrung des Paulus*. Hamerton-Kelly dismisses the wide acceptance of Kümmel's position as "fashionable" (122n.13), but does not address his arguments.

To summarize, it is in this chapter that Hamerton-Kelly seems to have the most trouble proving that Paul's target is the sacred violence *of Judaism*. Again and again Paul's thought is explicated by positing "the Jew" as its target; but that maneuver too often appears artificial.[29] At the same time, Hamerton-Kelly argues that Paul is concerned to "redeem the Law," "restoring the prohibition to its original loving intention" (105), establishing the "true meaning of the Torah as the prohibition of mimetic desire" (112).

What is lacking throughout the chapter is a sense of argumentative coherence in Romans, that is, of the function of each component part of the letter in an overall strategy to persuade a particular audience—in this case, of Gentile Christians. Scholars including Werner Georg Kümmel, Walter Schmithals, and J. Christiaan Beker have seen the letter's "double character"—by which they mean the problematic relationship between a predominantly Gentile-Christian audience (explicitly indicated in Rom 1:6, 13, 15, and in 15:14–16) and an argument preoccupied with the (Jewish) Law—as the central historical puzzle of the letter;[30] of all this Hamerton-Kelly says not a word. Why is Paul concerned to attack "the Jew" in a letter addressed to Gentiles? Why should he try to "redeem the Law" before such an audience, especially if the Law's function in prohibiting mimetic desire is also the function of the message of the *Cross*? What role do the diatribal interlocutions in Romans 2–3 play in such a letter: are they meant to convince *the Jew* of an insight into the Torah that was possible for Paul only in light of the Cross (104–5)?

I suggest that a possible solution to these questions presents itself once we abandon the supposition that Paul's concern in Romans *must* be to "indict Judaism." If, in fact, Paul believes that the original, "loving intention" of the Torah is the prohibition of mimetic violence (105)—a conviction he demonstrably shares with contemporary Jewish literature—why should the interpreter distinguish this insight from "Judaism" in Paul's thought? Why not suppose that Paul's dialogues with "the Jew" in Romans 2–3 are meant to establish this very insight *as Jewish*? On this suggestion, Paul's point would be to represent *as Jewish* a Girardian interpretation of the Torah—*in order to make another point* that Paul considers relevant to a Gentile-Christian audience. But here we anticipate a new topic: the interaction of Jew and Gentile-Christian in Romans.

---

29. Other examples are the introduction of 1 Thess 2:14–16 to explain Paul's supposed understanding of human idolatry in Rom 1:18ff (101), of the Jewish "rejection of the Messiah" (106), and of Jewish sacrifice (112).

30. See the discussions in Beker, *Paul the Apostle*; Kümmel, *Introduction to the New Testament*; and Schmithals, *Der Römerbrief als historisches Problem*.

What Is the Horizon of Paul's Hermeneutic of the Cross?

What difference does it make that Galatians and Romans were written to *Gentile* Christians? Despite the preponderance in Pauline interpretation of Luther's dichotomy between Law and Gospel, and Baur's historicization of that dichotomy in a scheme of conflict between early "Jewish" and "Pauline" Christianities, some interpreters are now insisting that a *Gentile-Christian* audience implies a distinct rhetorical situation for Paul's letters.[31]

If, in fact, Galatians addresses Gentile Christians who seek, not to become Jews, but to *Judaize*—to accept circumcision, and perhaps to observe other distinctive "ritual" commandments as well[32]—then we must be careful to distinguish Paul's arguments against a Gentile *misappropriation* of the Law from whatever Paul might say about his own encounter with the Law *within Judaism*. The clues to such distinctions lie on the surface of Galatians, where Paul expects Peter—a fellow Jew, not a Gentile sinner—to recognize the principle of justification by faith *as Jewish*.[33]

If, in fact, Romans addresses Gentile-Christians, and if Paul bases the moral exhortation in chapters 12–15 on the transformation accomplished in Christian baptism,[34] then it is reasonable to ask how what Paul says about the Torah and the Jews figures into that overarching argumentative structure. Romans 6 and, arguably, Romans 3 show that the Law can come up as an issue for Gentiles who know they do not have to keep it; Romans 11 shows that the fate of the Jews can come up as an issue for Gentiles who believe they have "replaced" the Jews in God's favor.[35]

But if in these two letters Paul is concerned to correct Gentile misapprehensions of the Law and of the fate of the Jews, it is methodologically unsound to assume that these letters will provide a straightforward account of Paul's understanding *of* Judaism.

Further, it would be more appropriate methodologically to direct Hamerton-Kelly's insights regarding the hermeneutic of the Cross toward the context in which Paul applies that hermeneutic, i.e., Gentile Christianity. Here I can only sketch prospective results of such an inquiry. In

---

31. Munck, *Paul and the Salvation of Mankind*; Stendahl, *Paul among Jews and Gentiles*; Gaston, *Paul and the Torah*; Tomson, *Paul and the Jewish Law*; Campbell, *Paul's Gospel in an Intercultural Context*.

32. See Gaston, "Paul and the Torah," in the book of the same name.

33. See Tomson, *Paul and the Jewish Law*, 62–68.

34. Hamerton-Kelly, *Sacred Violence*, 151; Furnish, *Theology and Ethics in Paul*, 101–6.

35. Campbell, *Paul's Gospel in an Intercultural Context*; Boers, "Problem of Jews and Gentiles."

Galatians, the hermeneutic of the Cross opposes a Gentile inclination to "supplement" their Christianity with the distinctive ritual markers of Torah; in this situation, mimetic rivalry is evident in the *Gentile* attitude toward the Law. In Romans, Paul must defend his hermeneutic of the Cross against a misconception of Jesus' death as an atoning sacrifice, a misconception that Paul apparently expects may be current among his *Gentile-Christian* audience, and that renders the ethical claims of the Torah irrelevant ("the more the trespass, the more the grace": cf. Rom 5:12–21). In this situation, Paul subordinates the revelation in Christ to the overarching principle of God's impartial justice (Romans 1–2), and relies on the impossibility of the Jew's mimetic rivalry against God (Romans 2; 7; 9–10)—an impossibility he considers self-evident *on Jewish terms*—in order to disarm the mimetic rivalry of the Gentile Christian against the Jew (Romans 11) and against God.

Is the Covenant with Israel a "Myth of Scapegoating"?

Just here I find a final occasion for dissent from Hamerton-Kelly's views. I found his discussion of "the dialectical role of the Jews in the history of salvation" (129–38) valuable, not least because he avoids the trap of "allegorizing" characters (Pharaoh, Jacob and Esau) into "Jews" and "Christians." He quite successfully shows that Paul refuses to allow either the Jews or the gentiles to exclude the other in a contest of mimetic rivalry. How surprising, then, to read Hamerton-Kelly wish that Paul's doctrine could be "radically reversed" (138)! He declares Paul's belief in Israel's election—an unreflected bit of Paul's "nostalgia"—to be "a myth of scapegoating." On this reconstruction, Paul could not deny Jewish involvement in Jesus' death, so he (acting out of overwhelming loyalty to his people) mythologized that involvement, making the Jews the unwitting servants of God's mysterious plan of salvation; he thus "covered up the responsibility of the Jews as representatives of all of us by blaming God for their rejection of Christ" (139).

I have already offered my doubt that 1 Thess 2:15–16 is genuine; without it, I find no evidence that Paul anywhere blames the Jews for the death of Jesus. He certainly regards them as refusing to accept Jesus as the Messiah *now*; but he says that situation is reversible, since God can—and will—save "all Israel" (Rom 11:26). Therefore, unless we are simply to equate distinctiveness with exclusivism and therefore with violence (and there is no reason why we should), I cannot see how Paul's belief in election or his insistence that God can save all Israel, despite their current disbelief, is a "scapegoat myth." Further, in the context of Romans 11, Paul's insistence is a clear and deliberate check on the mimetic rivalry of *Gentile Christians*; they—not Jewish opponents—provide the context for Paul's argument.

Hamerton-Kelly declares that Paul's doctrine of the remnant "can only be understood theologically" (137), by which I take him to mean that it is not merely a legitimizing myth for a particular group. How does this differ from Hamerton-Kelly's own "belief in the possibility of a new community" (184)? Can such hopes be entertained only in light of the Cross? Has Judaism no resources for overcoming mimetic rivalry, or the generative dynamics of sacred violence? Is it not conceivable that through his encounter with the Cross, Paul came to recognize as the "true meaning of the Torah" what others might recognize from within Judaism itself? The point of these questions is more specific: why is the hope Paul expresses under the category of "Israel's election" a regrettable concession to sacred violence, yet Hamerton-Kelly's hope for a new community is an innocent "preunderstanding"?

CONCLUSION

The preceding pages have focused upon areas where I differ from Hamerton-Kelly on matters of interpretation. Divergences on material questions are rather few, but nonetheless important: Did Paul blame the Jews for the death of Jesus? Did he cease to observe Torah? Could Jewish Christians eat with Gentile Christians without violating the Torah? But most often my dissensions have had to do with interpretations or connections supporting the thesis at the very heart of the book, that Paul's letters are pervasively occupied with a critique of Judaism.

My dissensions can be summarized briefly. In Hamerton-Kelly's view, Paul's "conversion" meant, first, recognizing the violence at the heart of Judaism, since Jesus was put to death by Jews for Jewish reasons; then recognizing the same violence in his persecution of Christians; and then (later, as a Christian apostle) recognizing the same violence in Jewish efforts to impose the Law on Gentile converts. Paul recognized that Judaism, like every other human religion, is a system of sacred violence; unlike other human religions, however, Paul's insight constitutes what in theological language could be called revelation.

I would argue—and my indebtedness to Hamerton-Kelly in these suggestions will be evident, divergences notwithstanding—that Paul came to see in the Cross the sacred violence in one political configuration of Judaism (the jockeying for power of the Judean Temple state), and to recognize that same violence in his persecution of Jews who proclaimed a crucified Messiah in the streets of Roman Syria. (I doubt that Paul persecuted Christians for having already drawn the conclusions regarding Torah observance that Hamerton-Kelly attributes to Paul's hermeneutic of the Cross.) In several of his letters we see that one of his chief concerns was to prevent the new, predominantly Gentile communities founded on the memory of the Cross from becoming structures of sacred violence, either through mimetically appropriating the boundary rituals of Judaism (Galatians) or through scapegoating Jesus Christologically, and the Jews salvation-historically (Romans).

On Hamerton-Kelly's view, those of us who stand as Paul's heirs in the culture of Gentile Christianity would do well to generalize Paul's critique of sacred violence—as he finds this violence in Judaism—to all human religion and culture, and thus to ourselves. On the view I have sketched, one of Paul's concerns was already to criticize the scapegoating mechanism of incipient Gentile Christianity itself, and to do so from the vantage-point of Torah; here the relevance for Christian readers will, I think, be more directly perceived.

2

Paul and the Spiral of Violence

IN 1987 RICHARD A. Horsley published a remarkable book, *Jesus and the Spiral of Violence*. Remarkable, first, because it drew on Horsley's own groundbreaking research regarding social realities in first-century CE Judea. Horsley was interested in the popular traditions that informed and inspired episodes of defiance and movements of resistance against Roman hegemony. Previous scholarly discussions of Jewish "messianic" expectation had relied primarily on specific titles used in literary sources (for example, the "messiah" in the Psalms of Solomon). In contrast, Horsley relied on reading historical sources, like Josephus's *Antiquities* and *Jewish War*, "against the grain" for indirect evidence of what social historians call "social banditry." Giving attention to the poor majority rather than to the cultured elite allowed Horsley to describe a reservoir of oral tradition, the "little tradition" of Israel's prophetic past, which fueled popular strategies of resentment, noncooperation, and occasional resistance of Rome.[1]

The book was remarkable, second, because these insights allowed Horsley to describe a very different picture of first-century Judean life. Against scholarly commonplaces about the benign nature of Roman Empire, its generally beneficial effects on subject populations, and the general acceptance of Roman hegemony among the Jews, Horsley demonstrated the systematic exploitation and violence of Roman conquest and extraction through taxation and tribute and, over against it, the contours of general unrest and dissatisfaction. These are the elements of what Marxist historians

---

1. Horsley, *Jesus and the Spiral of Violence*. A number of journal articles preceded this publication and were later the basis for Horsley and Hanson, *Bandits, Prophets, and Messiahs*. Those articles now appear in Horsley, *Politics, Conflict, and Movements*.

would call class struggle, smoldering beneath the calm surface presented by our sources. While some previous scholarship had accepted that surface picture at face value, Horsley urged us to look beneath that surface at the evidence of fundamental conflict. In particular, Horsley refused the scholarly habit of posing polar opposites, *either* acquiescence *or* violent warfare, the "Zealot option," as the only available alternatives in Judean society. Josephus's description of the "fourth philosophy" was Josephus's invention, a tendentious attempt to describe *all* opposition to Roman rule as irrational, murderously violent, illegitimate, and doomed. Instead, Horsley showed that the "philosophy" taught at the beginning of the first century CE by leaders like the scholars Judas of Galilee and Saddok the Pharisee, who organized resistance to Roman taxes, or the scholars Judas and Matthias, who organized the removal of Herod's golden eagle from the wall of the Temple as Herod lay dying, was an authentically Israelite teaching. This teaching insisted simply that God alone was owed absolute obedience. That teaching, which Josephus derided as a foreign infection of the Jewish *politeia*, was actually expressed in principled, strategic, but non-military campaigns to resist Roman claims on the people.[2]

Third, Horsley's book was remarkable because it placed Jesus of Nazareth squarely in this "little tradition" as an exponent of Israel's popular memory of free and egalitarian autonomy. Like other popular agitators, Jesus was able to gather crowds and lead them in a symbolically stylized campaign that entered Jerusalem itself; like other popular agitators, Jesus was hailed by crowds as "prophet" and "king" (though this popular, *practical* acclamation is very different, according to Horsley, from the refined messianic speculation of later literary sources); and like other popular agitators, Jesus was struck down by Rome.[3]

(The fact that the movement around Jesus nevertheless persisted and, in fact, expanded, is a historical puzzle at the heart of New Testament studies. That puzzle is usually conceived as the question of "Christian origins" and answered by reference to "the Easter experience," however that is understood. Horsley's own answer, reiterated in more recent studies, is that sayings in Q show that Jesus' followers viewed his death itself—apart from any conception of "resurrection"—as the martyrdom of their leader and found inspiration in that death.)[4]

2. Horsley, *Jesus and the Spiral of Violence*, chs. 1–5.

3. Horsley, *Jesus and the Spiral of Violence*, chs. 6–10. Horsley has continued this line of investigation in more recent studies: Horsley, *Jesus in Context*; Horsley, *Revolt of the Scribes*; Horsley, *Jesus and the Powers*; Horsley, *Jesus and the Politics of Roman Palestine*; and Horsley, *Galileans under Jerusalem and Roman Rule*.

4. See Horsley, *Jesus and the Powers*, chs. 9, 10.

Fourthly, Horsley opposed his understanding of Jesus as an agent of "social revolution" over against scholarly depictions of Jesus as a pacifist, in principled opposition to the violence of "the Zealot option." Oscar Cullmann had drawn a stark contrast between *Jesus and the Revolutionaries*; Martin Hengel had posed the question *Was Jesus a Revolutionist?* and answered, flatly, No.[5] These studies came out of a particular social context—the political turmoil of the 1960s in Europe, the global convulsions of decolonization as nations around the world threw off European colonial rule, and the possibility that European society as well would be transformed along democratic-socialist lines. This turmoil naturally affected European churches as well.

Horsley regarded earlier works on the question of Jesus and revolution as deliberate attempts to suppress any notion that the figure of Jesus could be enlisted for the cause of agitation for social change.[6] So he very deliberately posed Jesus as a figure of "social revolution." He did so, not only through a reexamination of the historical sources, but also through an explicit appeal to the theorization of violence by a Latin American exponent of the theology of liberation: Dom Hélder Câmara, bishop of Olinda and Recife, Brazil.

Câmara's description of a "spiral of violence" is at the heart of Horsley's book about Jesus. Over against the dominant ideological formation that included government and the corporately owned or government controlled media, an ideological formation that systematically depicts as "violence" only explicit destructive acts carried out against property, institutions, or persons in authority ("riots," "looting," etc.), Câmara insisted that the "fundamental" violence in contemporary society was the structural violence of economic and political oppression, a violence that deprives a society's majority of adequate food, shelter, medical care, employment, and education. This fundamental violence is invisible, however, within the perspective of the ideological system available through the media. According to Câmara, the episodes of violence that showed up on the evening news as "riots" or "looting" were often popular *responses* to the fundamental violence. These were expressions of a *second* violence, as deprived individuals seek to resist or oppose the machinery of their own oppression. The *third* violence—the use of force by police and security forces to suppress dissent and coerce submission—effectively reinforces the primary or fundamental violence but is seen within the ideological system as appropriate force rather than violence.

Horsley insisted that the question of "Jesus and violence" or "Jesus and revolution" could not adequately be addressed without a clear understanding

---

5. Cullmann, *Jesus and the Revolutionaries*; Hengel, *Was Jesus a Revolutionist?*

6. Personal conversation, April 2010.

of the spiral of violence in Jesus' society *and in our own*. That necessarily means that we take a good look at our own lenses: that we interrogate and analyze the dominant conceptions of force and violence that inform our biblical scholarship.

∾

I presume today that Câmara's analysis of "the spiral of violence" in contemporary society remains valid and as urgent as ever. It provides the necessary context in which we carry out theology and the interpretation of scripture.

My proposal today is that we can and should understand the apostle Paul and his mission within a similarly conceived "spiral of violence" in Roman society. In the time available I can only sketch an outline of the topics that would need to be included in such an approach to Paul.

First, such an approach to Paul will necessarily begin with a clear assessment of the nature of the Roman Empire as a "tributary agrarian empire," in transition to a slave-based economy. Land (owned by others than the people who worked it) and labor (performed by slaves who did not own their own bodies) were the chief sources of wealth. Roman aristocrats and emperors spoke frankly and readily about the fundamentally extractive and exploitive nature of the Empire; we should do no less.[7] This is "the first and fundamental violence."

Second, alongside ancient literary sources extolling the wondrous benefits of Empire we must pay equal attention to those sources that express resentment, resistance, and defiance, whether those sources are covert literary sources (like the Habakkuk Pesher with its scathing condemnation of "the Kittim"), records of overt rebellion (such as Tacitus's record of the British chief Boudicca's defiance), or Philo's careful alternation between frank defiance and diplomatic discretion. Here we see that the "second violence," resistance, normally had to be modulated, suppressed, or sublimated into eschatological fantasies of divine retribution. We need a theory that allows us to place our various sources in different sites on a single social landscape in which power—force—constrains and inhibits discourse. In recent work Horsley has promoted James C. Scott's discussion of "voice under domination" and of "hidden" and "public transcripts" as providing just such a theory.[8]

---

7. Lenski, *Power and Privilege*; de Ste. Croix, *Class Struggle in the Ancient Greek World*; on Roman sources see Elliott, *Arrogance of Nations*, 28–33.

8. Scott, *Weapons of the Weak*; Scott, *Domination and the Arts of Resistance*. It was at Horsley's insistence that I made my first exploration of the implications of Scott's work for the study of Paul in Elliott, "Paul and the Politics of Empire," in Horsley, *Paul*

Third, such an approach to our sources allows us to draw a more nuanced and complex picture of "Judean life under Roman rule." Awareness of class differences and class tensions and of the dynamics of imperialism require us to "complexify" our generalizations. For example, instead of taking at face value the celebration by Jewish apologists of the civic rights granted by Julius and Augustus Caesar, we should attend as well to the increasing role of anti-Judean attitudes and repressive policies under first-century emperors (the "third violence"). If we give attention to the dynamics of cultural accommodation and assimilation in the context of Roman colonialism and imperialism, we begin to realize how precarious the Jewish attempt to fit in with the "aura of *nomos*" became, during the decades of Paul's apostolic career.[9]

Fourth, it is against this background, then, that we should seek to understand aspects of Paul's career. This will include both his persecution of the early *ekklēsiai* in Judea and the turn-about that Christian tradition has popularly called his "conversion." Paula Fredriksen refutes a number of interpretations that attribute Saul's persecuting activity to "halakhic" motives. She argues instead that Saul's motives were political. He sought to protect Jewish communities from possible retribution or reprisal sparked by the incautious public proclamation of a crucified messiah. While it is easy enough to account for such "policing" efforts in terms of what we might call a Judean "realpolitik," grounded for example in the Sadducean elite in Jerusalem, we might equally well understand Saul the persecutor to have been motivated by an apocalyptic tradition in which resort to heavenly visions served to reinforce calls for "patience" and "endurance" under tribulation. Following Alan F. Segal's suggestions regarding Saul's participation in a visionary circle (*before* the apocalypse of Christ), I have proposed that we understand his persecution as motivated by the logic of just such apocalyptic visions. (Since God's heavenly agent still remains in heaven, the proper response of the faithful on earth is quiet patience—not agitation!) The unexpected (but *not* inexplicable) vision of *the crucified Jesus* as an exalted figure would necessarily have reversed that logic. The peculiar, and peculiarly volatile, mix of

---

and Politics, 17–39 (ch. 5 in Elliott, *Paul the Jew under Roman Rule,* forthcoming). See as well the essays gathered in Horsley, *Hidden Transcripts and the Arts of Resistance.* For refinement of Scott's method for application to ancient sources (rather than ethnographic studies) see Kittredge, "Reconstructing 'Resistance' or Reading to Resist," in Horsley, *Hidden Transcripts and the Arts of Resistance,* 145–56; and Elliott, *Arrogance of Nations,* 30–47.

9. See the "new Schürer"; Barclay, *Jews in the Mediterranean Diaspora*; Gruen, *Diaspora*; on Roman policy, studies by Slingerland, *Claudian Poilicymaking*; and Rutgers, "Roman Policy"; more generally, Greg Woolf's essays on "Romanization." The phrase "aura of *nomos*" is the very useful formulation of Taubes, *Political Theology of Paul.*

politics, violence, and apocalyptic vision awaits further exploration.[10] In terms of Câmara's scheme of the "spiral of violence," we should perhaps say that Saul the visionary had learned to sublimate into apocalyptic fantasy the impulses to resistance, the "second violence"—but that sublimation made him an accomplice in the "third," repressive violence, *until* this ideological repression and sublimation failed; he received a vision in which a victim of Rome's spectacular repressive violence was raised from the dead by Israel's God, neutralizing that third violence and promising an inevitable end to the foundational violence of empire ("he must reign until he has put all his enemies under his feet" [1 Cor 15:25 NRSV]).

Fifth, we would need to give some account of Paul's mission among the nations, or more precisely his mission *in support of the poor in Judea* among the nations, that understands that mission as a strategic alternative to direct political engagement with the Jerusalem regime itself. One of the startling facts about Paul's mission among the nations is that he declares this work to be intended for the benefit of his own people Israel (for example, Rom 11 and 15); he is tangibly involved with the apostolic community in Jerusalem; but he never mentions the political authorities in Jerusalem: kings, procurators, high priests, or Sanhedrin. The ruling authorities in Jerusalem are completely invisible in his letters—unless they are among the "rulers" and "authorities" that will be subjected to Christ's rule "at the end" (1 Cor 15); unless they are the "unbelievers" that he hopes to sway through the "offering of the nations" that he collects from the assemblies (Rom 15).

Paul's language of a heavenly *politeia*, practiced internationally, serving the anointed lord, is irreducibly political. This language points to a *politeia* of solidarity both across the boundary between Jew and non-Jew and under the authority of Israel's messiah who "rises to rule the nations" as well (Rom 15:12, quoting Isa 11:10). In this *politeia* of solidarity there is evidently no room for the continuing *politeia* of the Roman client regime in Jerusalem.

Sixth, it was important to Paul to maintain his congregations of non-Jews *as* holy and obedient representatives of "the nations," in fulfillment of prophecy, no matter the difficulties (in the forms of social ostracism and even "persecution") that this occasioned for his converts. He resisted the pressure in his congregations toward "judaizing," practicing selective works of law, on the part of his non-Jewish converts. With a few other scholars I believe this cannot be understood as pressure to convert to Judaism; otherwise the warning in Galatians 5, "you would have to keep the whole law," becomes nonsensical. Rather his non-Jewish converts appear anxious to

---

10. These comments summarize my proposal in Elliott, *Liberating Paul*, chs. 4 and 5. To date reviewers have not commented on those proposals.

escape harassment from their neighbors by claiming the exemption from civic ceremonies (and its accompanying idolatry) that Jews enjoy. That is, they wish to pass, socially, as Jews among their pagan neighbors, without actually becoming Jews.[11]

Some recent scholarship suggests that the "works-righteousness" Paul opposed was not a reference to Jewish halakah but referred to the pressure to conform to the regimens of Roman patronage and imperial cult, to "become Roman" through euergetism ("works"). (Recall that the definitive proclamation of the imperial gospel is the recitation of Augustus's "works," the *Res Gestae*.) While some Jews clearly sought to "make their way" in the Roman world by conspicuous euergetism, seeking to participate in the "aura of nomos" by seeking to identify Jewish practice with the highest civic ideals, Paul closes off this possibility for his congregations.[12]

Indeed, over the middle decades of the first century we can watch the bloom of that "aura of nomos" fade as Rome takes an increasingly antagonistic position over against Jews: in Tiberius's expulsion of Jews from Rome in 19 and his indulgence of Sejanus's anti-Jewish policies; in Gaius's indulgence of anti-Semitic slanders in the Roman court and his contemplated outrage against the Jerusalem Temple in 41; in Claudius's stern reprimand, later that same year, to the Jews of Alexandria for having dared to resist the bloody pogrom against them; and a few years later, in his expulsion of Jews from Rome again. To a thoroughly Hellenized Jew like Philo, these actions were shocking and incomprehensible. But it is hard for me to imagine Paul having been surprised by these events.

Neither participating in the civic cult nor seeking camouflage in the trappings of Jewish practice is allowed; membership in the *ekklēsia* is membership in the body of the crucified. He turns the eyes of his congregations not toward Rome, but toward Jerusalem and simultaneously toward heaven.

Seventh, the obvious exception to the picture I am drawing is Romans 13, and some account must be made of this passage. I remain baffled by it; it continues to thwart any straightforward attempt to interpret it. Regarding it, I am content to identify myself as a "militant agnostic": I don't know what it means, *and you don't either.*

I am unconvinced by attempts to portray this as the one place in Paul's letters where he envisions a structural role for Roman magistrates in God's benevolent administration of the world. I am tempted, but unconvinced by attempts to regard this as an interpolation, or as an intentional bit of irony

11. Gaston, *Paul and the Torah*; Gager, *Origins of Anti-Semitism*; Kahl, *Galatians Re-imagined*.

12. Kahl, *Galatians Re-imagined*; on the "aura of nomos," Taubes, *Political Theology of Paul*;

(or a part of a "hidden transcript") spoken over our heads but clearly audible to his intended audience; I see nothing in the letter to cue the audience to listen for irony. To attribute the passage's internal tensions to Paul's ethnic "hybridity" (as so many recent papers at the Society of Biblical Literature have attempted to do) seems to me to reduce Paul's thought to an unreflected expression of ethnicity.

As I have mentioned and written, I find most helpful Fredric Jameson's understanding of ideological constraint, which suggests to me that in his own ideological environment, certain thoughts were for Paul simply unthinkable. That Rome and its gods should be supremely sovereign was unthinkable; to imagine a world without rulers and imposed order was unthinkable; to imagine that direct defiance of Rome now would usher in the conditions of the messianic age was unthinkable. Only God can usher in those conditions.

But that means, I submit, that the "spiral of violence" continues to exercise an ideologically constraining force on Paul's thought. In the same way he simply cannot describe the fate of the Temple regime in Jerusalem, so he cannot describe the end of Roman imperium; he can only affirm a general hope that "every ruler and authority" will at last submit to Christ (1 Cor 15). For now, the believer must submit to *them*. In a similar paradox, the Spirit groans within the believer against the "subjection" of the created order (Rom 8)—but that means, against "the one who has subjected it" (*ho hypotaxas*, 8:20); that is, though for Paul the identification is literally unthinkable, *God*.

Here I think the point of analogy with our own age is most compelling. For us to understand the "spiral of violence" in our world requires us to recognize the ideological pressures around us and the ideological dimensions of our theological statements as well.

We live in a time when neoliberal capitalism appears absolute and its inevitability is generally unquestioned. Not long ago its triumph was announced as the "end of history."[13] If the subsequent terrorist attacks on the United States in 2001 convinced some people that history's consummation would have to be postponed until evil was finally defeated through protracted warfare, those attacks also diverted much popular energy from the global anti-neoliberal movement (with its slogan that "another world is possible").

Paul lived, and we live, in a time when absolutizing ideological claims are made for a particular political-economic order. Neither Paul nor we can identify the clear practical path to an alternative future (*how* is "another world possible"?). It is surely remarkable that some of the keenest interest in the figure of Paul comes today from non-theistic Leftists and Marxists who

---

13. Fukuyama, *End of History and the Last Man.*

identify precisely with his predicament: how do we affirm an alternative future when the present shows no evidence of its material conditions? Paul resorted at last to the language of "mystery"—but is that sufficient for our day?[14]

Paul's response was to mobilize people to an alternative allegiance, but he could only imagine this as possible because of a supreme *kyrios*, a "lord" who would ultimately defeat the *kyrios* Caesar. In our day, at least in the United States, the symbolic kyriarchy of Christian eschatology and the belief in a providential God often operate primarily to reinforce the civil religion; or else they serve, as often as not, to promote acquiescence and even a sense of futility. We thus find ourselves in a peculiar situation. On one hand, we may feel considerable sympathy with the figure of Paul; on the other, it is not helpful (and in fact may be counterproductive) simply to reaffirm his confidence in God's providence in our own day. How to give an account of Pauline "solidarity" with an afflicted creation and to affirm an alternative future without lapsing into the sort of deterministic language that only reinforces the status quo: that is the challenge that I believe faces us in the present moment.

14. I refer to the works of Jacob Taubes (*Political Theology of Paul*), Giorgio Agamben (*Time That Remains*), Alain Badiou (*Saint Paul*), Theodore Jennings (*Reading Derrida/ Thinking Paul*), and Slavoj Žižek (*In Defense of Lost Causes* and other works). Among responses to their works see the essays in Žižek and Milbank, *Monstrosity of Christ*; Caputo and Alcoff, *St. Paul among the Philosophers*; and Harink, *Paul, Philosophy*.

3

Strategies of Resistance and Hidden Transcripts in the Pauline Communities

James C. Scott's work on "everyday forms of peasant resistance" and on "hidden transcripts" of defiance among subordinate classes[1] has begun to have a welcome impact in biblical studies, especially as we continue to open our scholarship to the important questions arising out of postcolonial criticism. It's not surprising to find enthusiasm for Scott's work among scholars exploring the social currents around Jesus in agrarian Palestine: Richard Horsley and John Dominic Crossan have set Jesus squarely in the context of Galilean peasant unrest and social banditry.[2] Gerald O. West has discussed some of the political implications of Scott's work for teaching the Bible.[3]

The case appears quite different, at first glance, with regard to the letters of the apostle Paul. With the possible exception of Galatians, these letters are addressed to communities gathered in urban centers in the Roman world. We are now quite used to a standard picture (Abraham J. Malherbe called it a "new consensus")[4] of Paul's context as a richly textured urban society, characterized by a complex interaction of very different measures of social status. According to this now conventional view, Paul's congregations were populated by a cross section of first-century urban society, made up of individuals enjoying very different levels of wealth, legal status, education,

1. Scott, "Protest and Profanation"; Scott, *Weapons of the Weak*; Scott, *Domination and the Arts of Resistance*.

2. Horsley, *Jesus and the Spiral of Violence*; Crossan, *Historical Jesus*.

3. West, "Disguising Defiance"; West, *Academy of the Poor*.

4. Malherbe, *Social Aspects of Early Christianity*.

and other status indicators. The interaction of these different indicators is supposed to have resulted, for many of Paul's contemporaries, in a profound and pervasive sense of "status ambivalence."[5] The one group we should clearly *not* expect to find in these congregations, according to this consensus, is peasants; and the last person most of us would think of associating with the "hidden transcripts" of an underclass would be Paul himself. The apostle's reputed Roman citizenship (see Acts 16:37–38; 22:25–29; 23:27), apparent training in rhetoric, and what is often taken as thinly disguised condescension to the poor (what Gerd Theissen called Paul's "love patriarchalism"), surely betray an élite background and sympathies.[6]

My argument here, nevertheless, is that Scott's work on grassroots resistance and "transcripts" of defiance to hegemonic social pressures are of great value for our efforts to contextualize Paul's praxis and rhetoric. In what follows, I observe, first, that recent critiques of the just-sketched "new consensus" accompany suggestions that Paul's assemblies practiced alternative economic relationships at odds with the dominant patronage networks of the Roman Empire. I then address the methodological difficulty of appropriating Scott's work in peasant societies for the study of a different social reality, first-century urban centers. Finally, I discuss a surprising case—the passage Rom 13:1–7—where Paul's letter provides a glimpse into the sort of "hidden transcript" of defiance that Scott has so ably described.

PAUL AND THE PLIGHT OF THE URBAN POOR

Aspects of the received wisdom regarding the social circumstances in the Pauline congregations have recently been questioned. Insight regarding the "steep social pyramid" of Roman society has been buttressed by studies of the fundamentally "parasitic" nature of the Roman economy.[7] Drawing on that scholarship, others have questioned conventional generalizations about social status in the Pauline churches. Justin Meggitt's monograph on *Paul, Poverty and Survival* is a particularly important example of this trend.[8] Meggitt describes a globalizing Roman economy in which agriculture remained predominant, nearly 90% of the population living on or from

---

5. Meeks, *First Urban Christians*.

6. Theissen, *Social Setting of Pauline Christianity*; see also Judge, "Early Christians as a Scholastic Community"; Judge, "St. Paul and Classical Society"; Judge, "Social Identity of the First Christians."

7. MacMullen, *Roman Social Relations*; Garnsey and Saller, *Roman Empire*; de Ste. Croix, *Class Struggle in the Ancient Greek World*; Alcock, *Graecia Capta*.

8. Meggitt, *Paul, Poverty and Survival*.

the land, their labor harnessed by a form of "political capitalism" in which profit-making was squarely "in the hands of the élite" (47). In this economy, anything approximating a "middle class" was relatively insignificant (49); a wide gulf separated the very few rich and the very many poor. The vast majority endured at subsistence level—or below it, enduring an "absolute poverty" in which "the basic essentials necessary for supporting human life are not taken for granted but are a continuous source for anxiety" (5). The urban slums teemed with semi-skilled and unskilled workers, scrapping for occasional work to keep themselves just above the level of beggary and destitution. On Peter Garnsey's analysis, the provision of a regular grain dole in Rome, benefiting only male citizens—at most, a fifth of the population—highlights the general destitution in the city: "Most Romans . . . were poor."[9] Meggitt concludes that similar mass urban destitution would have been the case throughout the cities of the Empire.[10]

Most important for my purpose here, Meggitt shows that common generalizations about Paul's own social location, relative prosperity, and privilege have too often been based on anachronistic assumptions about Paul's social mobility and independence (75–97). The same is true of the assemblies he served (97–154). A wealth of close observations leads Meggitt to conclude that in absolute terms, *"Paul and the Pauline churches shared in this general experience of deprivation and subsistence. Neither the apostle nor any members of the congregations he addresses in his epistles escaped from the harsh existence that typified life in the Roman Empire for the non-élite"* (75); "the Pauline Christians *shared fully in the bleak material existence which was the lot of more than 99% of the inhabitants of the Empire"* (153, emphasis in original).

This is of course a conclusion very different from the older consensus that continues to dominate Pauline studies, and so Meggitt devotes an excursus to criticizing the methodology that informed that consensus (97–154). The cumulative effect of his case is clearly to shift the burden of proof onto those who would continue to present a "status-ambivalent," relatively middle-class portrait of the first urban Christians. Even with respect to Corinth—where the rhetoric of 1 and 2 Corinthians clearly addresses tensions running along a fault line of status and social power—Meggitt argues against the popular notion that the church included a significant number of wealthy, high-status individuals. Other interpreters have reached similar conclusions regarding the Corinthian congregation in particular, describing

---

9. Garnsey, "Grain for Rome"; Garnsey, "Mass Diet and Nutrition."

10. Meggitt, *Paul, Poverty and Survival,* 51–53; see de Ste. Croix, *Class Struggle in the Ancient Greek World,* 371.

social conditions as more difficult than earlier scholarship allowed, and highlighting the desperation that could feed tensions within the congregation. Richard Horsley, for example, describes Corinth as "the epitome of urban society created by empire," suggesting that Paul's congregation was drawn from

> a conglomeration of atomized individuals cut off from the supportive communities and particular cultural traditions that had formerly constituted their corporate identities and solidarities as Syrians, Judeans, Italians, or Greeks. As freedpeople and urban poor isolated from any horizontal supportive social network, they were either already part of or readily vulnerable for recruitment into the lower layers of patronage pyramids extending downwards into the social hierarchy as the power bases of those clambering for high honor and office expanded.[11]

ECONOMIC MUTUALITY VS. PATRONAGE

These recent studies not only relocate the Pauline congregations "downward" in social class; they also describe a deliberate economic practice fostered within and among these congregations as an alternative to the pervasive patronage system. Horsley finds the roots of the early Jesus movement's economic practice in "the horizontal economic reciprocity of village communities following the traditional mosaic covenantal ideal of maintaining the subsistence level of all community members" as enjoined in Leviticus 25.[12] He suggests that Paul's own refusal of support, deviating from the usual practice of the Jesus movement, may be ascribed to Paul's sensitivity, "as a former scribal 'retainer,'" to living off poorer communities (250). In Corinth, Paul confronted individuals "still attuned to the values of the patronage system." Beyond his personal refusal of patronage, however, "his larger concern may have been to prevent the assembly he was attempting to 'build up' from replicating the controlling and exploitative power relations of the dominant society." Paul's collection for Jerusalem indicates the *international* dimension of the practice he seeks to put in place (251).

Meggitt provides a more detailed description of the economic practices in the Pauline congregations as a survival strategy of "economic mutualism," characterized by relationships of mutual interdependence within and between communities and aimed at "promoting *material well being*."

11. Horsley, "1 Corinthians," 243.
12. Horsley, "1 Corinthians," 249–50.

This mutuality was embodied in relations of "horizontal reciprocity," as opposed to the "vertical reciprocity" of the patronage system.[13] Like Horsley, Meggitt also considers Paul's collection for Jerusalem the prime exhibit in the case, for it not only embodies direct relief to the economically poor in Jerusalem, but is "thoroughly *mutual* in its character." Paul makes the case clearly in his defense of the collection in 2 Cor 8:13–14: "I do not mean that there should be relief for others and pressure on you, but it is a question of fair balance between your present abundance and their need, so that their abundance may be for your need, in order that there may be a fair balance" (NRSV). Contributing to the needs of the Jerusalem church establishes a mutual relationship that could be reversed, should the precarious balance of food security shift and the Corinthians find themselves in need. Thus, Meggitt writes, "by meeting the needs of the Jerusalem congregation, the communities were contributing to their own long-term, economic stability."[14] To similar effect, Sze-Kar Wan has argued that the collection for Jerusalem expressed an alternative sociopolitical vision for a community "with its own economic principles and bases for structuring life." That vision "stood in opposition to and criticism of" the "political, social, and cultural hegemonic forces, expressions, and institutions" of dominant Roman society, "including the patronage system."[15]

It is just here, in the opposition between economic mutualism and patronage, that we find an important point of contact with Scott's work. These were not neutral alternative modes of social and economic organization, after all; rather, they served different and opposed interests. Much has been written about the ubiquitous *ideology* of benefaction (euergetism) and patronage in the ancient Roman world, an ideology that Meggitt observes was "created and practiced for the benefit of the élite, and not for the poor."[16] Meggitt declares that from the point of view of the poor, patronage relationships were "at best non-existent and at worst exploitative": they were "certainly not the all pervasive phenomenon so often assumed" in much New Testament scholarship, nor did they afford any "real opportunities to engender effective strategies for survival." Nevertheless, the *ideology* of

---

13. Meggitt, *Paul, Poverty and Survival,* 163–64; 157–58 (emphasis in original). Compare Crossan, *Historical Jesus,* 48–71.

14. Meggitt, *Paul, Poverty, and Survival,* 159–61.

15. Wan, "Collection for the Saints," 196.

16. Peter Garnsey, "Mass Diet and Nutrition," 166, has reminded us that common people very rarely appear as clients in the literary sources available to us; unless the poor had something the rich wanted, patronage relationships simply did not materialize. See also de Ste. Croix, *Class Struggle in the Ancient Greek World,* 334, 341–43, 362, 364–67, 372.

patronage—the (usually false) promise that individuals could better their lot by resorting to dependence on their superiors—was pervasive.[17] Crossan described it as "the dynamic morality that held society together"; de Ste. Croix called it "the mainspring of Roman public life."[18]

The ideology of patronage rests on the maintenance of a perceived universal social competition for resources. As Scott observes, this perception of social reality is represented as justifying systems of socio-economic relationships structured on *vertical* reciprocity, e.g., patronage, within the ideological construction of the dominant class:

> If the logic of a pattern of domination is to bring about the complete atomization and surveillance of subordinates, this logic encounters a reciprocal resistance from below. Subordinates everywhere implicitly understand that if the logic of domination prevails, they will be reduced to a Hobbesian war of all against all. Individual strategies of preferment are a constant temptation to members of subordinate groups. It is, in part, to encourage normative and practical defection [i.e., from solidarity within the subordinate community] that elites call forth the public acts of compliance that represent their authority. Also by such means elites create the loyal retainers, "trustees," and informers on whom they can rely.[19]

Scott continues that given the pressure of a dominant culture to coerce conformity, mutuality within subordinate communities must rely on "social incentives and sanctions." He refers to a "patrolling" within the social sites where resistance is imagined, a discipline exerted against "anyone who puts on airs, who denies his origins, who seems aloof, who attempts to hobnob with elites." In this way subordinate groups police conformity of speech, and sanction "a wide range of practices that damage the collective interest of subordinates."[20]

We can recognize immediately the applicability of Scott's observations to the Pauline congregations. Paul sought to enforce an ethos of mutuality with specific sanctions, for example enticing the Corinthians with the promise of praise if they contributed, threatening them with humiliation if they failed (2 Cor 9:1–5). Scott describes such "imposed mutuality" as

---

17. Meggitt, *Paul, Poverty, and Survival,* 166–9.

18. Crossan, *Historical Jesus,* 40; de Ste. Croix, *Class Struggle in the Ancient Greek World,* 65.

19. Scott, *Domination and the Arts of Resistance,* 128–29.

20. Scott, *Domination and the Arts of Resistance,* 129–30.

a "form of daily resistance" on the part of the subordinate community to outside pressures on relations of production and exchange.[21]

It follows that in the context of the ancient Roman city, we should expect economic mutuality as a survival strategy to involve some specific form of resistance to the social and economic pressures embodied in the ideology of patronage. Recent scholarship on Paul provides evidence of just such resistance. We have already noted Sze-Kar Wan's argument that the collection for Jerusalem involved a specific repudiation of the ideology of patronage. Peter Marshall has provided a careful analysis of the social conventions of "enmity" in 2 Corinthians, showing that in fact Paul strenuously resisted pressures from individuals in the Corinthian congregation to accept their patronage.[22] Mark Reasoner finds a similar repudiation of Roman codes of honor for the powerful and shame for the powerless behind Paul's talk of "strong" and "weak" in Romans.[23] And I have argued elsewhere, in general terms, that the rhetoric of Paul's other letters served similar purposes, reinforcing an egalitarian practice of mutuality in deliberate contradiction of the prevalent ideology and iconography of Roman power.[24]

IS ECONOMIC MUTUALITY "RESISTANCE"?

Even if we allow Meggitt's general case regarding the poverty in which most members of the Pauline congregations lived, however, we still face methodological challenges to moving from Scott's work on resistance *in peasant societies* to the sort of economic mutuality Paul encouraged in an *urban* social environment.

In the latter case, first of all, we are reading ancient letters: the sort of "thick" description and analysis of social interaction that an astute observer like Scott might carry out in a contemporary peasant society is not possible with regard to the Pauline congregations. We *believe* we are reading Paul's strategic response to one or another particular situation, based on his construal of the issues involved. Moving from text to situation is a very precarious enterprise, however. We are constantly reminded how much we do not know, and how much we can never learn without the methods available to participant observers. We cannot know what reactions these letters actually provoked in their intended audiences. Did Paul's hearers in fact

21. Scott, *Weapons of the Weak,* 261–65; *Domination and the Arts of Resistance,* 128–35.

22. Marshall, *Enmity in Corinth*; see also Chow, *Patronage and Power.*

23. Reasoner, *"Strong" and the "Weak."*

24. Elliott, *Liberating Paul,* 181–216.

realize the mutualism Paul urged on them? What did that look like? Did Onesimus's master accede to Paul's request, whatever that was? Did Paul's would-be patrons in Corinth have a change of heart?

We cannot answer those questions. Observing Paul's rhetoric is simply no substitute for a "thick" description of the common life of the Pauline congregations. Nevertheless, aspects of his rhetoric would have constituted a clear *ideological* assault on the values of the patronage system. His letters manifest a more ideologically "condensed" form of intervention than the Malaysian practices Scott describes precisely because the forms of exchange Paul seeks to promote are *not* already embedded in a community's life. To be sure, Paul's drawing on traditions of "horizontal reciprocity" from a village-based society may have evoked significant resonances for any of his readers familiar with such traditions in their own backgrounds. But judging from Paul's rhetoric, the practices he advocates are being formed *de novo,* in an urban context where otherwise unaffiliated individuals are gathering in private households to live out a *new* form of community.

Once we notice the frequency with which Paul evokes a clear social break with the past for individuals who have joined these communities (e.g., "turning to God from idols," 1 Thess 1:9), we will recognize that the mutuality being "preached" here is, in a sense, experimental. In this regard, Wayne A. Meeks spoke of the breaking of former social ties in the Pauline congregations and the establishment of "a new, fictive kinship," a transition that he remarks would have seemed "terribly subversive to the basic institutions of society."[25] We should expect this project to depend on more explicitly ideological appeals (that is to say, "theological" or "christological" appeals), rather than on the sort of implicit shared norms and practices that might be assumed by an established peasant community.

Another challenge is that since Paul's letters address not peasant communities, but congregations of *urban* poor, we should expect their strategies for survival to have been structurally different from those that established agrarian communities (like those Scott studied) would find workable. Meggitt himself makes the point: Referring to Peter Garnsey's work on famine and food in the Greco-Roman world, he observes that

> the poor who lived in cities could take only very limited *direct* action in the face of subsistence risk. For the most part they were reliant upon markets and market dependent shops for their foodstuffs and were therefore passive victims of problems of supply (whereas peasants had a number of adaptive agricultural

25. Meeks, *First Urban Christians,* 85–89.

mechanisms—risk buffering techniques—which could allow them to maintain better some kind of consumption stability.)[26]

For example, city dwellers were unable to rely on even modest food stockpiles to the extent peasants could have done. They could reduce their "liabilities" by removing dependents from their households; they could try to barter whatever meager possessions they had. But these were hardly reliable long-term strategies for survival.

By contrast, Scott could describe everyday routines of resistance in an established agrarian society, the forms of noncompliance and sabotage that constitute resistance against structural exploitation by landlords and employers. Part of the power of his analysis is that by numerous measures, Malaysia is, in his words, something of an "ideal" case, characterized by "an open, buoyant, capitalist economy with an abundance of natural resources," a relative absence of overcrowding, and "a state that is less predatory than most of its neighbors"—indeed, a state that works to moderate market pressures so as to maintain a domestic supply of rice, and at least to a modest degree, to redress poverty. In Scott's words, "If one had to be a peasant somewhere in Southeast Asia, there is little doubt that Malaysia would be the first choice by nearly any standard."[27]

In the local agrarian society Scott studied, there were "no riots, no demonstrations, no arson, no organized social banditry, no open violence"—none, that is, of the open forms of conflict we routinely associate with the term "peasant resistance." Malaysia did not offer examples of formally organized peasant resistance movements, and for just this reason could serve as an exception proving the rule that was the heart of Scott's argument: that resistance, or in the strongest terms, class struggle at the ideological as well as the material level, was the fabric of a "hidden transcript" in peasant society, well prior to its public expression. "The stubborn, persistent, and irreducible forms of resistance" Scott examined "may thus represent the truly durable weapons of the weak both before and *after* the revolution."[28]

By way of contrast, the economic pressures on the urban poor gathered in various first-century Roman cities were stark, and mass violence a regular occurrence. The chronicle of conquests in Augustus's *Res Gestae* hints powerfully at the social dislocation and economic disruption that military conquest, mass enslavements, and the subsequent "globalization" of the economy (i.e., the assimilation of local economies into the imperial economy) must have occasioned. Horsley observes that the relations

26. Meggitt, *Paul, Poverty and Survival,* 164–65.

27. Scott, *Weapons of the Weak,* 50–53.

28. Scott, *Weapons of the Weak,* 241–303 (emphasis in the original).

between Rome and Corinth, in particular, "exemplify the most extreme forms of Roman imperial practice and of the imperial society it produced," i.e. the sacking of Corinth in 146 BCE and Julius Caesar's repopulation of the city with "large numbers of urban poor from Rome."[29] Similarly harsh measures produced the Romanized economy in other cities, including Roman Judea, where the social dislocation was a major contributor to insurrection and revolt.[30] Stephen Dyson showed that native revolts against Rome could erupt in the interval between Roman military conquest of a territory and final administrative consolidation of the area's resources into the Roman economic system.[31]

In Rome itself, de Ste. Croix described rioting as the primary means through which the Roman *plebs urbana* could function as a "pressure group."[32] The notorious examples of civic violence in Alexandria in 38–41 and, later, in and around Rome itself, involved a volatile mixture of resentment of taxes and resentment of the Roman ruling class. That resentment could be shifted, with disastrous results, onto the most vulnerable population in the urban environment, an easily identifiable ethnic group caricatured in satire as rootless indigents: the Jews.[33]

It appears, then, that the Malaysian situation studied by Scott and the Roman urban context of the Pauline congregations might be placed at some distance from each other on what Scott himself describes as a "continuum of situations," from more to less explicit repression, allowing or evoking different forms and measures of resistance.[34] Paul's strategy, so far as we can tell from his letters, appears more *ideologically focused* than the Malaysian peasants' practices. To be sure, there is an ideological dimension to the expressions of resentment or defiance that Scott discovers as he moves into private, "off-stage" sites of peasant life, and the coherence of this ideological dimension encourages Scott to speak of a larger, fuller "hidden transcript" on which these expressions draw. In Paul's letters, by contrast, we see exhortations to specific practices regularly joined with ideological justifications, allowing us a fuller glimpse into the "hidden transcript" in the Pauline communities.

29. Horsley, "1 Corinthians," 242–43.

30. M. Goodman, *Ruling Class of Judaea.*

31. Dyson, "Native Revolts."

32. De Ste. Croix, *Class Struggle in the Ancient Greek World,* 357.

33. Gager, *Origins of Anti-Semitism*; Schäfer, *Judeophobia*; Slingerland, *Claudian Policymaking.*

34. Scott, *Weapons of the Weak,* 286.

AN INTERMEDIATE CASE:
PEASANT COMMUNITIES IN MODERN HAITI

A brief examination of a third situation—that of contemporary peasant organizations in the Haitian countryside, on whose behalf I was privileged to work in 2000–2001—provides a "bridge" example that I believe justifies plotting Malaysian peasant resistance and Paul's advocacy of economic mutuality as points on a single continuum. Like the Malaysian society Scott studied, Haiti's economy is largely agricultural; like Paul's Roman context, however, the people have experienced centuries of violence and exploitation, continuing in the present under U.S. hegemony.

Some 80 percent of Haiti's productive economy is agricultural, though the state has historically relied on export tariffs and, covertly, on the drug trade, which is still reportedly a source of income for some elements of the police apparatus. Haiti is in this regard a good example of the pattern Scott identifies in other developing countries, in which the state is forced to rely on levies on imports and exports, a pattern "in no small measure a tribute to the tax resistance capacities of their subjects."[35] In contrast to Malaysia, however, Haiti's experience as a former slave colony of the Spanish, then the French, then (after the tumultuous revolution of 1791–1804) a nation of freed slaves forced to return to fieldwork in virtual corvée labor, has decisively shaped Haitian history around the lethal interaction of a "predatory" state over against the nation. The predatory relationship was embodied in the sudden departure of President-for-Life Jean-Claude Duvalier in 1986, following mass demonstrations—organized by priests of the *ti legliz*, or liberation "little church"—that brought tens of thousands of Haitians into the streets of the capital. Duvalier fled the country aboard a U.S. military jet, carrying with him the entire national treasury, which he has since exhausted while living in France.[36]

The popular democratic movement that swept Duvalier from power also gained tremendous strength in the countryside, where hundreds of thousands of cultivators were organized into regional peasant organizations, each based in dozens of local cells, or *gwoupman*, of eight to ten cultivating households each. This bottom-up organizational structure, and an insistence on democratic functioning at each level of representation up to the regional level, has given the peasant communities a powerful and flexible instrument for working for their own goals. For just this reason, the peasant organizations and affiliated workers' organizations in the cities were targeted in the

35. Scott, *Weapons of the Weak*, 31.

36. See Trouillot, *Haiti, State against Nation*; on the Haitian Revolution, James, *Black Jacobins*; on more recent developments, Dupuy, *Haiti in the New World Order*.

late 1980s by a U.S. intelligence-gathering operation, run under the aegis of "in-country processing" for immigration applications, but modeled on the Vietnam-era "Operation Phoenix" (and reportedly run by several veterans of the Vietnam program). Violent suppression of the popular movement reached a climax during the brutal coup régime of Lt. Gen. Raoul Cedras and his colleagues (1991–94). Human rights reports speak of the "decapita- tion" of the democratic movement, a phrase not always metaphorical in its reference. Official estimates list five thousand men, women, and children murdered by the coup régime; the popular estimate is at least twice that. The Cedras régime has another notorious distinction: its systematic application of rape as a tactic of state terrorism was the first to be investigated under international law as a crime against humanity.[37] The impunity enjoyed by most of the torturers and murderers from the Cedras régime, continuing violence by heavily armed gangs of *zenglendo*, and repeated reports of coup attempts against the elected government by former military or police of- ficers, have created a climate of political insecurity.

There is also economic insecurity, and a collapse of food security for the poor, leading to what the United Nations Food and Agricultural Orga- nization (FAO) has described as the worst "depth of hunger" index in the Western Hemisphere. (The 2001 report, available on the UN FAO website, describes "depth of hunger" as the ratio of per capita daily caloric intake to expenditure.) Since the return (effected by U.S. Marines) of elected President Jean-Bertrand Aristide in 1994, the U.S. failed to deliver fifty million dollars in promised aid and blocked a $146 million loan from the Inter-American Development Bank (IDB) while the Haitian government was required to pay five million dollars as a "financing fee" for that aid. The elected gov- ernments of Aristide and his successor, Jean Preval, were put under pres- sure, from the U.S., the World Bank, and domestic opposition groups from the business sector (supported by U.S. government funds), to implement "structural adjustment" policies. These would convert the national economy from agricultural production to light assembly for export, along the lines of the *maquiladora* model imposed throughout much of Central America. The plan is known in the streets as *Plan Gwangou,* the "Starvation Plan."[38]

In this hostile environment, peasant organizations in the countryside have tried since 1994 to regroup in order to secure basic survival, security,

37. Advocates for Human Rights, *Another Violence against Women.*

38. Food and Agricultural Organization, *State of Food Security*; Dupuy, *Haiti in the New World Order*, ch. 7; Hallward, *Damming the Flood*, ch. 2; Robinson, *Unbroken Agony*, ch. 2.

and human rights needs in their zones. The vast majority of Haitian cultivators are small farmers, facing tremendous challenges:[39]

- a rapacious market in which they must sell their crops at rock-bottom prices to brokers or middlemen, who transport the food to urban markets at a huge profit;

- consequent lack of food security in their own agricultural communities;

- constant lack of resources to buy basic goods and services (clothing, fuel), leaving them at the mercy of predatory lending agencies that normally charge 20 percent interest per month (a practice popularly known as *kout ponya,* "a dagger to the heart");

- competition from the state-subsidized sugar and rice production in the neighboring Dominican Republic;

- a general lack of even basic agricultural equipment, exacerbated by a 1993 campaign by the Haitian Army to confiscate iron tools in the countryside, including mattocks and machetes;

- the remnants of a corrupt and predatory civil service, generally beholden to large landholders, the *chef seksyon;*

- apparent state indifference (an admitted improvement over active repression); and

- constant attrition from peasant communities as members give up on a failing agricultural economy and move to the cities in search of assembly work.

One 2001 report from field staff of the Haiti-based NGO for which I worked identified "demoralization" as the greatest obstacle faced by community organizers. To borrow a phrase from Scott: If one had to be a peasant somewhere in the Western Hemisphere, there is little doubt that Haiti would be the *last* choice by nearly every standard.

Nevertheless, hundreds of peasant organizations across the country have adopted consistent goals and a common survival strategy to address their situation. In several programmatic statements, these organizations have called for

- peasant control over the whole agricultural production process, and thus

---

39. Elliott and other staff of the Lambi Fund of Haiti, "Successful Strategies among Peasant Organizations in Haiti."

- control over food stocks for their communities, and fair prices for their crops;
- participation by all cultivators in grassroots cooperatives, in order to consolidate power;
- the appropriation of all unused state-owned land for cultivation;
- full agricultural reform throughout agricultural zones;
- fuller peasant participation in the decision-making processes that determine their living standards (including participation in state elections);
- ultimately, economic self-sufficiency within their communities.

The basic principles infusing these grassroots organizations include complete democratic functioning at every stage of organization; full community participation in all decisions affecting the life of the community, especially participation by women cultivators (who traditionally do more of the actual labor); complete transparency in all administrative processes affecting community life; and cross-fertilization with other peasant organizations, in order to share reflection and analysis on the most urgent needs in a zone, share successful strategies, and increase common morale—in Kreyol, *pou fe tet nou fò,* "to keep our heads strong."

Several aspects of the experience of these peasant organizations are instructive for my discussion of mutuality and resistance in the Pauline congregations.

First, I notice that the Haitian organizations regularly open a social space within their communities, and in meetings with other organizations in their zones, to reflect on their most urgent political and economic needs. These meetings normally combine discussions of very practical group concerns—regarding a group's operating funds, interpersonal relationships, the maintenance of tools and equipment—with penetrating socioeconomic analysis. At a conference for women cultivators in the summer of 2001, for example, thirty participants moved from a vigorous and insightful analysis of World Bank structural adjustment proposals to a discussion of how the participants could begin literacy courses. These meetings regularly involve a ceremonial sharing of food, singing (themes include invoking the Voudun *lwa,* and the importance of "weaving strength" through united effort), and dancing. There is a clear and consistent tone of commitment to the goals of the community: the participants are aware they are building something new, and that they need mutual support and encouragement to persist.

In addition, the reflections shared in the social space opened up within these communities constitutes what Scott has called a hidden transcript, most dramatically patrolled and protected during the 1991–94 coup regime, when community members were stationed at roads entering their village to watch for agents of FRAPH or the repressive *chef seksyon* apparatus.

Second, these organizations insist on full participation and complete transparency in community decision-making so that the sanctions used to enforce mutuality are clear and communally owned. This practice minimizes the possibilities for mismanagement or misappropriation of shared resources.

Third, these organizations are very clear about the social and economic practices they must *resist* in order to achieve a genuine mutuality. Usually one of their first goals is a pooling of funds to establish a modest micro-lending fund, a practice that community members quickly acknowledge is intended to free them from dependence on extortionary outside lenders. The model of grassroots agricultural development immediately and inseparably involves an explicit opposition to "structural adjustment" plans and the neoliberal ideology that undergirds them.

Fourth: while peasant organizations are eager to participate in decision-making processes in their zone, they are normally very cautious about the potential for partisan or electoral politics to fracture their communities. Some Haitians have described politics as their national sport; and even with the very best intentions, the Haitian state is years away from overcoming the patronage and nepotism that characterized Duvalierism. History has taught most peasant groups to be suspicious of state institutions. There is often a strong ethos that political energy is to be channeled into the *group's* activities; individual political aspirations are actively discouraged.

With appropriate qualifications, we can find rough parallels for all these practices in the Pauline *ekklēsiai*. In particular, the combination of *ideological critique* with *practices of economic mutuality* in the Haitian *gwoupman* provide a model for what I am proposing was the Pauline strategy of resistance. The Haitian practice clearly illustrates Scott's point that "it is precisely the fusion of self-interest," in the peasant's pursuit of basic material survival needs, "and resistance that is the vital force animating the resistance of peasants and proletarians." It is impossible, Scott declares, "to divorce the material basis of the struggle from the struggle over values—the ideological struggle."[40]

Unfortunately, by failing to connect specific economic practices in the Pauline congregations (mutuality, the refusal of patronage, the collection for

40. Scott, *Weapons of the Weak*, 295–97.

Jerusalem) with their ideological warrants, scholarship has too often presented just such a divorce. The mutuality that Paul sought to realize among the congregations he served involved the sharing of material resources and a conscious effort to avoid dependence on outsiders (1 Thess 4:11–12; Rom 13:8).[41] It also involved disciplines of resistance to specific exploitative practices inherent in the "political capitalism" of the Roman economic system.

PAUL'S RHETORIC AND
THE "VOICE UNDER DOMINATION"

As I mentioned above, one of the central insights of Scott's work is the observation that even in the absence of overt violence or rebellion, practices in Malaysian peasant society manifested aspects of a hidden transcript of defiance. That is, the resistance Scott observed was broad, systematic, and carefully managed to be largely invisible to "overseers." In barely detectable patterns of obstructive and resistant behavior Scott finds evidence of class struggle at both the ideological and material levels.

This aspect of Scott's work may be particularly fruitful for our interpretation of Paul's rhetoric. The last twenty years have seen an explosion in studies of the rhetoric of Paul's letters. Most of this work examines Paul's letters in terms of the categories discussed in the classical rhetorical handbooks. But these handbooks were written to describe and to prescribe effective communication among the powerful. The law court, the legislative assembly, the civic ceremonial: these are the arenas where political power was constructed and choreographed; and these are the only arenas in which the handbooks describe meaningful discourse as taking place.[42] We will look in vain in the handbooks for penetrating discussions of the rhetoric of the slave's groan, the prophet's denunciation, the apocalyptist's vision.

We may get further by using Scott's categories of "hidden" and "public transcripts" and the "voice under domination."[43] Scott is interested precisely in the difference between the "public transcript," i.e., "the open interaction between subordinates and those who dominate" (2), and the "hidden transcript," i.e., "discourse that takes place 'offstage,' beyond direct observation by powerholders" (4–5). The public transcript includes "the public performance required of those subject to elaborate and systematic forms of social subordination"; normally, for that reason, it will, "out of prudence,

---

41. See Elliott, *Liberating Paul,* 189–204.

42. Horsley, "Rhetoric and Empire"; Elliott, "Paul and the Politics of Empire," chapter 5 in Elliott, *Paul the Jew under Roman Rule,* forthcoming.

43. Scott, *Domination and the Arts of Resistance.*

fear, and the desire to curry favor, be shaped to appeal to the expectations of the powerful." Where the public transcript "is not positively misleading," Scott declares, it is nevertheless "unlikely to tell the whole story about power relations," since it is "frequently in the interest of both parties"—the subordinate and the dominant alike—"to tacitly conspire in misrepresentation." Social pressure produces "a public transcript in close conformity with how the dominant group would wish to have things appear."

As a consequence, "any analysis based exclusively on the public transcript is likely to conclude that subordinate groups endorse the terms of their subordination and are willing, even enthusiastic, partners in that subordination" (2). But such a conclusion would be false. "Virtually all ordinarily observed relations between dominant and subordinate represent the encounter of the *public* transcript of the dominant with the *public* transcript of the subordinate . . . Social science is in general, then, focused resolutely on the official or formal relations between the powerful and the weak" (13).

The hidden transcript, on the other hand, consists of "those offstage speeches, gestures, and practices that confirm, contradict, or inflect what appears in the public transcript." Scott is interested, not simply in identifying glimpses of hidden transcripts where they (occasionally) appear, but also in assessing the discrepancy *between* the hidden transcript and the public transcript as a way to measure "the impact of domination on public discourse" (4–5):

> The frontier between the public and the hidden transcripts is a zone of constant struggle between dominant and subordinate—not a solid wall. The capacity of dominant groups to prevail—though never totally—in defining and constituting what counts as the public transcript and what as offstage is, as we shall see, no small measure of their power. The unremitting struggle over such boundaries is perhaps the most vital arena for ordinary conflict, for everyday forms of class struggle. (14)

I find a striking illustration of what Scott describes as a partially "hidden transcript" in a speech given by the first democratically elected president of Haiti, Jean-Bertrand Aristide, on September, 27, 1991. Aristide had just been informed of plans for a military coup against him, which would remove him from power in a matter of hours. He addressed a crowd of supporters:

> Now whenever you are hungry, turn your eyes in the direction of those people who aren't hungry . . . Ask them why not? What are you waiting for? . . . And if you catch a [thief] . . . if you catch one who shouldn't be there, *don't hesitate to give him what he*

deserves [staccato for effect, repeated twice.] Your tool in hand, your instrument in hand, your constitution in hand. *Don't hesitate to give him what he deserves.* Your equipment in hand, your trowel in hand, your pencil in hand, your constitution in hand, *Don't hesitate to give him what he deserves . . .* What a beautiful tool! What a beautiful instrument! What a beautiful device! It's beautiful, yes it's beautiful, it's cute, it's pretty, it has a good smell, wherever you go you want to inhale it. Since the law of the country says Macoute isn't in the game [the 1986 Constitution forbade the participation of the former Duvalierist security apparatus in electoral politics], whatever happens to him he deserves, he came looking for trouble.[44]

The speech was widely condemned, especially by the U.S. government, as inflammatory, an incitement to mob violence. In particular, the comment that the "instrument" in the people's hands "has a good smell" was read by some observers as a veiled reference to "necklacing" (assassination by placing a burning tire around a political enemy's neck)—a suggestion that was quickly publicized as fact by the U.S. Embassy. Meanwhile supporters could accurately protest that the speech referred explicitly to the Constitution, and made no reference to violence. In Scott's terms, the "public transcript" allowed only a glimpse into an offstage transcript. In the fuller offstage transcript, the "tool in the people's hands" might have been a clear enough reference to the only means of resistance left at the disposal of the poor in the face of a military coup.[45]

The key question, of course, is how the analyst who stands *outside* the social location of the hidden transcript may recognize its reiteration beyond that location. Scott observes that occasionally what had been a hidden transcript comes to be expressed beyond the boundaries of the subordinate group, in a breach of the etiquette of power relations that carries "the force of a symbolic declaration of war" (8)—surely an appropriate expression in the case of Aristide's speech on the eve of a murderous military coup! It is only when the analyst can detect a *discrepancy* between the values expressed in speech, gesture, and practice of a subordinate group and the values that

44. This is the translation presented in Dupuy, *Haiti in the New World Order,* 128–29.

45. Hallward quotes veteran Haiti journalist Kim Ives's observation that in 1991, references to *Père Lebrun*—which could mean "necklacing" in particular—could also be taken more broadly as "code, or shorthand, for 'popular power,' 'street power' or 'popular vigilance.'" As Hallward summarizes, "resistance by all means necessary to prevent a further coup d'état" (*Damming the Flood,* 25–26).

dominate in the public transcript that the analyst may speak of an emergence or upsurge of a hidden transcript.

Scott speaks with optimism about the prospect thus opened up for the interpreter:

> The analysis of the hidden transcripts of the powerful and of the subordinate offers us, I believe, one path to a social science that uncovers contradictions and possibilities, that looks well beneath the placid surface that the public accommodation to the existing distribution of power, wealth, and status often represents . . . The analyst . . . has a strategic advantage over even the most sensitive participants precisely because the hidden transcripts of dominant and subordinate are, in most circumstances, never in direct contact . . . For this reason, political analysis can be advanced by research that can compare the hidden transcript of subordinate groups with the hidden transcript of the powerful and both hidden transcripts with the public transcript they share.[46]

On the other hand, Scott recognizes that his subject is "the often fugitive political conduct of subordinate groups." He admits that the "immodesty" of his goal "all but ensures that it will not be achieved except in a fragmentary and schematic form" (17). Nevertheless, any disguised or "offstage" political acts or gestures that we can identify help us to "map a realm of possible dissent":

> Here, I believe, we will typically find the social and normative basis for practical forms of resistance . . . as well as the values that might, if conditions permitted, sustain more dramatic forms of rebellion. The point is that neither everyday forms of resistance nor the occasional insurrection can be understood without reference to the sequestered social sites at which such resistance can be nurtured and given meaning. Done in more detail than can be attempted here, such an analysis would outline a technology and practice of resistance analogous to Michel Foucault's analysis of the technology of domination. (20)

---

46. Scott, *Domination and the Arts of Resistance*, 15.

A CASE STUDY IN "HIDDEN TRANSCRIPT":
PHILO OF ALEXANDRIA'S *ON DREAMS*

We may readily identify "hidden transcripts" in some Jewish writings from the Second Temple period. When the Habakkuk Pesher from Qumran refers to the Romans as "Kittim" (1QpHab, passim) or when the author of Mark's Gospel warns, "Let the reader understand" (13:14), we know we are in contact with a more extensive transcript that is largely hidden from view. We may never be able to recover these fuller transcripts, but we must recognize they are there. The situation is far more complicated, of course, in other materials that do not obviously bear the marks of a hidden transcript. But Scott urges us to imagine, not that the public transcript is "all that there is" on the social landscape, but rather that hidden transcripts are *constantly* "press[ing] against and test[ing] the limits of what may be safely ventured in terms of a reply to the public transcript of deference and conformity":

> Analytically, then, one can discern a dialogue with the domi-
> nant public culture in the public transcript as well as in the hid-
> den transcript. Reading the dialogue from the hidden transcript
> [when this is available] is to read a more or less *direct* reply, with
> no holds barred, to elite homilies . . . Reading the dialogue from
> the *public* oral traditions of subordinate groups requires a more
> nuanced and literary reading simply because the hidden tran-
> script has had to costume itself and speak more warily. It suc-
> ceeds best—and, one imagines, is most appreciated, too—when
> it dares to preserve as much as possible of the rhetorical force of
> the hidden transcript while skirting danger.[47]

I find a useful example of such a hidden transcript—"costumed," so to speak, as allegorical biblical interpretation—in Book 2 of Philo's *On Dreams*, to which E. R. Goodenough drew attention decades ago.[48] Philo's theme here is "caution" (*eulabeia*). Ostensibly treating Joseph's dream of sheaves of grain bowing down to him, Philo takes the occasion to describe the arrogant who "set themselves up above everything, above cities and laws and ancestral customs and the affairs of the several citizens," proceeding so far as to impose "dictatorship over the people," bringing "into subjection even souls whose spirit is naturally free and unenslaved" (*On Dreams* 2:78–79, trans. Colson and Whitaker).

---

47. Scott, *Domination and the Arts of Resistance*, 164–65 (emphasis in original).

48. Goodenough, *Introduction to Philo Judaeus*.

Note, first, that Philo's chosen medium, allegorical biblical interpretation, allows him a certain "deniability," a "disguise" for his political views.[49] And what are those views? Philo describes an unnatural imposition of dictatorship upon those who are naturally free. This theme, which has no basis in the text of Genesis, provides us a glimpse into a hidden transcript in which Philo participates. Immediately, however, he retreats (to protect the larger transcript from being divulged, or in Scott's terms, to avoid a "declaration of war"?). "Surely that is natural," Philo writes, for

> The man of worth who surveys, not only human life but all the phenomena of the world, knows how mightily blow the winds of necessity, fortune, opportunity, force, violence and princedom, and how many are the projects, how great the good fortunes which soar to heaven without pausing in their flight and then are shaken about and brought crashing to the ground by these blasts. And therefore he must needs take caution to shield him, . . . for caution is to the individual man what a wall is to a city. (*On Dreams* 2:81–82, trans. Colson and Whitaker)

Abruptly conforming to the "public" transcript, Philo describes necessity, fortune, opportunity, force, violence, and princedom as natural "phenomena of the world." So they seemed, also, to Roman elite authors like Cicero or Tacitus or Plutarch. But Philo has already indicated that these are *not* equally "natural" forces, for some represent the application of force on the part of human beings.

Of tremendous importance to our subject, Philo makes a distinction similar to Scott's distinction of "public" and "hidden" transcripts." "Caution," warns Philo, must be exercised preeminently by avoiding "untimely frankness" (*parrhēsian akairon*). Philo knows there are "lunatics and madmen" who "dare to oppose kings and tyrants in words and deeds." Interestingly, Philo does not say they are "lunatics" because they fail to recognize the inherent benefit of accepting their subordination to the imperial order (as the official transcript would define lunacy). Rather, they are lunatics because they fail to recognize just how harmful that order is: they fail, that is, to see that

> not only like cattle are their necks under the yoke, but that the harness extends to their whole bodies and souls, their wives and children and parents, and the wide circle of friends and kinsfolk united to them by fellowship of feeling, and that the driver can with perfect ease spur, drive on or pull back, and mete out any treatment small or great just as he pleases. And therefore

---

49. See Scott, *Domination and the Arts of Resistance,* 136–82.

they are branded and scourged and mutilated and undergo a
combination of all the sufferings which merciless cruelty can
inflict short of death, and finally are led away to death itself. (*On
Dreams* 2:83–84, trans. Colson and Whitaker)

Note that Philo's distinction of "caution" and "untimely frankness"
closely resembles Scott's distinction of "hidden" and "public transcripts":
"Tactful prudence ensures that subordinate groups rarely blurt out their
hidden transcript directly. But, taking advantage of the anonymity of a
crowd or of an ambiguous accident, they manage in a thousand artful ways
to imply that they are grudging conscripts to the performance."[50] Scott recognizes (as does Philo) that it is the "frustration of reciprocal action" that
informs the hidden transcript: "The cruelest result of human bondage is that
it transforms the assertion of personal dignity into a mortal risk. Conformity in the face of domination is thus occasionally—and unforgettably—a
question of suppressing a violent rage in the interest of oneself and loved
ones" (37).

Philo reports elsewhere that Roman tax gatherers have conducted
their work with particular savagery, especially against Jewish villages (*On
the Special Laws* 2.92–95; 3.159–63). Although he does not name Romans in
On Dreams, his rhetoric is brazen enough: The speeches Philo puts into the
mouths of the praiseworthy (2.93–95) are worthy of any Zealot call to arms.
The political subordination Philo describes is tantamount to living as brute
livestock, suffering torment and indignity until finally being butchered. No
reason for honoring the rulers is expressed here. Indeed, Philo interprets the
taunt of Joseph's brothers—"will you indeed reign over us? Not so!" (Gen
37:8, trans. Colson and Whitaker)—as the appropriately defiant speech
of the truly wise, to be spoken under circumstances that allow it (*Dreams*
2:93–94, trans. Colson).

Philo provides yet another glimpse of an offstage transcript when he
turns to an allegorical interpretation of Gen 23:7, describing Abraham's
obedience to the sons of Cheth. Although the text does not present these
terms, Philo insists that Abraham's obedience was compelled by "fear," not
"respect," playing on a well-known political topos:[51]

> For it was not out of any feeling of respect for those who by na-
> ture and race and custom were the enemies of reason . . . that he
> brought himself to do obeisance. Rather it was just because he

50. Scott, *Domination and the Arts of Resistance,* 15.

51. See Elliott, "Romans 13:1–7," 197–202; reprinted in Elliott, *Paul against the Nations,* 278–82.

feared their power at the time and their formidable strength and cared to give no provocation. (*On Dreams* 2.90, trans. Colson)

"To give no provocation" is the mark of true caution, true prudence, under domination. Just as a wise pilot will "wait" until storms pass over before setting sail; just as a traveler encountering a bear or a lion or a wild boar on the road will seek to soothe and calm the beast, so the wise citizen will manifest patience and deference to rulers (*On Dreams* 2.86–87, trans. Colson). All this is said obliquely, in the most general of terms, and while the comparisons are hardly flattering to rulers, neither are they specific or openly defiant enough to spark offense. (Josephus puts the same topos into the mouth of Agrippa, appealing to the rebels of Jerusalem to surrender: *Jewish War* 2.396.) At just one point does Philo allow the pretense that he is speaking in abstraction to slip:

> Again, do not we too, when we are spending time in the market-place, make a practice of standing out of the path of our rulers and also of beasts of carriage, though our motive in the two cases is entirely different? With the rulers it is done to show them honor, with the animals from fear and to save us from suffering serious injury from them. (*On the Special Laws* 2.91, trans. Colson)

Of course these qualifications come a moment too late. The distinction between rulers and brute animals is explicit but is undermined by everything else Philo has said about the brutality of rulers. And his insistence that "honor" is shown to rulers is belied by his preceding comment that fear, not honor, compels the outward deference of the subordinate.

"The sarcasm at the end is obvious," Goodenough writes—though not obvious enough to resolve the careful ambiguity of the whole passage:

> Philo has compared harsh rulers to savage and deadly animals throughout. When he mentions how in the marketplace the Jews have to make place for their rulers and the pack animals alike, it is part of the very caution he is counseling that he should distinguish between the two, once the rulers in Alexandria have been distinctly referred to, and say that one gives way out of honor to the rulers, but out of fear to the beasts,

thus maintaining the pretended deference to the legitimacy of Roman rule that is essential to the public transcript;

> But [Philo's] Jewish readers would quite well have understood
> that the reason Philo gave way to each was the same, because he
> knew that if he did not he would be crushed.[52]

That is, Jewish readers would have immediately picked up hints that seem merely incongruous in the treatise, but that make perfect sense within another, "offstage" transcript.

Here we see Philo explicitly distinguishing two transcripts: the "public" transcript of deference to the imperial order, and the "offstage" transcript of defiance, under the categories of "speaking most freely," or "boldness of speech" (*eleutherostomeito phaskein*), and speaking with "untimely frankness" (*parrhēsian akairon*). "When the times are right," when a social space is opened in which the "offstage" transcript can come onstage, the hidden transcript of defiance become public, then "it is good to set ourselves against the violence of our enemies and subdue it; but when the circumstances do not present themselves, the safe course is to stay quiet" (*On Dreams* 2.92, trans. Colson).

PAUL'S PARTICIPATION IN
AN APOCALYPTIC "HIDDEN TRANSCRIPT"

Despite the significant differences between the theological, cultural, and political stances of Philo and Paul, we may readily recognize aspects in Paul's letters of a similar hidden transcript of defiance and resistance toward Roman overlords. For example, while he will not tell the Corinthians what "a man" saw in the third heaven (2 Cor 12), he clearly expects them to recognize his reticence as the proper discipline of a true visionary.[53] Again, Paul can make oblique reference to "the time," "the hour," "the day" (Rom 13:11–13), obviously expecting these terse phrases to be meaningful to his hearers without elaborating the apocalyptic scenario to which they refer. Indeed, these apparently glancing references refer to a world of meaning that was obviously alive enough to his congregations.

Against a modern tendency to "demythologize" these apocalyptic elements and to insist that apocalyptic expectation had "lost its motive power" for Paul, J. Christiaan Beker insisted that apocalyptic expectation was "the central climate and focus of his thought."[54] Interestingly, Beker felt constrained to argue that case against the apparently disconfirming fact

---

52. Goodenough, *Introduction to Philo Judaeus*, 57.

53. Segal, *Paul the Convert*, 34–71.

54. Bultmann, *Theology of the New Testament*, 1:184; Beker, *Paul the Apostle*, 144.

that Paul "uses little of the traditional apocalyptic terminology," and shows no interest in "apocalyptic timetables, descriptions of the architecture of heaven, or accounts of demons and angels. He does not relish the rewards of the blessed or delight in the torture of the wicked" (145). It is nevertheless evident that Paul is familiar with those aspects of apocalyptic thought, and expected his readers to recognize his references to them. That is, they constitute elements of a larger worldview, a transcript that is not fully evident in the text of his letters.

More to our purpose here, Horsley has rightly observed that the Judean apocalyptic tradition functioned as a symbolic repertoire by which the Judean communities preserved their own identities by covertly rehearsing defiance of imperial regimes. "The scribal circles that produced this literature were able, through their revelations, creatively to envision a future for their society in freedom and justice beyond their present oppression under imperial rulers and/or their local client rulers . . . The fundamental message of most of this Judean apocalyptic literature . . . focused on future deliverance from imperial domination." Paul shares fully in that tradition.[55]

Using Scott's terminology, we might speak of a fully apocalyptic *off-stage* transcript to which Paul makes repeated references. Indeed, the very intentionality of apocalyptic or "revelatory" rhetoric is to refer to a reality not universally, or "publicly," evident; as Paul puts it, a reality that must be "revealed" as a "mystery" (Rom 11:25), but it is otherwise "unsearchable" and "inscrutable" (Rom 11:33). These observations lead to the suggestion that *every performance of one of Paul's letters, before a group constituted as an "ekklēsia," generated a social site for the rehearsal and reiteration of a hidden apocalyptic transcript.* This is, admittedly, a novel way to read Paul's rhetoric. Many scholars are more accustomed to taking the letters at face value, which explains the exertion with which Beker was compelled to argue his point, against a non-apocalyptic, "christocentric" interpretation of Paul. Interpreters easily gravitate to more self-evident language, and are tempted to minimize the importance of fragmentary glimpses into the fuller apocalyptic transcript; thus Dunn, for example, is forced in the face of Romans 13 to puzzle "why the apocalyptic character of the Thessalonian letters appears relatively isolated, and why Paul did not set out his theology on [apocalypticism] with greater coherence in the later letters, not least the more carefully laid-out Romans."[56]

The question is not whether, but where and how we may distinguish a hidden transcript in Paul's letters. One hermeneutical key is provided in the

---

55. Horsley, "Rhetoric and Empire—and 1 Corinthians," 95, 96–98.
56. Dunn, *Theology of Paul the Apostle*, 310.

way Paul describes his own apostolic presence by reference to the cross of Jesus, which Paul understands in a distinctively apocalyptic context. Just as the cross is "foolishness to those who are perishing," but "the power of God" to those who understand the hidden Pauline transcript (1 Cor 1:18–25), a "secret and hidden wisdom of God," concealed from the "rulers of this age" (1 Cor 2:6–8), just so Paul's own apostolic presence represents "a fragrance from death to death"—we might say, the smell of "dead meat"—among those who are perishing, but "the aroma of Christ to God," a "fragrance from life to life," among those being saved (2 Cor 2:15–16).

Here Paul makes use of a powerfully ironic metaphor, speaking of God in Christ "always leading us in triumph" (*thriambeuonti hēmas*). The public transcript regards Paul as simply a humiliated captive (e.g., in his arrest in Ephesus, 2 Cor 1:8–9); the hidden transcript reveals that even in such distress Paul is "captive" to God, and thus a manifestation of God's power. That here and elsewhere Paul establishes a distinction between public and hidden transcripts in terms borrowed from the ceremonial of the imperial cult suggests that the larger transcript of Paul's gospel is powerfully ironic and subversive of the imperial order.[57] The same conclusion may be drawn from Paul's pointed inversion of a slogan of Augustan propaganda, "*Pax et securitas*," in 1 Thess 5:2–4.[58]

GLIMPSES OF A HIDDEN TRANSCRIPT IN ROMANS 13:1–7

Another possible glimpse into the Pauline hidden transcript appears, surprisingly, in Rom 13:1–7. Here Paul's comments about the ruling authorities are far more reserved than that of other Jews under Roman rule (e.g., Josephus). As Meggitt observes, according to Paul, God "orders" the ruling authorities (*tetagmenai*, 13:1), "he does not ordain them."[59] There is no enthusiasm here for the divinely apportioned destiny of the Roman people, such as infects Josephus in *Jewish War* 2.350–358. Indeed, there is no recognition whatsoever of the commonplace—as old as Aristotle—that the world is "naturally" divided into rulers and ruled, masters and slaves. To the contrary, every soul is to be subject to "the authorities who are presently in charge" (*exousiais hyperechousais*, 13:1, my trans.), a participial phrase remarkable for the modesty of its claim.

57. See P. B. Duff, "Metaphor, Motif, and Meaning"; Elliott, "Apostle Paul's Self-Presentation," chapter 6 in Elliott, *Paul the Jew under Roman Rule*, forthcoming.

58. Koester, "Imperial Ideology and Paul's Eschatology in 1 Thessalonians."

59. Meggitt, *Paul, Poverty and Survival*, 186.

Paul's seemingly blithe expectation that the authority will reward good behavior and punish bad (13:3–4) and thus act as God's servant (*diakonos,* 13:4; *leitourgoi,* 13:6) is marred by two remarks: that the authority "does not bear the sword in vain" (13:4 NRSV), and that one therefore must "fear" the authority—not only in the instance that one does evil (13:4) but because fear is "owed" to the authority as such (13:7). These remarks are all the more startling in light of the commonplaces of Roman rhetoric. Propagandists like Cicero consistently held that fear and the threat of force was necessary only for insubordinate and uncivilized peoples. Citizens would naturally yield their happy consent. (Thus the wise statesman would be qualified in rhetoric, to persuade his peers, and in military skills, to coerce his subordinates: *De Republica* 5.6, 3.41.) The historian Velleius Paterculus similarly recognized that persuasion and forceful coercion were the twin instruments of social order (*History of Rome* 2.126). Later, Plutarch would distinguish the Romans' reliance on Fortune, the god who had ensured their countless military triumphs, with the Greek predilection for Wisdom or Prudence, the virtues of rhetorical persuasion (*Fortune of the Romans* 318). Nero's propagandists relied on this common distinction of persuasion and force to argue that strategies of coercion belonged to a bygone era: The emperor had come to power without resort to violence, and had thus ushered in a golden age of "Clemency," which "has broken every maddened sword-blade," and "Peace . . . knowing not the drawn sword" (Calpurnius Siculus, *Eclogue* 1.45–65).[60] The weapons of earlier wars were mere historical curiosities (Einsiedeln Eclogues, lines 25–30). Seneca even had the emperor declare, "With me the sword is hidden, nay, is sheathed; I am sparing to the utmost of even the meanest blood; no man fails to find favor at my hands though he lack all else but the name of man." Seneca gushed that so noble a ruler need not fear for his own protection: "The arms he wears are for adornment only" (*De Clementia* 1.3; 13.5).[61]

Clearly Paul has a different view. The Roman sword is still wielded, provoking terror (*phobos,* 13:4). Thus one's posture must be one of "subjection:" or "subordination" rather than revolt (13:2). Just here we may detect a glimpse of a "hidden transcript" in the Pauline *ekklēsiai,* expressed in terms very similar to Philo's carefully calculated remarks in *On Dreams.* While Roman propaganda leads us to expect that a beneficiary of the Roman order would extol *consent* and *agreement* (cf. *syneidēsis,* 13:5), Paul speaks, with what would have sounded like the ingratitude of the uncivilized, of two alternatives: *subjection* (*hypotassesthai*) or *revolt* (*antitassesthai; anthistēmi*).

---

60. Text in J. W. Duff and A. M. Duff, *Minor Latin Poets,* 1:222–23.
61. Text in Seneca, *Moral Essays,* 1:356–59, 1:398–99.

His declaration that "rulers are *not* a fear [*phobos*] to the good work, but to the evil," is in line with Roman propaganda, as is the remark that the one working good will thus avoid having to "fear the authority" (13:3); only the evil doer has reason to fear (13:4). But then Paul exhorts his readers to return what they "owe" to others: to some, fear (*phobos*), to others, honor (*timē*, 13:7). And then he insists that his readers "owe no one anything except love" (*agapē*, 13:8)!

Given the exuberant currents of political rhetoric in the Neronian age, Paul's phrases encouraging submission are remarkably ambivalent. I suspect that in a Roman official's ear, Paul's language would have seemed to offer a peculiarly grudging compliance, rather than the grateful contentment of the properly civilized. Scott cites Zora Neale Hurston's observation that the verbal art of subordinate groups is often characterized by "indirect, veiled, social comment and criticism"; note also his remarks on the rhetoric of "grumbling," which always "stops short of subordination—to which it is a prudent alternative."[62]

Despite the proximity of the "riots" that, in Suetonius's view, justified police action against "the Jews" (Suetonius, *Tiberius* 43), and of recent unrest over taxes in Rome and nearby Puteoli (Tacitus, *Annals* 13.48), we cannot tell from this distance whether Paul in fact considered an attempted uprising to be an imminent danger. (His reference to paying taxes in 13:6–7 has been read this way.) Any reasonable Jew could have imagined what the probable imperial response would have been to even modest popular agitation, however.

Perhaps we should read Rom 13:1–7 as part of an ad hoc survival strategy in an impossible situation;[63] Dunn calls it the "realism of the little people who had the most to lose" in the event of civil unrest.[64] Paul's "eschatological realism"—a realism determined by the unwavering conviction that God had raised the crucified Jesus from the dead—was never an otherworldly realism. Paul was at least as adroitly political a creature as Philo, whose insistence on discerning the political moment in his allegorical treatise *On Dreams* sounds surprisingly modern. "When the times are right," Philo wrote, "it is good to set ourselves against [*anthistanai*] the violence of our enemies and subdue it: But when the circumstances do not present themselves, the safe course is to stay quiet." Otherwise, one risks sharing the fate of those who have been "branded and beaten and mutilated and suffer

---

62. Scott, *Domination and the Arts of Resistance*, 153, 155–56.

63. See Meggitt, *Paul, Poverty and Survival*, 155–78.

64. Dunn, *Theology of Paul the Apostle*, 679–80.

before they die every savage and pitiless torture, and then are led away to execution and killed" (*On Dreams* 2:83–92, trans. Colson and Whitaker).

The modest remarks in Rom 13:1–7, or in the second book of Philo's *On Dreams,* are hardly unusual. Indeed, such "realistic caution" was required of "all people of the Empire."[65] What is remarkable is how out-of-step this caution would have sounded to ears accustomed to the exultant themes of Roman eschatology. In effect, Paul declares: "The empire is as dangerous as it has ever been. Nothing has changed. Exercise caution."

Paul expresses no fantasy that the powers that be are about to vanish in a miraculous puff of smoke, but neither are they permanent (13:11–12). The Christian's arena of responsibility is much closer, in any event, for the Christian must be diligent for the common good (12:3–21) and fulfill the obligation of mutual love (13:8–10). The "hinge" between the "argument" of the letter, Romans 1–11, and the exhortative material in chaps. 12–15, is the broad exhortation to resist conformity to the world (12:2). This resistance clearly involved, for Paul, a defiance of the empire's ideological insolence, by which it sought to legitimize a brutal rapacity (i.e., to "suppress the truth," 1:18.[66]

Whether or not this last suggestion regarding Rom 13:1–7 prevails, it should be evident enough from the preceding that James Scott's work holds out tremendous promise for a new critical approach that will contextualize Paul within the dynamics and ideology of Roman imperialism. Perhaps the effort will also contribute to greater awareness of our own situation vis-à-vis the imperial cultures and ideological pressures that surround us today.

65. Goodenough, *Introduction to Philo Judaeus,* 54–62.

66. See Elliott, *Liberating Paul,* 190–95.

4

An American "Myth of Innocence" and Contemporary Pauline Studies

I BEGIN WITH A brief reminiscence.[1] Several years ago the Society of Biblical Literature met in Washington, DC, and a friend and I took the opportunity to visit the United States Holocaust Museum there. We were both deeply impressed with the care and thoughtfulness that had gone into well-crafted, deeply moving, informative, and solemnly captivating exhibits. I did not expect to be *surprised* by the information in the exhibits, but one news photo from the *New York Times* took me aback. It showed a rally of thousands of Americans in Time Square, calling on the United States government to take decisive action on behalf of endangered European Jews.[2]

What surprised me was the realization that there had been large-scale, organized popular agitation in the United States, both before and during U.S. entry into World War II, pressing the government to do more than it was doing to alleviate the suffering of Europe's Jews. Not having lived during the War, I realized, I had relied for my imagination of that time on official and semi-official accounts—and on warm images like Norman Rockwell's paintings of the *Four Freedoms* or the post-war *Brotherhood of Man*—accounts and images that implicitly identified my nation with the cause of

1. I wish at the outset to acknowledge my debt to colleagues from whom I have learned so much: Pamela Eisenbaum, John G. Gager, Lloyd Gaston, and Mark Nanos. These scholars have helped to move all of us toward a new understanding of Paul, especially in relation to his contemporary Judaism.

2. Gilbert discusses two New York protests, in 1933 and 1938 (*Holocaust*, 33, 74). The museum exhibit may have featured yet another—indicating the relative frequency of such demonstrations.

freedom and justice. I had naively accepted as self-evident the notion that one of the reasons the United States went to war in Europe was to free European Jews. Though I am quite used to the observation in my own time, I wasn't prepared for the realization that ordinary citizens in the 1930s and '40s had actually been far ahead of their government in this regard.

I had unconsciously accepted a key element in the dominant national mythology, what Richard T. Hughes labels the myth of America as an "Innocent Nation."[3] This particularly volatile mythology became especially powerful in the twentieth century, informing the nation's entry into and conduct of two world wars and countless other regional wars. The immediate power of the myth derives, Hughes argues, in part from the fact that the United States "really did face great evil in the twentieth century." But the dramatic convergence in the early twentieth century of two other mythic themes—of America as "Nature's Nation" and as a "Millennial Nation," or in the terminology of comparative religion, of "*Urzeit* and *Endzeit*"—"preclude[d] any meaningful sense of history in the United States." By identifying itself so completely with a mythic primordial golden age and a millennial consummation, "America lifted itself, as it were, above the plane of ordinary human history where evil, suffering, and death dominated the drama of human existence. Other nations were mired in the bog of human history, but not the United States."[4] The paradoxical effect of this mythology of innocence is that when other nations declined to acknowledge U.S. claims to innocence, or when American actions and policies belied those absolutist claims, the United States failed to distinguish fantasy from reality. "In this way, while proclaiming its innocence and the purity of its motives, America—like the other nations of the world—also fell into the guilt of history."[5]

Hughes documents how the mythology of American innocence governed Woodrow Wilson's campaign to summon popular support in the U.S. for entering World War I, and decades later, Franklin Roosevelt's efforts "to portray the Axis forces as fundamentally demonic and America as fundamentally good." The mythic scope of the national vision prevails in official rhetoric down to our own day.

As for the post-war years, as Roosevelt had contrasted "biblical" America with "pagan" Nazism, so post-war American culture understood the new "Cold War" situation as a conflict between "godless Communism" and the prevalence in America of a "deeply felt religious faith." The phrase comes from President Dwight Eisenhower, who famously declared in 1954

3. Hughes, *Myths America Lives By*.

4. Hughes, *Myths America Lives By*, 154–55.

5. Hughes, *Myths America Lives By*, 163.

that "our government makes no sense unless it is founded on a deeply felt religious faith—and I don't care what it is."[6] Hughes cites historian William Lee Miller's observation regarding what he called the emerging American emphasis on "religion-in-general": "Depth of feeling is the important thing, rather than any objective meaning. One might say that President Eisenhower, like many Americans, is a very fervent believer in a very vague religion."[7]

I doubt that any of this depiction sounds foreign to us today. That President George W. Bush could declare, during the 2000 campaign, that Jesus was his "favorite political philosopher," though he was incapable of naming a single political idea he had learned from Jesus, suggests that the "very fervent belief in a very vague religion" persists as a value in American culture.

I recall as a child passing highway billboards, printed in stately letters, exhorting Americans to "attend the church or synagogue of your choice." The message sank in that in *this* country—in contrast to Nazi Germany or Soviet Russia—Jews and Christians lived side by side as neighbors, enjoying full rights and accepting one another, in part because they shared a commitment to a *common* religion, a peculiarly American religion, "Judeo-Christianity." In contemporary controversies over monumental displays of the Ten Commandments on public property we hear much of the same emphasis, not on Judaism or Christianity but on a "Judeo-Christian" foundation for the nation. Within this mythic framework, reports of occasional incidents of anti-Jewish prejudice were always understood as isolated exceptions to the rule, the result of individual bigotry, places where the light of enlightened American egalitarianism had not yet reached. After all, this was the land where Sammy Davis Jr. and Barbara Streisand were *famous and successful stars.* Not infrequently, I heard that observation elicit the response, "I didn't even know they were Jewish."

As to other celebrated heroes of the American spirit, like Charles Lindbergh or Henry Ford,[8] many of us might honestly have added, "we didn't even know they were aggressively anti-Semitic."

I trust some aspects of my reminiscence are familiar enough that we can recognize the broad symbolic themes of national self-representation in the last half of the twentieth century. And I hope we can detect some irony in the observation that the best demonstrations of this inclusive atmosphere have been American Jews who are—*just like everybody else.* That is: in this

---

6. Hughes, *Myths America Lives By*, 171.

7. Miller, *Piety along the Potomac*, 34.

8. On Ford, see now Baldwin, *Henry Ford and the Jews.*

popular understanding of "religion-in-general" that supports the mythology of America as an "innocent nation," Jewish *difference* is downplayed; Jewish participation in "religion-in-general" is welcomed and celebrated.

THE SURPRISING PERSISTENCE OF THE "NEW PERSPECTIVE ON PAUL"

I discuss Hughes's idea of a myth of American innocence in order to draw attention to two important aspects of our current situation in Pauline studies. My proposal, briefly, is that certain important historical questions about Paul remain unanswered, and an inadequate and unconvincing reading of Paul remains dominant, not so much because of any historical probability as because of its congeniality to contemporary cultural values.

As we all know, the 1970s saw the publication of several groundbreaking, paradigm-shattering books on Paul, including works by Rosemary Radford Ruether, Krister Stendahl, and E. P. Sanders.[9] In the wake of these significant works, scholars began to recognize the need for a "new perspective" on Paul. What came to be called the "Lutheran" reading—a scholarly convention of enormous value to Protestant dogmatics because it juxtaposed Paul's central theological theme, "justification by faith," with a supposed "Jewish doctrine" of "justification by works of law"—now appeared to be theologically problematic, morally complicit in Christian anti-Judaism, and historically untenable as well. Of course these arguments had been raised by other scholars in previous decades—one thinks especially of works by G. F. Moore and Samuel Sandmel[10]—but they didn't obtain the *traction* of the books by Ruether, Stendahl, and Sanders in wider scholarship, implicitly shaped as it had been by Christian dogmatic presuppositions.

With Sanders's sustained argument that Judaism contemporary with Paul simply did not imagine or practice anything like "works-righteousness" as a "pattern of religion," the whole edifice of conventional Pauline theology threatened to collapse. Paul appeared at least an inconsistent thinker. Sanders himself concluded, famously, that Paul had "thought backward, from solution to plight," to reach his conclusion that salvation through Christ and through "works of law" were incompatible. Paul then presumably shifted gears and "thought forward" when he wrote something like the letter to the Romans, arguing toward conclusions that he had already assumed as premises.

9. Ruether, *Faith and Fratricide*; Stendahl, *Paul among Jews and Gentiles*; Sanders, *Paul and Palestinian Judaism*.

10. Moore, *Judaism in the First Three Centuries*; Sandmel, *Genius of Paul*.

The result is logically incoherent argumentation on the apostle's part. Other scholars soon followed that general line of interpretation. Paul was practically incapable of coherent thought, reproducing theological slogans that had proven to be successful in a particular "niche market," i.e., among Gentile Christianity;[11] or else he was an enthusiastic convert to a new religious community who had taken over their presuppositions, in a fundamentally irrational process, as his own.[12]

Still other interpreters sought to take seriously Sanders's demonstration about the untenability of Jewish "works-righteousness" as a foil for Paul's thought, without, however, accepting Sanders's unattractive conclusions about Paul's theology. Following Stendahl's lead, they shifted the terms of the argument. It was not Jewish *works-righteousness* Paul opposed, but *Jewish opposition to Paul's law-free mission among gentiles*. When Paul argues against Jews and Judaism, as many scholars persist in holding he does in Romans and Galatians, it is not Jewish "legalism," but Jewish "exclusivism" or "ethnocentrism" or "cultural imperialism" that he opposes. The broader implied story here—as presented, for example, by James D. G. Dunn[13]—is that Paul began to preach a law-free gospel to Gentiles in a mission endorsed by the Jewish apostles in Jerusalem. Only later, when other Jews *opposed* Paul's mission out of their own chauvinistic and xenophobic assumptions, did Paul craft the theological polemic against "justification by works of the law" that we find in Romans and Galatians.

At first glance, this "new perspective on Paul" (as Dunn coined it) appears to breathe new life into the view, put forward a century earlier by William Wrede and Albert Schweitzer,[14] that justification by faith was (at least initially) not the center of Paul's theology, but only a defensive "rearguard action" against Jewish opposition. Indeed, the "new perspective" bears strongest resemblance to the *old* "dialectical" perspective of F. C. Baur, who interpreted all of early Christian history as the working out of a great conflict between Pauline "universalism" and "Jewish particularism."[15]

It bears note, however, that Baur, Wrede, and Schweitzer understood their readings as dramatic *alternatives* to the dominant theological interpretation of Paul. Today, in contrast, the "new perspective" offers an explicitly theological interpretation of the apostle. Like Baur, the "new perspective"

---

11. Räisänen, *Paul and the Law.*

12. Segal, *Paul the Convert.*

13. Dunn, "New Perspective on Paul"; Dunn, *Theology of Paul the Apostle.*

14. Wrede, *Paul*; Schweitzer, *Mysticism of Paul the Apostle.*

15. Baur, *Paul the Apostle of Jesus Christ*; see now Hafemann, "Paul and His Interpreters."

understands Paul's doctrine of justification by faith as fundamentally a theological affirmation of *inclusion,* and as a *defensive reaction* against Jewish opposition to inclusion. Paul's universalism is made to bear the theological burden that previously was borne by the "Lutheran" paradigm.

A CRITICAL ASSESSMENT

Since opposing Paul's inclusive gospel to "Jewish exclusivism" has become the common currency of Pauline interpretation today, it behooves us to ask whether this development is an advance in understanding the apostle's theology. Several observations suggest that it is not.

1. Proponents of the "new perspective" have been unable to meet the standard set by Sanders for documenting the prevalence of Jewish "exclusivism" in Paul's day. True enough, Jewish identity was defined in part by ritual boundary markers, but these markers (e.g., Sabbath observance, circumcision, *kashrut*) also defined modes of *inclusion* and *welcome* into the Jewish community.[16]

2. As Richard A. Horsley has observed, generalizations about Jewish "exclusivism" conform to "the theologically determined metanarrative of the field, the replacement of the overly political and particularistic religion 'Judaism' by the purely spiritual and universal religion 'Christianity.'"[17] However stereotypical and prejudicial, they persist in aspects of the "new perspective."[18] Mainstream Christian interpretation too often fails to rise above pejorative assumptions that Jewish identity and observance *per se* are problematic for Paul, constituting (for example) the "weakness" of the "weak in faith" of Romans 14.[19] No less prejudicial is the theological habit, stretching from Bultmann to Käsemann and beyond, of allegorizing "the Jew" in Paul's thought as a cipher for sinful or boastful humanity.[20]

3. Yet another grave challenge to the "new perspective" comes from the efforts of scholars, among them Lloyd Gaston, John G. Gager, Stanley K. Stowers, and Mark D. Nanos, to demonstrate not only that Paul's letters to the Romans and Galatians are *addressed* to Gentiles, but that the argument in both letters addresses *Gentile concerns* or *Gentile*

16. Fredriksen, *From Jesus to Christ,* 142–53.
17. Horsley, "Submerged Biblical Histories," 154.
18. Deidun, "James Dunn and John Ziesler."
19. Critiqued in Nanos, *Mystery of Romans,* 88–119.
20. Critiqued in Boyarin, *Radical Jew,* 209–14.

misunderstandings, not Jewish or Jewish-Christian attitudes.[21] It is widely acknowledged that Paul's warning to the Gentile believers in Rome not to "boast" over Israel (Romans 11) is the climax of the letter. Many scholars have retreated from this insight, however, insisting that "this cannot explain the whole of the letter," because the heart of the letter is a "debate" or "critique" or "attack on Judaism."[22] If, however, as I and others have argued, the whole of the letter's argument can be related to that goal; and if (as Gaston and Gager have argued) Galatians can be read successfully as directed against *Gentile* "Judaizing," then much of the need to "import" a supposedly exclusivistic Jewish opposition evaporates.[23]

4. To my mind, these are serious objections, and I would reasonably expect proponents of the "new perspective" to want to address them head-on. Surprisingly, the familiar lines of the "new perspective" are more often simply reasserted, without engagement with recent challenges. My question is, simply, *why*—why does so theologically and historically vulnerable an interpretation continue to hold sway in scholarship? To be sure, the "new perspective" represents an attempt to get beyond what now (in the wake of Sanders's work) appear as the prejudicial characterizations of Jewish "works-righteousness"; but does it simply replace those characterizations with equally prejudicial characterizations of Jewish "exclusivism"? Why do interpreters simply modify older answers to Sanders's question, "What [in Paul's view] is wrong with Judaism," rather than ask whether that line of inquiry is appropriate to Paul's thought in the first place?[24]

THE PROBLEM OF
PAUL'S ALLEGED "DOUBLE STANDARD"

I want to pose one more question about the current state of Pauline studies. I participate in the "Paul and Politics" SBL section, where we have for

---

21. Gaston, *Paul and the Torah*; Gager, *Origins of Anti-Semitism*; Gager, *Reinventing Paul*; Stowers, *Rereading of Romans*; Nanos, *Mystery of Romans*; Nanos, *Irony of Galatians*.

22. For example, Beker, *Paul the Apostle*, 74–76.

23. Elliott, *Rhetoric of Romans*; Gaston, *Paul and the Torah*; Gager, *Origins of Anti-Semitism*; Stowers, *Rereading of Romans*, 21–34.

24. See Eisenbaum, "Paul, Polemics, and the Problem of Essentialism"; also Nanos, "Paul and Judaism."

several years explored the role of imperial ideology and culture in Paul's environment. We have been surprised again and again to discover how little attention has been paid in conventional scholarship to some of the themes we are discovering, and how often a discussion of "Paul's politics" begins and ends with banal generalities about Romans 13 and obedience to the state. Other cultures—including, notably, German Protestantism, South African churches, and circles of Latin American liberation theology—have long realized the problematic nature of Romans 13 and have sought to bracket the passage in discussions of "Paul's politics." In Anglo-American scholarship, however, discussion often begins and ends with this passage.

Added to the canonical portraits of Paul as an "apostle of subordination"—the champion of subordination of women and of slaves (in Colossians, Ephesians, 1 Timothy and Titus)—the resulting impression is of what Elaine Pagels called a curious "double standard" on the part of the apostle: To continue observing kosher laws is to deny "the freedom for which Christ died," but to continue observing social, political, and marital laws and conventions remains acceptable, even commendable. Although the "new humanity" has transformed the entire relationship between Jews and gentiles, Paul does not allow it to challenge the whole structure of the believers' social, sexual, and political relationships.[25]

Given more time, I would want to quarrel—I *have* quarreled—with aspects of this characterization, especially its dependence on pseudo-Pauline texts for its generalizations.[26] As a depiction of conventional readings of Paul, however, it is accurate. Notice the terms in which this picture is couched. "Freedom" from the law—from determinate Jewish identity—is a good thing, Jewish difference apparently being an onerous burden. At the same time, our bookshelves groan beneath the weight of volumes explaining why Paul simply did not care about other forms of liberation.

How do such generalizations survive, let alone thrive in contemporary scholarship? Is it just the force of habit, the weight of received wisdom?

I suspect not. I suspect that the pressure comes rather from what Shawn Kelley has called the "racialized discourse" of modern biblical studies, dependent as it is (through F. C. Baur) on Hegel's hierarchy of absolute, enlightened universalism (= European culture) and primitive, irrational, tribal ethnocentrism (= the Other in Africa, Asia, and the Middle East). Drawing importantly from Edward Said's exposure of "orientalism" as the construction of Western imperialist culture, Kelley, and Richard Horsley before him, point out the close genealogical resemblance between Hegel's

25. Pagels, "Paul and Women," 545.

26. Elliott, *Liberating Paul,* 25–90.

"orientalism" and modern biblical scholarship's "Othering" of Judaism. The intriguing puzzle here is that such "orientalizing" patterns should persist, so powerfully, precisely in the social environment (North America) where they have been so decisively called into question.[27]

I suspect the ready dichotomy of "inclusion" and "universalism" against "exclusivity" and "ethnocentrism" is particularly convenient, comfortable, and seemingly self-evident to modern readers, *especially* in the American context, where a deeply felt *generic* religiosity and the ideal of inclusiveness are paramount values. Dale B. Martin observes that in post–World War II America the racism of Nazi Germany was so thoroughly stigmatized that race and nation are no longer acceptable categories for discussing Judaism: "the dominant category has become 'culture.'"[28] Is it surprising that American scholarship on Paul should attribute a similar "discovery" to the apostle Paul?

I also suspect that the enduring attraction of the picture of Paul's "social conservatism" owes much to the dominance of an American myth of innocence, which precludes even the interest in searching for a "Pauline politics" beyond the endorsement of the status quo and subordination to the powers that be (Romans 13). Hughes argues that we will only make progress toward democratic goals when we face and begin to counteract the myth of American innocence in U.S. culture. I ask whether we need to apply the same lesson to Pauline scholarship, and (to appropriate Schweitzer's discussion of historical-Jesus research) stop trying to drag Paul into our own time and cultural situation. We have seen important efforts to understand Paul as a *Jew* of his own time, including understanding him as devoutly Torah-observant.[29] The Paul and Politics section continues to sustain new insights into aspects of Paul's thought and praxis that cannot be assimilated with the ideology of Roman Empire. Both lines of investigation pull us away from the convenient synthesis of the "new perspective" and generalizations regarding Paul's "social conservatism"; they may also lead us into an important understanding of the apostle as a man of his own time.

27. Kelley, *Racializing Jesus*; Horsley, "Submerged Biblical Histories."

28. Martin, "Paul and the Judaism/Hellenism Dichotomy," 59.

29. Davies, *Paul and Rabbinic Judaism*; Jervell, *Unknown Paul*; Tomson, *Paul and the Jewish Law*; Nanos, *Mystery of Romans*; Nanos, *Irony of Galatians*.

5

Marxism and the Postcolonial Study of Paul

The originality of Marxist criticism . . . lies not in its historical approach to literature, but in its revolutionary understanding of history itself.

—Terry Eagleton[1]

Those of us for whom the Bible's operative vision is of a divine "option for the poor" must confess that only Marxism and its offspring have given political form to that vision.

—David Jobling[2]

Marxist interpretation of any part of the Bible has been a rarity. Even today, after the end of the Soviet Union and the dramatic dissolution of the Soviet bloc in Eastern Europe, we might expect the name "Marxist" to appear less inflammatory than before those events and even, at least in some academic circles, to enjoy a certain éclat. Yet only a few brave Hebrew Bible scholars, notable among them Norman K. Gottwald, Roland Boer, and David Jobling, routinely identify themselves in their work as Marxist critics.[3] Elements of Marxist criticism may be more widely known as they

1. Eagleton, *Marxism and Literary Criticism*, 3.
2. Jobling, "'Very Limited Ideological Options,'" 192.
3. Gottwald, *The Tribes of Yahweh*; Boer, "Western Marxism and the Interpretation

have passed, perhaps unrecognized by readers, under other names, such as "socio-literary" or "ideological criticism."[4]

The case is similar in New Testament studies, where those scholars who attempt a serious engagement with Marxist theory and methods have generally demurred from identifying their work as Marxist or from any explicit, sustained engagement with Marxism. More often such engagements are presented under the headings of "political" or "liberative" or "materialist" interpretation, or as readings "from the margins" or "from below."[5] So, for example, Richard Horsley has done much to advocate and to advance political, counter-imperial, and "people's history" interpretations of various aspects of early Judaism and Christianity, yet so far as I know, he nowhere describes his own work as Marxist in orientation.[6] Again, although Steven Friesen has offered a sustained critique of the ideological blind spots in "capitalist criticism" of the New Testament, he does not suggest Marxist criticism as an alternative; instead he pleads that we "move beyond the capitalism/Marxism argument," without pausing to describe what the Marxist side of such an argument might sound like.[7]

Those interpreters who have called most explicitly for a full complement of analytical methods that include distinctively Marxist categories of class and mode of production (whether or not they are identified as such) speak from what continue to be regarded, in mainstream (or in Elisabeth Schüssler Fiorenza's trenchant phrase, "malestream") North American biblical scholarship, as "contextualized" or "perspectival" approaches that combine feminist, gender, and postcolonial criticism.[8] Schüssler Fiorenza's neologism *kyriarchy* is increasingly recognized as an apt way to conceive of the overlapping systemic hierarchies of class, gender, race/ethnicity, colonialism, and sexuality in the ancient world and our own.[9] Yet as she and others observe, such pleas for complex, "multi-axial" methods have most

of the Hebrew Bible"; Boer, "Marx, Postcolonialism, and the Bible"; Jobling, "'Very Limited Ideological Options.'"

4. Gottwald, *Tribes of Yahweh*; Gottwald, *Hebrew Bible*; Yee, *Poor Banished Children of Eve*; Yee, "Ideological Criticism."

5. On materialist or "non-idealist" approaches to the Bible, see Kahl, "Toward a Materialist-Feminist Reading"; Lopez, *Apostle to the Conquered,* 7–11. Kahl names 1960s Europe as the formative environment for the scholars whom she discusses.

6. See, among many works, Horsley, "Submerged Biblical Histories"; Horsley, *Christian Origins.* "People's history" was pioneered by British Marxist historians; see the concise retrospective of Crossley, *Why Christianity Happened,* 5–18.

7. Friesen, "Poverty in Pauline Studies," 336–37.

8. For example, Yee, *Poor Banished Children of Eve*; Kwok, *Postcolonial Imagination and Feminist Theology*; Marchal, *Politics of Heaven,* ch. 1.

9. Schüssler Fiorenza, *Power of the Word,* 1.

often been met with a studied silence or marginalization by a discipline more interested (as we should expect, in late capitalism) in the proliferation of difference than in concerted thinking and action in terms of class solidarity.[10]

ELEMENTS OF MARXIST INTERPRETATION

Given the relative unfamiliarity with Marxist themes in the field of biblical studies, it might be useful to distinguish Marxist historiography, with which this essay is concerned, from Marxist philosophical theory and Marxist political action, with which it is not. (Many contemporary Marxists in the "New Left" would urge a similar distinction between the Marxist legacy as mobilized in democratic socialist movements and the legacy of Leninism-Stalinism.)[11] I follow G. E. M. de Ste. Croix in understanding "Marxist" historiography as a way of describing past (and present) societies that gives foremost attention to the dynamics of *class* and *class struggle*. By *class* I understand the pattern of relationships between human beings in a society as they are mutually involved in the process of production, whether the relationships involve property or labor. *Class struggle* consists in the exploitation that characterizes those relationships and resistance to that exploitation.[12] Though Marx's particular focus was the industrial capitalism of nineteenth-century England, he was also keenly interested in tracing the dynamics of class struggle throughout history.[13] Following Marx's insights, de Ste. Croix had no trouble describing those dynamics in the Roman world. The propertied class derived the economic surplus that "freed them from the necessity of taking part in the process of production"—not from wage labor, as in contemporary industrial capitalist society, but from unfree labor of various kinds, such as slavery.[14] Imperialism, whether in the undeniably different forms of ancient Rome or in the modern world, is but "a special

10. Marchal, *Politics of Heaven*, ch. 1. Fredric Jameson understands "postmodernism" and the proliferation of difference as a function of capitalism's continuing mutation: *Postmodernism*.

11. See Therborn, *From Marxism to Post-Marxism?* The question of "exonerating" Marx for the crimes committed in his name is of course contested; see Kolakowski, *Main Currents of Marxism*.

12. De Ste. Croix, *Class Struggle in the Ancient Greek World*, 31–33.

13. A point ably made by de Ste. Croix (*Class Struggle in the Ancient Greek World*, 23–25); on the reception of Marx (or lack of it) among classical scholars, see ibid., 19–23.

14. De Ste. Croix, *Class Struggle in the Ancient Greek World*, 39, 133–47.

case" of extraction and exploitation, involving "economic and/or political subjection to a power outside the community."[15]

Quoting liberally from Marx's writings, de Ste. Croix provides helpful correctives to the popular misrepresentation of Marx's ideas as imposing a strict "economic determinism"[16] and to the erroneous assumption that class struggle can be said to exist only when and where self-conscious classes are engaged in explicitly political struggle.[17] The correctives are important. As de Ste. Croix observes, the nearly "complete . . . lack of interest" displayed by English-language historians of the Greco-Roman world issues as much from ignorance or misunderstanding of Marx's ideas as from overt rejection of them.[18] He takes care nevertheless to observe that, to scholars satisfied with the present order, there is reason enough for avoidance of the sorts of questions Marxism raises:

> Whereas descriptions of ancient society in terms of some category other than class—status, for instance—are perfectly innocuous, in the sense that they need have no direct relevance to the modern world . . . an analysis of Greek and Roman society in terms of class, in the specifically Marxist sense, is indeed . . . something *threatening,* something that speaks directly to every one of us today and insistently demands to be applied to the contemporary world.[19]

It is one thing to identify aspects of class struggle in the ancient world and another to describe what a Marxist investigation of the New Testament writings might look like. Obviously, for such an investigation the role these writings subsequently played as the sacred Scriptures of the Christian religion must in no way be allowed to limit or qualify the application of historical methods. As Fredric Jameson declares in his essay on Marxist interpretation, "The convenient working distinction between cultural texts that are social and political and those that are not"—for example, religious texts—"becomes something worse than an error: namely, a symptom and a reinforcement of the reification and privatization of contemporary life" that is "the tendential law of social life under capitalism." By contrast, Marxist

---

15. De Ste. Croix, *Class Struggle in the Ancient Greek World*, 44; on Roman imperialism, see chs. 6–8.

16. De Ste. Croix, *Class Struggle in the Ancient Greek World*, 25–28.

17. De Ste. Croix, *Class Struggle in the Ancient Greek World*, 36, 57–66.

18. De Ste. Croix, *Class Struggle in the Ancient Greek World*, 19–20.

19. De Ste. Croix, *Class Struggle in the Ancient Greek World*, 45 (emphasis in original).

interpretation insists that "there is nothing that is not social and historical—indeed, everything is 'in the last analysis' political."[20]

Marxist interpretation of texts makes use of accepted historical- and
literary-critical methods, but with a clear conception of the ideological
character of cultural texts. Jameson describes three distinct operations in
such interpretation. In the first, narrowly historical phase, a text is understood as a symbolic act, an attempt to resolve specific contradictions in a
historical situation. Because Marxism understands culture to be generated
by the deep contradictions inherent in class struggle that correspond to a
particular mode of production, and because these contradictions are evidently still unresolved in the history of which we, too, are a part, the situ-
ational character of the text cannot be the final object of our interpretation.
Thus Marxist criticism does not end where some applications of historical
criticism leave off. Rather, in a second phase, we must regard the text as an
attempt at ideological closure, at resolving the unresolvable—those deeper
material contradictions that have generated the ideological framework in
which a text necessarily operates. The text "maps the limits of a specific
ideological consciousness and marks the conceptual points beyond which
that consciousness cannot go."[21] So understood, the text points to a broader
semantic horizon, the social order that is the expression of class struggle
in a particular period. In this second phase of interpretation, the object of
investigation is "the great collective and class discourses" of that period, of
which the text "is little more than an individual *parole* or utterance."[22]

But because the text inheres, as we do, in "a single great collective story,
a single vast unfinished plot," the final horizon of interpretation is nothing
less than "the ultimate horizon of human history as a whole."[23] The text as
parole and the class discourse or *langue* of which it is an utterance point, in a
particular place and time, to "the coexistence of various sign systems which
are themselves traces or anticipations of modes of production," which are
themselves always in flux and tension. The final phase of Marxist interpretation points to the historical possibilities for transformation and "cultural
revolution" latent in those tensions.[24]

20. Jameson, *Political Unconscious*, 20.

21. Jameson, *Political Unconscious*, 47.

22. Jameson, *Political Unconscious*, 76.

23. Jameson, *Political Unconscious*, 19–20, 76; see further 83–88.

24. Jameson, *Political Unconscious*, 76; see 88–96. On the vexed debates over the
category "mode of production," see Jameson, *Political Unconscious*, 89–90; also Boer,
Marxist Criticism of the Bible, 229–46.

MARXIST INTERPRETATION OF EARLY CHRISTIANITY

What now appears as a virtual "dividing wall" between New Testament scholarship and Marxism was not a fixed barrier from the beginning. Frederick Engels was keenly interested in early Christianity as "a movement of oppressed people" with "notable points of resemblance with the modern working-class movement"—including its power to attract both the dispossessed and a variety of charlatans eager to prey upon them.[25] Karl Kautsky applied Marxist principles to a much more expansive discussion of the "foundations of Christianity."[26] According to Kautsky's account, Jesus mounted an abortive rebellion that the Gospel writers subsequently covered up; his execution makes sense only on that basis.[27] The organization that Jesus established before his death—an incipient communism among the free proletariat of Jerusalem—survived him: indeed it was "the vitality of the community" that "created the belief in the continued life of their Messiah."[28] Once the movement spread beyond Palestine into the Diaspora, it immediately attracted non-Jews among the lower classes, but the tension between the movement's originally Jewish nationalist impulses and its proletarian appeal across ethnicities became acute.

The figure of Paul was central for Kautsky's account. Paul represented the dynamic that accelerated the spread of Christianity as a proletarian movement unmoored from its Jewish character.[29] This was ultimately a short-lived moment, however, for a number of reasons. First, the destruction of Jerusalem "stifled the last popular force in the Empire" so that afterwards "there was no longer any basis for an independent class movement of the Jewish proletariat."[30] Second, the urban poor and slaves could never achieve a community of production like that which enabled the Jerusalem movement to thrive. Their movement—deprived of any meaningful way to practice the community of production or of goods beyond common meals[31]—became increasingly "subservient and even servile" after the destruction of Jerusalem. It declined into "the budding Christian opportunism

25. Engels, "On the History of Early Christianity."

26. Kautsky, *Foundations of Christianity*, 86.

27. Kautsky, *Foundations of Christianity*, 310–14.

28. Kautsky, *Foundations of Christianity*, 322–23.

29. Kautsky, *Foundations of Christianity*, 328–29.

30. Kautsky, *Foundations of Christianity*, 334–35.

31. Kautsky, *Foundations of Christianity*, 352–53.

of the second century," which would, at last, "raise the spineless obedience of the slave to a moral duty."[32]

Aspects of this remarkable account of Christian origins find definite, albeit diverse, echoes in more recent works, such as Gerd Theissen's distinction of the "radical theocratic" ethic of the Palestinian Jesus movement from the "familial love-patriarchalism" of the urban Hellenistic mission, where the itinerant ideal "retreats almost completely."[33] Another example is Justin Meggitt's description of the economic "mutualism" that Paul encouraged as a valuable "survival strategy" at the subsistence level for the urban poor, who could not otherwise draw on collective resources as peasants could.[34] Though we find very different estimations of the material circumstances of the Pauline assemblies in Theissen ("a certain degree of prosperity") and Meggitt ("a bleak existence"), both sustain Kautsky's focus on how those material circumstances differed from the situation of the Palestinian Jesus movement.

Since Kautsky's work, however, we have not seen a similarly comprehensive account of the rise and fall of early Christianity as a social revolutionary movement. Nor have we seen as incisive a discussion of the Pauline mission as a fateful tactical blunder in that movement's advance. By advancing too quickly toward a *symbolic* unity of urban proles across ethnic and provincial boundaries, Kautsky argued, the movement overreached its *material* base. Without the clear example of a community of goods that Jerusalem had provided, these communities quickly lost their character as a class movement.

THE CURIOUS ABSENCE OF MARXIST CONCERNS IN NEW TESTAMENT SCHOLARSHIP

Kautsky represents the keen interest among some early Marxists in the origins of Christianity. If his account is not immediately familiar to New Testament scholars today, it is not because it lacks either coherence or currency with the critical scholarship of his time. The explanation lies elsewhere.

James Crossley describes a general "fear of and hostility to Marxism" in a discipline that remains dominated by Christian theological interests.[35] Karl Barth's dialectical theology and his general suspicion of any socialism

---

32. Kautsky, *Foundations of Christianity*, 354–55.

33. Theissen, *Social Setting of Pauline Christianity*, 36–37.

34. Meggitt, *Paul, Poverty and Survival*, ch. 5 ("Survival Strategies").

35. Crossley, *Why Christianity Happened*, 9.

that was not avowedly "Christian" certainly played a role in this outcome.[36] So did the powerful influence of anti-Communist ideology, manifested both as pressure on the churches and as dissension within the churches. As a result, although in the last forty years scholarship on the social circumstances of the Pauline assemblies has developed into a robust field, it has done so despite the almost complete neglect of questions of class and class struggle. The fact that New Testament scholars routinely sound warnings against the "danger" of Marxist approaches even though such analysis remains virtually nonexistent should alert us to the presence of ideological currents within the discipline.[37]

As Steven Friesen has shown, Adolf Deissmann's generalizations at the beginning of the twentieth century about the "mixed" social makeup of Pauline Christianity, which he described as a "cross-section" of society drawn from "the middle and lower classes," have exercised a disproportionate influence on subsequent scholarship.[38] Although Wayne Meeks and Abraham Malherbe have hailed a "new consensus" since the 1970s that has replaced the older views of Deissmann, Friesen has shown that their views in fact represent the mainstream consensus of twentieth-century New Testament scholarship, a view that is essentially a continuation of Deissmann's thesis.[39] This mainstream consensus has mostly marginalized the topic of poverty, whether by (a) ignoring it completely, (b) trivializing it by extolling the virtues of a putative first-century economic expansion, or (c) elaborating sophisticated social-scientific models that simply erase class from consideration.[40] The last strategy, dominant since the 1970s, has paid more attention to "social status," but, as Friesen has observed, "economic inequality . . . never gained a foothold as a significant topic of conversation."[41] To the contrary, "our preoccupation with 'social status' is the very mechanism by which we have ignored poverty and economic issues."[42] To Friesen's critiques of social-status modeling we might add a

36. Crossley, *Why Christianity Happened*, 3–5; Theissen, *Social Reality and the Early Christians*, 9–13.

37. Crossley, *Why Christianity Happened,* 11, citing Luise Schottroff and Horrell, "'Not Many Powerful,'" 278–79.

38. Friesen, "Poverty in Pauline Studies," especially 326–27. See Deissmann, *Paul,* 241–43.

39. See Meeks, *First Urban Christians*; Malherbe, *Social Aspects of Early Christianity*; and now Still and Horrell, *After the First Urban Christians*.

40. Friesen, "Blessings of Hegemony," 122–24.

41. Friesen, "Blessings of Hegemony," 124–25.

42. Friesen, "Blessings of Hegemony," 124–25. For further discussion, see Elliott, "Diagnosing an Allergic Reaction" (Chapter 6 in this volume).

critique of cultural-anthropological scholarship that has advanced a static, functionalist view of first-century society at the expense of any attention to class or class struggle.[43]

Common to these discussions of social realities in the Pauline churches is the refusal "to engage in economic analysis."[44] There are sufficient data to carry out such analysis, as Friesen, Meggitt, and Peter Oakes have recently shown in important studies.[45] But apart from these and similar efforts, the general pattern in scholarship on Paul's communities is clear: if poverty is generally ignored, oppression and class conflict are unmentionable.[46] Friesen relates this mind-set to the broader formation of academic disciplines in the twentieth century, when Fordist industrial capitalism created the need for an educated professional-managerial class. The progression of scholarly discussions of poverty in the Pauline churches (or the systematic avoidance of such discussion) is, Friesen suggests, only one instance of a larger pattern: "Higher education taught future professionals to accept and to overlook economic inequality, and Pauline studies did so as well."[47] Friesen calls this pattern of interpretation "capitalist criticism."

MARXISM AND POSTCOLONIAL CRITICISM

In contrast to "capitalist criticism" as practiced and taught in the metropolitan centers of the West, one might expect postcolonial criticism to readily and systematically embrace the tenets of Marxism. After all, imperialism, and especially the "impressive ideological formations" that undergird and impel it, lies at the heart of postcolonial criticism,[48] and Marx (and to an even greater extent, Lenin) had already theorized imperialism as the extension of class struggle. Moreover, early critics of colonialism like Frantz

43. I have in mind Malina and Pilch, *Social-Science Commentary on the Letters of Paul,* especially 393; and Malina, *New Testament World,* 97. For critiques of their positions, see Elliott, "Diagnosing an Allergic Reaction" (Chapter 6 in this volume).

44. Friesen, "Poverty in Pauline Studies," 357.

45. Friesen, "Poverty in Pauline Studies," 357. Friesen's work gives statistical precision to the argument of Meggitt (*Paul, Poverty and Survival*). These ideas are taken up in Peter Oakes's discussion of living space in Pompeii (*Reading Romans in Pompeii*). Meggitt's work provoked strong reactions from advocates of the alleged "new consensus"; see responses by Dale B. Martin (Martin, "Review Essay") and Theissen, "Social Structure of Pauline Communities" in *Journal for the Study of the New Testament,* and Meggitt's response (Meggitt, "Response to Martin and Theissen") in the same issue.

46. Friesen, "Poverty in Pauline Studies," 335.

47. Friesen, "Blessings of Hegemony," 125–27.

48. Said, *Culture and Imperialism,* 9.

Fanon, W. E. B. Du Bois, and C. L. R. James were avowed Marxists. Fanon called for nothing less than socialist revolution as the only viable path to decolonization.[49] More recently, Aijaz Ahmad has invoked Marxism to raise a similarly trenchant critique of the "mystificatory character" of much postcolonial discourse, which effaces the socialist cause in its celebration of national decolonization.[50] Nevertheless, the postcolonial criticism of the last few decades has so largely ignored Marx and Marxism as to give some observers the impression that its proponents wish to "dump" Marx and "forget Marxism."[51]

In her introductory text on postcolonial theory, Leela Gandhi provides a lucid summary of the intellectual "genealogies" that lie behind this debate.[52] Although a long history of Marxist interpretation has insisted that colonialism is at least "a necessary subplot" in the expansion of European capitalism, postcolonial analysts rarely acknowledge their "genealogical debt" to Marxism, claiming closer affinity to Foucauldian poststructuralism. Because Marxism has generally focused its attention on class struggle as manifested in European industrial capitalism, some postcolonial critics have argued that it fails to do justice to the distinctiveness of the colonial experience in other parts of the world. They also protest that the Marxist claim to have uncovered a single dynamic shaping universal history is but another form of European cultural imperialism. Thus, Dipesh Chakrabarty protests that in Marxism as well as other European philosophical traditions, history remains the discourse through which the West construes the rest of the world in terms of its own narrative: "Europe remains the sovereign, theoretical subject of all histories, including the ones we call 'Indian,' 'Chinese,' 'Kenyan,' and so on."[53] From their side, Marxists insist that privileging the experience of colonialism obscures the genuine similarities and shared interests among oppressed classes who may not have experienced colonization, or may not have experienced it in the same way.[54] Further, because Marxists regard class solidarity across national and ethnic boundaries as the only possible engine of historical transformation, they see the characteristic

49. Fanon, *Wretched of the Earth*.

50. Ahmad, *In Theory*, ch. 8; quotation from 317.

51. Boer, "Marx, Postcolonialism, and the Bible," 166–67.

52. Gandhi, *Postcolonial Theory*.

53. Gandhi, *Postcolonial Theory*, 24–26, 170–71. Chakrabarty, "Postcoloniality and the Artifice of History," 1.

54. This protest is raised especially against postcolonial critics, who fail to distinguish adequately between former colonies like the United States or Australia and other formerly colonized nations: see Gandhi, *Postcolonial Theory*, 167–70; against Ashcroft et al., *Empire Writes Back*.

postcolonial emphasis on the formation of distinctive subaltern subjectivities as a dangerous distraction from the necessary *collective* resistance to political and cultural domination.

The Marxist protest is occasionally phrased in terms that approach *ad hominem* attacks on postcolonial interpreters, as when Arif Dirlik declares that postcolonialism is what happens "when Third World intellectuals have arrived in the First World."[55] Gandhi and Spivak respond that despite the unavoidable challenges of "positionality," the postcolonial interpreter ensconced in Western academia nevertheless has a genuine "political vocation" to precipitate the sort of dialogue between Western and non-Western academies that can "think a way out of the epistemological violence of the colonial encounter."[56]

MARXISM AND POSTCOLONIAL NEW TESTAMENT STUDIES

Because the topic of empire is at the heart of postcolonial criticism, it is not surprising that New Testament critic Fernando Segovia has named as the "first dimension of a postcolonial optic" an analysis that contextualizes Jewish and early Christian texts within "the reality of empire, of imperialism and colonialism."[57] One would therefore expect to find postcolonial and Marxist perspectives to be closely allied within the discipline. But here again, much postcolonial New Testament interpretation has shown a striking disinterest in Karl Marx's theories, if not outright hostility to them.[58] As Roland Boer quips, "One is more likely to come across Groucho or Harpo Marx in the writings of biblical critics who have taken up postcolonial theory or, indeed, postcolonial critics who have written about the Bible."[59]

Elaborating much of the same genealogy of postcolonialism that Leela Gandhi has described, Boer laments the eclipse in postcolonial biblical criticism of an understanding of history as the arena of class struggle. Instead, the Bible's historical role in the colonial project of "civilizing" the "native"

55. Dirlik, "Postcolonial Aura." Ahmad offers similar criticisms in Ahmad, *In Theory*. See also Gandhi, *Postcolonial Theory*, 27–28, 56–57.

56. Spivak, *Outside in the Teaching Machine*; Gandhi, *Postcolonial Theory*, 54–63, 176.

57. Segovia, "Biblical Criticism and Postcolonial Studies," 56.

58. Perhaps the most dramatic opposition appears in K.-K. Yeo's postcolonial interpretation of 1 Thessalonians, where he dismisses Marxism as an expression of "the spirit of the anti-Christ" (in Patte, *Global Bible Commentary*, 500).

59. Boer, "Marx, Postcolonialism, and the Bible," 170.

and the associated indigenous project of "decolonizing the Bible" have been elevated to primary status. As a result, postcolonial critics have occupied themselves with a search for "counter-hegemonic moments in canonical texts" rather than "the kind of work that begins to make sense of the anti-colonial movements and wars of independence." Boer asks whether imaginative textual "interventions" will "remain ultimately futile, absorbed into the dominant system?"[60]

This concern echoes the more general critique of postcolonial critics as third-world intellectuals who "have arrived" in first-world academia.[61] It would be unfair, however, to apply such generalizations indiscriminately to postcolonial feminist theologians like Kwok Pui-lan or Musa Dube, who have repeatedly discussed the intersection of overlapping domains of class, gender, and ethnic oppression and the need for a broad solidarity in inter-related struggles for liberation.[62] It is nevertheless appropriate to pose this concern as a "test," as theologian Catherine Keller does, for postcolonial interpreters. Keller asks whether postcolonial theory is used in such a way as "to relativize any revolutionary impulse, to dissipate the political energy of transformation, to replace active movements of change with clever postures of transgression."[63]

Of course, the decolonization of the Bible is not primarily a phenomenon of Western academia. It is an integral component also of the praxis carried out in local sites of emancipatory struggle, such as apartheid South Africa, where the Bible was an important part, perhaps the most important part, of the symbolic repertoire. Nonetheless, David Jobling ably characterizes such sites as offering "very limited ideological options." The work of decolonizing the Bible requires distinguishing the message(s) of the Bible from the colonizing project brought by European missionaries, but this work is not usually at the forefront of broad popular movements for liberation. Rather it remains the case that "the Bible's location is often—surely *most* often—some form of church."[64] Churches themselves are sites

---

60. Boer, "Marx, Postcolonialism, and the Bible," 170. Boer (pp. 171–74) takes the prodigious work of R. S. Sugirtharajah as a particular example of the eclipse of Marx and the abandonment of Marxist methods as thoroughly dispensable.

61. See, for example, Gandhi, *Postcolonial Theory,* 59–60; Spivak, *Outside in the Teaching Machine,* 56–57.

62. Kwok, *Postcolonial Imagination*; Dube, *Postcolonial Feminist Interpretation of the Bible.*

63. Keller, *God and Power,* 103.

64. Jobling, "'Very Limited Ideological Options,'" 187; the phrase comes from Mofokeng, "Black Christians, the Bible and Liberation," 40. On the role of the Bible in popular struggles, see especially West, *Academy of the Poor.*

of "very limited ideological options" because they are often divided in their political commitments (where such commitments are even expressed) and because "the Bible/Christianity has tended heavily to be on the wrong side of the colonial/postcolonial struggle."[65] Both Marxism and those churches that practice the decolonization of the Bible can provide resources for local liberative struggles, Jobling argues, not least because those involved in local struggles often "need some sort of organized view of the outside world which confronts them" such as Marxism and Christianity—"two inveterately globalizing mindsets"—provide. But we should hardly expect them to be adopted in equal measure for the same reason that Alistair Kee noted concerning theologies of liberation: churches will not readily embrace Marx's critique of *religion* while pursuing a *theological* decolonization.[66]

We see, then, that postcolonial biblical critics in Western academia—especially those located in theological institutions—occupy a particularly complex, precarious position. They represent their own decolonized nations to the Western academy, yet their incorporation often hinges on their position as expressions of "exotic culture." They represent peoples who remain politically, culturally, or economically oppressed, yet they do so as faculty members at prestigious Western universities and seminaries. They represent often vibrant decolonized churches to a post-Christendom Western ecclesiastical establishment that is often more concerned about its survival than about political transformation. And even if they embrace socialist politics—something that one should hardly assume—that same Western Christian establishment assimilates them as emblems of institutional commitment to multiculturalism rather than as advocates of class struggle. Given the political economy of Western theological higher education, we should not be surprised to find postcolonial biblical criticism more often emphasizing themes of acceptance across cultural difference than of revolutionary class consciousness. An exception to this pattern can be seen in the many subaltern women who have spoken out courageously against the multiple oppressions of ethnic, colonial, class, and gender discrimination despite the compounded jeopardies that these oppressions place upon them.[67]

---

65. Jobling, "'Very Limited Ideological Options,'" 189.

66. Jobling, "'Very Limited Ideological Options,'"190. Kee, *Marx and the Failure of Liberation Theology.*

67. Keller speaks to these multiple jeopardies and for the necessity of a relational ethic of "just love" rather than of ideological purism (*God and Power,* 107–11).

MARXIST CHALLENGES FOR
THE POSTCOLONIAL INTERPRETATION OF PAUL

To date, distinctly Marxist categories of analysis such as *class* and *class struggle* have been mostly marginalized in postcolonial interpretations of Paul in favor of conversations about imperial ideology, colonial identity, and hybridity.[68] Rather than adding another survey of postcolonial literature to those presented elsewhere, I would like to offer a list of challenges that Marxism poses to postcolonial interpretation as well as to more conventional "capitalist" modes of criticism.

Class, Class Struggle, and Ideology

The cornerstone of contemporary Marxist historiography is the correlation of the ideological representations in a particular culture with the economic relations inhering in the current mode of production.[69] With regard to the early Roman Principate, we are dealing with a transition from an agrarian, tributary mode of production to an increasing reliance on slave labor, as conquests occasioned the incorporation of more and more slaves into an expanding imperial economy. The first mode of production correlates with the temple state, of which "religion" and the prerogatives of (divine and human) monarchy (evoked by the term "sacred kingship") were the indispensable ideological apparatus. But the expanding empire faced a more complex ideological challenge. A society that is based on slave production depends on the careful maintenance of a symbolic system of difference: citizens must be distinguished from noncitizens, free persons from slaves, conquerors from conquered. Bodies that enjoy a presumption of freedom from being shackled, flogged, pierced, and crucified must be distinguished from those that do not. In the Roman era, this distinction was represented visually through an elaborate iconographical system that encoded as natural the power differentials inhering in gender and class relationships as well as

---

68. See, for example, the variety of essays on the letters of Paul in Segovia and Sugirtharajah, *Postcolonial Commentary on the New Testament Writings.* While economic realities are discussed in several of the essays on Pauline Letters, nowhere does the reader encounter a sustained discussion of class relations based in the organization of material production.

69. On mode of production, see Boer, *Marxist Criticism of the Bible,* 244–45; Jameson, *Political Unconscious,* 89–90; de Ste. Croix, *Class Struggle,* 29–35; on the Roman economy, see Garnsey and Saller, *Roman Empire,* 3–5. These paragraphs are more fully developed in Elliott, *Arrogance of Nations,* 28–30, 156–59; and Elliott, "Ideological Closure in the Christ-Event," 144–45 (see Chapter 7 in this volume).

those distinguishing Romans from other peoples. The distinction was also rehearsed ritually at various sites including the temple or shrine, the arena, and places of crucifixion.[70]

Symbolic representations of the spectacular violence, invincible military might, and inevitability of Roman hegemony were already abundant during the Republic. Under the Principate, these images expanded to include the elaborate ideological representation of the emperor. Beginning with Augustus, the emperor was portrayed simultaneously as a peace-bringing monarch and devoted high priest (symbolizations appropriate to an agrarian mode of production) and a benevolent householder, guardian of domestic morality, and pious father of his people (legitimizations essential to the slaveholding class in a slave-based mode of production). These crucial innovations in the iconographic, literary-poetic, and ideological representations of Augustus were appropriated and adapted by his successors, who asserted both genealogical and theological claims to his legacy, relying particularly on the symbolization of the emperor as *divi filius*, "son of the divine one."[71]

From a Marxist point of view, the correlation between prevailing economic relationships and dominant ideological representations cannot be sundered. For this reason, discussions of the class position of Paul and the members of his assemblies, class-conscious analyses of particular economic practices—what Justin Meggitt has called "mutualism," the only "survival strategy" left to the urban poor—and examination of Paul's resistance to patronage overtures from higher-class individuals are of primary importance.[72] But the interpretation of these economic practices should not be separated from an ideological understanding of Paul's proclamation of a crucified and risen Christ, as if the former were incidental or merely pragmatic mechanisms for sustaining the assemblies as *religious* groups

---

70. On iconography, see Zanker, *Power of Images*; for application to the interpretation of Paul, see Lopez, *Apostle to the Conquered*; and Kahl, *Galatians Re-imagined*.

71. I argue that this ideology is the immediate context of Romans in Elliott, *Arrogance of Nations*, ch. 1.

72. On the location of Paul and the vast majority of his congregations among the poor, see Meggitt, *Paul, Poverty and Survival*, ch. 4; on mutualism, Meggitt, *Paul, Poverty and Survival*, ch. 5. I compare Meggitt's argument with analogues in contemporary rural Haiti in Elliott, "Strategies of Resistance and Hidden Transcripts," Chapter 3 in this volume. On Paul's resistance to patronage, see Chow, *Patronage and Power*; on his repudiation of the logic of asymmetrical obligation that was the basis of patronage, see Reasoner, *"Strong" and the "Weak."* On the collection, see Georgi, *Remembering the Poor*; Wan, "Collection for the Saints as an Anti-colonial Act." On the radicality of Paul's economic practice, see Stubbs, "Subjection, Reflection, Resistance"; Welborn, *That There May Be Equality*.

that were primarily concerned with beliefs in the latter. For Paul to insist that Christ took "the form of a slave" and "became obedient to the point of death—even death on a cross" (Phil 2:7–8), and that God's action in raising this "doulomorphic" messiah from the dead made possible the filiation of a new and free people as the "children of God" (Rom 8:12–21) is an unmistakable expression (in the language of Jewish apocalypticism) of solidarity with the lowest classes, akin to what contemporary liberation theologians call the "preferential option for the poor."[73]

Ethnicity and Imperialism

Recent Western interpretation of Paul—especially under the banner of the "New Perspective"—has emphasized themes of multicultural and multiethnic tolerance and inclusion as Paul's legacy for the contemporary world. After landmark studies in the 1970s showed the traditional theological opposition of Paul's doctrine of justification to a supposed Jewish works-righteousness to be historically untenable and morally bankrupt,[74] many interpreters, chastened by those studies, adopted an alternative exposition of Paul's gospel as a form of advocacy for "the inclusion of Gentiles" and the "legitimization of the Gentile church." A corollary of the emerging "New Perspective on Paul" was a new explanation of "what, in Paul's view, was wrong with Judaism," which focused on circumcision, kashrut, and Sabbath observance as badges of identity and thus as expressions of characteristically Jewish "ethnocentrism," nationalism, or "exclusivism."[75] Ethnic tensions between Jews and non-Jews have been proposed as the chief concern motivating Paul's letters to the Romans and Galatians.[76]

The New Perspective has proven quite popular, in part because of its congeniality to the Western liberal celebration of multicultural difference,[77] but it has also met significant criticism. Even when carefully phrased in terms

73. See now Sobrino, *No Salvation outside the Poor*; Elliott, *Arrogance of Nations*, ch. 5 and epilog.

74. Stendahl, *Paul among Jews and Gentiles*; Sanders, *Paul and Palestinian Judaism*; Sanders, *Paul, the Law, and the Jewish People*.

75. See Dunn, "New Perspective on Paul," and Dunn, *Theology of Paul the Apostle*; further bibliography and discussion are available online at http://www.ThePaulPage.com.

76. See, for example, Walters, *Ethnic Issues in Paul's Letter to the Romans*; Esler, *Conflict and Identity in Romans*; Esler, *Galatians*.

77. See Campbell, *Paul's Gospel in an Intercultural Context*; Barclay, "'Neither Jew nor Greek'"; Esler, *Galatians*, 235–39 (on "the intercultural promise of Galatians"); Park, *Either Jew or Gentile*.

of a conflict between "universal" and "exclusivistic" trends within Judaism rather than as a wholesale conflict between Pauline Christianity and Jewish religion, some of the interpretations associated with the New Perspective have purchased a contemporary theological or cultural relevance for Paul at a high price. Too often they rely on derogatory (and generally undocumented) characterizations of Judaism—especially when Paul is the only named example of the supposed "universalistic" strain in Judaism.[78] Similarly, Jewish feminist scholars have criticized Christian feminist, liberationist, and now postcolonial interpreters for constructions of early Christianity that end up "blaming the Jews for the birth of patriarchy."[79] Attempts to portray Pauline Christianity as being "non-ethnic" or transcending ethnicity face decisive critiques, first, for being unavoidably supersessionistic,[80] and, second, for failing to give full respect to Paul's own Jewish identity.[81]

It is important to recognize that more is at stake here than the perpetuation of inexcusable stereotypes regarding Judaism. In her essay on decolonizing feminism, Chandra Talpade Mohanty notes that "multicultural" analyses in the metropolitan West often bypass an analysis of power relations. She calls for a "fundamental reconceptualization of our categories of analysis so that [ethnic] differences can be historically specified and understood as part of larger political processes and systems."[82] To similar effect with regard to New Testament postcolonial scholarship in particular, Tat-siong Benny Liew highlights the often hidden role that power differentials play in Western discourse on ethnicity and race.[83]

Marxist interpretation poses an additional challenge to the "universal" Paul, asking whether such interpretations are purchased at the price of a studied silence over issues of class, exploitation, and class struggle and a fully historical contextualization of the constructions of ethnicity in Paul's era. Explicit attention must be given to the scope and contours of

78. A good critique of the New Perspective can be found in Deidun, "James Dunn and John Ziesler." Interpretations directed in part against it include Nanos, *Mystery of Romans*; Boyarin, *Radical Jew*; and Eisenbaum, *Paul Was Not a Christian*.

79. See Plaskow, "Anti-Judaism in Feminist Christian Interpretation"; Heschel, "Anti-Judaism in Christian Feminist Theology"; Schottroff et al., *Feminist Interpretation*, 55. On the same dynamic in postcolonial studies, see Levine, "Disease of Postcolonial New Testament Studies"; Kwok, *Postcolonial Imagination*, 93–99.

80. See Buell and Hodge, "Politics of Interpretation"; Hodge, "Apostle to the Gentiles"; Elliott, *Arrogance of Nations*, 47–50.

81. Eisenbaum criticizes the tendency of some New Perspective scholarship to read Paul as ethnically or culturally Jewish—as a Jew "*kata sarka*"—but as theologically Christian (Eisenbaum, "Paul, Polemics").

82. Mohanty, *Feminism without Borders*, 193.

83. Liew, "Margins and (Cutting-)Edges."

"Romanization" in the early Principate as the cultural and political means for assimilating provincial elites into the imperial system, as well as to the ways in which patronage and the civic cultus served that assimilation.[84] Mark Reasoner has described a "Roman ethnocentrism," involving integrated codes of strength and weakness, honor and shame, class and status, and patronage and obligation, as the immediate context of Paul's letter to the Romans.[85] Similarly, but with greater theoretical emphasis on the interplay of imperial, class, and gender inequalities, Davina Lopez and Brigitte Kahl have offered insightful studies of Paul's mission, and of Galatians in particular, as posing an alternative to Romanizing constructions of ethnicity as membership in either conquering or conquered peoples.[86]

Judaism and the Law

The political interpretation of Paul that was pioneered among Latin American liberation theologians has recovered the political dimension of Paul's gospel as the advocacy of *dikaiosynē,* that is, of *social justice.* José Porfírio Miranda declared social justice to be the "revolutionary and absolutely central message of Romans," a message "customarily avoided by exegesis." He argues that Paul's critique of "law" involves a more generalized critique of the effect of sin and idolatry within civilization, "whose most characteristic and quintessential expression is the law."[87] Elsa Támez has also offered a sustained critique of the doctrine of justification by faith as conventionally understood, declaring it to be "good news more for the oppressors than for the poor."[88] Similar generalized readings of Paul's comments on law, informed by deconstruction rather than liberation theology, have been offered by Theodore Jennings and Alain Badiou.[89]

Although these readings expand Paul's critique to include the oppressive structures of imperial civilization, they do not remove "the Jews" from Paul's rhetorical crosshairs; rather they risk *inflating* the role of "the Jews" into a symptom of a larger societal pathology against which only Paul's gospel of justice is the antidote. For Miranda, the "civilization" that Paul criticizes under the name of law includes Jewish civilization as well, against

---

84. Key studies include Woolf, "Becoming Roman, Staying Greek"; Woolf, "Beyond Romans and Natives"; Gordon, "From Republic to Principate."

85. Reasoner, *"Strong" and the "Weak."*

86. Lopez, *Apostle to the Conquered*; Kahl, *Galatians Re-imagined.*

87. Miranda, *Marx and the Bible,* 152, 160.

88. Támez, *Amnesty of Grace,* 20–22.

89. Jennings, *Reading Derrida/Thinking Paul*; Badiou, *Saint Paul.*

which Miranda poses "evangelization, begun by Jesus and continued by the Church" as alone "God's instrument for causing faith and therefore justice" in human beings.[90] For Támez, Paul levels against "the Jews" the accusation of presuming on "the privilege of the law" and thus perverting it, creating an "inversion of values" in society.[91] Badiou for his part emphasizes Paul's "rupture with Judaism"[92] and argues that Paul sought to free the gospel "from the rigid enclosure within which its restriction to the Jewish community would confine it."[93]

However unintentional these reinstatements of pejorative characterizations of Judaism may be, they highlight the need for a careful rhetorical-critical analysis of Paul's alleged indictment of "the Jew," which may turn out to be something other than an indictment after all.[94] From a Marxist viewpoint, such analysis at the level of rhetoric or ideology must be joined with careful attention to the social and political options available to Jews in the first-century imperial situation, especially as these changed critically in the course of particular crises. This correlation of ideology with sociopolitical options provides the proper interpretive context for Paul's letters.[95]

Furthermore, there are grounds for reconsidering Paul's categorical repudiation of vindication through "works," traditionally understood as his critique of a characteristic Jewish "works-righteousness," for which historical substantiation has proven elusive. Careful attention to Roman imperial ideology and the ideology of patronage and euergetism has shown that these factors provided the context for a lively "theology of works" in Paul's day. Indeed, the "works" of the divine Augustus were celebrated in monuments across the empire.[96] Scholars have used the term "Romanization" to

---

90. "Sin, although it entered the world because of the guilt of one man, has become structured into human civilization itself, whose most characteristic and quintessential expression is the law" (Miranda, *Marx and the Bible*, 182; cf. 174). Miranda declares that Jesus, Paul, and the Gospel writers all perceived the redaction of the Torah to include laws within the exodus theophany as the "artifice of the later legislators" (Miranda, *Marx and the Bible*, 158).

91. Támez, *Amnesty of Grace*, 101–2.

92. Badiou, *Saint Paul*, 35 (emphasis added).

93. Badiou, *Saint Paul*, 13.

94. Elliott, *Rhetoric of Romans*; Elliott, *Arrogance of Nations*, chap. 3.

95. Elliott, "'Patience of the Jews,'" ch. 5 in Elliott, *Paul the Jew under Roman Rule* (forthcoming) Elliott, "From Background to Foreground," ch. 6 in *Paul against the Nations*; Elliott, *Arrogance of Nations*, chs. 3–4.

96. On the importance of "works" (*erga*) as distinguishing "people of exceptional merit, esp. benefactors," see the revised entry in Danker et al., *Greek-English Lexicon*, 390, and Danker, *Benefactor*; on their importance to Augustus's self-presentation, see the *Res Gestae*; on the Augustan ideology of works, Galinsky, *Augustan Culture*,

describe incorporation into (a) the system of euergetism; (b) the people
of the Romans, who were destined to rule the world; and (c) filiation to
Augustus, who recapitulated the virtue of his pious ancestor Aeneas, the
founder of the Roman people. Against this background, Paul's multiple repudiations of patronage, idolatry, and ethnic hierarchy, together with his
radical proclamation of filiation to a rival "father" and "lord" through the
Jewish ancestor Abraham, seem to cohere as a repudiation of the key elements of Romanization. This in turn suggests a very different context for
interpreting Paul's comments on "works." In fact, several recent interpreters
have argued that the Roman ideology of euergetism (as an instrument of
Romanization), rather than Jewish belief or practice, was the primary target
of Paul's critiques of "works" in Galatians and Romans.[97]

Gender, Class, and Empire

Postcolonial feminist interpreters have insisted on the importance of at-
tending to the multiple overlapping and intersecting dimensions of power
relations in the Roman world, including gender, class, and status (for example, slave or free, citizen or noncitizen).[98] While Marxist interpretation
of the place of women in Pauline Christianity has sometimes focused on the
subordination codes in the pseudo-Pauline writings (including the interpolation in 1 Cor 14:34–35) to the exclusion of wider considerations,[99] postcolonial and feminist interpreters have generally been careful to distinguish
these texts from Paul's genuine letters. This has not stopped them, however,
from identifying and assessing the kyriarchal codes and subordinationist
themes in Paul's own letters that became so useful to subsequent shapers of
the Pauline legacy.[100]

   Antoinette Clark Wire's reconstruction of the social experience of Corinthian women prophets is a landmark work, applying gender and rhetorical criticism to 1 Corinthians as well as a nuanced consideration of social
status. Wire describes the early Principate as a period in which the power

93–100; on patronage and cultus as modes of incorporation into the ideology of imperial benefaction, see Gordon, "From Republic to Principate."

   97. See Kahl, *Galatians Re-imagined*, ch. 5; Elliott, *Arrogance of Nations*, 138–41.

   98. Marchal, *Politics of Heaven.*

   99. De Ste. Croix, for example, devotes most of his admittedly "brief and oversim-
plified" discussion of women in the Greek and Roman world (*Class Struggle in the
Ancient Greek World*, 98–111) to a withering critique of "Christian attitudes toward
women," for which the pseudo-Paulines are his chief exhibits.

   100. See Wire, *Corinthian Women Prophets*; Kittredge, *Community and Authority*;
Kwok, *Postcolonial Imagination*, 89–93; Schüssler Fiorenza, *Power of the Word*, ch. 3.

of the senatorial order was weakened relative to the rise of provincial elites. Drawing on Mary Douglas's model of "grid" and "group" social forces, she characterizes the Principate as a "weak group/low grid" society. As Wire summarizes the situation, "In provincial cities like Corinth, if taxes were paid, external controls were basically absent, and honor fell on whoever could generate wealth and connections. Achieved status bypassed attributed status in importance."[101] In this context, and as an effect of what she describes as Augustus's "liberalizing" reforms of marriage laws, Wire proposes that lower-status women in Corinth would have experienced at least a broadening of opportunities for increased status while Paul—as someone reared in the "relatively 'strong group/high grid' system of councils, courts, and synagogues" of the Hellenistic East—would have experienced a diminution of privilege and status. She correlates the disparity between the women prophets' gain and Paul's loss of status with the difference between their "theologies and ethics." This disparity provoked Paul's restrictive rhetoric in his "first" letter to the Corinthians.[102]

Wire's reconstruction might be challenged on two fronts. First, because she and Elisabeth Schüssler Fiorenza (among others) accept 1 Cor 14:34–35 as genuine, they read the entirety of the letter's rhetoric as Paul's highly nuanced effort to rein in the efforts of independently minded "women of spirit."[103] Others, however, regard the passage as an interpolation and consequently read the letter's rhetoric as directed not against women but against elite *male* members of the assemblies.[104]

Beyond these text-critical and rhetorical-critical issues, the Marxist insistence on class analysis suggests that we must give careful consideration to the multifaceted gender, class, and social-status effects of the Pax Augustana and of Augustus's marriage legislation in particular. While Roman aristocrats may have complained about the *nouveaux riches,* this does not mean that there was a broad democratization of wealth or privilege. Instead, models of Roman patronage suggest that any expansion of opportunities was limited to a relatively tiny elite in the provinces, where such opportunities served as incentives to promote conformity and assimilation to the well-defined expectations of Romanization—even if they did not inculcate in a figure like Petronius's Trimalchio the decorum expected of true nobility.[105]

101. Wire, *Corinthian Women Prophets,* 191. Mary Douglas's model of "grid" and "group" forces is presented in Douglas, *Natural Symbols.*

102. Wire, *Corinthian Women Prophets,* 181–95; 217–19.

103. Wire, *Corinthian Women Prophets,* 229–32; cf. Schüssler Fiorenza, "Rhetorical Situation and Historical Reconstruction."

104. See Marshall, *Enmity in Corinth*; Elliott, *Liberating Paul,* 52–54, 204–14.

105. See MacMullen, *Roman Social Relations,* 44–45, 114; de Ste. Croix, *Class*

Further, Karl Galinsky has observed that Augustus's reforms of marriage laws "aimed particularly at the governing classes": they were designed to regularize sexual, family, and property relationships, rewarding productive marriages with access to patronage. The laws thus incorporated more wealth into the patronage system and thereby presented a more uniformly "moral" governing class to the provinces. The net effect was to draw ambitious upper-class women more closely into marriages.[106] This understanding of the social effects of the early Principate seems at variance with the "liberalizing" effects of Augustan legislation that Wire posits for the Corinthian women prophets. It also suggests that urban society in the early Principate should be described as "high grid/high group," as described in other studies of Roman patronage (grid) and Romanization (group) in Corinth.[107] Despite these qualifications, Wire's correlation of different social experiences (that of Paul and of others in the *ekklēsiai*) with theological expression is an important advance. Clearly this is an area where more thorough exploration by postcolonial, feminist, and Marxist analysis is desirable.

Empire and Ideology

Kwok Pui-lan observes that "Paul's political stance toward the state and empire has long been a bone of contention among biblical scholars and theologians," who usually turn quickly to Rom 13:1–7.[108] Some interpreters continue to take this passage as a straightforward endorsement of the Roman Empire (as did Kautsky).[109] More attentive exegesis has long recognized that there are tensions both within this passage and between Paul's statements here and his much less sanguine estimation of the "rulers of this world" in other places.[110] Counter- or "anti-imperial" interpretations of Paul have sometimes pointed to reservations in Paul's language in Romans 13—for

---

Struggle in the Ancient Greek World, 341–43, 364–67, and passim. For Trimalchio, see Petronius's *Satyricon*; for the contemporary challenge of distinguishing true nobility from the "nouveaux riches" under globalized capitalism, Žižek (*Living in the End Times*, 4 n. 3) cites Marcel Proust's reference to the unwritten, informal habits that always mark true nobility, even when the external marks of hierarchy are abolished.

106. Galinsky, *Augustan Culture*, 128–38.

107. In addition to works cited above, see Alcock, *Graecia Capta*.

108. Kwok, *Postcolonial Imagination*, 90.

109. So Blumenfeld, *Political Paul*, 378–94; Kautsky, *Foundations of Christianity*, 336.

110. Ernst Käsemann regarded it as "an alien body in Paul's exhortation," though he did not consider it an interpolation (as others have) (*Commentary on Romans*, 352); see also Keck et al., "What Makes Romans Tick."

example, reading *tetagmenai* (13:1) in a restrictive sense, or suggesting that he regards governing authorities as "servants of God" *only insofar as* they promote the good and punish evildoers (13:4). Others have found Paul's statements so modest, when compared with the effusive claims of imperial propaganda, as to seem like demurrals (my own earlier proposal) or even intentional irony.[111] John Marshall has deployed Homi Bhabha's discussion of the phenomenon of *hybridity* among colonized peoples to propose that we read the passage as evidence of Paul's own cultural hybridity, which leads him to speak here in favor of affiliation with Rome and elsewhere about alienation from the colonizing power.[112] Meanwhile, more theologically oriented interpreters continue to insist that the passage is not problematic if read through an appropriately theological and pastoral lens rather than from an inappropriately political perspective. In their view, Paul was not opposed to Caesar's empire "because it was an empire," but rather because he rejected "paganism in all its shapes and forms."[113] Paul's concern, according to this approach, was fundamentally to safeguard the church.[114]

None of these interpretations of Rom 13:1–7 enjoys consensus, and the tremendous weight that this passage continues to carry in interpretation means that there is no consensus regarding Paul's attitude toward the Roman Empire. I persist in thinking that exegesis of Paul's letters must be combined with the fullest possible understanding of Paul's ideological context, including contemporary Roman ideological themes concerning obedience, faith, the virtues of the emperor, the destiny of peoples, and so on. I have also argued that interpreters of Paul must develop an approach to "intertextuality" that considers Roman imperial ideology and iconography to be as much a part of Paul's rhetorical "context" as Israel's scripture.[115] But the impressive tradition of Marxist theory regarding ideology and what Fredric Jameson calls ideological constraint suggests that we shift the object of our interpretive efforts from "Paul's thought" or "Paul's attitude" or even "Paul's theology"—as if any of these could be explored as a coherent system

111. Elliott, "Romans 13:1–7 in the Context of Neronian Propaganda"; Carter, "Irony of Romans 13."

112. Marshall, "Hybridity and Reading Romans 13." Ronald Charles pursued a similar argument in his paper at the 2009 SBL annual meeting, "A Bhabhaian Reading of Paul as a Diasporic Subject of the Roman Empire."

113. See Wright, "Paul's Gospel and Caesar's Empire," 164, on the "background" of Paul's concern for church unity.

114. Dunn, *Theology of Paul the Apostle*, 675. I concur that concern for the safety of the assemblies—but more especially Jews as a particularly vulnerable population—is Paul's motive in the passage (Elliott, *Liberating Paul*, 221–26).

115. Elliott, "'Blasphemed among the Nations'"; Elliott, *Arrogance of Nations*, 40–43.

of representation, free of the constraining force of culture—to the ideological, and more specifically *kyriarchal* texture of Paul's rhetoric. Marxist
ideological theory suggests that we should understand Paul's rhetoric as a
particular *parole* or utterance within a field of forces determined, ultimately,
by the power relations of Roman imperialism. The tensions within those
power relations are expressed as tensions and even contradictions within
Paul's rhetoric—for example, between a God who subjects the world to futility and a Spirit who agitates within the world against just that subjection
(Rom 8:21–23), or between a declaration that the one who does right has
nothing to fear from the governing authority and the exhortation to return
fear (*phobos*) to that same authority (Rom 13:3, 7).[116] Such a shift away from
Paul's thought or theology as the object of attention will likely be resisted
or rejected by scholars who are invested in preserving a view of theological discourse as an autonomous domain. It may be welcomed, however, by
those who are ready to understand Paul as a full participant in the nexus of
material forces that we call history.

A FUTURE FOR MARXIST CRITICISM?
A CHRISTIAN-MARXIST CODA

Given the ideological and institutional limitations that circumscribe much
of biblical scholarship in Western academia, there is no reason to expect
that Marxist theory will ever take the interpretive world by storm—not
even the small portion of that world that is postcolonial-critical scholarship on Paul. Even in secular universities free from ecclesiastical pressures,
Marxist theory is usually confined to political science curricula; religious
studies programs are conceived without any reference to Marxist categories.
Departmental commitments to multicultural, multiethnic, gender-critical,
and postcolonial perspectives that emphasize the theorization of cultural
difference and hybridity have been hard won; the same level of commitment
to applying Marxist theory to class-based analysis is rare.

Even deliberate invocations of Marxist theory, for example, in literary
criticism, are inadequate in the eyes of some Marxists. Aijaz Ahmad regards
the explosion of "theory" following the radical impulses of the 1960s as the
result of efforts to domesticate, in institutional ways, the very forms of political dissent which those movements had sought to foreground, to displace an
activist culture with a textual culture, to combat the more uncompromising

116. Elliott, *Arrogance of Nations*, 50–57; on ideology, see Jameson, *Political Unconscious*; Eagleton, *Ideology*; Rehmann, "Ideology Theory"; Rehmann, *Einführung in die
Ideologietheorie*.

critiques of existing cultures of the literary profession with a new mystique of leftish professionalism, and to reformulate in a postmodernist direction questions that had previously been associated with a broadly Marxist politics.[117]

The decline (or "defeat" or "collapse") of socialist politics marked a fateful development for Marxist theory. Göran Therborn discusses "Marxism's broken triangle," by which he means the former interrelation under the umbrella of Marxism of "a historical social science, . . . a philosophy of contradictions or dialectics, [and] a mode of politics of a socialist, working-class kind." The last of these, socialist politics, "disintegrated in the course of the 1980s." The future of Marxist theory, Therborn suggests, will be shaped more by the vicissitudes of Western liberal academia than by any future revival of socialist politics.[118]

There is more than a little irony, then, in the development of a new interest in the figure of Paul as "our contemporary" on the part of Marxist or "dialectical materialist" philosophers in Europe, including Alain Badiou, Giorgio Agamben, and Slavoj Žižek. While *theological* interpreters struggle to find meaningful ways to translate Paul's (evidently failed) apocalyptic vision into the present, Paul is being rediscovered as a kindred spirit by just those thinkers who confront the collapse of socialist politics as a crisis of meaning.[119] They agree that the long twentieth-century experiment in centralized state power has ended in decisive failure. They also freely concede that they do not have the formula for a future without capitalism's pathologies. Their writings speak more of existential ache than of dogmatic certainty. Badiou asks how "the communist hypothesis," the notion that "the logic of class . . . is not inevitable, [that] it can be overcome," can be reasserted. He affirms a single, simple truth—that "there is only one world," of rich and poor, oppressor and oppressed, together. The vision of a world in which capitalism triumphantly unfolds to the betterment of all humanity is a delusion that can be maintained only by walling off the reality of the poor.[120] Similarly, Slavoj Žižek declares that "the defining problem of Western Marxism" has been "the lack of a revolutionary subject," so that Marxists have "engaged in a constant search for others who could play the role." He

---

117. Ahmad, *In Theory*, 1. Terry Eagleton provides a similar assessment of theory for its own sake in Eagleton, *Literary Theory*, 205.

118. Therborn, *From Marxism to Post-Marxism?* 116–19.

119. Badiou, *Saint Paul*; Žižek, *Fragile Absolute*. On the debate among philosophers, theologians, and biblical scholars, see Žižek and Milbank, *Monstrosity of Christ*; Caputo and Alcoff, *St. Paul among the Philosophers*; and Harink, *Paul, Philosophy*.

120. Badiou, "Communist Hypothesis."

muses that perhaps "waiting for another to do the job for us is a way of rationalizing our inactivity."[121]

Badiou's and Žižek's readers have been left unsure about how exactly Paul offers the answers to their questions. How, for example, might one appropriate Paul's "revolutionary subjectivity" (Badiou) in the present? Perhaps aspects of Paul's praxis show us the hallmarks of a truly revolutionary community: economic mutualism; resistance of the delusional claims of imperial ideology; and the continual *anamnēsis* of Jesus and incorporation into his destiny as one condemned to non-being by the powers of this world but alive to a genuine future.[122] But where are the material conditions for the rise of such a revolutionary community? Theologian of liberation Jon Sobrino writes that such a future is *ou-topia,* an impossible place if imagined as an extension of the present, seen from within "the civilization of wealth." From the perspective of the poor, however, "'utopia' means a dignified and just life for the majorities"; it is *eu-topia,* "that 'good place' that must exist." It emerges, Sobrino declares, from the "civilization of solidarity" practiced among the poor.[123]

Such ruminations might be dismissed as romantic—a dismissal Sobrino himself takes great pains to refute. The question of revolutionary agency nevertheless remains an acute problem not just for the theology of liberation but for all forms of Marxist theory as well and, in fact, for any project that seeks a realistic vision of an alternative to the evident hegemony of capitalism's predatory globalization.[124]

One of the lessons that Christianity must learn from Marxism is to relinquish the evasions and sublimations of these questions that have traditionally been made possible by escape into dogmatic speculation. The most urgent task for those among Paul's interpreters who participate in the struggle to realize "another world"—especially those who work in situations of privilege today—may be, at the very least, to embrace in their work the ancient apostolic imperative to "remember the poor" with some measure of Paul's own eagerness (Gal 2:10).

---

121. Žižek, "How to Begin from the Beginning."

122. I have elaborated these suggestions in two lectures to the International Seminar on St. Paul sponsored by the Society of St. Paul in Ariccia, Italy, in April 2009. See Elliott, "Paul between Jerusalem and Rome"; and Elliott, "Liberating Paul."

123. Sobrino, *No Salvation outside the Poor,* 61; Elliott, *Arrogance of Nations,* 161.

124. The question of revolutionary agency is at the heart of Hardt and Negri's explorations in Hardt and Negri, *Empire*; and also in Hardt and Negri, *Multitude.* Especially in the wake of U.S. wars in Iraq and Afghanistan, the authors have been stoutly criticized for their argument that the role of nation-states is increasingly irrelevant; see Balakrishnan's review, "Virgilian Visions," and Borón, *Empire and Imperialism.*

6

Diagnosing an Allergic Reaction
The Avoidance of Marx in Pauline Scholarship

THE MEDICAL METAPHOR IN my title is somewhat misleading. My topic is the remarkable rarity of explicit reference to Marxism or Marxist categories in New Testament scholarship and Paul scholarship especially. But in the following remarks I do not so much offer a single diagnosis as I observe a range of symptoms and propose several possible diagnoses for consideration.

Marxist interpretation of any part of the Bible has been scarce.[1] Even today—when, after the dramatic dissolution of the Soviet Union and the end of the Eastern Bloc in Europe, we might expect the name "Marxist" to appear less inflammatory than before those events—only a few brave Hebrew Bible scholars, notable among them Norman Gottwald, Roland Boer, and David Jobling, routinely identify themselves in their work as Marxist critics.[2] Elements of Marxist criticism may be more widely known as they have passed, perhaps unrecognized by readers, under the names "socioliterary" or "ideological criticism."[3] The case is similar in New Testament studies, where those scholars who propose "political" or "liberative" or

---

1. See Boer, "Western Marxism and the Interpretation of the Hebrew Bible"; Boer, "Marx, Postcolonialism, and the Bible"; Boer, "Twenty-Five Years"; Elliott, "Marxism and the Postcolonial Study of Paul" (Chapter 5 in this volume). Soviet-era Marxist scholarship on early Christianity was briefly reviewed (and dismissed) by Kowalinski, "Genesis of Christianity."

2. For example, Gottwald, *Tribes of Yahweh*; Gottwald, *Hebrew Bible*; Boer, "Marx, Postcolonialism, and the Bible"; Jobling, "'Very Limited Ideological Options.'"

3. Yee, "Ideological Criticism"; Yee, *Poor Banished Daughters of Eve.*

"anti-imperial" readings or interpretation "from below" or "from the margins" generally do so without identifying their work explicitly as "Marxist."[4]

One might ask, So what? After all, Norman K. Gottwald has reportedly observed that there is a high level of "*implicit* Marxism" in biblical studies, meaning that scholars increasingly give attention to ideology, economic and political realities, and the role of empires and resistance to them.[5] So what difference does it make if such discussions go on without anyone *explicitly* naming Marx or Marxism? The difference, I think, is that unless terms are defined in specific relationship to recognizable categories like those provided in Marxist thought—especially categories like class and mode of production—"social and economic realities" may be discussed in such general, imprecise, and vague ways that they may mean very different things to different interpreters, as some of the following remarks may begin to illustrate.

Simply for purposes of contrast I note that thirty years ago Geoffrey de Ste. Croix published a monumental discussion of *The Class Struggle in the Ancient Greek World*, including the Roman Empire. He explicitly applied Marxist categories and adapted them in thoughtful ways to present a coherent and wide-ranging account. De Ste. Croix defined *class* as referring to the pattern of relationships in a society by which human beings are mutually involved in the process of production (whether that involves property or labor relationships); *class struggle* describes the conflict between the exploitation that characterizes those relationships and resistance to that exploitation.[6] Following and developing Marx's own insights into ancient history,[7] de Ste. Croix showed that in the Roman world, the propertied class derived

---

4. For an exception that proves the rule see West, *Academy of the Poor*. On materialist or "non-idealist" approaches to the Bible, see Kahl, "Toward a Materialist-Feminist Reading," and Lopez, *Apostle to the Conquered*, 7–11. Kahl names 1960s Europe as the formative environment for the scholars she discusses. Boer discusses what appears to be the careful avoidance of Marxist study of the Roman world among New Testament scholars ("Zeal of G. E. M. de Ste. Croix"). Perhaps no single scholar has done more to advocate and advance political, counter-imperial, and "people's history" interpretations of various aspects of early Judaism (including the Jesus movement) and early Christianity than Richard A. Horsley—not only through his own writing but by mobilizing the work of other scholars (see his edited volumes *Paul and Empire*; *In the Shadow of Empire*; *Paul and Politics*; *Paul and the Roman Imperial Order*; *Christian Origins*)—yet so far as I know he nowhere describes his own work as Marxist in orientation. "People's history" was pioneered by British Marxist historians: see the concise retrospective in Crossley, *How Christianity Happened*, 5–18. Parenti, *Assassination of Julius Caesar*, applies the method to ancient Rome.

5. See Boer, "Twenty-Five Years," 316.

6. De Ste. Croix, *Class Struggle in the Ancient Greek World*, 31–33.

7. De Ste. Croix, *Class Struggle in the Ancient Greek World*, 23–25, 19–23.

the economic surplus that "freed them from the necessity of taking part in the process of production" through exploitation; not through wage labor, as in contemporary industrial capitalist society, but through un-free labor of various kinds, including slavery as well as the expropriation of agricultural labor through taxation.[8] De Ste. Croix described Roman imperialism as the extension of class-based extraction and exploitation,[9] and devoted several chapters to the ideology of imperialism as the expression of class warfare.

I recognize that even these definitions are the subject of lively debate among Marxist historians.[10] They are nonetheless useful for drawing attention, first, to the fact that Marxist categories *can* in fact be applied to the world studied by New Testament scholars, with impressive results; and second, to what is therefore the even more remarkable silence—one is tempted to say, the *studied* silence—regarding class and class struggle in New Testament studies. I turn next to a brief inventory of the different forms such silence takes.

THE SOUNDS OF SILENCE

The first way New Testament scholarship has avoided matters of class has been to practice an embarrassed reluctance to discuss them. That is, scholars sometimes acknowledge Marxism without giving it the sort of serious consideration that might offend polite society. I take as an example the landmark study by Meeks.[11] To his credit, early in the book Meeks recognizes that Marxists "have made important contributions to our understanding of ancient society"—but he never tells us what those contributions might be. Instead, that statement serves only to qualify his larger point that "the Marxist reading" of early Christianity, at least in its "crude popular versions," has been "reductionist."[12] Meeks never tells his reader whether there is any other kind, leaving the possible impression that *any* Marxist analysis will inevitably be "crude" simply because it is Marxist.

When Meeks later turns to "social stratification" in the ancient Roman world, he helpfully distinguishes class, order (*ordo*), and status, but then

8. De Ste. Croix, *Class Struggle in the Ancient Greek World*, 39, 133–47.

9. De Ste. Croix, *Class Struggle in the Ancient Greek World*, 44; on Roman imperialism, chs. 6–8.

10. Roland Boer offers insightful interaction and critique of de Ste. Croix especially around categories of mode of production and "un-free labor" (see Boer, *Marxist Criticism of the Bible*; and Boer, "Zeal of G. E. M. de Ste. Croix"). On the definition of ideology see Eagleton, *Ideology*; Rehmann, *Einführung in die Ideologietheorie*.

11. Meeks, *First Urban Christians*.

12. Meeks, *First Urban Christians*, 3.

immediately declares that the category of "class is not very helpful." This is because "in the everyday speech of popular sociology" it is used imprecisely to refer primarily to income and because, "for Marx, class was determined by relation to the means of production, *yielding only three*: landlords, capitalists, and workers."[13] "None of these definitions [of class] is very helpful in describing ancient society," he continues, "for they lump together groups who clearly were regarded in antiquity as different." Note, first, that the one sentence in the book that passes for a summary of Marxist thought is inaccurate. *In modern industrial capitalism,* Marx distinguished capitalists and workers as *two* opposed classes; landowners were not a third class in capitalism but were opposed to the landless serfs who worked the land in a *previous* economic system, feudalism. Marx was very careful to distinguish the different configurations of class struggle related to the dominant means of production in different historical epochs; Meeks doesn't bother. Why not? Because, he says, people in ancient Roman society did not categorize people into just two classes.

That is a remarkable argument. Can one imagine, as an analogy, a sociologist of contemporary U.S. society refusing to use the category "race" because different people use the term differently in everyday conversation, or because we recognize a plurality of ethnic and cultural identities? Meeks does not consider whether a more precise definition of class (such as Marx *actually* supplied) might be useful. Nor does he ask whether the multiplicity of overlapping ways in which people in the first century perceived status might be correlated with deeper dynamics of unequal economic relationships (as de Ste. Croix has in fact demonstrated, with encyclopedic detail). Instead, Marx's understanding of class is glancingly mentioned, inaccurately described, and summarily dismissed, within a few lines—and not mentioned again. This approach allows the scholar to appear to extend an undeserved generosity (in giving Marx any mention at all) and simultaneously to remain decorously circumspect (in protecting delicate readers from having to trouble themselves any further about "crude" Marxism).

THE SURPRISING (AND DISTRACTING) PREEMINENCE OF THE "MIDDLE CLASS"

A second way scholars have avoided a careful analysis of class relations has been to perpetuate a description of the Pauline churches as constituting a "cross-section" of Roman society. In contrast to MacMullen's description of a "very steep social pyramid" with a few fantastically rich people at the top

---

13. Meeks, *First Urban Christians*, 53 (emphasis added).

and the great mass of the people at the bottom,[14] New Testament scholars have more usually affirmed, in between the very rich and the very poor, the existence of a broad and significant "middle class" of artisans, merchants, laborers, and higher-status slaves. If there were "not many" wise, powerful, or nobly-born members of the church in Corinth (1 Cor 1:26–27), this argument goes, there were at least a few. It follows, at least by implication, that Marxist jargon about oppression and class struggle simply doesn't apply, either to the early churches or to the wider society around them.

Meeks and Malherbe have hailed this description as a "new consensus," beginning in the 1970s, and as an innovation that broke with a more "proletarian" description of the Pauline churches that they attributed to Adolf Deissmann.[15] As Steve Friesen has shown, however (and I gratefully depend on Friesen's work on this and the following point), this history of scholarship is inaccurate. Friesen suggests that Malherbe, Meeks, and others may have assumed their views constituted a divergence from Deissmann's because they misunderstood his language about the "lower strata." He points out, first, that although Deissmann's language about *die unteren Schichte* is routinely translated into English as "the lower classes," in early twentieth-century German political debate the term *Schichte* (which he translates "strata") did not carry the specifically Marxist connotation of *Klasse,* "class," and was deliberately used as an alternative to the latter term. Second, he suggests that although Deissmann used the phrase to refer to "the entire population of the empire except the small ruling elite," later interpreters like Malherbe and Meeks erroneously assumed that he meant by the phrase to refer *only* to the lowest strata;[16] they thus mistakenly attributed to him the view that the churches came from "the poor and dispossessed of the Roman provinces."[17]

Instead of an "old" and "new" consensus, "there was simply a twentieth-century consensus" among most Western scholars that the members of Paul's churches "represented a cross-section of society, coming mostly from the middle and lower sectors of society, with some members from the higher sectors."[18] Furthermore, Friesen shows that this "cross-section"

---

14. MacMullen, *Roman Social Relations,* 90.

15. Meeks, *First Urban Christians*; Malherbe, *Social Aspects of Early Christianity*; Deissmann, *Das Urchristentum und die unteren Schichten.* Meeks and Malherbe attribute much of the alleged "new consensus" to the work of Gerd Theissen, whose early landmark essays are collected in *Social Setting of Pauline Christianity.*

16. Friesen, "Poverty in Pauline Studies," 326. Malherbe, *Social Aspects of Early Christianity,* 31; Meeks, *First Urban Christians,* 51–52.

17. Meeks, *First Urban Christians,* 52.

18. Friesen, "Poverty in Pauline Studies," 325; Friesen, "Blessings of Hegemony," 119.

portrayal of the apostle's churches goes back to Deissmann himself. He had already emphasized Paul's greetings to and from "fairly well-to-do Christians," including sponsors of house churches "who cannot have been poor," and described the churches as made up of "men and women from the middle and lower classes," meaning from all but the tiny minority who were spectacularly wealthy.[19] It originally served an explicit political agenda: to repudiate a Marxist "proletarian" history of early Christianity that was on the ascendancy early in the twentieth century.[20]

Despite its political agenda, however—or should we perhaps say, because of it?—the cross-section characterization of the Pauline churches has become the reigning consensus. Elsewhere, Friesen surveys a dozen New Testament introductions published between 1904 and 1975 and finds that they generally depict a robust Roman economy and an upwardly ambitious middle class in what we might call boosterish terms. He concludes that "the twentieth-century mainstream consensus on economic issues in the Pauline assemblies was tedious. There was little progress on the topic [of poverty] and little curiosity about it."[21]

CHANGING THE SUBJECT

Friesen also points to what I count as a third way New Testament scholars have avoided the topic of economic class: by changing the subject, emphasizing instead the complex interaction of different measures of social status and status inconsistency.[22] Although the increased focus since the 1970s on

19. Deissmann (*Paul,* 241–43); see Friesen, "Poverty in Pauline Studies," 326–27.

20. Deissmann was active in an ecclesiastical campaign to blunt the advance of the Marxist Social Democratic Party in Germany in which Karl Kautsky was prominent. Friesen observes ("Poverty in Pauline Studies," 327) that "Deissmann's major statement on the social status of the early assemblies was written for the 1908 meeting of a politically oriented Lutheran organization," the Evangelisch-sozialer Kongress, which had as one of its goals "to stave off the dramatic advances of the Marxist Social Democratic Party in Germany." As Friesen summarizes the majority of addresses at that Congress, including the comments of the presider, Adolf von Harnack: "the social description of Paul's assemblies was intertwined with a determined effort to deny a need for structural change in German society . . . Most of them maintained that the gospel could transform the lower classes without disrupting the status quo because the gospel brought inner enlightenment and peace to individuals . . . Social stratification was not a problem, [dissenting voices] were told, and poverty was not important. The churches simply needed to do a better job of caring for the souls of individuals in order to win back the hearts and minds of the German working class" (Friesen, "Poverty in Pauline Studies," 330–31). Theissen offers a similar history: *Social Reality and the Early Christians,* 3–8.

21. Friesen, "Blessings of Hegemony," 121.

22. On status inconsistency see Meeks, *First Urban Christians,* 22–23 and passim.

questions of social status produced some important insights, it also means, Friesen writes, that "economic inequality . . . never gained a foothold as a significant topic of conversation."[23] To the contrary, "our preoccupation with 'social status' is the very mechanism by which we have ignored poverty and economic issues." That is not because our methods are more sophisticated than our predecessors', however. Friesen argues that social status as currently defined is unmeasurable because it involves the interaction of at least ten variables for which we do not have the sort of comparative data that would allow us to quantify their interaction—even for the small percentage of members of the Pauline churches whom we can name. So why do we prefer dealing with admittedly "impressionistic" generalizations regarding "status inconsistency" over actual economic analysis (such as that carried out by Marxists)? Friesen regards that preference as evidence of "an unacknowledged bias": "Instead of remembering the poor, *we prefer* to discuss upwardly mobile individuals and how they coped with the personal challenges of negotiating their ambivalent social status."[24] Friesen proposes (and I agree) that we should label this systematic bias "capitalist criticism": "after all, why should the burden of self-disclosure fall only on the shoulders of Marxist critics?"[25]

THE CULTURAL-ANTHROPOLOGICAL MODEL OF A "LIMITED GOOD" SOCIETY

A fourth way of avoiding discussion of class is to deny its relevance outright. In their social-scientific discussion of "religion, economics, and politics" in the environment of Paul's churches, Bruce J. Malina and John J. Pilch observe that in the New Testament period, "neither religion nor economics had a separate institutional existence, and neither was conceived as a system on its own, with a special theory of practice and a distinctive mode of organization . . . Nowhere do we meet the terminology of an economic 'system' in the modern sense. There is no language implying abstract concepts of market, monetary system, or fiscal theory."[26]

All this appears true enough, at face value; but it begs the interpretive question. *Why* should "the terminology of an economic 'system' in the modern sense" be the criterion for our understanding of what qualified as the economic dimension of ancient life? If the ancients did not theorize

23. Friesen, "Blessings of Hegemony," 124–25.

24. Friesen, "Poverty in Pauline Studies," 332–35 (emphasis in original).

25. Friesen, "Poverty in Pauline Studies," 336.

26. Malina and Pilch, *Social Science Commentary on the Letters of Paul*, 393.

"economics" in such narrow terms as came to prevail in the nineteenth century—when economics came increasingly to be defined as an autonomous
field of professional, "scientific" study, properly isolated from any interaction with social, political, or ideological dimensions of life—then is it simply
to be ignored by the contemporary interpreter as if it did not exist?[27]

Nor is this rather peculiar observation sufficient reason why, among
the many cultural "reading scenarios" offered in their *Social-Science Commentary,* Malina and Pilch provide no entries for *poverty* or *class.* The depiction of an idealized model of "Mediterranean" or "peasant society" (they use
the terms interchangeably)[28] should not derail the investigation of actual
economic and political realities, which existed whether or not the ancients
theorized them in modern, abstract ways.[29] (I note that Malina and Pilch do
not hesitate to discuss "alternative states of consciousness" simply because
the ancients didn't speak that way.) Furthermore, even as a high-altitude
theoretical construct, their model of "Mediterranean society" fails to account for the abundant data from the Roman world. Their observation that
economic relations were "embedded" in kinship systems might be valuable
for an ideal description of traditional village society, but does not account
for urban society in the Roman Empire, where "kinship" could be manu-
factured (through adoption); or for the Roman imperial economy, which
senators and emperors were able enough to describe in terms of systematic
extraction of wealth from the provinces.[30] In contrast to the approach taken

27. I owe this insight to Roland Boer (personal conversation), who refers to Wallerstein, *Modern World-System, IV*, 261–64.

28. Crossley ("Jesus the Jew since 1967") observes that "Mediterranean" also appears interchangeable with "Middle Eastern" in a number of social-science studies—not
only yielding imprecision but also allowing for egregious stereotyping of contemporary
"Middle Eastern culture" as well.

29. Malina and Pilch conclude that "ancient Rome elites did not have an idea of
juridical relations among various peoples. Instead Roman statesmen dealt with other
peoples in terms of good faith based on the analogy of patron-client relations. *Rome
was patron, not holder of an empire*; it wanted persons to behave like clients" (*Social-
Science Commentary on the Letters of Paul*, 393 [emphasis added]). But that conclusion would have come as a surprise to Cicero, Caesar, or Augustus, who spoke frankly
enough about the empire Rome held.

30. In the early second century Aelius Aristides sought to launch his rhetorical
career by praising such extraction, though he was shrewd enough to describe the conquered continents as "offering up" their wealth to Rome. He described the continents
surrounding the Mediterranean as continuously "offering [Rome] in full measure
what they possess"; the profusion of produce from India and Arabia suggested that
"the trees in those lands have been stripped bare . . . If the inhabitants of those lands
need anything, they must come here [to Rome] to beg for a share of what they have
produced" (*Panegyric on Rome*). In the first century, the author of the Apocalypse condemned Rome for such extraction (Rev 18:1–24); and from the third century comes the

by Malina and Pilch, the challenge of a Marxist approach is to be far more comprehensive and less reductionist than this purported "cultural-anthropological" approach in defining and understanding "economics."[31]

In his textbook on *The New Testament World*, Malina goes even further. Under the banner of "cultural anthropology," he describes "the first-century Mediterranean world" as one in which the terms *poor* and *rich* were not expressions of "'class' or economic rank at all." He declares that most people in this world "worked to maintain their inherited status, not to get rich."[32] This, too, begs the question: How, then, should we account for the amply documented individuals who considered the acquisition of exorbitant fortunes a matter not only of personal ambition but of the destiny of the "best people"? In the world Malina describes—the world of *peasant* honor—such people simply did not exist: "the honorable persons would certainly strive to avoid and prevent the accumulation of capital."[33] By definition, then, those persons who in fact accumulated vast amounts of capital could only have been what Malina calls "the dishonorable rich," those "beyond the pale of public opinion."[34] But this again begs the question: On what grounds should we categorize the rich, who are prominently named in countless monuments and inscriptions as benefactors of their cities, as "beyond the pale of public opinion"? Why are they not an integral part of the "world" Malina seeks to describe? The avaricious elite who actually shaped the material conditions in which the rest of the population lived simply vanish from discussion: They have no place in the only "New Testament world" in which Malina has any interest. "Peasants consider all persons in their society as 'equal,'" he writes; but he does not even attempt to substantiate that generalization, let alone explain how such purported egalitarianism relates to the competition for honor.[35] The facts that honor and shame could function as the motivating sanctions within the fundamentally unequal relationships of the patronage system, as evidenced in contemporary criminal syndicates as well as among the ancient Roman elite, or that patronage-clientage was a chief mechanism by which village-based agricultural production could be harnessed to the extractive schemes of Roman imperialism, are here ruled out

---

declaration that "the cities are set up by the state in order . . . to extort and oppress" (a Talmudic saying cited by MacMullen, *Roman Social Relations*, 34).

31. Another insight owed to Roland Boer (personal communication).
32. Malina, *New Testament World*, 97.
33. Malina, *New Testament World*, 97.
34. Malina, *New Testament World*, 98.
35. Malina, *New Testament World*, 99.

of discussion.[36] In reality, however, there were not two different worlds, that of the bucolic village of peasant equals somehow living their own lives far from the madding rush of urban and imperial politics. There was one world, and in it, village-based agriculture was expropriated through mechanisms of inequality that favored the grotesquely rich.[37]

Furthermore, because he never mentions actual material realities like daily caloric intake, living space, and life expectancy, Malina can declare that "we simply cannot get any idea" what New Testament authors might have meant when they referred without further qualification to "the poor." He knows, of course, that plenty of New Testament passages describe the poor as suffering hunger, thirst, indebtedness, physical incapacitation, or dispossession, but these characterizations point us not to structural dynamics in an actual economy (since, according to Malina's logic, the ancients were incapable of the concept, and thus it cannot play any role in our analysis) but to "some unfortunate turn of events or some untoward circumstances."[38] Poverty, on this account, is always accidental and by definition temporary. "The poor would not be a permanent social standing"—that is, a *class*—"but a sort of revolving category of people who unfortunately cannot maintain their inherited status. Thus day laborers, peasants, and beggars born into their situation were not poor persons in first-century society."[39]—Unless, one wonders, they constituted the very group referred to throughout the New Testament simply (and, to Malina, inscrutably) as "the poor"! Malina's peculiar reticence is all the more striking when we observe that, even

36. To confine ourselves to recent scholarship on the context of Romans, Reasoner (*"Strong" and the "Weak"*) discusses the use of pejorative terms like "weak" or "shameful" as designations by the economically powerful of the powerless; Jewett (*Romans*) discusses honor and shame as crucial values of exploitative Roman imperialism. Herzog (*Parables as Subversive Speech*) discussed the Roman expropriation of the wealth produced by Galilean agriculture as the necessary context for understanding Jesus' parables. Hanson and Oakman (*Palestine in the Time of Jesus*) offer an accessible discussion of the unequal and exploitative aspects of Galilean society.

37. Compare Alain Badiou's repudiation ("The Communist Hypothesis," 38–39) of the ideological assertion of two different worlds, one where capitalism produces wealth and another where—paradoxically—misery prevails, as the result of the moral or cultural deficiency of the poor. Instead Badiou insists: "there is only one world."

38. Malina, *New Testament World*, 99–100.

39. Malina, *New Testament World*, 100. Malina precludes any consideration of class or class struggle: further, "you will find no capitalist or communist work ethic in the New Testament. Nor will you find any program of 'social action' aimed at the redistribution of wealth *or anything of the sort*" (*New Testament World*, 97 [emphasis added]). It is surprising to see other social-science interpreters discuss Marxist historians alongside Malina's views without observing tensions between them (for example, Oakman, "Ancient Economy").

without the benefit of sophisticated "economic" models, classical historians have found sufficient evidence to name the poor in the first century straightforwardly as a "class."[40]

THE POLITICS OF "EXASPERATION"

One last form of what James G. Crossley has called a general "hostility to Marxism" in New Testament studies[41] is the refusal of Marxist categories as morally repugnant. I take as an example Ben Witherington's review of my own book, *The Arrogance of Nations,* in which I made use of a Marxist understanding of ideology to read Paul's letter to the Romans. In an otherwise insightful, appreciative, and helpfully critical review, Witherington declared my use of Marxist categories "especially exasperating" because of his own experience "teaching in various countries that have been laid waste by communism, countries in which the poor were certainly not better served by any form of Marxist government than by capitalism or democracy, countries in which, in fact, Christianity was banned, oppressed, persecuted, and martyred by Marxist governments."[42]

I won't quarrel here with Witherington's experience or perceptions but I question what seems to me a remarkable double standard. As a matter of fact, the poor have *also* been ill served by *anti*-communist governments; Christian "delegates of the word" have been arrested, tortured, and "disappeared," on an industrial scale, also by nominally Christian, "democratic," pro-capitalist, U.S. client regimes in Central America in the 1980s. Should we repudiate any of the methods of what Friesen calls "capitalist criticism" because of that sordid history?—And why doesn't that question enter the calculation? There are as many democratic Christians who abhor U.S. imperialism as there are Western Leftists who repudiate Stalinism and the Shining Path.[43] Why, then, should we accept a single stark alternative: *either* embrace the ideals and ideology of democratic capitalist nations (ignoring the actual effects of their policies) *or* side with the devastating actions of nominally Marxist centralized governments (whatever their relation to Marxist concepts and principles)? Does my use of a tool of Marxist criticism necessarily mean that I have ("exasperatingly") chosen the wrong side?

This sounds less like analysis than like a test of loyalty. I am reminded of feminist activist Florynce Kennedy's response to a heckler who shouted at

40. E.g., MacMullen, *Roman Social Relations,* 88–120.

41. Crossley, *How Christianity Happened,* 9.

42. Witherington, review of Elliott, *Arrogance of Nations.*

43. Eagleton, *Literary Theory,* 195; Crossley, *How Christianity Happened,* 13–14.

her, "what are you, a lesbian?" She answered, "what are you, my alternative?" My point is that we are *not* limited to narrow, false dichotomies. But why do we act as though we are?

TOWARD A DIAGNOSIS

I turn at last to consider some possible explanations for what I suggest is a fairly systematic avoidance of Marxist analysis.

One overused answer is that Marxism—or indeed *any* political interpretation—is simply inappropriate to the New Testament writings because they are fundamentally *religious* or *theological* texts.[44] The argument is, in its own way, reductionistic.[45] Moreover, it appears, from the point of view of a Marxist critic like Frederic Jameson, to be "something worse than an error: namely, a symptom and a reinforcement of the reification and privatization of contemporary life" that is "the tendential law of social life under capitalism." Rather, Marxist interpretation insists that "there is nothing that is not social and historical—indeed . . . everything is 'in the last analysis' political."[46] At the very least, the fact that a political reading *can* be carried out, often with surprising insights, shows that the

---

44. This was a point of remarkable agreement in a staged "debate" between John Barclay and N. T. Wright at the 2008 Society of Biblical Literature. Ironically, the two names routinely intoned over this verdict, Karl Barth and Reinhold Niebuhr, were both far more aligned with socialism than their contemporary fans usually acknowledge or allow (see, e.g., Hunsinger, ed., *Karl Barth and Radical Politics*). The long famine of social-scientific approaches to the New Testament between the 1920s and the 1970s is usually attributed in part to the influence of Karl Barth and dialectical theology after World War I. The formidable resistance shown to any social-scientific or "sociological" approach to Paul by his theological defenders, a resistance often waged in Barth's name, has determined the course of subsequent twentieth-century scholarship or, put more forcefully, has impeded its progress (see Crossley, *How Christianity Happened,* 3–5; Theissen, *Social Reality and the Early Christians,* 9–13). As John Cort summarizes the conundrum presented by "Barth the ambiguous": "The Christian could be, *should* be, socialist, but not *religious* socialist: the old distinction without a difference" (Cort, *Christian Socialism,* 207–13). Niebuhr's own turn from avowed Marxism to a more pragmatic Christian Realism never involved an explicit renunciation of socialism, only of the (officially pacifist) socialist parties on offer, but the turn was sufficient to signal "the epitaph of organized Christian socialism in the United States" (Cort, *Christian Socialism,* 276–77). From the 1960s on, his heritage has been disputed by "left" and "right Niebuhrians"—the latter insisting that Christian Realism required a robust militarism and endorsement for capitalism, even over Niebuhr's protests (see Dorrien, *Soul in Society,* ch. 4).

45. As rightly seen by Meeks, *First Urban Christians,* 3!

46. Jameson, *Political Unconscious,* 20.

insistence on maintaining a "pure" textual preserve for theological privilege is arbitrary.

A second possible answer is that the events of 1989–90 proved Marxism to be hopelessly obsolete, disproven, and thus irrelevant for interpretation. The verdict that with the triumph of Western capitalism we had arrived at the "end of history" was especially popular in the months just before September 11, 2001; now pundits have slipped back into the reassuring Manichaean tropes of a potentially endless "clash of civilizations." This is not the occasion for debating that proposition.[47] I simply want to observe (what I think the pages of the *Wall Street Journal* document on a daily basis) that the consummation of human history in the triumph of capitalism is not all it's sometimes cracked up to be. More importantly, we must distinguish Marxist *historiography,* Marxist (or neo-Marxist) *philosophical theory,* and Marxist *politics* (and, prominent Marxists would argue, distinguish Marxist politics from the centralized totalitarian capitalist states that claimed the Communist mantle in the last half of the twentieth century).[48] Especially in the present moment, the relevance of Marxist criticism should be measured by its explanatory power—not least, its impressive capacity to account for the effects of actually existing capitalism.[49]

A third, more compelling answer points us to the political economy of biblical studies within the contemporary Western academy. Time allows me only to mention historical studies (cited by Friesen 2008) that correlate the development of twentieth-century Fordist industrial capitalism and its need for an educated professional-managerial class with the emphases of twentieth-century higher education (including biblical studies). Notable among these is Wallerstein's observation that through the creation of history and economics as isolated, autonomous academic disciplines, the Western world "studied itself [and] explained its own functioning, the better to control what was happening."[50] As Friesen summarizes the point, "higher education taught future professionals to accept and to overlook economic inequality."[51] If that was the general direction of the humanities, it was manifest in the "capitalist criticism" of the New Testament as well,

---

47. See Fukuyama, *End of History and the Last Man*; and Huntington, *Clash of Civilizations and the Making of a New World Order*; in opposition, Achcar, *Clash of Barbarisms*; and Chomsky, *Hegemony or Survival*.

48. Therborn, *From Marxism to Post-Marxism?* 116ff.

49. See, among other diagnoses, Klein *Shock Doctrine*; Davis, *Planet of Slums*; Harman, *Zombie Capitalism*.

50. Wallerstein, *Modern World System, IV,* 264.

51. Friesen, "Blessings of Hegemony," 125–27.

in which economic analysis is avoided, poverty is ignored, and oppression and class conflict are virtually unmentionable.[52]

A number of scholars have offered complimentary analyses in their trenchant criticisms of postcolonial literary criticism as a "safely" post-revolutionary enterprise;[53] of "religious studies" as a discipline segregated from sociopolitical history;[54] and of biblical scholarship as the post-enlightenment project to insulate the Bible from secular criticism by surrounding it with an aura of cultural privilege.[55] Similar pressures in postcolonial theological studies have been analyzed by Catherine Keller[56] and, in liberation theology, by Ivan Petrella.[57] All these analyses point to-

---

52. Friesen, "Poverty in Pauline Studies," 331–37, 357.

53. Aijaz Ahmad writes that such developments have served "to domesticate, in institutional ways, the very forms of political dissent which those movements had sought to foreground, to displace an activist culture with a textual culture, to combat the more uncompromising critiques of existing cultures of the literary profession with a new mystique of leftish professionalism, and to reformulate in a postmodernist direction questions which had previously been associated with a broadly Marxist politics" (*In Theory*, 1; compare Eagleton, *Literary Theory*, 205). Leela Gandhi discusses the particular dilemma faced by postcolonial critics from decolonized nations who find positions in first-world academia—where they may be valued more as emblems of an institution's commitment to (ethnic) "diversity" than of social revolution (Gandhi, *Postcolonial Theory*).

54. Asad, *Genealogies of Religion*; Fitzgerald, *Ideology of Religious Studies*; Shedinger, *Was Jesus a Muslim?*

55. Moore and Sherwood, *Invention of the Biblical Scholar*.

56. Catherine Keller wonders whether postcolonial theory has a place only so long as it can be adapted "to relativize any revolutionary impulse, to dissipate the political energy of transformation, to replace active movements of change with clever postures of transgression" (Keller, *God and Power*, 103).

57. Ivan Petrella asks whether the profusion of "contextual" liberation theologies and the focus on identity and hybridity serves to obscure the fundamentally determinative fact of economic deprivation. He argues that liberation theologians around the world share a single material context—the poverty of the majority of the world's people—and a single theological context—the failure of liberation theologies to deal successfully with that material reality. Despite their profusion, contextualized theologies remain "powerless to face the spread of zones of social abandonment. They're powerless because the upsurge of race, ethnicity, gender, and sexuality as organizing axes for liberation theology has blurred the fact that material deprivation, that is, the deprivation that comes from one's class standing in society, remains the most important form of oppression" (Petrella, *Beyond Liberation Theology*, 80–81). In too much liberation-theology *writing*, he protests, global *economic* marginalization "recedes from view while the *theological* exclusion" of one or another group "comes to the forefront . . . Helping people become theologians is given priority over helping people lift themselves from social misery. Obviously, a class choice has been made": the result "is not a theology of liberation, it is a theology of inclusion for the middle class" (Petrella, *Beyond Liberation Theology*, 95–96).

ward the cultural climate in which New Testament scholarship is carried out.

More is involved than self-censorship or personal reticence among contemporary academics, of course. In 1988, Noam Chomsky and Edward S. Herman described a "propaganda model" of the "political economy of the mainstream media."[58] I suggest that their model works as well to describe the various ideological apparatuses that shape our perceptions of what may be thought, written, taught, and learned in higher education and biblical studies in particular. Their "propaganda model" includes the instruments of "flak," with which I would identify the systematic, well-funded efforts of organizations like Fox News (where Glenn Beck notoriously fulminated against churches that taught "the social gospel" and against the insidious liberation theology of President Obama), David Horowitz's "Freedom Center" (which polices "liberal" thought on university campuses), and the Institute for Religion and Democracy (which has mounted devastating pressure campaigns against faculty members at church-affiliated institutions of higher education as well as progressive church organizations).[59] I suspect a number of teachers in religious-studies and theological classrooms could recount episodes in which the effects of such "flak" mechanisms were felt.

The question facing biblical interpreters is whether we will acquiesce in those pressures or resist them—but the first step is to name them. As President of the Society of Biblical Literature, years ago Elisabeth Schüssler Fiorenza called members to a politically engaged scholarship; she has renewed that plea by calling for cooperation in liberative efforts across boundaries of denominational and religious affiliation, across the divide between "believer" and "unbeliever,"[60] in a collaboration similar to what Roland Boer has called "the worldly Left."[61] That plea, I contend, is not only appropriate to our present situation but may also allow us to attend to an important dimension of Paul's own work. However we may construe the adequacy or inadequacy of his own practice, he named as

58. Herman and Chomsky, *Manufacturing Consent*, updated ed.

59. The IRD was founded in 1981 by neoconservative theologians and provided initial funding by conservative foundations and, in 1985, by the U.S. Central Intelligence Agency. The Institute's website is www.theird.org; a brief introduction to its antagonistically conservative agenda is provided by Political Research Associates at Clarkson, "Battle."

60. See Schüssler Fiorenza, "Ethics of Biblical Interpretation"; Schüssler Fiorenza, *Rhetoric and Ethic*; Schüssler Fiorenza, *Power of the Word*; and Schüssler Fiorenza *Democratizing Biblical Studies*.

61. Boer, *Rescuing the Bible*, ch. 2.

the horizon of his apostleship a priority that he claimed to share with the other apostles in Jerusalem: "to remember the poor" (Gal 2:10). Marxist criticism offers the analytical tools that allow us to take that horizon seriously in our exploration of Paul and the early Christian movement.

7

Ideological Closure in the Christ-Event

A Marxist Response to Alain Badiou's Paul

A PARADOX

At the church I serve as part-time priest, St. Paul's on the Hill, a great stained-glass window looms over the altar rail depicting St. Paul "on the Hill" of Mars, the Areopagus in Athens (Acts 17). The Parthenon in the background identifies the location; the gorgeous hues of sunset indicate evening is at hand. The philosophers have departed, laughing derisively at Paul's notion of the "resurrection of the dead," gone to seek better entertainment elsewhere. As one approaches the altar rail, one is left in the small company of enlightened souls who remain, bowing reverentially in prayer.

Fig. 7.1. *Paul on Mars Hill.* **Stained glass. Tiffany Studios, 1903.**
Photo by the author.

The contemporary scene in Paul studies offers a peculiar reversal of that biblical tableau. Those Christians today who haven't given up on Paul as the arrogant homophobe, the patriarchal male chauvinist, the authoritarian apostate Jew, the apostle of the status quo—even those who style themselves Paul's loyal sympathizers—often seem hard pressed to make the case that the apostle's apocalyptic theology has anything meaningful to say to our time until it has been thoroughly demythologized. It has proven much easier for theologically oriented Paul scholars to focus on the inclusion of "Gentiles" and the legitimization of the "Gentile mission" as the core of Paul's gospel and thus to read him as the champion of those good liberal ideals of universalism, inclusiveness, and multicultural tolerance (as opposed to narrow ethnocentrism and tribalism.)[1] Much of contemporary discussion around the "New Perspective" turns on the question whether we can proclaim Paul's gospel of inclusion without indulging in that ancient Christian habit of attributing its opposite, "exclusivism" or "ethnocentrism," to Paul's

1. The late Krister Stendahl set the agenda for decades of Paul scholarship when he argued that the purpose of Romans was to argue for the legitimacy of the Gentile mission: Stendahl, *Paul among Jews and Gentiles,* 23–40; Stendahl, *Final Account,* ix.

own people, the Jews of the Roman world. The best critical voices in the New Testament guild, prominent among them the late Lloyd Gaston, have called on us to renounce that habit.[2] It nevertheless remains sorely tempting for "multicultural" and "postcolonial" readings to enthuse about Paul's distance from the narrowly tribal thinking of his Jewish contemporaries. That temptation indicates that we have not yet thought seriously enough about the political and ideological context of Paul's thought and praxis.[3]

But now a new crowd has resolutely taken their stand beside Paul: they are precisely those philosophers (or self-styled "anti-philosophers")— distant descendants of the Areopagus crowd?—who have no interest at all in what Alain Badiou calls the "fable" of the resurrection of the dead.[4] To some theologians this new crowd of enthusiasts, including Badiou, Jacob Taubes, Giorgio Agamben, and Slavoj Žižek, appear as impertinent interlopers, "poaching" on the rightful territory of theology and exegesis as practiced within the Christian church.[5] On these terms, the philosophers are criticized for doing theology poorly. For Paul J. Griffiths, for example, they are objects of "Christian pity and concern" because, despite their erudition, they stubbornly and irrationally resist the only true answer to their questions, which is to be found in "the peace given by explicit knowledge

2. Gaston, *Paul and the Torah*. Gaston modeled for the guild of Pauline scholarship the restless intellectual curiosity and moral gravitas that refuses to be placated by conventional wisdom, not least in his insistence on the principle that "it makes a difference" whether Paul's audience was "Gentiles or Jews." I therefore find all the more ironic his presumption, without argument, that "Paul's major theological concern" was "the justification of the legitimacy of the Gentile mission" (6).

3. The voluminous literature on the "new perspective" seems to increase daily, as documented by the invaluable website *The Paul Page* (www.thepaulpage.com). The fountainhead of the "new perspective" is the essay by James D. G. Dunn, "New Perspective on Paul"; see also Dunn's magisterial *Theology of Paul the Apostle*. Critiques include Denise Kimber Buell and Caroline Johnson Hodge, "Politics of Interpretation"; Hodge, "Apostle to the Gentiles"; Eisenbaum, "Paul, Polemics"; and Tat-Siong Benny Liew, "Margins and (Cutting-) Edges." I offer my own alternative to the "new perspective" in Elliott, *Arrogance of Nations*.

4. Badiou, *Saint* Paul, 4–5. Badiou, styling himself an "anti-philosopher," takes his own place rhetorically alongside Paul at the Areopagus, over against contemporary philosophical projects: Badiou, *Saint* Paul, 58. Other radical thinkers showing recent interest in Paul include Taubes, *Political Theology* (German original 1993, compiled from lectures given in 1987); Agamben, *Time That Remains*; Žižek, *Fragile Absolute*; and Jennings, *Reading Derrida/Thinking Paul*.

5. Gignac employs the metaphor playfully: "Taubes, Badiou, Agamben," 156. Jennings describes how the reading of Romans in particular "has largely been restricted to a confessional/ecclesiastical ghetto of doctrinal interest" and pleads for engagement with philosophical readings: *Reading Derrida/Thinking Paul*, 1. Robbins also discusses the dynamics of a certain territoriality within New Testament and theological "guilds" when confronted by keenly interested outsiders: Robbins, "Politics of Paul."

of the God of Abraham," and communion with the church catholic. It is "the Church here below," Griffiths declares, that most fully embodies the community free of political and economic domination that philosophers like Žižek seek.[6] Similarly, theologian Daniel M. Bell protests that Badiou fails to grasp a central truth at the heart of Christianity: that the salvation he seeks is possible only through "ontological union" with Israel's messiah, which makes possible "humanity's being taken up into the divine life of the Trinity." According to Bell, it is not philosophical analysis but the church's works of mercy that offer the fullest resistance to capitalism's depradations.[7]

At just this point an interested onlooker might well wonder whether these theologians are looking at the same church "here below," a church that is—at least in the United States—so integrated into capitalist society that Žižek is hardly alone in finding it quite irrelevant to the radical project. In a post-Soviet world, it may be tempting to compare the *achievements* of what were once actually existing Marxist states with Christian *theory*; on the other hand, comparing Marxist *theory* with the *achievements* of actually existing ecclesiastical institutions offers considerably less room for Christian self-congratulation.[8] Ward Blanton makes the point from the perspective of Christian theology when he writes, with genuine respect, of the "unexpected hodge podge of neo-Paulinists" who, quite outside of the boundaries of any religious community, have been

> able to do what mainline Protestantism in the U.S. has not been able to do, namely, to contest in a committed, clear, and thoughtfully aggressive way the hegemony of an American Christendom that has become little more than a crutch for the sometimes faltering conscience of U.S. imperialism abroad . . . Christianity risks today being the false conscience of an imperial system of staggering proportions.[9]

I take that assessment to be accurate precisely as a *theological* summation of what Blanton calls the "difficult Pauline *krisis*" confronting churches in the United States today. Caught up in currents of self-delusion, churches may believe they are "doing their own thing" faithfully and independently of the powers that be. But, Blanton protests, it is precisely the Pauline "demand

---

6. Griffiths, "Christ and Critical Theory," 46, 50, 54–55.

7. D. M. Bell, "Badiou's Faith and Paul's Gospel," 108.

8. Years ago, a cherished economist colleague at the College of St. Catherine made the point with regard to Haiti: "if the saturation of Christian missionaries per square mile were ever going to make any difference to actual living conditions under capitalism, anywhere in the world, we should have seen it first in Haiti."

9. Blanton, "Disturbing Politics," 5.

for actuality" that indicts the ineffective hand-wringing of a complacent church: "it is precisely that moment when Christendom laments the unfortunate war, the unfortunate policy, the unfortunate dead—known and unknown—that one must be haunted by this shocking Paulinist motif: to say, to feel, even to speak the liberating word is *not* the same thing as doing it."[10]

Blanton insists that it is precisely the "atheistic fighting neo-Paulinists" who are "doing it"—that is, opening up a space where "genuine lines of contestation" with imperialistic powers may be drawn. The greater offense that these radical philosophers present to mainstream liberal theology is that they are not just "unbelievers," adamantly uninterested in the abstractions of Christian doctrine. They are resolute leftists, implacable advocates of what Badiou calls "the Communist hypothesis," opposed to the capitalist world order in which so many Christians in the West are relatively comfortable, if not entirely content. And the radicals now claim that Paul is one of *them,* a "militant figure," an "activist" committed to "large-scale struggle," busy organizing little enclaves of those who will serve as "vectors of a new humanity."[11] In his name, they call us not to an intensified religiosity but to a political militancy with which U.S. churches are in general acutely uncomfortable. Suddenly, theological liberals who thought they were Paul's last, truest friends are put in the unfamiliar position of being offended by a scandalous Pauline gospel!

PAUL "OUR CONTEMPORARY"

Why are these less-than-religious thinkers interested in Paul, of all people?

The "Present Evil Age"

It is important to recognize the context in which the appeal to the figure of Paul is made: namely, the particular crisis that recent decades have presented *for adherents of dialectical materialism.* However convincing Marx's analysis of capitalism, history has not turned out the way his theories suggested. Socialist revolutions have taken place in the wrong places, generated by the wrong classes, and ushering in centralized states that have shown not the least tendency toward "withering away." History has presented committed Marxists with a conundrum as powerful as any cognitive dissonance faced by the first believers in the risen Christ's imminent return. In this

10. Blanton, "Disturbing Politics," 5.

11. Badiou, *Saint Paul,* 2, 20, 21.

"time of radical reaction,"[12] characterized by disorientation on the Left and the collapse of any sense of alternative to the existing capitalist order, the "communist hypothesis"—that "the logic of class . . . is not inevitable"—seems chimerical, vanquished by the cold hard facts of history. Badiou is by no means the only Marxist to point out the consequences:

> What is at stake in these circumstances is the eventual opening of a new sequence of the communist hypothesis. But it is clear that this will not be—cannot be—the continuation of the second one [from 1917 to 1976]. Marxism, the workers' movement, mass democracy, Leninism, the party of the proletariat, the socialist state—all the inventions of the 20th century—are not really useful to us anymore. At the theoretical level they certainly deserve further study and consideration; but at the level of practical politics they have become unworkable.[13]

The proposed explanations (from a Marxist point of view) are as familiar as the question itself. The proletariat failed to mobilize because of the success of "ideological state apparatus" (Louis Althusser), or more subtly, the cultural hegemony of the ruling class (Antonio Gramsci); and capitalist culture itself has proven almost infinitely adaptable to new challenges, chameleon-like (Fredric Jameson).[14] Badiou observes that in the new order in the West, "the left no longer frightens anyone"; rather the slogan of the day is *Vivent les riches,* and to hell with the poor."[15] But the promises of capitalism are empty: the collapse of the Berlin Wall has not ushered in "a single world of freedom and democracy"; rather, "the world's wall has simply shifted: instead of separating East and West it now divides the rich capitalist North from the poor and devastated South. New walls are being constructed all over the world . . . the 'unified world' of globalization is a sham."[16]

The "empty universality" of capital means that the enemy of a true and vital human particularity is not a single homogeneous culture, as the liberal vision of multicultural diversity would have it. Instead, the wide range of human particularities are themselves rendered commodities to be trafficked in one niche market after another. The commodification or "communitarization of the public sphere" means that in place of "the law's transcendent neutrality" or any unifying vision of a common good shared

12. Peter Hallward uses the phrase to situate Badiou's work: *Badiou,* xxxi.

13. Badiou, "Communist Hypothesis," 37.

14. See Terry Eagleton's lucid discussion, *Ideology;* Fredric Jameson, *Postmodernism.*

15. Badiou, *Saint Paul,* 7; on our current situation, 6–13; see also Badiou, "Communist Hypothesis," 29.

16. Badiou, "Communist Hypothesis," 38.

by all—a true *political* universal—the capitalist ideological order offers only a cockpit wherein the voices of various marginalized groups may compete against one another for momentary attention. Capitalism's universalism is hollow because it enfranchises only those who submit themselves to the inexorable logic of the market. Law becomes a device for distinguishing those to whom material resources may be allocated, for a price, from those who must be excluded.[17] Human well-being is not the measure of economic health; rather the free flow of *capital*, which requires increasing restriction on the movements of human beings, is.

Against this false universality, Badiou seeks a true universality, one that can be *collectively* affirmed as a universal truth such as the declaration, "There is only one world." But such an affirmation flies in the face of the evidence around us. It "is not an objective conclusion. It is performative: we are deciding that this is how it is for us." For me to decide "that all belong to the same world as myself" requires, is nothing else than, an absolute *political commitment*.[18]

Giorgio Agamben similarly exposes the fraud of the capitalist claim to universalism. In *Homo Sacer* he argues (taking up Michel Foucault's discussion of biopolitics, but revising it) that the sign of sovereign power is always "the production of a biopolitical body," by which he means a body for which the very conditions of life have become the object of political demarcation and boundary-making. While Aristotle declared that the human is a "political animal," Agamben argues that sovereign power consists in the power to decide not only what is the proper sphere of political activity, but also what is excluded from politics and law. In the modern state, the decision to *include* as a political object what had previously been excluded as "natural"—to render the very condition of life a matter of political contest—is "the original activity of sovereign power." Inverting Aristotle, for whom the proper distinctiveness of the human animal was its *logos,* its power to communicate, Agamben declares that modern sovereign power is manifest in the production of life-forms incapable of communication. The Nazi death-camps are for Agamben the inevitable end of this "biopolitics," representing the sheer and arbitrary determination of which objects shall be included and which excluded from the conditions for life. They are "the space where the exception begins to become the rule," where the production

---

17. Badiou has the French situation particularly in mind, where the popular slogan "France for the French" requires "the persecution of those people arbitrarily designated as the non-French" (*Saint Paul,* 8). Here I find invaluable the analysis provided in Mike Davis's magisterial study *Planet of Slums*.

18. Badiou, "Communist Hypothesis," 38–39.

of non-living beings—the walking dead, the mute *"Musselmänner"*—is the inevitable outcome.[19]

In our own day, the language of "extraordinary rendition," in which a sovereign state reserves the sovereign authority to declare a permanent state of exception to its own laws, in this case regarding torture, shows the relevance of Agamben's analysis.[20] And it begs an Agambenesque question: what is the *ordinary* rendition of human beings, if not the creation of mute objects of capital's sovereign power? If, for Agamben, the work of "biopower" in the Nazi death camps was to create the lifeless walking form of the *Musselman*,[21] we may ask whether the industrial-scale transformation of Muslims into *"Musselmänner"* in prisons like Abu Ghraib is the signal characteristic of sovereign power in our own day. And theologically, we must ask what relation can exist between such production of *Musselmänner* and the embodiment of Christ in our world.[22]

Fig. 7.2. Abdou Hussain Saad Faleh, prisoner under U.S. military custody at Abu Ghraib, Iraq (the "Hooded Man"), and Staff Sgt. Ivan Frederick II, Nov. 3, 2004; photo by Sabrina Harman. U. S. Government photograph.

19. Agamben, *Homo Sacer*.

20. As used in the United States, "extraordinary rendition" refers to the state's exercise of sovereign authority to remove human beings to other nations where they are subjected to torture that remains illegal in the rendering state (the U.S.)—though the latter has proven to be a quite malleable category. Agamben helps us to understand the significance of a previously secret 2003 executive finding by the U.S. president that while no legal constraint barred the executive branch from authorizing torture, he "declined" to provide such authorization "at this time." See Hersh, *Chain of Command*, 5.

21. See Agamben, *Homo Sacer*, ch. 7.

22. Though it is beyond the scope of this essay, important resources for such discernment are Cavanaugh, *Torture and Eucharist*; and Ellacuría, "Crucified People."

Fig. 7.3. Matthias Gothart Grünewald, *The Mocking of Christ*, 1503; commons.wikimedia.org.

The Body of Christ

When Badiou declares that Paul is "our contemporary," it is in part because he finds a precise parallel between Paul's situation and ours. But it is also because he finds in Paul the ideological gesture, the performance, of a "universal truth" that militates against the ideological constraints of Paul's situation and our own.

Both Paul's situation and ours are characterized, Badiou declares, by "the destruction of all politics," evident in the legal usurpation by the Principate of the political structures of the Republic, and in our own day by a parliamentary-democratic system that carefully insulates the economic order from popular will, that is, from politics. (He is speaking of Europe; the

constitutional crisis in the United States is arguably more severe.)[23] Though
Badiou does not expand on the comparison, a number of valuable recent
studies of the economic, military, and ideological aspects of Roman Empire
confirm its aptness.[24] We may go further, however, in light of Agamben's
insistence that "biopower" is the characteristic of sovereignty not only in the
modern age but in the age of the Roman Empire as well. But if the homol-
ogy between an anti-politics (Badiou), or the sovereign exercise of biopower
against bare life (Agamben), in Paul's day and our own is important for our
appropriation of Paul today, it is even more important for us to recognize
that the fundamental ideological requirements of Roman imperialism are
directly opposed in Paul's representation of the body of the crucified-and-
risen Christ in the world.

In Marxist terms, we may identify the "cultural dominant" of the Roman Empire in terms of a transition from an agrarian, tributary mode of
production to a reliance on slave labor.[25] If "religion" and the prerogatives of
(divine and human) monarchy were the indispensable ideological apparatus
of the tributary state (what Marx called the "Asiatic" mode of production),
a society expanding to include more and more territory (and thus more
and more agrarian production) in an economy increasingly reliant on slave
labor faced a more complex ideological challenge. A slavery society depends
upon the careful maintenance of a symbolic system of difference: citizens
must be distinguished from noncitizens, free from slaves—and conquerors
from conquered. In the Roman era, the distinction was represented visually
through iconography and rehearsed "ritually" through sites as distinct as
the civic arena and extra-urban sites of crucifixion. A specific symbolic code

23. Badiou, *Saint Paul,* 7 and passim; Badiou, "Communist Hypothesis," 31–32.

24. See Garnsey and Whittaker, ed., *Imperialism in the Ancient World*; de Ste. Croix,
Class Struggle in the Ancient Greek World, especially chs. 6 and 7; Garnsey and Saller,
Roman Empire; Price, *Rituals and Power*; Zanker, *Power of Images*; and Galinsky, *Augustan Culture*. Richard A. Horsley brought these insights together with applications by
New Testament scholars to Paul and his letters in Horsley, ed., *Paul and Empire*; I have
relied on these and other studies in my own effort to situate Paul's thought and practice
in the context of Roman imperialism: see Elliott, *Liberating Paul*; and Elliott, *Arrogance
of Nations*.

25. See Roland Boer's excellent discussion of "the question of mode of production"
in *Marxist Criticism of the Bible,* 229–46. Norman K. Gottwald applies the Marxist
understanding of modes of production to ancient Israel's history in Gottwald, *Hebrew
Bible*. Fredric Jameson points out that Marx's presentation of a "sequence" of modes
of production must be adapted to recognize the possible simultaneity of incompatible modes of production, some ascendant, some vestigial, and others only anticipated:
Jameson, *Political Unconscious,* 89–102. Boer's and Jameson's discussions inform my
own proposals regarding the ideological constraints in Paul's day in Elliott, *Arrogance
of Nations,* 29–30; 156–59.

distinguished those who could not be tortured or crucified from those who could. But in our own day as well, the ritualized distinction between powerful captor and powerless captive, the production of mute biopolitical bodies as a gesture of sovereign power, is just as important as in a slave-based economy. This is true whether or not the distinction is publicly displayed—but of course it *is*, as in the photos from Abu Ghraib, where the abject misery, humiliation, and injury of the prisoners stands in the sharpest possible relief to the consistently relaxed postures and smiling, smug comportment of the captors.

My point is not to draw a sentimental equivalence between the crucified Christ and contemporary prisoners at Abu Ghraib, although theologically the comparison bears sustained reflection. My point is to compare in both situations, ancient Rome and our own, the dynamics of sovereign power to generate "necessary" exclusions from its own laws, and the ideological apparatus that justified these exclusions.

In the Roman Empire, the careful distinction of bodies that could and could not be tortured went hand in hand with an elaborate ideological representation of the emperor as benevolent monarch, a supreme patron, father, and priest; that is, the symbolization dominant in an *agrarian* mode of production overlapped with and in part was used to routinize and legitimize the symbolization dominant in a *slave* mode of production.

This is the necessary ideological context in which alone we can fully understand Paul's proclamation of a crucified and risen Christ. Paul insists (and scholars agree this is his own contribution to whatever preexisting Christian traditions he inherited) that Christ took "the form of a slave" and "became obedient to the point of death—even death on a cross" (Phil 2:7–8).[26] That phrase has traditionally been taken to refer generically to Christ's appearance *as a human being,* but surely refers more pointedly to the manner of his death, the shameful subjection to a *slave's* death by crucifixion. Such a death publicly reinscribed on certain bodies the status of slave/conquered and thus reinforced the routinization of the symbolic cultural dominant. For Paul to proclaim that just such a body, inscribed in death as slave by the power (Agamben might stipulate, the *biopower*) of the Empire, had been raised from the dead by God, and that this divine act established the true filiation of a free people regardless of their ascribed status in the Roman symbolic economy: this was inherently and irreducibly subversive.[27] So, for that matter, was what we must assume was Paul's defiant

26. See Dunn, *Theology of Paul the Apostle,* 244–52.

27. The characterization of Paul's proclamation as "subversive" has recently found potent substantiation in the arguments of Davina C. Lopez, *Apostle to the Conquered,* and Brigitte Kahl, *Galatians Re-imagined.* Both studies focus attention on the ideological

practice of *performing* the "dying of Jesus" as crucified, whatever form that performance took, for it repeatedly embodied a counter-representation of status.[28] As Paul puts it in 2 Corinthians 2:14–16 (NRSV):

> But thanks be to God, who in Christ always leads us in triumphal procession, and through us spreads in every place the fragrance that comes from knowing him. For we are the aroma of Christ to God among those who are being saved and among those who are perishing; to the one a fragrance from death to death, to the other a fragrance from life to life.[29]

These contours of Paul's proclamation, which indicate its direct and inescapably antagonistic engagement with aspects of Roman imperial ideology, are surely important to understanding what he means by affirming Christ's resurrection. They are ideological dimensions that Badiou unfortunately fails to address because of his general dismissal of the resurrection as "fable."[30] Just this dismissal brings down on Badiou the criticism of Christian theologians who consider that he has thrown out the Pauline baby with the bathwater (and betrayed his own inconsistency regarding the "truth event").[31] This is an apt criticism, but not because Christian theologians possess some additional datum that Badiou refuses to acknowledge, as though resurrection were a discrete episode given to us in history. The proclamation of resurrection, the *concept* of resurrection, makes sense—it has meaning—only within a symbolic context, what many of us would call a *mythological* context, that points inexorably forward to a consummation of history that Paul, for one, considered absolutely *real.*[32] Badiou dismisses the reality of the resurrection-as-discrete-episode apparently without recognizing its place in that larger apocalyptic understanding of the real. Of course,

character of Roman iconography, which displayed the power of Rome in part through the representation of subjected and defeated bodies.

28. Paul's initial proclamation was an "exhibition" of Christ crucified (Gal 3:1 NRSV); his apostolic presence was a "carrying in the body the death of Jesus" (2 Cor 4:10); the Eucharistic assembly was a proclamation of "the Lord's death until he comes" (1 Cor 11:26).

29. The metaphor implies that Paul is a *conquered prisoner* of Christ: see P. B. Duff, "Metaphor, Motif, and Meaning"; Elliott, "Apostle Paul's Self-Presentation."

30. A point Badiou repeats, for example when he emphasizes that "the event that [Paul] takes to identify the real *is not* real" (Badiou, *Saint Paul*, 58).

31. So Griffiths rightly points to "a persistent lack of clarity in Badiou's understanding of truth," if "Paul's proclamation of Christ resurrected can be true even if Christ was not in fact resurrected . . . There is a conundrum here that Badiou does not resolve" ("Christ and Critical Theory," 52).

32. Here of course I am guided by the force of J. Christiaan Beker's argument in *Paul the Apostle.*

this observation hardly gives Christian theologians an upper hand, since they can no more point to the *evidentness* of history's consummation than can Badiou. Indeed, given the apocalyptic coordinates of Paul's affirmation of a risen Christ, any theological appropriation of Paul should accept as a theological-critical axiom—in the most *materialist* terms—Paul's own exclamation in 1 Corinthians: if Christ has not been raised, "if for this life only we have hoped in Christ," if, that is, the resurrection does *not* point inexorably to a *real* consummation of history, then "we are of all people most to be pitied" (1 Cor 15:19). If Badiou's Paul is the "master of the gesture,"[33] so at last, so far as the course of history to date would indicate, is the Christian's Paul.

What does that gesture mean? Read in apocalyptic terms, Paul's proclamation of Jesus' resurrection means, inevitably I think, that the "biopower" of the state is *not* sovereign, that its totalizing claims can be resisted (for, indeed, the proclamation is itself such resistance). The formation of a community whose collective subjectivity depends upon the failure of the state's totalizing claims over their allegiance is inherently subversive. For such a community to practice an economic mutualism that crossed, and thus annulled, the distinctions *slave vs. free* or, implicitly, *conqueror vs. conquered* would have constituted the performance of a genuine collective universalism such as Badiou describes.[34]

The Body of Christ and Jewish Bodies

Badiou goes a different way. Rather than exploring the inherent political significance of Jesus' death and resurrection in opposition to the very totalizing ideology that used crucifixion as an indispensable signification,[35] Badiou focuses—as so much of Protestant theological interpretation has focused—on the dichotomy "Jew/Gentile" and the supposed exclusion

---

33. Griffiths, "Christ and Critical Theory," 52.

34. On the significance of the practice of mutualism as a survival strategy among the poor, see Meggitt, *Paul, Poverty and Survival*; on the collection, Sze-Kar Wan, "Collection for the Saints as an Anti-colonial Act," 206–10. I use the qualifier "implicitly" above because we can speak only with some ambivalence of the distinction "conqueror vs. conquered" being overcome in the Pauline churches: in Corinth, for example, there is evidence of members of the Roman elite joining with much lower-status believers in the congregation, but the resulting tensions make Corinth the test case. Welborn addresses precisely this test case in *That There May Be Equality*.

35. Jennings criticizes Badiou on just this point, for missing the unmistakable political aspects of crucifixion and therefore of resurrection as well: Jennings, "Paul and (Post-modern) Political Thought."

inherent in Jewish law. What Paul sought, Badiou muses, was "to drag the Good News . . . out from the rigid enclosure within which its restriction to the Jewish community would confine it." (He goes on to insist that Paul sought to free the gospel from the constraints of Roman law, too, but this rather theoretical assertion is not pursued, and remains incidental to his project.)[36] More important for him is the assertion that "Paul emphasizes rupture rather than continuity *with Judaism.*"[37] Rather paradoxically, Badiou seeks to distance himself from the anti-Semitic and supersessionist aspects of the Christian theological tradition, but for him, as for much of Christian theological scholarship, especially the liberal Protestant scholarship aligned with the "New Perspective" on Paul, Pauline universalism is fundamentally and inevitably opposed to Jewish "exclusivism." "Jewish discourse is a discourse of exception" over against "Greek discourse," which is the discourse of a natural (or naturalizing) totality.[38] These two discourses are bound up with each other, indeed they "are the two aspects of the same figure of mastery": "In the eyes of Paul the Jew, the weakness of Jewish discourse is that its logic of the exceptional sign is only valid *for* the Greek cosmic totality. The Jew is in exception to the Greek."[39] In the place of this relationship of totality-and-exception Paul affirms a universalism based in the event. The central problem of Paul's thought is, for Badiou, the question, "What is it in this resurrection, this 'out from the dead,' that has the power to suspend differences? Why, if a man is resurrected, does it follow that there is neither Greek nor Jew, neither male nor female, neither slave nor free man?" (referring to Gal 3:28).[40]

The direction in which I pointed above answers the last part of this question: that is, it follows quite clearly within an apocalyptic logic that if a *crucified* man is resurrected, there is neither slave nor free man, since resurrection *means* a divine intervention that ruptures the very system of significations that oppose slave and free, men and women. Badiou restricts himself to the first opposition, Greek nor Jew, because he takes it to be homologous with the opposition in contemporary French politics between the false universalism of a totalizing nationalistic identity and the identity politics of minority groups;[41] also because he considers it central to Paul's thought.

36. Badoiu, *Saint Paul,* 13.

37. Badiou, *Saint Paul,* 35 (emphasis added).

38. Badiou, *Saint Paul,* 41–42.

39. Badiou, *Saint Paul,* 42.

40. Badiou, *Saint Paul,* 73.

41. Badiou, *Saint Paul,* 12–13.

Here Badiou follows what some of us regard as a flawed tradition of Protestant scholarship going back at least to F. C. Baur. He reads Paul in opposition to a "Jewish Christian faction" in the early church and declares it *"impossible to overestimate* the importance of the incident at Antioch" (Gal 2:11–14).[42] To the contrary, however, such "overestimation" happens all the time: indeed it has long been a mainstay of Protestant dogmatics. "Paul *never stops telling us*," Badiou writes, "that the Jews are looking for signs and 'demanding miracles,' that the Greeks are 'looking for wisdom' and asking questions, that the Christians declare Christ crucified."[43] To the contrary, however, Paul makes the statement *only once,* at 1 Cor 1:22–25; he first opposes Jews not to "Greeks" but to *ethnē,* those from among the nations ("Gentiles" in the NRSV); and in the context of that rhetorically freighted argument it is clear that it is the Greek/"ethnic" clamoring for wisdom, rather than a Jewish proclivity for signs (let alone a Jewish "exclusivism," which Paul does not name here), that is his target in the Corinthian assembly.

My point is simply that Badiou, like so much of Protestant scholarship, wrongly places a supposed opposition to Judaism, Jewish identity, and the "exceptionalism" of Jewish law as such at the center of Paul's thought. He consequently overemphasizes the significance of passages where Protestant scholarship is accustomed, rightly or wrongly, to read the traces of that opposition.[44] Against these well-worn habits, pioneering scholars like Lloyd Gaston have insisted that we must read Paul's letters, and what he says about the law in them, first in terms of their intended effect among *non-Jewish* audiences who are tempted to misinterpret or to misuse that law for their own, *non-Jewish* purposes.[45] Jewish scholars have insisted that Christian interpreters of Paul renounce the morally unacceptable practice of trading on historically inaccurate stereotypes about Jewish boasting, works-righteousness, exclusivism, and so on.[46] And attention to the political context of the Roman Empire and Roman imperial ideology has allowed us to see the oppositions of "Jew and Greek," "Greek and barbarian," *Ioudaioi* and

---

42. Badiou, *Saint Paul,* 22–26 (emphasis added).

43. Badiou, *Saint Paul,* 58 (emphasis added).

44. Characteristic is Günther Bornkamm's insistence that in all of his letters, "Paul's opponent is not this or that section in a particular church, but the Jews and their understanding of salvation" (Bornkamm, *Paul,* 11–12). It is no surprise that Badiou selects Bornkamm's book as one of two books on Paul which he recommends to his readers, the other being *Saint Paul* by Stanislas Breton (3).

45. Gaston, *Paul and the Torah.*

46. Fundamental here are Fredriksen, *From Jesus to Christ;* Boyarin, *Radical Jew;* and Nanos, *Mystery of Romans.*

ethnē, not as a single ethnic or religious binary but as positions within a more complex configuration of identities in Roman imperial culture.[47]

PAUL AND THE IDEOLOGICAL GESTURE

These criticisms are meant not to disqualify Badiou's deployment of Paul but to suggest ways in which that deployment might be set on different grounds, grounds both more historically defensible and more congenial to Badiou's own political purposes.

I have already suggested that Paul's proclamation of the resurrection of a *crucified* messiah was irreducibly political in its implications, reversing and neutralizing the significations on which the slave mode of production (and the Roman imperial order based upon it) relied. Badiou moves in this direction when he discusses, with reference to 1 Cor 1:18-29, the cross for Paul as the event that renders "the philosophical logos incapable of declaring it."

> The most radical statement in the text we are commenting on is in effect the following: "God has chosen the things that are not [*ta mē onta*] in order to bring to naught those that are [*ta onta*]." That the Christ-event causes nonbeings rather than beings to arise as attesting to God; that it consists in the abolition of what all previous discourses held as existing, or being, gives a measure of the ontological subversion to which Paul's antiphilosophy invites the declarant or militant.[48]

Badiou is concerned here to oppose Paul to efforts to domesticate or accommodate the event into a positive *philosophical* logos. But the same point can be made over against a *political* logos, that is, against a totalizing ideology such as that of the Roman Empire (or of contemporary capitalism, or for that matter of contemporary Christianity's accommodation to the capitalist order). Badiou's philosophical-political universal truth—that "there is only one world"—can indeed be drawn from Paul, and *has* been drawn from this specific Pauline text, though without reference to Badiou. Expounding upon the thought of martyred Jesuit theologian Ignacio Ellacuría, Jon Sobrino has distilled Paul's claim regarding God's creation of a new community out of "things that are not"—a political *creatio ex nihilo*—into a single theological axiom: *ex pauperes nulla salus,* "no salvation outside [or apart

---

47. Here the decisive works are Lopez, *Apostle to the Conquered*; and Kahl, *Galatians Re-imagined*; see also Elliott, *Arrogance of Nations*, ch. 1.

48. Badiou, *Saint Paul*, 46–47.

from] the poor." Sobrino's seminal work makes clear that the universal truth at the heart of the Pauline gospel is no philosophical abstraction but is realized in an alternative politics, the civilization of human solidarity that is the civilization of poverty.[49]

The civilization of poverty can of course be perceived and analyzed, from structuralist or functionalist perspectives, as one segment—even a necessary or inevitable segment—of society ordered according to the regime of capitalism. To declare, as Sobrino does, that the civilization of poverty is a sign of the world's future, a *utopian* sign, will seem, from within the thought-world of capitalist ideology, nonsensical, fantastic, *merely* "utopian." It will seem as much an empty, formal "gesture" as Badiou's appeal to a resurrection without a risen body.

But Badiou and Sobrino alike have a precedent in these seemingly utopian gestures: Paul himself. A Marxist understanding of the ways ideological forces constrain cultural expression—and the ways a countervailing force opposes and resists those ideological forces—allows us to see the ideological gesture in Paul's thought and praxis.

Quoting Karl Marx, Fredric Jameson describes the ultimate horizon of interpretation as "the collective struggle [in history] to wrest a realm of Freedom from a realm of Necessity." The consequence is that it is "something worse than an error" to distinguish "political" texts from non-political, for example "religious," ones. Such a categorical distinction is symptomatic of the pervasive logic of capitalism, which relegates to the private sphere what would otherwise be collective visions and imaginings of an alternative future ("utopia") as it usurps for itself the public arena of political action. Because (according to Jameson's Marxist cultural theory) the ideological forces arising in any social order act to constrain collective imagination, including what may be thought or imagined in the production of texts (like Paul's letters), the interpreter's task is to identify the ways in which a text has been constrained by ideology. But because the ultimate horizon of interpretation is not the static operation of ideological necessity but the *struggle* between the dominant ideological forces and the human strivings and imaginings that those forces operate to limit and channel, the interpreter's task is also to trace and tease out the impulses at work in the text that seek to work against ideological closure, impulses that "remain unrealized in the surface of the text." Those impulses, Jameson argues, arise from what may be described as a collective "political unconscious."[50]

49. Sobrino, *No Salvation outside the Poor.*
50. Jameson, "On Interpretation."

That Paul's thought is constrained by the ideological forces prevailing in the early Roman Empire is evident in his assertion of a coming "lord" (*kyrios*) who "rises to rule the nations" (Rom 15:12). Of course, that *kyrios* is the messiah, consequently a lord other than Caesar—a fact that has led some interpreters to conclude that Paul's gospel is at least implicitly opposed to the claims of Roman imperial propaganda.[51] But the alternative that Paul imagines to Rome's evil rule—to a "bad kyriarchy," we might say, doomed to destruction (1 Cor 2:8; 15:24–25)—is not a completely different social configuration, but a "good kyriarchy," the rule of a *benevolent* lord. That Roman kyriarchy might come to an end without the ascendancy of a new and better kyriarchy and that the world might be configured in a way completely free of the rule of a monarch—these notions were for Paul and, we may presume, for countless others of his time, apparently unthinkable.[52]

But there is better evidence for ideological constraint on Paul's thought. He declares in Romans that the world has been "subjected to futility" and "bondage to decay," meaning that *God* has subjected it (Rom 8:20–21). Yet God's Spirit also militates *against* that subjection through the "groaning," as of a woman in labor, of a creation yearning for liberation, and agitates among those who wait for "the glorious liberation of the children of God" and "the redemption of our bodies" (8:22–23). Thus, for Paul, God is simultaneously the source of the world's coming liberation, and the one who has imposed the present subjection (8:20). The tension between these statements—a tension Paul does not mitigate, indeed a tension of which he actually seems unaware—is, following Jameson, an expression of the deeper, unconscious tension generated by the "restless" energy of a collective unconscious militating against the ideological constraints of the environment (Roman imperial ideology). Paul's apocalyptic assertion that "the appointed time has grown short" (*ho kairos synestalmenos estin*, 1 Cor 7:29) may be typical of an apocalyptic way of thinking (compare Mark 13:20, "if the Lord had not cut short those days . . ."); but it is the nature of the assertion *as ideological gesture* that bears attention.

The apocalyptic assertion is an attempt to achieve a standing place over against the ideological force of Roman realized eschatology, which declares constantly that history has reached its decisive climax in the supremacy of Rome and the triumph of "the Roman people." Against this ubiquitous claim Paul can only announce a "mystery" (Rom 11:25): that God has—inscrutably, invisibly—intervened in history, interrupted its progress. God has subjected the world to a "futility" that renders any attempt to read the

---

51. For example, Wright, "Paul's Gospel and Caesar's Empire."

52. See on this point Elliott, *Arrogance of Nations*, 50–57.

future from present circumstances not only futile, but counter to the *real* future that God alone will bring about. Present circumstances (meaning the *apparent* triumph of Rome and the *apparent* relegation of Israel to the vanquished peoples of the earth) can only deceive the senses; only the one who perceives according to reason (*logos, logismos*)—meaning, reason *shaped by divine event*—can perceive that real future. The argument in Romans 9–11—I would argue, the argument of the whole letter—is an example of what the "New Rhetoricians" call an argument by *dissociation of concepts,* here the dissociation of what *appears* true, given present circumstances, from what is *real.*[53]

That rhetorical trope-as-ideological-gesture was a commonplace among Paul's Jewish contemporaries, to judge from Philo of Alexandria and the author of 4 Maccabees.[54] But it is also a rough ancient analogue for the truth-procedure Badiou describes, the truth procedure for which Badiou appeals in a contemporary world in which capitalist ideology claims to have reached "the end of history."[55] That claim causes a profound "disorientation" in the present to men and women "imprisoned within the temporality assigned us by the dominant order"; the words are Badiou's, but they might be Paul's. "What takes courage is to operate in terms of a different *durée* to that imposed by the law of the world," says Badiou. "You know what time it is . . . The night is far gone, the day is near," says Paul.[56]

A Christian posture that claims to hold the truth of resurrection as a discrete possession fails to recognize the character of Paul's proclamation as ideological assertion, as one moment in a *struggle* against the ideological hegemony of the imperial order. For Paul, that struggle was couched in the language available to him, that of Jewish apocalypticism. In our own time, many of us are unused to thinking according to the cosmological and kyriarchal fabric of apocalypticism. Those who often claim to have recovered the *terms* of Paul's response in a literal way have often advocated a theistic determinism that legitimates political quietism and acquiescence—postures we can scarce afford, given "the impending crisis" (*tēn enestēsan anankēn,* 1

---

53. See Perelman and Olbrechts-Tyteca, *New Rhetoric,* 411–59; Elliott, *Arrogance of Nations,* 83–85; 50–57.

54. In 4 Maccabees the Greek tyrant appeals to the defiant Jews to listen to reason (*logos*); they reply that they *are* listening to reason, the tyrant is being *alogos.* Their minds are informed by the law, that is, the Torah. Philo similarly challenges his reader to perceive not with the bodily senses, that "discern [only] what is manifest and close at hand," but to perceive with *logismos,* which will reveal the divine providence in human history (*Embassy* 1–3). See Elliott, *Arrogance of Nations,* 146–50.

55. So Fukuyama, *End of History.*

56. Badiou, "Communist Hypothesis," 41; Rom 13:11–12.

Cor 7:26). We need instead to recover the character of Paul's proclamation (and of the practices of which it was a part, including the economic mutualism of his assemblies) precisely as ideological gestures of defiance—or in theological terms, as signs of a heavenly citizenship (Phil 3:20). Toward that end, Alain Badiou may be an indispensable guide.

8

The Philosophers' Paul and the Churches

THE OCCASION FOR THIS volume is one of the most remarkable recent developments in scholarship on the apostle Paul: the surprising attention being paid to Paul by a number of European and North American philosophers who find the apostle a model for their politically radical but non-theistic programs. The development is all the more surprising when we recall how some earlier philosophers, chief among them Frederick Nietzsche, presented themselves as the cultured despisers of Paul's form of Christianity.[1]

Each of the other essays in *Paul in the Grip of the Philosophers* [see n. 1] has addressed a particular philosopher who has engaged the apostle's legacy. The focus in those essays has been to describe and to evaluate diverse appropriations of the apostle, asking whether one or another philosopher has offered new insight into Paul's thought. My purpose here is different. I wish to shift attention from "the philosophers" and their interpretation of Paul to the Church and to Christian responses to the philosophers.

Such a prospect confronts several challenges. The first is bound up with that reference to "the Church," capitalized rather audaciously to indicate a single coherent entity—a common enough usage in theology, but one that must appear to beg the question today. I mean that amid contemporary U.S. churches, denominational differences pale in comparison with the metastasizing diversity of alternatives, from storefront missions to "emergent" coffee houses and full-service Christian megaplexes. Those "mainline" denominations that remain are often polarized by campaigns and agendas conceived in think tanks and driven by lobbying groups and full-spectrum

---

1. Frick, "Paul in the Grip of Continental Philosophers." References in this essay to "this volume" are to Frick, ed., *Paul in the Grip of the Philosophers*.

Christian broadcasting, especially vibrant on the right. Protestants are now outnumbered by people affiliated with no religious faith.[2] Mainline congregations compete for the adherence of their own members with the cultural axiom that religion is a matter of intensely personal preference. The enormous growth of what we may call "spirituality" industries manifests the triumph of capitalist values, as religious symbols are transformed into infinitely customizable consumer commodities. To speak in such a context of "the Church" as a coherent and singular reality must seem wistfully nostalgic, perhaps even retrograde.

Further, until now, the subject of this volume has been of interest chiefly to individual scholars and, perhaps, their advanced students in philosophy, theology, and biblical studies, individuals who have been drawn to the topic by their own personal and professional interests. "The philosophers' Paul" appears as the subject of analysis at the narrow intersection of these academic disciplines, not beyond it. I am unaware of official ecclesiastical responses to the work of any of the philosophers discussed here, or of any prospect that such statements might be forthcoming. Even if a number of the scholars involved in recent discussions of this topic have been self-consciously doing theology on behalf of "the Church," broadly defined, or working in ecclesiastically affiliated institutions of higher learning, the diversity of their responses—ranging on occasion from enthusiasm to condescension to alarm toward one or another of the philosophers in question—points up the fallacy of construing them together as a single, univocal "Christian response."

Finally, although in recent years I have offered my own criticisms of one or another aspect of a philosopher's reading of Paul,[3] I readily concede that I am neither fluent in contemporary philosophy nor, although I am a priest in the Episcopal Church, do I hold any sort of ecclesiastical or academic rank that would qualify me to do anything as audacious as speak broadly for "the Church."

My purpose here is necessarily more modest. I wish to point again to the wider radical project in which several of the contemporary philosophers are currently engaged as the proper context in which their appropriations of Paul must be understood and evaluated. Further, I propose that the failure, or at least reluctance, of some theologians to enter into that context, to step, so to speak, onto the philosophers' home turf, is symptomatic of a wider presumption of privilege on the part of Christian theology. That presumption

2. Pew Research Center, "'Nones' on the Rise."
3. See Elliott, "Marxism and the Postcolonial Study of Paul" and "Ideological Closure in the Christ-Event" (Chapters 5 and 7 in this volume).

is itself a case in point of the perilous contemporary ideological situation to which the philosophers wish urgently to draw our attention. At last I wish to suggest that the apostle Paul himself offers, mutatis mutandis, a way out of the presumption of epistemic privilege that so dominates and distorts much Christian theology today.

THEOLOGICAL CRITIQUE BY DISMISSAL

In a spate of conferences and publications over the last decade, groups of theologians, philosophers, and biblical scholars have gathered to interact with selected works by Jacob Taubes, Giorgio Agamben, Alain Badiou, Slavoj Žižek, Walter Benjamin, and others grouped under the category of continental philosophy.[4] This energetic activity suggests that the work of "the philosophers" has become the sort of *cause célèbre* for some in these circles—and the *bête noir* for others—that René Girard's work on "sacred violence" presented beginning in the 1990s.[5] The reaction has not been uniformly enthusiastic. Alain Gignac pointed out the potential for a certain professional resentment when he playfully described Taubes, Badiou, and Agamben as "poach[ing] in the hunting grounds of theologians and exegetes"; and sure enough, others have observed a note of "indignation" among theologians and exegetes posing as Paul's ecclesiastical defenders.[6]

The implication of metaphors like "poaching" or "expropriation" is that Paul is *properly* interpreted by the theological "insiders," indeed, that he is their property. It follows that atheists, no matter how erudite, can have no "proper" claim on the apostle. It is this proprietary presumption,

4. See Odell-Scott, *Reading Romans*; Caputo and Alcoff, *St. Paul among the Philosophers*; Harink, *Paul, Philosophy*.

5. Girard's works (including *The Scapegoat, Violence and the Sacred*, and, with J. M. Oughourlian, and G. Lefort, *Things Hidden since the Foundation of the World*) inspired Williams, *Bible, Violence, and the Sacred*, and in particular connection with Paul, Hamerton-Kelly, *Sacred Violence*. The Colloquium on Violence and Religion (COV&R) was founded in 1990 to explore implications of Girard's theory and continues its work today (see http://violenceandreligion.com/about-covr), in part through its journal *Contagion*. For an early response especially to Robert Hamerton-Kelly's book, see my essay "Paul and the Lethality of the Law" (Chapter 1 in this volume).

6. Gignac, "Taubes, Badiou, Agamben," 156; similarly, Robbins, "Politics of Paul," describes a certain "territoriality" on the part of theological and biblical scholars defending "their" Paul against interlopers. New Testament scholar Stephen Fowl ("Very Particular Universalism," 119) has observed "a rather indignant attitude" toward the philosophers among Paulinists; theologian Paul J. Griffiths ("The Cross as the Fulcrum of Politics," 180) invokes the analogy of "despoilers of the Egyptians" to describe Giorgio Agamben as reading Paul "from without" or "from outside"—"insiders" here being identified with church theologians and New Testament scholars.

this note that Paul "belongs" to the theologians, that I want here to contest; not because I think the theologians' interest in the apostle is illegitimate, but because the rush to defend Paul from dialectical materialists and their ilk appears to me a symptom of the very predicament that the dialectical materialists are laboring to diagnose. My purpose here is to point in the direction of a more fruitful interaction with the philosophers on the part of "the Church."

Some theologians have argued not only that the philosophers in question should not claim to interpret Paul because he is not properly their subject but that the effort is doomed from the start; they *cannot* understand him. On this account, the philosophers fail to grasp fundamental and central aspects of Paul's thought because they cannot comprehend a reality in which, because of their lack of faith, they do not participate. So Jens Zimmermann has argued that "unbelieving" philosophers inevitably "fail to grasp" the irreducibly theological categories that are "the very fabric of Paul's thinking": concepts like "Christology," "transcendence," and "new creation" in Christ. Zimmermann insists he is not raising a mere "matter of interpretive preference"; the choice of these *theological* categories is grounded in the Christian's "ontological participation in" the new creation and new humanity that have been opened up in Christ.[7] In earlier essays, J. Paul Griffiths and Daniel M. Bell argued that precisely because the philosophers are not Christians, they have consistently failed to recognize as a fundamental truth that the only satisfactory answer to their quests is "the peace given by explicit knowledge of the God of Abraham," available only through communion with the Church, through which humanity is "taken up into the divine life of the Trinity." The only true and worthy radicality, they asserted, is to be found in the familiar embrace of the Church's liturgical and charitable practices.[8]

Alas, this argument is made more often on cozily theoretical than on empirical grounds. One is left to wonder whether the philosophers (and others) might be more amenable to persuasion if "actually existing" Christian worship on any given Sunday morning gave just a bit more evidence of its alleged revolutionary potential. In the absence of such evidence, the theological critics seem, to my ear at least, to protest too much. Indeed, such

7. Zimmermann, "Hermeneutics of Unbelief," 235–36.

8. Griffiths, "Christ and Critical Theory," 46, 50, 54–55; D. M. Bell, "Badiou's Faith and Paul's Gospel," 108. Both express a certain amount of condescension toward the benighted non-Christians, Griffiths naming them objects of "Christian pity and concern." Creston Davis, in Milbank et al., *Paul's New Moment*, expresses a similar enthusiasm for the Eucharistic liturgy as an "Incarnational" reality through which union with the Trinity is achieved. Surprisingly, he attributes these thoughts to the apostle Paul.

theological critiques of the philosophers resemble a sort of defensive action, rather like that of a body's immune system rushing to guard against a foreign contaminant. But, as anyone who has suffered from hay fever knows, the body's allergic and defensive mobilizations can sometimes be out of any proportion to the actual danger posed by a foreign body.

Similarly, the nervous zeal with which some have rushed to demonstrate that, at one or another point, the philosophers have misinterpreted the apostle's thought, or that they have not kept up with the latest developments in the professional exegetical literature, seems misplaced. Admittedly, I have offered my own criticism elsewhere of Alain Badiou's appropriation of Paul (in *St. Paul: The Foundation of Universalism*), arguing that Badiou relies on an untenable essentializing of "Jewish" and "Greek" discourses that theological and exegetical scholars still struggle—quite rightly—to disavow.[9] I also argued, quite apart from questions of the historical veracity or verifiability of the resurrection of Jesus, that in its original apocalyptic context, the symbolization of the Messiah's resurrection bore far more *political* potential than Badiou recognized. But my goal in that effort was to *augment* the relevance of Badiou's argument, not to deny or disqualify it from the outset as insufficiently "theological."

Those who strive to make the latter case appear to miss the point. The philosophers neither claim nor aspire to give a comprehensive account of Paul's *theological* thought. Rather, they are trying to describe, and if possible to model, a radical militancy appropriate and necessary to our present situation. To reduce this to a matter of "theology" is to evade the greater responsibility to which the philosophers seek to call us all.

From the start of his book on Paul, Alain Badiou has made clear that he is indifferent to the more sublime dimensions of the apostle's theology. The resurrection of the Messiah, admittedly central to Paul (for it is to this single statement that, Badiou cheerfully admits, Paul "reduces Christianity"), is "precisely a fable" in which it is "rigorously impossible to believe."[10] For his part, Slavoj Žižek makes clear that his interest in Christianity is not in any of its dominant contemporary expressions but in its "perverse core," which he finds crystallized in Jesus' cry of dereliction from the cross (Mark 15:34):

> When Christ dies, what dies with him is the secret hope discernible in "Father, why hast thou forsaken me?": the hope that there *is* a father who has abandoned me. The "Holy Spirit" is the

---

9. See Blanton, "Mad with the Love of Undead Life"; Elliott, "Ideological Closure" (Chapter 7 in this volume).

10. See Badiou, *Saint Paul*, 4–5.

community deprived of its support in the big Other. The point of Christianity as the religion of atheism is not the vulgar human-ist one that the becoming-man-of-God reveals that man is the secret of God (Feuerbach et al.); rather, it attacks the religious hard core that survives even in humanism, even up to Stalinism, with its belief in History as the "big Other" that decides on the "objective meaning" of our deeds.[11]

What Žižek here calls the "point of Christianity" is a "perverse core" because it is a perversion of the "core" of Christianity as most Christians historically have understood it. Indeed, in Žižek's own words, the "core" he poses as the proper object of philosophy is the substitution of a "religion of atheism" in the place of a belief in God. This "core," Žižek continues, can be redeemed

only in the gesture of abandoning the shell of [Christianity's] institutional organization (and, even more so, of its specific reli-gious experience). The gap here is irreducible: either one drops the religious form, or one maintains the form, but loses the es-sence. That is the ultimate heroic gesture that awaits Christian-ity: in order to save its treasure, it has to sacrifice itself—like Christ, who had to die so that Christianity could emerge.[12]

Evidently, then, Badiou and Žižek are chiefly interested in selected ele-ments of Christian, and especially Pauline, theology because they perceive there elements of a radical subjectivity that they wish to extricate from the deadening context of contemporary Christianity, rather as one might pull smoldering embers from the cool bed of a dying fire to fan them into flame. Just as evidently, neither philosopher imagines contemporary Christian churches as providing the tinder (to extend the metaphor) for the fire they wish to see cast upon the earth. In the face of Žižek's call for renunciation, for "dropping the religious form," it seems hardly to the point to protest that Badiou or Žižek (or others of the philosophers) have failed to be adequately Christian in their theologizing. Theology—as a separate domain only cir-cumstantially related to the political—is not the point.

11. Žižek, *Puppet and the Dwarf*, 171. He introduces the paragraph by declaring it is "the point of the book."

12. Žižek, *Puppet and the Dwarf*, 171. Žižek returns to this interpretation of the cross in "Meditation on Michelangelo's *Christ on the Cross*."

THE COMMUNIST IMPERATIVE

What Badiou and Žižek wish (to limit ourselves to these two, though a simi-lar argument could be extended to other of the philosophers) is to inspire a truly "revolutionary subjectivity." As he has described it in other writings, Badiou's goal is the performative revival in our day of "the communist hypothesis":

> What is the communist hypothesis? In its generic sense, given in its canonic *Manifesto*, "communist" means, first, that the logic of class—the fundamental subordination of labour to a dominant class, the arrangement that has persisted since Antiquity—is not inevitable; it can be overcome. The communist hypothesis is that a different collective organization is practicable, one that will eliminate the inequality of wealth and even the division of labour.[13]

It is wrong, Badiou argues, to regard this hypothesis as "utopian." It is just as wrong to judge the value of the communist hypothesis by the rela-tively brief and ultimately failed experiments of authoritarian Eastern bloc governments in the twentieth century; its legacy is much older.[14] "As a pure Idea of equality, the communist hypothesis has no doubt existed since the beginnings of the state. As soon as mass action opposes state coercion in the name of egalitarian justice, rudiments or fragments of the hypothesis start to appear."[15]

The agenda to which Badiou calls us "during the reactionary interlude that now prevails" includes recognizing that conditions in our own day more nearly resemble the pre-revolutionary nineteenth century than the twenti-eth. That is, we today confront "vast zones of poverty, widening inequalities, politics dissolved into the 'service of wealth,' the nihilism of large sections of the young, the servility of much of the intelligentsia." Badiou seeks "to renew the existence of the communist hypothesis, in our consciousness and on the ground."[16]

For his part, borrowing a (pseudo-)Pauline phrase from Ephesians 6:12, Žižek declares, at the outset of a lengthy discussion of "living in the

13. Badiou, "Communist Hypothesis," 34–5.

14. "Utopian" aspects of Paul's thought were the subject of a special joint session of the Paul and Politics and Pauline Soteriology Groups of the Society of Biblical Litera-ture at the annual meeting in 2011. Papers by me, Douglas Harink, Douglas Campbell, and Theodore Jennings will be published in a forthcoming volume. I thank Susan East-man and Ross Wagner for their energy in pulling together this session.

15. Badiou, "Communist Hypothesis," 34–5.

16. Badiou, "Communist Hypothesis," 41–42.

end times," that today, "our struggle is not against actual corrupt individuals, but against those in power in general, against their authority, against the [capitalist] global order and the ideological mystification which sustains it."[17] It is necessary, Žižek argues, always to "maintain the precise reference to a set of social antagonisms which generate the need for communism." This understanding of communism is "still fully relevant": "Marx's good old notion of communism not as an ideal, but as a movement which reacts to actual social antagonisms." It is further necessary not only to recognize, but to participate in those conflicts: "It is not enough to remain faithful to the communist Idea—one has to locate it in real historical antagonisms which give to this Idea a practical urgency. The only *true* question today is: do we endorse the predominant naturalization of capitalism, or does today's global capitalism contain antagonisms powerful enough to prevent its indefinite reproduction?"[18]

If Žižek uses the term "communist" somewhat less readily than Badiou, it may be, in part, because he, too, does not want his cause to be confused with the centralized state experiments of Eastern Europe in the last half of the twentieth century[19] and, in part, because he insists we must be not less, but *more* radical than Marx.[20] The critique of the political economy of our age remains an urgent task, but according to Žižek, Marx's tendency to represent the future as unfolding according to an inexorable materialist determinism not only has been disproved by history; it is theoretically too reliant on the mechanistic claims of nineteenth-century capitalism itself.[21] On this point, Žižek is taking part in an intense, wide-ranging, and long-standing deliberation carried on amidst the political Left today. But this is a conversation of which all too few theologians and church leaders are aware and with which still fewer are conversant. This is unfortunate. The social moment that Žižek describes is also where the Church lives, and moves, and has its being.

17. Žižek, *Living in the End Times*, xv.

18. Žižek, "How to Begin from the Beginning."

19. Žižek, "How to Begin from the Beginning," 218–19 (though just here Žižek speaks frankly of the need today to "reactualize the communist Idea," and of participating in "the communist struggle"). See also Eagleton, *Literary Theory*, 195.

20. Ward Blanton compares Žižek's "peculiarly complex intertwining of the 'old and the new'"—particularly with regard to the Marxist heritage—with that of Paul; see Blanton, "Mad with the Love of Undead Life."

21. "What Marx conceived as Communism remained an idealized image of capitalism, capitalism without capitalism" (Žižek, *Year of Dreaming Dangerously*, 134). Lawrence Welborn argues that Walter Benjamin's similar repudiation of the "antiquarian approach" to history informed Jacob Taubes's reading of Paul (Welborn, "Jacob Taubes—Paulinist, Messianist").

The Left entered a period of profound crisis—the shadow of the twentieth century still hangs over it, and the full scope of the defeat is not yet admitted. In the years of prospering capitalism, it was easy for the Left to be a Cassandra, warning that our prosperity is based on illusions and prophesizing [sic] catastrophes to come. Now the economic downturn and social disintegration [that] the Left was waiting for is here; protests and revolts are popping up all around the globe—but what is conspicuously absent is any consistent Leftist reply to these events, any project of how to transpose islands of chaotic resistance into a positive program of social change.[22]

It is just this aspect of the philosophers' contemporary work that demands and deserves the serious attention of U.S. churches, whether or not that attention takes the form of engagement with the philosophers themselves. In the United States today, in the absence of a coherent and compelling narrative of our situation issuing from a well-arrayed Left, that ideological vacuum has been filled by competing arguments about how the capitalist machinery can best be carbureted to achieve "job creation," "deficit reduction," and "financial stability" without interfering with the putative sovereignty of a "free market." Challenges to the fundamental axiom of capitalism's necessity—that it is the *only* imaginable mechanism for "wealth creation"—now generally go unmentioned and appear to have become unthinkable. Indeed, our atmosphere has become so choked with the doctrinal assertions of Neoliberalism that hardly anyone bothers to pose the question empirically, as a proposal for genuine controlled experimentation. (The "controlled experiment" provided by history, that is, by decades of virtually unchecked Neoliberal policies, is presumably irrelevant to the question, for example, whether corporate profits fueled by tax-break subsidies should not already have revived the "private sector.") Instead, as Immanuel Wallerstein has observed, those exerting the most control over the machinery of contemporary capitalism have also taken the most care to protect it from political evaluation or from the sort of modification ("reform") that might make the stuff of campaign promises actually feasible. They appear more interested in securing their own privilege through ongoing structured inequality, rather like robbers who weight down the throttle of a runaway train before leaping free with their ill-gotten loot.[23]

22. Žižek, *Year of Dreaming Dangerously*, 133.

23. Immanuel Wallerstein observes that in the present moment of "structural crisis," "those in power will no longer be trying to preserve the existing system (doomed as it is to self-destruction); rather, they will try to ensure that the transition leads to the construction of a new system that will replicate the worst features of the existing

We should, with Žižek, perceive here the "shameless cynicism of the existing global order," which perpetuates both the ongoing immiseration of the world's majority, not least through the imposition of "austerity" measures, and the constant ideological obfuscations of its true nature under the guise of "news" and "information." That world order is now so pervasive as to seem *natural* to us.[24] It is difficult to imagine a concerted popular effort to stand against the tide; it is difficult to imagine that such efforts, when they *do* take organized form as they have, for example, in the Occupy movement, will escape being framed by corporate media as the pointless antics of the idle and self-absorbed.[25]

My purpose here is not to offer a detailed diagnosis of our situation at this stage of hyper-capitalism, as the overheated mechanism threatens to come unmoored and fly apart (to borrow just one of Žižek's vivid images for our time). It is to name the context of political struggle in which Badiou and Žižek seek to engage us as the "proper" context in which their references to the revolutionary subjectivity of the apostle Paul must be understood.

In their preference for a more safely distant and hagiographic approach to the apostle, various exegetes and theologians may gallantly protest that Paul simply was not *that* kind of fellow! But it would be much more to the point of the conversation to which Badiou and Žižek invite them for exegetes and theologians to propose a *better* social site than Pauline studies where truly revolutionary subjectivity may instead be found. For Badiou and Žižek, Paul is a *pointer*, like a finger pointing at the moon. To focus on the pointer—rather than the target at which it points—is to miss their intention.

That, alas, is a challenge that too few theologians appear interested in taking up. There are important exceptions, of course, as some of the essays

---

one—its hierarchy, privilege, and inequalities. They may not be using language that reflects the demise of existing structures, but they are implementing a strategy based on such assumptions" ("New Revolts against the System"). The train robber analogy is my own.

24. On the "naturalizing" function of ideology, with appropriate discussion of the heritage of Antonio Gramsci and Louis Althusser, see Eagleton, *Ideology*; and Rehmann, "Ideology Theory."

25. In the course of 2011 and 2012, left-leaning journals like *Mother Jones* and the *Nation* published a number of articles attempting to discern the future of the Occupy movement. Social anthropologist David Graeber proposed that Occupy Wall Street "allowed us to start seeing the system [of the financial industry] for what it is: an enormous engine of debt extraction . . . 'Financialization,' then, is not just the manipulation of money. Ultimately, it's the ability to manipulate state power to extract a portion of other people's incomes"; it follows that a debt resistance movement would strike at the very heart of the mechanism (Graeber, "Can Debt Spark a Revolution?").

in this volume demonstrate. For another example, Creston Davis begins a volume of essays drawn from a 2002 international conference by observing,

> At a point when the capitalist world is coming apart at the seams, we may pause and ask ourselves: what has happened to serious leftist protests against the unjust and dehumanizing logic of global capitalism? For the last few decades, any attempt to criticize the inner dark logic of capitalism has been simply dismissed as passé (or un-American). But now, as we perch precariously on the brink of total financial-capitalistic collapse, we may wonder why and under what cultural conditions true critique from the Left have been systematically marginalized into non-existence.[26]

How can such a "critique from the Left" be revived and nourished? Davis's own answer is that "theology (and the Christian tradition) serves as a wellspring capable of funding a materialist politics of subjective truth." He intends through his project "to challenge the American bourgeois interpretation of Christian faith that simply hands over the world to the corporation without a fight."[27]

Such combative language will seem the appropriate register of response to any reader who recognizes our current era as a time of unremitting class warfare being waged from the top. But for just that reason, Davis's positive proposal is all the more perplexing. He continues simply by referring his reader to the Church's Eucharistic practice: "The liturgy is the material participation in the active ontological movement of the world's mediation of itself through which the world returns nonidentically to itself in the everlasting glow of God's glory."[28] However moving some Christians may find such descriptions of the liturgy, infused as they are with Orthodox tropes of mystical participation in the divine life of the Trinity, others may well ask whether the insatiably aggressive and irreducibly material corporate domination of "the world," which Davis has already invoked as his concern, has really met its match here. One may as well ask whether Davis has met his own stated theological criterion of "incarnational materiality," according to which "without the material . . . all simply remains in the ether of speculation."[29]

I name Davis because he explicitly recognizes the challenge posed to theology by Badiou and Žižek. He seeks to bring the theological resources

26. Davis, Introduction, 1.
27. Davis, Introduction, 4.
28. Davis, "Subtractive Liturgy," 167–68.
29. Davis, "Subtractive Liturgy," 150.

of the church's tradition into engagement with the material struggle being waged around us. (This is a struggle, we should note, in which the world's poor majority have been hard pressed, long before some of us who are more comfortable in the first world suffered imperiled mortgages and deteriorating retirement funds.) I also refer to Davis because the key of his response—a quasi-mystical description of the Eucharistic liturgy—appears, despite his intentions, more fogbound in speculative abstraction than another time-honored, venerable, and doughty response to capitalism offered, not really so long ago, by the churches.

THE STRANGE SILENCE
IN CONTEMPORARY CHURCHES

That other response, in a word, is socialism.[30] Almost a century ago, before his appointment as Archbishop of Canterbury, William Temple could declare, "socialism is the economic realization of the Christian Gospel."[31] It is some measure of our current situation that "socialist" is no longer a banner carried by church leaders, but a term of reproach to be hurled against any of them who dare to deviate from "free-market" orthodoxy, as did Archbishop Temple's successor, Rowan Williams, for example, when he opposed harsh austerity measures that were presented as "welfare reform" in Britain.

The history of socialism is one side of the history of class struggle; the other side is the history of massive, systematic opposition to and repression of even moderate social-democratic impulses.[32] The history of socialist movements in and alongside Christian churches is well documented;[33] it is often rehearsed along one or the other of two dominant narratives. The first is a narrative of progress, describing how—despite a series of failures on the part of self-styled Christian socialists to stand, at crucial points, alongside working-class movements—many of their professed values nevertheless helped to ameliorate the worst upper-class antagonisms, to inform the eventual platforms of parties like Labor (U.K.) and the Democratic Party (U.S.), and thus indirectly to shape the eventual construction of state welfare in the

30. This would be an appropriate place for a lengthy excursus distinguishing "socialism" from "communism"; I ask the reader instead to settle, for purposes of my argument, for a rough interchangeability of terms in which either embodies Badiou's minimal criteria for a "communist hypothesis": the refusal of the "logic of class" wherein labor is subordinated to the interests of a dominant class.

31. See Cort, *Christian Socialism*, 169–72.

32. Zinn, *People's History of the United States*.

33. E.g., Cort, *Christian Socialism*; on the legacy of the social gospel movement in the United States, Dorrien, *Soul in Society*.

twentieth century.[34] The second narrative is an admonitory tale in which the history of Christian socialism is remembered through its decisive repudiations by towering theological intellects such as Karl Barth and Reinhold Niebuhr. For such defenders of the faith, we are told, theological liberalism, the Social Gospel, and other social-ethical impulses in Christianity were too optimistic, idolatrously arrogant about human capacity to reshape the world, and insufficiently "realistic" about human depravity.[35] It seems not to matter that in these rehearsals, the repudiations are routinely exaggerated and unmoored from their historical contexts; that the continuing and equally comprehensive critiques of capitalism offered by these same theologians are downplayed or ignored; or that the so-called "free market" seems to have its own checkered track record, at best, so far as offering any restraint on human depravity is concerned. In these ways, the question *What might a contemporary Christian refusal of the logic of class or the inevitability of inequality look like?* may be studiously avoided.

The contestations over these theological legacies, like the repeated rebukes of liberation theologians issuing from the Vatican, appear to be something other than academic disputes after all.[36] They replicate much larger systematic efforts in Western capitalist societies not only to criticize the effectiveness of "actually existing" socialist experiments but to announce their fundamental unthinkability.

We may observe the effects in higher education as well, where historians have documented the decisive influence of Fordist industrial capitalism in shaping and redirecting academic institutions and curricula toward the production of an efficient managerial class, dedicated to the smooth function of expanding industry and generally as unmoved by the interests of the poor as they have been hostile to the organized efforts of the working class.[37] Steven Friesen has convincingly applied these observations to explain the otherwise mysterious absence of poverty in general, and poor people in particular, in the New Testament scholarship produced during the twentieth century. Friesen has proposed we identify the resulting scholarship—no less shaped by ideological commitments than "feminist" or "postcolonial criticism"—as "capitalist criticism."[38]

34. So, with regard to the Anglican Left, Markwell, *Anglican Left*.

35. The debate about Niebuhr's legacy is long and intricate: a helpful recent entrée is Rasmussen, "Was Reinhold Niebuhr Wrong about Socialism?"

36. Key texts are helpfully gathered in Hennelly, *Liberation Theology*; and O'Brien and Shannon, *Catholic Social Thought*.

37. Friesen, "Blessings of Hegemony," points to the studies by Menand (*Marketplace of Ideas*) and Ohmann (*Politics of Knowledge*).

38. Friesen, "Blessings of Hegemony"; see also Friesen, "Poverty in Pauline Studies."

In the fall of the Berlin Wall and the collapse of the Soviet Union, some Westerners saw the "end of history," meaning its culmination in the triumph of a single world order so inevitable that meaningful alternatives could no longer be imagined. Terry Eagleton has chronicled the corresponding retreat, through the 1990s, of the humanities and social sciences from describing an alternative politics to theorizing the diversity of ethnic and gender identities.[39] Similarly, the rise of postcolonial theory, often regarded in biblical studies as at the forward edge of progressive thought, has also been criticized as a convenient place where analytical tools and perspectives developed in genuinely revolutionary movements have been "parked," at a safe distance from political conflict. The effect, Aijaz Ahmad has written, has been

> to domesticate, in institutional ways, the very forms of political dissent which those movements had sought to foreground, to displace an activist culture with a textual culture, to combat the more uncompromising critiques of existing cultures of the literary profession with a new mystique of leftish professionalism, and to reformulate in a postmodernist direction questions which had previously been associated with a broadly Marxist politics.[40]

The aggressive formation of a reactionary corporate-capitalist ideological regime has deformed the life of the church as well. Decades ago, lawyer and Episcopal theologian William Stringfellow observed that in the U.S. civil polity,

> the church becomes confined, for the most part, to the sanctuary and is assigned to either political silence or to banal acquiescence. Political authority in America has sanctioned this accommodation principally by the economic rewards it bestows upon the church. The tax privilege, for example, to which the church has acceded, has been a practically conclusive inhibition to the church's political intervention save where it consists of applause for the nation's cause. Furthermore, the tax preference, or political subsidy, the church has so long received has enabled,

39. Terry Eagleton, *After Theory*, noting the irony of the academic focus on marginality, remarks that, for the socialist, "the true scandal of the present world is that almost everyone in it is banished to the margins. As far as the transnational corporations go, great masses of men and women are really neither here nor there" (20).

40. Aijaz Ahmad, *In Theory*, 1. See also Eagleton, *Literary Theory*, 205; and Leela Gandhi, *Postcolonial Theory*. On the fateful break of the former triangular bond between Marxist political action, theory, and historiography, see Therborn, *From Marxism to Post-Marxism?*

perhaps more than anything else, the accrual of enormous, if unseemly, wealth. In the American comity, the church has gained so huge a propertied interest that its existence has been overwhelmingly committed to the management of property and the maintenance of the ecclesiastical fabric which that property affords.[41]

Stringfellow wrote before the rise of the "Neoconservative" policies of Reagan and Thatcher or the "Neoliberalism" of the "Washington Consensus." He wrote before the rise of a well-funded and politically aggressive religious right in the United States, devoted to "taking the country back" for a Christian quasi-theocracy and to demonizing even moderate gestures toward social democracy through institutions like the notorious Institute for Religion and Democracy. In the ensuing decades, the dynamics Stringfellow described have only been magnified. Denominational social service and public policy advocacy agencies have suffered attrition, due in significant part to the withdrawal of funds by disgruntled congregations. (To be sure, even sympathetic observers have questioned their efficacy, given the structured indifference of the systems from which they sought ameliorative reforms.)[42] Especially after the financial crisis of 2008, church and denominational budgets are severely constrained, their real estate and investment portfolios so eroded that what Stringfellow called "the management of property" and the "maintenance of the ecclesiastical fabric" has become a matter of triage in many places. Meanwhile, the ideological atmosphere has become so poisonous that right-wing pundits can identify even the language of "social justice" as the hallmarks of socialism and Christian heresy, claims no less influential for being absurd.[43]

Such popular demagoguery is an easy target for ridicule. The fact remains, nevertheless, that while Stringfellow could observe that the churches were left room only to champion "the nation's cause," today the nation's cause is fused with the cause of corporate capitalism.

41. Stringfellow, *Conscience & Obedience*, 102–5.

42. The authors in Sedgwick and Turner, *Crisis in Moral Teaching in the Episcopal Church*, describe a "crisis in moral teaching in the Episcopal Church" in which moral teaching has come to mean resolutions directed to government, advocating specific policy recommendations, rather than moral reasoning directed to the faithful. Their theological critique corresponds in important ways with the political analysis of "non-hegemonic" anarchist thinkers like Richard J. F. Day, *Gramsci Is Dead*, who argues that the liberal impulse to petition hegemonic structures for "reform" simply reinforces the hegemony of those structures.

43. One notorious example is Fox News mouthpiece Glenn Beck's broadcast, "The State of Religion in America," July 2, 2010.

The effects of these ideological currents on even self-identified progressive or liberationist academic theological disciplines bear sober reflection as well. For example, theologian Catherine Keller has pointed out that postcolonial theory can be deployed in theological work "to relativize any revolutionary impulse, to dissipate the political energy of transformation, to replace active movements of change with clever postures of transgression."[44] Similarly, theologian Ivan Petrella observes a withdrawal from materialist politics in the present profusion of "contextual" liberation theologies, where preoccupations with ethnic and gender identities and with "hybridity" have often obscured the more fundamentally determinative fact of economic deprivation.

As Petrella points out, liberation theologians around the world (along with all other theologians) share a single material context—the poverty of the majority of the world's people—and a single theological context—the failure of liberation theologies (along with all other theologies) to deal successfully with that material reality. Despite their profusion, contextualized theologies remain "powerless to face the spread of zones of social abandonment. They're powerless because the upsurge of race, ethnicity, gender, and sexuality as organizing axes for liberation theology has blurred the fact that *material deprivation, that is, the deprivation that comes from one's class standing in society, remains the most important form of oppression*."[45]

It is a perverse irony of our time that not only is so basic an assertion rare in liberation theology; the realities of class antagonism, the exploitative nature of capitalism, and the mystifying power of "market" ideology are also virtually unspeakable in much Christian theological discourse, including theological discussion of "the philosophers"—although Jesus of Nazareth did not hesitate to declare that one "cannot serve both God and mammon" (Matt 6:24).[46]

AN ETHIC OF RELINQUISHMENT

I do not mean here simply to argue that Christians, and especially Christian theologians, should embrace socialism (not that there would be anything

44. Keller, *God and Power*, 103.

45. Petrella, *Beyond Liberation Theology*, 80–81 (emphasis added).

46. It bears at least passing notice that, writing earlier in the twentieth century, F. Hauck could describe *mamōnas* as conveying "the demonic power immanent in possessions, surrender to [which] brings practical enslavement" (Hauck, "μαμωνος," 389); at the century's end, M. Wilcox could simply generalize that "'mammon' is not inherently evil" and restrict his observations on Jesus' words to their linguistic derivation and consistency across the Synoptic tradition (Wilcox, "Mammon," 490).

wrong with that; it is simply an argument for another occasion). Neither do I mean to argue that the writings of philosophers (or "anti-philosophers") like Alain Badiou, Giorgio Agamben, or Slavoj Žižek are only comprehensible when they are read by others who share their dialectical-materialist convictions. The latter argument would simply invert the insistence, mentioned above, that the philosophers cannot understand *Paul* without becoming Christians; but either argument surrenders faith in the capacity of human language and understanding to the pseudo-logic of doctrinal assertion.

I mean simply to deny the claim made by some theologians (and, I suspect, harbored implicitly by others) that the philosophers are doing something *improper*, something illegitimate, when they approach Paul from the perspective of dialectical materialism, as if they are wrenching Paul from his "proper" place—the domain of Christian theology. Badiou refers to this premise when he mentions a "Church dialect" governing the interpretation of Paul and repudiates it, one might say, from the outside.[47]

It is from *within* the theological "guild," however, that Mark Lewis Taylor has offered the most trenchant argument for exposing and disavowing this distinctive "dialect." Taylor distinguishes "Guild Theology" from what he seeks to articulate as "the theological." Guild Theology "is usually marked by some discourse of transcendence, that is, a thinking across (*trans-*), which involves a going above, a climbing (*scandere*), beyond the finite, somehow to another dimension above world and history."[48]

The traditional and enduring hallmark of Theology is precisely the claim to be dealing with the transcendent, with a reality categorically unlike all "merely" immanent, "merely" historical, "merely" material reality. This hallmark is evident in most contemporary affirmations of the relevance of Christian symbols, and in most of the ways in which those guild members whose professional responsibility it is to manage the interpretation of those symbols seek to represent their usefulness. What Corey D. B. Walker has written regarding so-called Radical Orthodoxy might be applied more generally to other streams of liberal and postliberal theology as well: namely, that theological projects are often "indebted to and predicated on historical and traditional flows of *conceptual certainty, epistemic privilege* and *theoretical imperialism* that masks the exploits and consolidations of political and intellectual power"—precisely by means of these projects being endowed with an aura of the unassailably transcendent.[49]

47. Badiou, *Saint Paul*, 26.
48. Taylor, *Theological and the Political*, 14.
49. Walker, "Theology and Democratic Futures" (emphasis added).

The claim to epistemic privilege is evident in every protest that theological truth cannot and must not be "reduced" to merely secular or political truth. Such protests effectively fracture truth, polarizing the theological and the political as fundamentally different domains. The claim to epistemic privilege is evident, Taylor suggests, whenever ecclesiastical voices protest the encroachments of a perilous "secularism" or express a longing to perpetuate Christian beliefs and practices "within some Christian haven, thinking them protected from the challenges of secular thought, of other religions, or of the plurality of other Christian cultural readings."[50]

The fundamental error in such longing is precisely the assumption that "the theological" may be preserved by insulating it from the political, when in fact the opposite is the case. In our contemporary situation—the context of global capitalism and the corresponding ideological representations in which we live, move, and have our being—the categorical polarization of the theological and the political functions to protect the political sphere from the disruptive potentialities of religious symbols, that is, the symbols traditionally assigned to the domain of theology. Theology is thus rendered politically irrelevant, *reduced,* precisely to a zone carefully demarcated and ideologically policed as *non-political.* (It is also ironic that this happens just as some members of the theological Guild struggle to reassert their cultural relevance in university humanities departments and other sites of public deliberation. Surely such relevance can only be purchased, if it is still available, at a price.)

Taylor's analysis allows us to predict that Guild Theology will be best received when it conforms to the ideological constraints of late capitalist culture. Equally predictably, those forms of Christianity will thrive in the present environment that continue to truck in the rhetoric of free enterprise, individual initiative, and an economic version of double predestination in which humanity is neatly divided into those worthy of a share in the world's material resources and those who are unworthy. If present ideological trajectories continue, just as predictably, the "liberal" extreme for church and theological academy alike will consist in advocating equality and tolerance amid a plurality of diverse identities. To the extent that state and civil societal structures already manage the competition among identities within acceptable limits, liberal Christianity may be able to demonstrate its *congeniality* to liberal society, even if it is increasingly hard pressed to demonstrate its *necessity* even to its own members.[51] But a Christian theol-

50. Taylor, *Theological and the Political,* 2.

51. The perceived decline of "liberal" or "mainstream" Christianity as compared to a resurgence of Evangelical Christianity, especially in the United States, is a major concern to congregations, seminaries, denominational structures, and theological

ogy whose sails are carefully trimmed to tack with the prevailing ideological winds will not play a significant role in the history of class struggle in the twenty-first century. And the presumption of such a theology to stand in judgment of "the philosophers," without engaging the urgent contemporary context in which the philosophers seek to make their intervention, seems more than ungracious: it seems, in the worst sense of the word, merely academic.

The posture of claiming the epistemic high ground in the name of the apostle Paul has a long history (and, we may expect, a vibrant enough future). But it is not the only way to remember or engage the apostle's legacy. At what we may, in retrospect, recognize as a climactic point in his career, Paul wrote to the non-Jewish majority in the *ekklēsiai* in Rome to warn them against "boasting" over an apparently defunct Israel (the "branches" that had apparently been "broken off": Rom 11:13–25).[52] New Testament scholars increasingly recognize that this passage comes at the rhetorical climax of the letter, a climax that begins with a sudden, intensely emotional self-disclosure in Rom 9:1–4.

What is less often observed is that the poignancy of Paul's words in Rom 9:1–4 derives in no small part from the emotionally reassuring tone of his previous comments in 8:15–39. Paul has assured his (predominantly non-Jewish) readers that they are recipients of the love of God, that the Spirit testifies that they are true children (*huioi*) of God, that "nothing can separate" them from God's love. Now—abruptly—he invokes the same testimony of the Spirit in his own heart, but goes on to express his earnest wish that he might be "cut off" from Christ for the sake of his kinfolk. "They are Israelites," he declares, and to them belong—rightfully and first—all the benefits that Paul has just assured his readers were also *theirs*.[53]

I draw from this evocative passage a model to which Paul's theological guardians might well aspire as they warily contemplate the approach of the non-theistic philosophers. We know from this same letter that Paul himself was not shy when it came to claims of epistemic privilege. He declared a "mystery" to the Romans concerning God's plan toward Israel and

---

publishers alike. My comments here are meant to apply to the *theological* academy Terry Eagleton's analyses of the humanities academy more generally (see especially *Literary Theory*, 169–208, and *After Theory*).

52. I have argued elsewhere that Paul is here confronting a perception among non-Jews in the *ekklēsiai* that was shaped by the contemporary themes of Roman imperial ideology, especially concerning the supremacy of the Roman people over others and the evident status of Jews as *victi* ("the vanquished") (Elliott, *Arrogance of Nations*, chs. 3, 4).

53. On the force of this single rhetorical unit across Romans 8–9, see Elliott, *Rhetoric of Romans*, 261–64; and Elliott, *Arrogance of Nations*, 114–19.

the nations (11:25–27)—a mystery, one presumes, not given to any other mortal until Paul shared it. But that transcendent knowledge concerns the priority in God's purpose of those who are not presently "in Christ," who indeed "shall be saved" apparently *without* being incorporated "in Christ." By wishing *himself* outside of Christ, *for their sake*—more broadly, for the sake of a world now held in subjection (8:18–25)—Paul provides an even better prototype for Žižek's vision of Christianity's "perverse core" than Žižek himself offered.

"It is possible today," Žižek wrote, "to redeem this core of Christianity only in the gesture of abandoning the shell of its institutional organization (and, even more so, of its specific religious experience) . . . That is the ultimate heroic gesture that awaits Christianity: in order to save its treasure, it has to sacrifice itself—like Christ, who had to die so that Christianity could emerge."[54] Such flourishes are unlikely to endear Žižek to the Guild of professional theologians. But they do have a precedent, and a Pauline precedent at that. The assertion that Christ "had to die so that Christianity could emerge" is possible only in theological retrospect. But Paul was explicit enough in his own rhetoric, however imaginary the "heroic gesture" he made, and this allows us some poetic license. Might professional "Paulinists" follow Paul best by following just such a gesture of renunciation, abandoning their claims to transcendent knowing for the sake of a wider human and cosmic solidarity—as we, along with an imperiled world, face "the end times"?[55]

54. Žižek, *Puppet and the Dwarf*, 171.
55. Žižek, *Living in the End Times*.

9

Economic Realities
in the New Testament World

WHILE I SHARE IN general the interest of other scholars to build, expand, and develop lasting exchanges across "bridges in New Testament interpretation," in one area—the study of economic realities in the first-century world—I think it more important to sound a note of caution regarding indiscriminate traffic along certain familiar routes.

UNKNOWN UNKNOWNS

As fellow veterans of the New Testament Studies classroom may attest, the greatest obstacle to student learning is often not what students don't yet know, but what students presume they *already* know about the Bible on the basis of whatever measure of religious training they have received. In my own experience, that is especially the case where economic realities in the New Testament world are in question.

I have found that discussing the agrarian-tributary economic system,[1] patronage and clientage,[2] or the "steep social pyramid" in Roman society[3] is relatively easy, perhaps because those are usually new ideas for students. But it's proven much more difficult, for example, to suggest that Jesus'

---

1. Gerhard Lenski's work has been especially influential: *Power and Privilege*; G. E. M. de Ste. Croix's *Class Struggle in the Ancient Greek World* is indispensable on this and many other points.

2. Wallace-Hadrill, "Patronage in Roman Society."

3. MacMullen, *Roman Social Relations*, 80.

words at table in Bethany, that "the poor you will always have with you," might be an allusion to the command in Torah always to *care* for the poor: "There will always be poor people in the land. Therefore I command you to be openhanded toward your fellow Israelites who are poor and needy in your land" (Deut 15:11). The point is fairly well established in scholarship;[4] Mark's version even makes the point explicit, having Jesus continue, "and whenever you will you can do good to [the poor]" (Mark 14:7). But many students are more accustomed to hearing the statement as an oft-repeated truism about the inevitability and intractability of poverty in the U.S. That, they presume, is what the saying *"really"* means. Indeed, poverty activist Liz Theoharis reports that this single verse is the most powerful "stopper" text she has encountered in years of work in U.S. churches.[5]

Nor have undergraduates been receptive to the suggestion that the (deutero-)Pauline admonition "if any would not work, neither let them eat" (2 Thess 3:16) might have been directed at the indolent rich in Roman society, or to the socially ambitious "climbers" who preferred to attach themselves to wealthy patrons rather than to support themselves through labor. The possibility has academic pedigree.[6] Interestingly, the principle was also axiomatic for V. I. Lenin, who understood it as an indictment of the wealthy who profited from the labor of others; he declared it "the prime, basic, and root principle of socialism."[7] But most of my students haven't read Lenin. Older students may have heard the verse used against the poor by the likes of arch-conservative preacher Jerry Falwell. Younger ones, to the extent they attend to Congressional proceedings, may have heard any number of Republicans cite the passage on the floor of the House of Representatives more recently.[8] Either way, students "just know" what the saying *really* means.

In more than a quarter century of teaching in undergraduate and graduate classrooms, I have yet to discuss the figure of the tax collector Zacchaeus (Luke 19:1–10) without at least one student volunteering to sing

4. Matt 26:11 NIV; Mark 14:7. *The Synopsis of the Four Gospels* (ed. Kurt Aland) lists Deut 15:11 as the background for Jesus' words in every occurrence. (I've cited the NIV, where the wording in English is most similar to the text in Deuteronomy.)

5. The Rev. Liz Theoharis, PhD, reports that over twenty years of activism, she has heard this text used, "on nearly a weekly basis, . . . to argue that doing anti-poverty work is futile because poverty is inevitable and can never be ended" (Theoharis, "Reading the Bible with the Poor").

6. See McGinn and Wilson-Reitz, "2 Thessalonians vs. the *Ataktoi*."

7. Lenin, "On the Famine: A Letter to the Workers of Petrograd."

8. Michelle Goldberg observed that the verse from 2 Thessalonians had played a prominent place in floor speeches during the 2013 legislative session (Goldberg, "Poverty Denialism").

about the "wee little man" they learned about in Sunday School. They usually learned little else about him. They were never encouraged, for example, to compare Zacchaeus's response to Jesus to that of the rich ruler who appears just a few verses earlier (18:18–27), or to wonder about the significance Luke gives the scene by placing it at the end of the travel narrative (19:28).

When I teach the parables of Jesus, we discuss William R. Herzog II's argument that Jesus' authentic parables, once they have been freed from their redactional frames in Matthew, Mark, and Luke, can be read as a "subversive pedagogy." Herzog argues that Jesus used parables to describe succinctly the oppressive economic realities in first-century Galilee.[9] I've found Herzog's work cited only sporadically in subsequent studies of the parables.[10] That might mean his argument is not yet well known; or it might indicate that other scholars are reluctant to imagine that the Gospel writers distorted the parables to a dramatic degree even as they handed them on. Regardless, undergraduate and graduate students in my courses have often rejected Herzog's thesis out of hand. Jesus simply *couldn't* have meant that the laborers who worked in the vineyard all day should have been paid more (Matt 20:1–16). The whole point of the parable, these students are unshakably sure, "is *spiritual*. Everyone gets the same."

LOST IN TRANSLATION

My point is not to complain about the level of my students' preparedness or any lack of curiosity on their part. Some of the brightest and most engaged students have trouble imagining that economic realities, of all things, might be at the heart of one or another passage in the New Testament. Nor do I wish to suggest that these students have all been brainwashed by authoritarian church leaders or that religious education as such is the extent of the problem. True, churches must own their responsibility for acquiescence in the rise of an aggressive religious right and for promoting often insipid religious education ("Zacchaeus was a wee little man . . ."). But many of my students who are convinced the Bible's message is purely "spiritual" have no religious affiliation or background at all. Even if *they* are not religious, however, these students are certain that the New Testament writings *are*.

And who can blame them? That is often the explicit message of their textbooks, which insist that the New Testament writings are *religious* writings, from *religious* communities, about *religious* matters.[11] The presumed

9. Herzog, *Parables as Subversive Speech*.

10. An important exception is Schottroff, *Parables of Jesus*.

11. This is not only the approach of avowedly "confessional" introductions (e.g.,

spiritual focus of the texts means that material realities are, at most, second-ary, of only marginal importance. It follows that studying economic realities misses the primary point of the texts.

Even the Bibles in students' hands may incline them arbitrarily toward a spiritualizing interpretation. In the Parable of the Laborers in the Vine-yard, for example, the NRSV tells us that the landowner agreed with the first hired laborers for "the usual daily wage" (Matt 20:2), then offered to pay others "whatever is right" (20:4). At the end of their workday, he paid them all "the usual daily wage," and the first-hired grumbled at it (20:10). They are rebuked by the landowner: "Friend, I am doing you no wrong; did you not agree with me for the usual daily wage?" (20:13). The NRSV translation makes clear that while the laborers were unreasonable and ungrateful, the landowner was eminently fair. That is what we should expect, after all, in an allegory about God's unmerited mercy to human sinners, which may well have been Matthew's intended meaning in retelling the parable. Indeed, commentators almost universally follow this line.[12]

But the fix is in. The NRSV translators reveal in textual notes that they have repeatedly supplied "the usual daily wage" where the Greek has sim-ply "a denarius" (δηνάριον). Nowhere else, however, in the New Testament does the NRSV render δηνάριον with "the usual daily wage,"[13] and for good reason. There is only sparse and indirect evidence to suggest that a denarius *was* "the usual daily wage" in first-century Palestine—whatever that phrase might have meant in the absence of anything like minimum wage laws or bureaus of economic statistics.[14] Rather, commentators in general appear to

Carson and Moo, *Introduction to the New Testament*). The authors of a prominent historical-critical textbook emphasize from the start "the necessity of viewing and seeking to understand those writings as products of *an ancient religious community* and its leaders"; the *religious* character and claims of the texts are their focus (Spivey, et al., *Anatomy of the New Testament,* 7th ed., xv (emphasis added).

    12. Craig A. Evans accepts the equation, "a denarius, the 'usual daily wage,'" without comment (Evans, *Matthew*, 350).

    13. The coin is simply "a denarius" in the NRSV at Matt 22:19 // Mark 12:15 // Luke 20:24. The earlier RSV read "denarius" at Matt 20:2 but specified in a text note that "the denarius was a day's wage for a laborer."

    14. Earlier commentaries and recently Ulrich Luz (*Matthew 8–20,* 530) have pointed to Tobit 5:15 as evidence that the denarius was the "daily wage," but the coin in Tobit is a drachma, not a denarius, and it is not a "living wage," it is what Tobias offers the angel Raphael (in disguise) as a bonus for accompanying his son on the road, *in addition to his daily expenses* (τὰ δέοντά σοι). James S. Jeffers cites Luke 10:35, where the Samaritan "assumes that two denarii will cover most of the costs of several days' food and lodging at a country inn" (*Greco-Roman World of the New Testament Era,* 152): but in fact the Samaritan does not specify what the denarii will cover and expressly promises to pay the balance of expenses when he returns. Otherwise Jeffers simply relies on the parable

have stipulated the value of the proposed wage based on their assumption that the landowner in Jesus' parable is both fair and generous (for how else could he represent God?).[15] The NRSV has simply taken the point to an extreme, incorporating a *possible* gloss into its published translation—lest its readers be left to explore the parable's meaning on their own.

Herzog argues, to the contrary, that the behavior of the landowner is what we should expect of a representative of a powerful landholding elite who had gained new lands through foreclosure, displacing peasants and creating a large unemployed population in the process. He makes successive trips to the agora to hire a few unemployed laborers at a time, in all but the first instance failing to specify wages. The landowner is evidently trying to minimize his costs by paying the least he can get away with. If he can find workers hanging about the agora an hour before sundown, then "those workers have no bargaining power," Herzog observes. The landowner's offer is a "take it or leave it proposition": he has the power in the situation.[16]

Further, Herzog (and Luise Schottroff before him) point to Cato's admonition to the overseer of an estate that "he must not hire the same day-laborer or servant or caretaker for longer than a day" (*On Agriculture* 5.4). The effect, and probable intention, of such advice would be to suppress wage and employment expectations in the potential labor force.[17]

---

of Matthew 20 to identify the denarius as "a generous day's wage for farm workers" (151), but this is circular reasoning that begs the question. Others cite Tacitus, *Annals* 1.17, where a legionnaire incites his comrades to mutiny unless their pay is increased to a denarius a day (and Pliny declares that this has "always" been soldier's pay, *Natural History*. 33.3); but of course these are troops who need not pay for their own food or housing out of that stipend. Otherwise it is notoriously difficult to ascertain the "buying power" of a denarius in the period. Luz discusses Mishnaic references to daily expenses and concludes that if a denarius was in fact a daily wage, "day laborers had a hard life," even if they did not have to support families (*Matthew 8–20*, 530). See Oakman, "The Buying Power of Two Denarii"; I thank K. C. Hanson for bringing this essay to my attention.

15. Davies and Allison discuss the parable under the rubric "the Generous Employer" (*Gospel according to St. Matthew*, 3:67–78). Ulrich Luz's rehearsal of Protestant and Catholic scholarship shows general unanimity through history regarding this reading (Luz, *Matthew 8–20*, 526–30). Beyond the assumption that he is powerful, wealthy, and generous, "so strong is the assumption" among interpreters that the landowner "is a God figure that he merits little attention" (Herzog, *Parables as Subversive Speech*, 84–88).

16. Herzog, *Parables as Subversive Speech*, 86.

17. Russell Morton asserts, to the contrary, that the point of "story parables" such as this one is to portray "shocking," "unrealistic" behavior in order to represent divine mercy. The landowner's generosity in giving "the daily wage" (a translation Morton asserts, without defense) "would not be convincing in a real-world situation, leaving the owner hard pressed to hire anyone to work in the vineyard the following year" ("Parable

(I note that the dynamic is of course completely familiar in U.S. cities today. When the SBL met in Baltimore, Maryland, the indefatigable Noelle Damico and Crystal Hall organized a "poverty tour" of the downtown area, introducing participating scholars to local activists and organizers. One stop was on a street corner where men and women were lined up along the curb, waiting to be hired for the day. Several of them explained to us that they had been on custodial crews at the nearby sports stadium until new owners can-celled their contract; now, some of them were called back, sporadically, to do the same work for a day, but at much lower wages and without benefits. When, with this same parable in mind, I asked one man whether it would matter if he were called up at the beginning or toward the end of the day, he replied, "all the same to us, man. The game is rigged so they"—he threw his head in the direction of the stadium—"keep all the money.")

Whatever the incidental evidence for the value of a denarius, then, there is no basis for considering the pay offered to unemployed men for a day's labor to be in any way "usual" or regular, let alone what we would con-sider a "livable wage." It was meant to enlist the laborers' effort on the spot, not to provide any level of subsistence either for them or for their families. One should expect, to the contrary, that a landowner "should try to put day laborers in as weak a position as possible when it comes to wages,"[18] and that is what our landowner appears to have done.

That reading makes perfect sense to any reader familiar with the pow-er dynamics of contemporary wage negotiations.[19] No one would imagine that references to compensation in traditional folk songs—"Oh, it's work all day for the sugar in your tay";[20] "They fairly mak' ye work for your ten and nine"[21]—were straightforward indications of "the usual daily wage." Indeed, the contexts of both songs make clear the workers' grievance over unlivable

---

and Proverb," 436b). On the powerful presumption that parables are *always* depictions of divine grace, Morton thus rules that *by definition* parables cannot describe actual real-world behavior; it follows that the denarius *must be* the "usual daily wage." I note that Herzog's work is cited in Morton's bibliography, but his thesis is never discussed.

18. Schottroff, "Human Solidarity and the Goodness of God," 133.

19. In one discussion of the parable with a church audience, some years ago, a wom-an raised strong objections to the way the laborers in Matthew's parable were treated: "equal pay for equal work, that's all that workers want." A man seated near her replied that she simply misunderstood the parable. In the ensuing discussion, she identified herself as the union organizer leading a strike at a local factory; he identified himself as the owner of the factory.

20. "Drill, Ye Tarriers": words by Thomas Casey, music by Charles Connolly, pub. 1888.

21. "The Jute Mill Song," by Mary Brooksbank, early twentieth century.

wages.—*But so do the laborers in Jesus' parable*; and hearing a foreman retort that the wages paid are fair and just! should hardly change our minds.

Furthermore, if we imagine that unemployed laborers such as are portrayed in the parable were likely to have been former peasants who had been displaced from their land by such landowners, and if we further presume that the total sum paid to them for harvesting the estate in a single day would have been dwarfed by the landowner's profit, we might hear his self-justifying protest that he can "do what I choose with what belongs to me" as an infuriating taunt. We might also be led to regard their complaint with more sympathy.

But such considerations are decisively precluded by the NRSV's substitution of "usual daily wage" for δηνάριον.

There is a pattern in all the examples I've mentioned. Students are simply following the signals given them by religious communities, political and cultural leaders, textbook authors, and even the translators of the Bibles in their hands when they perceive biblical texts as concerned with "religious" truths and innocent of economic perspectives.—Or more accurately: they regard the texts as devoid of economic perspectives *that differ in any way from the dominant ideology of global capitalism*. It is clear enough to them, after all, that there *are* individuals in economically straitened circumstances in the Bible, but they tend to regard these as individuals who have made poor choices and thus failed to take advantage of the opportunities available to them, like the day laborers who freely agreed to work for "the usual daily wage." The Matthean parable becomes, in this view, a beautifully condensed representation of the wonders of the "free market." Enough is available for everyone, if only those who own the wealth in a society are free to do with it as they wish and workers accept what "the market" provides.

THE AIR WE BREATHE

Indeed, we should hardly expect anything else, given the pervasive constraints on the common imagination imposed by what theorist Mark Fisher calls "capitalist realism."[22] One of Fisher's themes, borrowed from Fredrick Jameson and Slavoj Žižek, is that "it is easier to imagine the end of the world than the end of capitalism,"[23] an observation that should alert scholars of

22. Fisher, *Capitalist Realism*.

23. Fisher, *Capitalist Realism*, 2. Already in 1995, liberation theologian Franz Hinkelammert wrote, "There exists only one lord and master, and only one system"; the empire of global capitalism "is everywhere . . . The consciousness that an alternative exists is lost. It seems that there are no longer alternatives" ("Crisis of Socialism in the

ancient apocalyptic literature that their field has been swallowed whole by contemporary capitalist culture.

As the nation's "iconic book," the Bible has long played a unique role in legitimizing and sacralizing the dominant culture in the United States.[24] Polls over two decades have shown, however, that it is more often regarded as sacred, inerrant, and foundational to national morality than it is actually read, or its contents understood, by Americans.[25] The ready explanation is that the Bible is playing an *ideologically* important role, independent of citizens' familiarity with its contents.

Historians and sociologists have given substance to that explanation by developing a robust understanding of American civil religion.[26] One of the earliest analysts of that religion, Robert N. Bellah, identified one of its most powerful elements as a fervent individualism that came, with the rise of industrial capitalism, to be posed antithetically to social and economic collective effort. As a result, socialism came to be identified as "the American taboo," posed in the twentieth century as the opposite of "free enterprise." This polarization took place largely on the basis of emotion rather than a rational "choice between alternate ways to order a new industrial economy." Such was the power of the dominant ideology that few have asked whether "the giant corporate bureaucracy that was the reality of late American capitalism" could aptly be described as "free enterprise."[27]

I speak of *ideology,* following Terry Eagleton, to describe the ways social interests are not only expressed but rationalized, legitimated, universalized, and naturalized in such a way that their historical contingency and particularity are erased.[28] As David Harvey has shown, neoliberal ideology, the reigning formation of capitalist ideology since the 1970s, has prevailed, not because it has reliably prescribed the workings of a successful economic order, but despite its failure to do so. That is, neoliberal economic theory has routinely failed at critical moments when massive public subsidies have

Third World").

24. Marty, "America's Iconic Book."

25. Marty, "America's Iconic Book," 5–6, citing Elwell's discussion of Gallup Poll results (Elwell, "Belief and the Bible"). A 2013 survey by the American Bible Society found similar results: C. K. Bell, "Poll: Americans Love the Bible." See also Chancey et al., *Bible in the Public Square.*

26. For an informative and concise historical introduction to American civil religion, see Hughes, *Myths America Lives By.*

27. Bellah, *Broken Covenant,* ch. 5.

28. Eagleton, *Ideology,* 50–61. Eagleton discusses different ways the term has been understood even within the Marxist critical tradition. Antonio Gramsci's discussion of hegemony in his *Prison Notebooks* is important to the understanding of ideology used here.

been required to keep private-corporate interests from suffering the disastrous consequences that would ensue in an *actual* "free market." (It should not escape notice that disastrous consequences are in fact suffered, but by others, notably, by vulnerable human populations, who are encouraged to see their plight as the salutary discipline of "austerity.")[29] "The main substantive achievement of neoliberalization," Harvey observes, "has been to redistribute, rather than to generate, wealth and income" through a dynamic he labels "accumulation by dispossession."[30] In the previous century, billionaire Andrew Mellon described the dynamic (in terms of a fantasy that persists in dominant media today) as "assets return[ing] to their rightful owners."[31]

The neoliberal project has never won popular approval, nor even been openly proposed through democratic processes. Rather, the rhetoric of "freedom" and individualism have persuaded the majorities in countries like the United States to accept neoliberal policies as if they served their most vital values.[32] Harvey sums up his history by observing that

> there is abundant evidence that neoliberal theory and rhetoric (particularly the political rhetoric concerning liberty and freedom) has . . . all along primarily functioned as a mask for practices that are all about the maintenance, reconstitution, and restoration of elite class power.[33]

It is within this ideological project that the Bible has served its useful purpose. It seems perfectly natural that the "iconic book" of a sacred capitalist order should itself express capitalist themes. That is a simple truism to followers of myriad televangelists of the "Gospel of Wealth" like Kenneth Copeland, Creflo Dollar, Joel Osteen, and Paula White, to name only a few of the more spectacular celebrities. *Of course* the Bible preaches capitalism and its virtues, they maintain: "Free market capitalism" is the economic system that God wills. The clear implication is that advocating anything less than unfettered "free-market" policies is not only un-American: it is heresy. So, beginning in the 1980s, right-wing "flak" operations like the Institute for Religion and Democracy targeted center-left scholars in mainstream seminaries for harassment and intimidation.[34] In much the same rut, in 2010,

---

29. Harvey, *Brief History of Neoliberalism*.

30. Harvey, *Brief History of Neoliberalism*, 159.

31. Harvey, *Brief History of Neoliberalism*, 163, quoting Wade and Veneroso, "Asian Crisis," 21.

32. Harvey, *Brief History of Neoliberalism*, ch. 2, "The Construction of Consent."

33. Harvey, *Brief History of Neoliberalism*, 188.

34. The IRD website is at www.theird.org; alternative viewpoints are available at www.rightwingwatch.org and in the writings of Sara Diamond, beginning with her

Fox News talking head Glenn Beck urged his listeners to "run" from their churches if they heard talk of "social justice," which Beck regards as code for forced collectivism in the spirit of Stalin.[35] In the overheated, triumphalist atmosphere that has prevailed after the fall of the Berlin Wall in 1989 and the collapse of the Soviet Union in 1991, even the most progressive churches have refrained from using terms like "Leftist" or "socialist" to describe their economic prescriptions. Christian socialism, once a potent movement, has become the heresy that dare not speak its name.[36]

"The Gospel of Wealth" was the title of Andrew Carnegie's 1889 essay urging plutocrats to a generous but judicious philanthropy, by which he meant a solicitude careful not to encourage "the slothful, the drunken, the unworthy."[37] The Gospel of Wealth, or "Prosperity Gospel," is the public theology of an ascendant Religious Right in the U.S. today, but in reality, its promises of prosperity for all the faithful mask an underlying agenda of preserving the wealth of the few who already own most of it. Historians and journalists have traced how, under the banner of free enterprise, Evangelicals have been mobilized against Franklin D. Roosevelt's "New Deal,"[38] Lyndon B. Johnson's "Great Society,"[39] and the specter of a progressive movement that carried Barack Obama to the presidency.[40]

As Naomi Klein has brilliantly shown us, however, the reigning gospel of neoliberalism is not a theology derived from scripture. It is rather a "free-market fundamentalism" that plunders the Bible for fantasies of disaster and destruction, even as it literally capitalizes on human catastrophe to "wipe the slate clean" so that a new, more profitable world can be created.[41]

Nor is this a gospel of universal salvation. Immanuel Wallerstein predicts shrewdly that in the present "age of transition," "those in power will no longer be trying to preserve the existing system (doomed as it is to

exposé in *Spiritual Warfare*.

35. See Fox News, "'Glenn Beck': State of Religion in America"; and Grant, "Glenn Beck: 'Leave your Church.'"

36. *Sojourners* magazine dared to break the largely self-imposed silence with Danny Duncan Collum's essay, "Should Christians Be Socialists?" See also Cort, *Christian Socialism*.

37. Carnegie, "Gospel of Wealth."

38. Sutton, *American Apocalypse*, ch. 8.

39. Diamond, *Roads to Dominion*.

40. Mayer, *Dark Money*.

41. Klein, *Shock Doctrine*. I sought in an earlier essay to juxtapose Paul's implicit theology of creation and eschatology with Klein's description of neoliberal ideology as the dominant theology of our age: Elliott, "Creation, Cosmos, and Conflict in Romans 8–9." (See also Chapter 11 in Elliott, *Paul against the Nations*.)

self-destruction); rather, they will try to ensure that the transition leads to the construction of a new system that will replicate the worst features of the existing one—its hierarchy, privilege and inequalities."[42] A *Guardian* reporter at the 2015 World Economic Forum in Davos, Switzerland, listened as one speaker, a former hedge fund manager, revealed that members of his class were "already planning their escapes" from the twin catastrophes of economic inequality and irreversible climate change (along with whatever social disruption these would cause).[43] Those who have profited most from the rising economic tide know best that it will not "lift all boats."[44]

A Marxist or Gramscian understanding of ideology would suggest that we should expect, in this situation, that the Bible as the nation's iconic book would be read in ways that marginalize and delegitimize any collective action directed toward changing economic relationships. "God's economics," on this view, focus exclusively on the "spiritual" values of the pious individual, the thrift and hard work of those who presumably have attained righteous wealth by exercising their God-given "freedom" (or enjoy the benefits of the virtuous exertions of their ancestors). Correspondingly, the poor are implicitly (or, often, explicitly) described as those who have failed to exercise their own freedom wisely.

THE BIBLE AND THE DYNAMICS OF POVERTY

The picture I have just described is quite different from the study of economic realities in the ancient world that has been advanced in biblical studies over the last generation. Norman K. Gottwald's *The Tribes of Yahweh* inaugurated a new age in the ideological criticism of the Hebrew Bible.[45] Gottwald showed that a range of different and, often, opposite representations of wealth and poverty appear on the surface or embedded beneath the biblical texts, due to the tumultuous dynamics of class struggle that generated them. His work, informed by Marxist theory, has proven enormously influential in the study of ancient Israel and early Judaism.[46] A comparable approach to the New Testament was pioneered by Richard A. Horsley, whose *Jesus and the Spiral of Violence* used a conflict model of social-scientific analysis

42. Wallerstein, "New Revolts against the System," 37.

43. Hogg, "As inequality soars."

44. See now Rieger, *No Rising Tide.*

45. Gottwald, *Tribes of Yahweh.* Gottwald developed his history into a textbook: Gottwald, *Hebrew Bible.*

46. See also Jobling et al., *Bible and the Politics of Exegesis*; Boer, *Marxist Criticism of the Hebrew Bible*; Boer, *Tracking the Tribes of Yahweh.*

to describe the political, social, and economic violence inherent in the imperial situation in first-century Judea.[47] Individually and together, Gottwald and Horsley played early and decisive roles in shaping an explicitly political exegesis of the Bible.[48]

Horsley has sparked or fanned into flame important conversations around related themes, often inviting scholars from outside the biblical studies guild to meet and interact with biblical scholars. Topics so addressed have included the political economy of peasant societies under domination (exploiting the scholarship of James C. Scott);[49] the dynamics of Roman imperial domination, ideology, and hegemony through images and ritual (interacting with G. E. M. de Ste. Croix, Simon R. F. Price, Paul Zanker, and Karl Galinsky);[50] and the character of the Roman economy and its effects in generating and sustaining poverty (relying on de Ste. Croix, Keith Hopkins, and Richard Saller and Peter Garnsey).[51] During the same years, Horsley has actively pursued connections with historiographic currents in postcolonial criticism and "people's history."[52] He has mounted sustained criticism of the dominance of structuralist-functionalist sociology in contemporary New Testament studies.[53] (He has, of course, also ranged into other important questions around ancient media, memory, and orality that have been taken up by other scholars.)

In an important sense, Horsley personally embodies the theme of "bridging" different fields of scholarship to bring new light to bear on the New Testament writings and the history behind them, not only in his own scholarship but also in the way he has, with an infectious enthusiasm, assembled circles of scholars to explore these connections with him. He has been instrumental in starting new sections of the Society of Biblical Literature to examine conventional knowledge about Apocalypticism and

47. Horsley, *Jesus and the Spiral of Violence*; see also Horsley and Hanson, *Banits, Prophets, and Messiahs*.

48. See Gottwald and Horsley, *Bible and Liberation*. Other scholars also played important roles, for example Luise Schottroff, Wolfgang Stegemann, and Halvor Moxnes.

49. Scott, *Weapons of the Weak*; Scott, *Domination and the Arts of* Resistance; Horsley, *Galilee*; Horsley, *Hidden Transcripts*.

50. Garnsey and Whittaker, *Imperialism in the Ancient World*; de Ste. Croix, *Class Struggle in the Ancient Greek World*; Price, *Rituals and Power*; Zanker, *Power of Images*; Galinsky, *Augustan Culture*; Horsley, *Paul and Empire*; Horsley, *Paul and Politics*; Horsley, *Paul and the Roman Imperial Order*.

51. Hopkins, *Conquerors and Slaves*; de Ste. Croix, *Class Struggle in the Ancient Greek World*; Garnsey and Saller, *Roman Empire*.

52. Horsley, "Submerged Biblical Histories"; Horsley, *Christian Origins*.

53. See Horsley, *Sociology and the Jesus Movement*. Horsley's critique relies on Gouldner, *Coming Crisis of Western Sociology*.

Wisdom, Paul and Politics, Poverty in the Biblical World, and Economics in the Biblical World. In the latter sections, most relevant for my purposes here, he has encouraged close interaction with particular contemporary economic theorists as well: Charles McDaniel, David Graeber, Thomas Piketty, and others.[54] To the extent one today finds intelligent discussions of material realities—social, political, and economic—in the world around the New Testament, it is not unusual to find Richard Horsley involved in the conversation, if not spurring it on.

It is nevertheless the case that much of mainstream New Testament scholarship proceeds while giving minimal attention, at best, to material realities and to economic conditions in particular.

The point has perhaps best been documented with regard to the social setting of the apostle Paul and his assemblies (ἐκκλησίαι). Important questions about Paul's own social status and the status(es) of members of the assemblies, especially in Corinth (where our textual and archaeological evidence seem most promising), have preoccupied scholars for more than a century.[55] Nevertheless, Justin J. Meggitt has shown decisively that the sort of broad generalizations about middling social status in Paul's assemblies that were common at the end of the twentieth century were based on uncritical acceptance of elite ancient sources, which manifested a profound bias against and contempt of the poor. The result has been a tremendous underestimation of poverty and an exaggeration of prosperity in Paul's environment.[56]

What was then hailed as a "new consensus" described a mixed social status in an assembly in Corinth. This picture was based on the inference that if "not many" in Corinth "were wise . . . , powerful, . . . well-born" (1 Cor 1:26), surely "some were."[57] But as Steven Friesen has shown, with effect similar to Meggitt's work, this "new consensus" was neither new nor compelling. Friesen argues that the Corinthians, and Paul himself, in general lived much closer to the level of mere subsistence.[58] He goes on to

54. See McDaniel, *God & Money*; Graeber, *Debt*; Piketty, *Capital in the Twenty-First Century*.

55. It must suffice here to name a few classic works: Deissmann, *St. Paul*; Malherbe, *Social Aspects of Early Christianity*; Theissen, *Social Setting of Pauline Christianity*; Meeks, *First Urban Christians*. See now Blanton and Pickett, *Paul and Economics*.

56. Meggitt, *Paul, Poverty and Survival*.

57. Malherbe spoke of a "new consensus"; Theissen and Meeks are usually considered its representatives as well (see footnote 55, above).

58. Friesen, "Poverty in Pauline Studies." Friesen offers his own adjusted scale of social status in Friesen, "Prospects," 362, 364. See also Still and Horrell, *After the First Urban Christians*; and Oakes, *Reading Romans in Pompeii*, among other important studies in the recent conversation.

demonstrate that the "new consensus," and the general focus in "social-scientific" study on a multi-factored *social status* in the Pauline assemblies, effectively *erased* poverty from the historical agenda throughout much of the twentieth century. Indeed, the poor make scarce appearances, and are discussed minimally when they do show up, in the standard textbooks in the New Testament literature. The explanation, Friesen argues, has little to do with the ancient evidence or with the logic of social-scientific model-ing. The measure of wealth "is, after all, the most important component of social status," but it is nevertheless "the one least likely to be addressed systematically by New Testament scholars."[59] More plausibly, he argues, "our preoccupation with 'social status' is the very mechanism by which we have ignored poverty and economic issues."[60]

A more likely cause for that preoccupation, Friesen suggests, is an "unacknowledged bias" directly related to the ideological atmosphere of late capitalism. He attributes the tendency of textbook authors to "portray the Roman Empire with a booming economy" and to minimize poverty to the context of higher education in the industrial and post-industrial U.S., where "the primary function of the American professoriate" has been "to train members of the professional-managerial class." That is, Friesen summarizes, "higher education taught future professionals to accept and to overlook eco-nomic inequality, and Pauline studies did so as well."[61] As a result, Friesen proposes that we describe the mainstream of twentieth-century New Testa-ment scholarship as "capitalist criticism." "After all," he asks, "why should the burden of self-disclosure fall only on the shoulders of Marxist critics?"[62]

Perhaps the most dramatic example of the phenomenon Friesen iden-tifies, the relative absence and silence of the poor in New Testament scholar-ship (though not in the ancient texts), appears in several social-scientific textbooks on the New Testament. In the *Social Scientific Commentary on the Letters of Paul,* one finds concise discussions of social-scientific theories and social realities under the label "reading scenarios." Notably, there are no "reading scenarios" for "the poor," "poverty," or "class" (let alone "class struggle"). Under the heading "Religion, Economics, and Politics," we are informed that "economics," at least, does not bear discussion:

> Neither religion nor economics had a separate institutional existence, and neither was conceived as a system on its own, with a special theory of practice and a distinctive mode of

59. Friesen, "Prospects," 362, 364.

60. Friesen, "Poverty in Pauline Studies," 332–35.

61. Friesen, "Blessings of Hegemony," 125–27.

62. Friesen, "Poverty in Pauline Studies," 336.

organization. There is no language implying abstract concepts of market, monetary system, or fiscal theory.[63]

Consequently, there is no further discussion of economic realities anywhere in this "social-science commentary." Another volume, the *Social Science Commentary on the Synoptic Gospels,* has an entry for "Rich, Poor, and Limited Good," which has the task of explaining that "rich" and "poor" are merely matters of relative *perception,* not reflections of actual material conditions.[64] Where other classic historians find ample basis for describing the Roman economy as predatory and extractive, our "social-science" authors explain that

> ancient Rome elites did not have an idea of juridical relations among various peoples. Instead Roman statesmen dealt with other peoples in terms of good faith based on the analogy of patron-client relations. Rome was patron, not holder of an empire: it wanted persons to behave like clients.[65]

That rather rosy description might have surprised Romans like Cicero, Julius Caesar, or Augustus, who were able enough to describe the right of the Romans to exercise *imperium* over all whom they conquered.

Bruce J. Malina goes even further in his textbook entitled (ironically enough) *The New Testament World.* The terms *poor* and *rich* were not expressions of "'class' or economic rank at all," he informs us. Most people in the Mediterranean world "worked to maintain their inherited status, not to get rich."[66] That statement should leave us wondering how our literary sources from the Roman world came to be filled with the ambitions of people who considered the acquisition of tremendous wealth the right and duty of the *optimates,* the "best people." Malina suggests such people simply did not exist: "the honorable persons would certainly strive to avoid and prevent the accumulation of capital."[67] We can only conclude that the individuals who we know accumulated vast amounts of capital could only have been what Malina calls "the dishonorable rich," those "beyond the pale of public opinion";[68] but then we should be at a loss to explain the ubiquitous

---

63. Malina and Pilch, *Social-Science Commentary on the Letters of Paul,* 393. I have drawn some of this material from my own earlier critique of Malina's work, "Diagnosing an Allergic Reaction" (Chapter 6 in this volume).

64. Malina and Rohrbaugh, *Social-Science Commentary on the Synoptic Gospels.*

65. Malina and Pilch, *Social-Science Commentary on the Letters of Paul,* 393.

66. Malina, *New Testament World,* 97.

67. Malina, *New Testament World,* 97.

68. Malina, *New Testament World,* 98.

honorary inscriptions that celebrated the calculating beneficence of these same wealthy individuals.

"Peasants consider all persons in their society as 'equal,'" Malina writes, apparently oblivious to the evidence of peasant humiliation, obsequiousness, and veiled resentment toward their superiors compiled decades ago by classicist Ramsey MacMullen.[69] Malina seeks to paint an idyllic portrait of villages filled with happy peasants squabbling fiercely but harmlessly over honor, far away from the predations of the landlords and tax collectors who fill the actual Roman sources.

At length, Malina declares that "we simply cannot get any idea" what New Testament authors meant when they referred to "the poor."[70] He surely knows that any number of New Testament passages describe the poor as suffering hunger, thirst, indebtedness, disease, physical incapacitation, and dispossession of homes and possessions, but these cannot by definition point us to anything called "poverty," he implies, since the ancients had no word for it. (This, too, is a surprising announcement, since MacMullen supplied an ample vocabulary in both Greek and Latin.) Of course, Malina admits, there were people referred to as "poor," but this was only because they had encountered "some unfortunate turn of events or some untoward circumstances."[71] Poverty, on Malina's view, is always accidental and, by definition, temporary. "The poor would not be a permanent social standing" (like a *class*) "but a sort of revolving category of people who unfortunately cannot maintain their inherited status. Thus day laborers, peasants, and beggars born into their situation were not poor persons in first-century society."[72]

Such categorical denial is perplexing. The New Testament repeatedly refers without further specification to "the poor" as if they were an identifiable class of people, but Malina insists the category could only have referred to an ever-shifting population of people suffering only temporary setbacks. At length, however, Malina cannot restrain himself from admonishing the contemporary student, "You will find no capitalist or communist work ethic in the New Testament. Nor will you find any program of 'social action' aimed at the redistribution of wealth or anything of the sort."[73] One cannot help wondering whether Malina's tendentious appreciation of economic realities in the past has been influenced by his political views regarding the present.

69. Malina, *New Testament World,* 99; MacMullen, *Roman Social Relations,* 88–120.

70. Malina, *New Testament World,* 99.

71. Malina, *New Testament World,* 100.

72. Malina, *New Testament World,* 100.

73. Malina, *New Testament World,* 97.

Malina's work is only an egregious example of a much wider pattern in New Testament scholarship: a pattern of inattention to, or dismissal or denial of poverty and its causes. This pattern is one element of what Friesen calls "capitalist criticism." Of course, the observation hardly allows us to discern the political inclinations of individual scholars as diehard advocates of unfettered "free-market" capitalism. But the limited interest among the scholarly mainstream in certain economic realities seems to correlate with a disinterest in taking seriously any alternative interpretations, for example socialist or Marxist interpretation, if we are to judge by the short shrift such alternatives are given in leading academic works.

In *The First Urban Christians*, for example, Wayne A. Meeks acknowledges that Marxists "have made important contributions to our understanding of ancient society"; but he never tells us what those contributions might be. He declares that "the Marxist reading" of the New Testament, at least in its "crude popular versions," has been "reductionist," but he offers no further discussion, so we never learn whether he recognizes any other kind.[74] Later, when he turns to discussing "social stratification" in the ancient Roman world, he declares that the category of class is "not very helpful" for analysis because "for Marx, class was determined by relation to the means of production, yielding only three: landlords, capitalists, and workers," categories not readily mapped onto antiquity.[75] Further, class is not helpful, Meeks declares, because the ancient Roman classification of the top *ordines*, the senatorial and equestrian orders and local aristocracies, comprised only a tiny fraction of the general population, and Meeks is avowedly interested in discussing a broad Roman "middle class" (though he would be hard-pressed to find it defined in the ancient literature).[76]

In fact, Marx offered a clear and subtle discussion of class based in power differentials and in its relationship to the means of production. He recognized that in the Roman world, ownership of land and slave labor were the decisive factors in generating wealth and power. Capitalists and workers were the *two* classes he identified in later, industrial society. It is remarkable to see Marx's clear discussion so distorted, then abruptly dismissed, in a work pretending to give the Marxist perspective a serious hearing.[77]

To take another example, in his inaugural lecture at the University of Edinburgh, surveying "Questions for the Discipline" of New Testament

---

74. Meeks, *First Urban Christians*, 3.

75. Meeks, *First Urban Christians*, 53.

76. Meeks, *First Urban Christians*, 53. "The category [of *ordo*] does not have much discriminating power for the sorts of groups we are investigating."

77. Elliott, "Diagnosing an Allergic Reaction" (Chapter 6 in this volume).

studies, Larry W. Hurtado declared as a truism that "we cannot really study the New Testament writings without engaging *the religious affirmations and issues that constitute their contents* . . . In fact, it is difficult to imagine what sort of scholar could successfully be disinterested in the religious import of the New Testament."[78] In another lecture on the future of the discipline, Hurtado showed scarce interest in political interpretation of any kind. He declared that Marxist interpretation was but a short-lived "fashion" that had suffered a "precipitous decline" after the 1980s, at least so far as he had been able to determine after a few minutes with a Google search algorithm.[79] "Postcolonialism," now a venerable tradition after half a century of criticism, was unlikely to catch hold over the long term, Hurtado asserted, since most non-Western biblical scholars were self-identified church members and thus more concerned, he presumed, with "Christian faith and practice" than with issues of liberation. (He did not explain why these were mutually exclusive alternatives.) Although his theme was "future prospects in New Testament studies," Hurtado had nothing to say about feminist, economic, or "empire-critical" interpretation; the rest of his lecture was taken up with traditional exegetical topics like the "Son of Man" debate and the nature of Q.

My point is that for much of mainstream New Testament studies, the lack of interest in poverty in the ancient world seems to go hand in hand with marked indifference toward (and relative ignorance of) any perspective that would direct attention precisely to class differences and tensions, such as Marxist criticism does. Though this neglect is sometimes excused on the grounds that the New Testament writings are "really" about *religion*, not material concerns, that has not prevented keen academic interest in "social status." Rather, the lack of interest in poverty and the indifference toward Marxist or ideological criticism appear to be the twin components of what Friesen calls "capitalist criticism." This dominant perspective is not shaped by the ancient sources, which supply ample data for any interpreter ready and able to tease out the lineaments of class relationships (as Marxist historians have readily done). It appears rather to be an unreflected expression of capitalist ideology.

78. Hurtado, "New Testament Studies at the Turn of the Millennium," 170, 171 (emphasis added).

79. Hurtado, "Fashions, Fallacies, and Future Prospects."

THE TROUBLE WITH BRIDGES

If the preceding observations point to a certain myopia in biblical studies, it is not, I argue, the result of a blinkered preoccupation with the biblical texts alone. In terms of the metaphor "bridges of interpretation," it is not the case that biblical studies operates within a closed ivory tower, carefully separated from its environs by an ideational moat and in need only of a good sturdy drawbridge or two. To the contrary: As far as economics goes, New Testament studies is more like a broad field, flooded by the dominant ideological currents of capitalism. In this particular case, biblical scholars do not need to build "bridges" to other disciplines so much as we need (to extend the metaphor) to construct dikes and canals so as to redirect those ideological currents away from harming human communities.

Instead, the values and presuppositions of capitalist ideology have so influenced the field as to predetermine which data are relevant and how they should be understood. Indeed, the discipline of biblical studies is increasingly discussed and practiced as an auxiliary of capitalist discourse.

In a series of studies, Charles McDaniel has described the deleterious effects of the massive shift of the U.S. and global economies toward the financial sector since the 1970s.[80] Financialization has distorted economies, injured the poor, and eroded the very structures of civil society that in McDaniel's view might offer the best resources for withstanding its effects.

> While debate continues concerning its overall impact, financialization of the economy has been accompanied by undeniable changes that many see as destabilizing: further widening in the distribution of income, acceleration of commodity price volatility, explosion of government deficits, increases in corporate and household indebtedness, and a pervasive short-termism in corporate management policy designed to maximize "shareholder value" often at the expense of other values and interests.[81]

Financialization, which McDaniel regards as the latest phase in "capitalism's evolutionary course," has reshaped fundamental aspects of economic life:

---

80. McDaniel teaches in the interdisciplinary core at Baylor University and edits the journal *Journal of Church and State*. He is the author of McDaniel, *God & Money*; "Theology of the 'Real Economy'"; and McDaniel, "Financialization and the Changing Face of Poverty," 24. McDaniel presented his views at the SBL Economics of the Biblical World section in November 2014, and I offered one of several responses; I am grateful to him for the exchange.

81. McDaniel, "Financialization and the Changing Face of Poverty," 192.

> Financial innovation . . . carries with it a whole new set of values
> and assumptions about the nature of work, the composition and
> allocation of wealth, and the role of financial intermediation in
> economic development.[82]

The last impact is especially deleterious to efforts to alleviate poverty:

> What is of particular concern is that changes in the global finan-
> cial system are rendering the world economy less able to address
> conventional poverty such that efforts toward its elimination,
> which some believe possible through the spread of market capi-
> talism, have diminished in priority . . . Dreams of eradicating
> poverty are fading not because capitalism has proven incapable
> of producing sufficient output to feed and clothe the world, but
> rather because its evolution has led to structural unemploy-
> ment, extreme concentrations of wealth, and government bud-
> get deficits that weaken the ability of developed nations to aid
> those that lag behind.[83]

The language McDaniel uses here is worth noting. Although he is keenly aware of the negative effects of financialization, he describes it not as the result of the effect of specific orchestrated decisions and policies made over decades by bank and financial executives and legislators acting in collusion (although he is presumably aware of that history), but as the latest phase in capitalism's "evolution."[84] This language accords with the "naturalizing" effect of capitalist ideology itself. "The world economy" is posed here as the chief character in a global drama, inclined to "address" and "eliminate" poverty, but rendered helpless by an evolutionary development beyond its control. "Developed nations" are also named as apparently benign forces that intend to aid those who "lag behind" capitalism's inexorable advance, but are similarly hindered by financialization, as by a decades-long natural disaster. Such language affords no account of the role developed national governments have in fact quite deliberately played in accelerating the financialization of the world economy at the expense of poorer nations.

Elsewhere in the same essay, McDaniel admits that the collapse of the U.S. housing market in 2008 was the result of "a collaborative effort among governments, lending firms, credit rating agencies, and consumers themselves who have taken advantage of historically unprecedented access to

---

82. McDaniel, "Financialization and the Changing Face of Poverty," 193.

83. McDaniel, "Financialization and the Changing Face of Poverty," 195.

84. Later in the same article McDaniel speaks again of financialization as "a natural development in our capitalist evolution" (McDaniel, "Financialization and the Changing Face of Poverty," 211).

credit in their pursuit of the 'good life.'"[85] There *are* human beings responsible for the crisis, then: not policy makers, as one might have surmised
from the historical record, but *consumers*. Given McDaniel's own extended
discussion of the complexity and opacity of debt-bundling instruments,
however, one wonders just how culpable ordinary consumers were for as-
suming debt obligations for which banks and regulatory agencies readily
and systematically approved them. Capitalist theory leads him at length to
insist that "financialization results as much from the demand as the supply
side of the equation. *It is consumers who insist on unrealistic returns* as much
as the professionals in financial services who devise intricate instruments to
achieve those returns who today protract the problem." Curiously, he offers
no evidence that the financial crisis was caused by the pernicious demands
of greedy consumers.[86]

McDaniel is so impressed with the scale and scope of the crisis brought
on by financialization that he doubts any change from within the economic
system can be meaningful. "Solutions to these problems must come from
beyond the economic system."[87] The economy itself "knows no turning back
of its own devices . . . Financial innovation likely will continue along the
present course, absent some 'external shock' capable of reorienting values."[88]
He doubts that any regulatory regime, at least as imaginable within contemporary Neoliberal polity, will be of any significant effect. "[R]eal change
of the kind needed to ethically reinvigorate the industry will not come from
within the system."[89]

As the italicized phrases reveal, McDaniel holds out no hope for any
systemic change to the financialized economy because he cannot imagine
any alternative: *political action outside of or in opposition to the Neoliberal
order is for him unthinkable.* The most we can hope for is to temper the
financial industry with "religious values," and for this McDaniel looks to
religious communities and traditions. "Theological resources" must be mar-
shaled "to aid the 'definancialization of global culture.'" By this he means
not that the financial configuration of the economy itself might be altered

85. McDaniel, "Financialization and the Changing Face of Poverty," 193. Elsewhere
McDaniel attributes "regulatory inaction and ineptitude" to "the embedding of regulatory authorities in a highly politicized economy that is inclined toward preserving the
status quo" ("Theology of the 'Real Economy,'" 26–27).

86. McDaniel, "Theology of the 'Real Economy,'" 28 (emphasis added).

87. McDaniel, "Financialization and the Changing Face of Poverty," 192 (emphasis
in original).

88. McDaniel, "Financialization and the Changing Face of Poverty," 206.

89. McDaniel, "Financialization and the Changing Face of Poverty," 211 (emphasis
added); McDaniel, "Theology of the 'Real Economy,'" 26–28.

(as any self-respecting version of socialism, including religious varieties, would demand), but that the financial industry might be redirected by an emphasis on a set of values other than greed. Inexplicably, he describes our predicament as a crisis of rampant "materialism" in which even sacred institutions are caught up in "exaggerating material welfare above all else."[90] (One might reasonably have characterized the problem instead as the material self-indulgence of a tiny elite at the expense of the material deprivation of the world's majority.) He hopes for the "possible re-communalization of investment in ways that . . . might . . . broaden responsibility for its ethical consequences"[91] or, as he puts it elsewhere, that "religious traditions can make a positive contribution to economic ethics by developing theological and moral principles to guide believers in investment decisions and commercial activity generally."[92]

McDaniel diagnoses the problem, then, as a crisis of values.[93] Because of the inherent "fallibility" of "human beings and their institutions," the market economy is susceptible to "unintended consequences" or, at worst, to "criminal activity and corruption"[94] (or, as he elsewhere puts it with more restraint, "the ill-advised actions of a few rogue traders").[95] The solution is for religious communities to encourage their members—who are conceived primarily as *consumers* and *investors*—to be guided by "biblical values." And what are these? McDaniel finds in Proverbs 3:7 a "call to right relationship with the Creator and a reminder of the limits of human reason."[96] From the story of the Tower of Babel (Genesis 10), McDaniel derives a generalized warning about "human pretention."[97] Adam and Eve's mistake in "acting

---

90. McDaniel, "Financialization and the Changing Face of Poverty," 196; again, 198; 207 (a "purely materialistic society").

91. McDaniel, "Financialization and the Changing Face of Poverty," 210.

92. McDaniel, "Theology of the 'Real Economy,'" 16. "Theologically based definitions of real economic production are needed to help *guide adherents in consumption and investment decisions* and to provide substance to criticism of financialization by religious leaders" ("Theology of the 'Real Economy,'" 18 (emphasis added).

93. Financialization "carries with it a whole new set of values and assumptions about the nature of work, the composition and allocation of wealth, and the role of financial intermediation in economic development" (McDaniel, "Financialization and the Changing Face of Poverty," 193).

94. McDaniel, "Financialization and the Changing Face of Poverty," 207.

95. McDaniel, "Financialization and the Emerging Monopoly on Public Discourse," 24.

96. McDaniel, "Financialization and the Emerging Monopoly on Public Discourse," 19.

97. McDaniel, "Financialization and the Emerging Monopoly on Public Discourse," 19–20.

out of 'perceived' self-interest" is comparable to a faulty investment decision based on "greed and self-concern."[98] He invokes the insistence in other texts that "the land" belongs to YHWH (e.g., Leviticus 25) to counteract financial methods that have "further loosened the essential human connection to the land." The Jubilee command and the petition for forgiveness of debts in the Lord's Prayer hardly suggest the illegitimacy of debt as such; rather, they are lessons that "all are indebted, no matter how blessed with material wealth."[99]

Fundamentally, biblical texts point to "spiritual values" that transcend the merely material: so in Luke 19, "Zacchaeus was not required to give away all his possessions; *the turn that led to his salvation was a spiritual one* that caused him to reflect on his transgressions and view his wealth in a new light." It follows that "Christians are not called to be destitute but rather to acknowledge *the radical inferiority of material possessions to spiritual gifts*."[100] (It bears note that McDaniel's distinction between "material" and "spiritual" values, and the possibility of Christians making themselves "destitute," do not arise in Luke's story. They seem rather to reflect McDaniel's concerns, and, perhaps, a general anxiety among the "ownership class" that obedience to Jesus' commands might be materially costly.) As to the role of that story in Luke's larger narrative—in particular, the way Zacchaeus's exuberant action in giving to the poor and making whole everyone he had abused economically counterbalances the refusal of the rich ruler to follow Jesus by selling everything he had and giving it to the poor (Luke 18:18–27)—McDaniel breathes not a word.

In these essays by McDaniel, other biblical texts that one might have thought would play a role in informing "biblical values" regarding the economy play no role. We hear nothing of Amos's excoriations against the oppressive rich, or James's; nothing regarding the "apostolic communism" of the early Jerusalem congregation (Acts 2) or Paul's insistence on an equality that satisfies the material need of the neighbor (2 Corinthians 8–9). Other teachings of Jesus—parables of foolish (Luke 12:13–21) or negligent rich people who ignored the plight of the poor around them (Luke 16:19–31); his condemnation of officials who "eat up the property of widows" (Luke 20:45–21:4)—are scarcely evident.[101]

98. McDaniel, "Financialization and the Emerging Monopoly on Public Discourse," 20.

99. McDaniel, "Financialization and the Emerging Monopoly on Public Discourse," 20–21.

100. McDaniel, "Financialization and the Emerging Monopoly on Public Discourse," 21–22.

101. This generalization should be qualified: the parable of the rich fool (Luke 12:13–21) is briefly mentioned as reinforcing the lesson drawn from the parable of the

At length, McDaniel proposes to discuss what he considers "Jesus' most direct teaching with respect to capital."[102] One might expect a treatment of the command to the rich young man/rich ruler, which caused such alarm in the disciples. Or one might imagine that the most obvious candidate is Jesus' succinct dictum, "You cannot serve God and money" (REB) or "mammon" (Matt 6:24; Luke 16:13 RSV), where the particular character of money as competing with God for human allegiance or worship ("service," δουλεῖν) is explicit. Admittedly, even this saying has been "devalued" in twentieth-century scholarship.[103] But it plays no role at all in McDaniel's discussions. He means instead the Parable of Talents (Matt 25:14–30). "Jesus' most direct teaching with respect to capital" is, in part, "a call to wise investment," but more than that: it is about "the necessity of risk-taking for the Kingdom of God": "Risk must be taken to achieve ultimate ends."[104]

We should not at last be surprised that what McDaniel finds in the Bible are chiefly resources to guide prudent and humane investment. He understands the value of religious tradition, including Christian theology and ethics, as its potential to "humanize discourse"; to awaken human beings to "more inherently communal aspects of money management"; to "bring public discourse back into balance."[105] "New theologies are needed to engage the issues at the heart of the present crisis: risk, return, scarcity, efficiency, financial complexity, and contribution/reward"—that is, preeminently

---

talents (see next note).

102. McDaniel, "Financialization and the Emerging Monopoly on Public Discourse," 23.

103. In 1942, F. Hauck wrote that while the Semitic *mammôn* could be used in a neutral sense for "possessions," money, in a way "free from ethical objection," it also appears in Jewish tradition with "an ignoble sense and is used in censure." In the admonitions of Ethiopian Enoch (chs. 94–105), the love of (unrighteous) mammon is opposed to the love of God, as in Jesus' teaching. Indeed, the term conveys the "demonic power immanent in possessions" in the logion under consideration (Hauck, "μαμωνας,"388–89). "This realistic view of the actual facts makes it impossible for Jesus to think of earthly possessions with religious optimism or to regard them as a mark of special divine blessing" (389–90). Decades later, however, the "demonic power immanent in possessions" had by some capitalist miracle been bleached out of them; so Max Wilcox could simply state that *mammon* was "the normal word for 'wealth,' 'money,' in Mishnaic Hebrew," and "is not inherently evil." Otherwise Wilcox was concerned only with the word's etymology (Wilcox, "Mammon," 490).

104. McDaniel, "Financialization and the Emerging Monopoly on Public Discourse," 23–24. Elsewhere McDaniel argues that the parable "has implications for concepts like entrepreneurship and responsible risk-taking" ("Theology of the Real Economy," 22).

105. McDaniel, "Financialization and the Emerging Monopoly on Public Discourse," 19, 26.

questions of financial prudence.[106] McDaniel is confident that capitalism it-self was originally "created and deployed for human ends"—an assumption that does not stand up well to history.[107] He hopes now that a recourse to re-ligious values will reorient the financial industry, "transforming" its culture in such a way as to "stabiliz[e] the global economy."[108] The ultimate goal is to renew "virtue" among financial professionals: "it will likely take another ref-ormation of the investment community to reestablish stability."[109] The prob-lem with financialized capital is, at root, an understandably human desire (on the part of investors) to seek exorbitant short-term gains. "Religion is an institution uniquely positioned to ground investor expectations in ways that can be more effective than acts of regulatory agencies."[110]

These quotations should suffice to show that this is a thoroughly *capi-talist* vision of the role of religious tradition and of the Bible in particular.

Remarkably, McDaniel's keen insights into the pervasive and distorting effects of financialization include tracing its corruptive reach into ecclesias-tical life. He knows that "economic rationalism . . . has worked its way into even our most sacred institutions."[111] He recognizes that "greed is infused through the church, as the people of the church in most parts of the world are immersed in economic systems that are based on greed."[112] A dramatic example that McDaniel repeatedly invokes is the Church of England's com-mitment of much of its investment portfolio and clergy pensions to hedge funds prior to 2008.[113] He urges that we must recognize "capitalism's pen-etration into our religious institutions and its possible weakening of voices that might call attention to corruption and injustice."[114] He never explains how this corruptive influence within theology and the churches should be mitigated or reversed, however, so that they might fulfill the virtue-renew-ing, moderating, and "stabilizing" roles he envisions. Nor, as should be evi-dent at this point, does he imagine that the theological or biblical traditions might offer resources for any *alternative* to the capitalist system.

106. McDaniel, "Theology of the 'Real Economy,'" 21.

107. McDaniel, "Theology of the 'Real Economy,'" 9; see Boer and Petterson, *Idols of Nations.*

108. McDaniel, "Theology of the 'Real Economy,'" 27.

109. McDaniel, "Theology of the 'Real Economy,'" 28.

110. McDaniel, "Theology of the 'Real Economy,'"28.

111. McDaniel, "Financialization and the Changing Face of Poverty," 196.

112. McDaniel, "Financialization and the Changing Face of Poverty,"209, quoting Premawardhana, "Greed as Violence," 226.

113. McDaniel, "Financialization and the Changing Face of Poverty," 209; McDan-iel, "Theology of the 'Real Economy,'" 15.

114. McDaniel, "Financialization and the Changing Face of Poverty," 209.

That failure is an apparent indication that capitalist ideology has established the horizons of the possible so far as McDaniel is concerned. After
all, it is possible for theologians to operate on other premises: for example,
in Latin America and the Caribbean, where it is commonplace for observers to distinguish actual "free markets" from the compulsory globalization
imposed by international organs like the IMF and World Bank.[115] But if capitalist ideology has set the limits not only of what is politically and economically possible but of the role of theological and biblical traditions as well, we
should properly label McDaniel's argument another example of "capitalist
criticism."

CONCLUSION

In the case of economic realities in the New Testament world, it appears that
the chief obstacle to more comprehensive interpretation is not the failure of
New Testament scholars to read more widely in other fields, as the metaphor
of "bridging" disciplines implies. As we have seen, the situation is rather that
aspects of the ancient world are emphasized or neglected according to their
suitability to the dominant interpretive scheme of Neoliberal capitalism.
More adequate interpretation—that is, more adequate to the ancient subject
and to contemporary contexts alike—will depend, not so much on seeking
out contemporary research and models in economic theory, dominated as
this is by capitalist ideology, as by contemplating alternatives to that ideology. The problem is not one of disciplinary specificity but of ideological and
political standpoint.

But that problem is remedied, readily enough, by adopting a different
standpoint: moving, for example, to stand in sympathy and solidarity with
the global majority who are not the cheerful beneficiaries of Neoliberalism,
but its victims. Here too, Richard A. Horsley has been an example and a
guiding light to many, even as he has pointed continually to the vast work
lying ahead of us. We who have worked with him and learned from him
(and so many others) can best express our thanks by carrying forward that
work.

115. See Correa, "Globalization and the World Trade Organization"; similarly Aristide, *Eyes of the Heart,* 9–10.

10

Socioeconomic Stratification and the Lord's Supper

(1 Corinthians 11:17–34)

PAUL'S ADMONITION OF THE Corinthian faithful regarding their practice of the Lord's supper (1 Cor 11:17–34) has long attracted attention from those interested in the historical origins of the Eucharist.[1] In recent decades, it has become a focus for theologians discussing the theory and practice of the Eucharist in global contexts of socioeconomic disparity and oppression. In this same period, some New Testament scholars have applied social-scientific models to the same passage, seeking evidence regarding the socioeconomic status of members of Paul's assemblies (ἐκκλησίαι) and explaining the conflict around the Corinthian supper in terms of socioeconomic stratification within the assembly.

The question of socioeconomic status in the Pauline churches receives direct attention in other essays in this volume.[2] My interest here is with the conclusions interpreters have drawn from Paul's admonition in 1 Corinthians 11. Those conclusions do not float in their own abstract world, however, and so it is important to describe the wider social and ecclesial context in which they appear.

---

1. See for example, Crockett, *Eucharist*; O'Loughlin, *Eucharist*.

2. Blanton and Pickett, *Paul and Economics*. See also Meggitt, *Paul, Poverty and Survival*; Friesen, "Poverty in Pauline Studies"; Friesen, "Blessings of Hegemony"; Longenecker, "Socio-Economic Profiling."

THE EUCHARIST AS A SITE OF CONTESTATION

The last half of the twentieth century saw dramatic historical developments worldwide. The aftermath of the Second World War, including the plight of millions of displaced and refugee persons and the devastation of European Jews by the Nazis, brought increased attention to human rights, a concern expressed in the formation of the United Nations and the promulgation of the Universal Declaration of Human Rights. The dawn of the nuclear age with the U.S. atomic bombing of Japanese cities and the ensuing arms race with the Soviet Union evoked international concern to slow and reverse the threat of nuclear annihilation. The international rhetoric of democracy and human rights, along with the debilitation of various European powers, fueled decolonization movements that swept through Africa, Asia, and Latin America. The economic and military ascendancy of the United States cast a shadow over all these developments, even as spiraling prosperity for a global minority sharpened the perception of growing economic and political inequality nationally and internationally. For all these reasons, social and political questions of justice and equality were becoming the coin of worldwide interaction.

These dramatic changes were reflected in theological developments, from the foundation of the World Council of Churches to the Second Vatican Council and beyond. In particular, changes in the theological understanding of the Eucharist included the recovery of its original eschatological horizon[3] and of the rich symbolic and narrative repertoire of relevant biblical materials;[4] a shift in emphasis from "ontological" questions (e.g., regarding Christ's "real presence" in the Eucharist) and the individual efficacy of the sacrament to its social context and corporate efficacy;[5] and a reorientation of the Eucharist's significance toward questions of human need, especially global hunger.[6] Orthodox theologians emphasized the Eucharist's central and formative role in constituting the church in its authentic missional stance "for the life of the world."[7] Theologians of liberation elucidated its proper role in forming communities dedicated to the project of human

3. Wainwright, *Eucharist and Eschatology.*

4. Commission on Faith and Order, *Baptism, Eucharist and Ministry;* Commission on Faith and Order, *Baptism, Eucharist and Ministry, 1982–1990.*

5. Juan Luís Segundo attributes this shift in emphasis to the conciliar documents of Vatican II: Segundo, *Sacraments Today,* 124.

6. Examples are Hellwig, *Eucharist and the Hunger of the World;* and Grassi, *Broken Bread and Broken Bodies.*

7. Schmemann, *For the Life of the World;* Zizioulas, *Eucharistic Communion and the World.*

emancipation.[8] Early in this period, political theologian Johann B. Metz called the Eucharist a "subversive remembrance."[9] More recently, Andrea Bieler and Luise Schottroff argued that its practice presents an "alternative economy" to the omnivorous Neoliberal construction of the human as *homo oeconomicus*, conformed to market demands as consumer or producer in the ubiquitous flow of capital.[10]

This increased emphasis on the social dimension of the Eucharist has been intertwined with the theme of judgment upon social inequality. The World Council of Churches ecumenical statement on *Baptism, Eucharist and Ministry* (1982) boldly declared:

> The eucharistic celebration . . . is a constant challenge in the search for appropriate relationships in social, economic, and political life . . . As participants in the eucharist, therefore, we prove inconsistent if we are not actively participating in this ongoing restoration of the world's situation and the human condition. The eucharist shows us that our behavior is inconsistent in the face of the reconciling presence of God in human history: we are placed under continual judgment by the persistence of unjust relationships of all kinds in our society, the manifold divisions on account of human pride, material interest and power politics, and, above all, the obstinacy of unjustifiable confessional oppositions within the body of Christ.[11]

Liberation theologians as well understand the Eucharist as a social imperative. So Victor Codina:

> In the eucharist we not only commune with Jesus, but with his Kingdom project; we not only edify the church but anticipate the banquet of the Kingdom. Thus the eucharist is inseparable from the fellowship of love and service . . . For this very reason a eucharist without real sharing, as occurred in Corinth, "is not the Lord's supper" (1 Cor. 11:20–21). The patristic tradition corroborates this dimension of the eucharist, which is not only ecclesial but social: the offerings of the faithful for the poor; the presence of the slaves and the exhortation for their manumission; the preaching of the Fathers on justice and the defense of the poor; the liturgical excommunication of public sinners, who

---

8. Segundo, *Sacraments Today*; Codina, "Sacraments," 671–72.

9. Metz, "Future in the Memory of Suffering," 19; Metz, *Faith in History and Society*, 88–89.

10. Bieler and Schottroff, *Eucharist*, ch. 3.

11. Commission on Faith and Order, *Baptism, Eucharist and Ministry*, 14.

must be reconciled with the church in order to be readmitted to eucharistic communion.[12]

Or, as J. M. Castillo has put it succinctly, "Donde no hay justicia no hay eucaristía."[13]

When theologians and church leaders have drawn such connections between the Eucharist, social justice, and judgment, they have relied on the single biblical text where these themes are combined: the apostle Paul's discussion of the "Lord's supper" in 1 Cor 11:17–34. There Paul rebuked the Corinthian assembly because, in his words,

> when you come together it is not for the better but for the worse . . . When you come together it is not really to eat the Lord's supper. For when the time comes to eat, each of you goes ahead with your own supper, and one goes hungry and another becomes drunk. What! Do you not have homes to eat and drink in? Or do you show contempt for the church of God and humiliate those who have nothing? (1 Cor 11:17, 20–22 NRSV)

Paul went on to invoke the tradition of Jesus' words at the supper "on the night when he was betrayed," then warned, "whoever, therefore, eats the bread or drinks the cup of the Lord in an unworthy manner will be answerable for the body and blood of the Lord" (11:27 NRSV). He concluded,

> So, then, my brothers and sisters, when you come together to eat, wait for one another. If you are hungry, eat at home, so that when you come together, it will not be for your condemnation. About the other things I will give instructions when I come. (11:33–34 NRSV)

The theme of judgment on social injustice has been developed in an especially acute way by William T. Cavanaugh in his argument for a robust practice of excommunication of the architects of social evil. Cavanaugh has in particular view the practice of torture carried out by military officers and state security officials in Augusto Pinochet's regime—men who continued not only to attend Mass, but quite possibly to receive Communion in the company of their victims and their families.[14] Cavanaugh grounds his argument in part in 1 Cor 11:17–34.

> Paul would exclude from the Eucharist those who fail to "discern the body," meaning not only Christ's sacramental body but

---

12. Codina, "Sacraments," 671.

13. Castillo, "Donde no hay justicia no hay eucaristía."

14. Cavanaugh, *Torture and Eucharist*, 260.

especially his ecclesial body (1 Cor. 11:29). The specific sin Paul addresses in this passage is the "humiliation" of the poor by the rich, who eat their fill when the community gathers while others go hungry (11:21-2). According to Paul this is not simply sin against individuals but "contempt for the church of God" (11:22). The rich bring divisions into the church, and thus threaten the visibility of the body of Christ. Exclusion of the offenders from the Eucharist is meant to restore the church as a sign of reconciliation by leading the offenders to change their conduct (11:31-2). If they do not repent, exclusion from the Eucharist also safeguards the witness of the church by anticipating the Lord's final judgment, when His own will be separated out from the world (11:32).[15]

While Cavanaugh's argument focused on a specific and extreme case, one might reasonably extend the argument to other crimes and other regimes. For example, we might propose that those who committed torture at U.S. military facilities at Abu Ghraib or Guantánamo or Baghram Air Field should be made excommunicate from any churches of which they are members, along with the architects and apologists of torture programs and those who knowingly permitted their execution through benign neglect.[16] Excommunication generally is understood as an act of grace in an extreme circumstance, intended to move the impenitent sinner to repentance and ultimate reconciliation. Cavanaugh insists that it is also a discipline guaranteeing the integrity of the "body politic" that is the church.

Such a robust understanding of the insoluble connection between the Eucharist and justice stands at some distance from the more sedate solemnities of broad swaths of U.S. church life, as it does from the cerebral reflections of much academic scholarship and even from church-based activism against torture.[17] Indeed, proposing the exclusion of accused torturers from the Eucharist in U.S. churches would likely result in the (further) polarization

15. Cavanaugh, *Torture and Eucharist*, 246.

16. In April 2003, the Greek Orthodox priest in charge of the Church of the Nativity in Bethlehem barred Iraq War architects George W. Bush, Donald Rumsfeld, Tony Blair, and Jack Straw from entering his church "forever" (reported in the *Jordan Times*, April 4, 2003). In December 2014, after the U.S. Senate's report on torture at military sites was published, a German human-rights group filed war-crime charges against Bush, Rumsfeld, and Dick Cheney, as reported by *Democracy Now!* Richard Clark, the top U.S. counterterrorism official under President George W. Bush, declared that their actions "probably" constituted war crimes (Ashtari, "Former Counterterrorism Czar").

17. The National Religious Coalition against Torture enrolls faith congregations in lobbying efforts to ban torture by U.S. military and government officials; it does not include excommunication of torturers in its agenda (www.nrcat.org).

of churches along political and ideological lines. If some Christians found the proposal compelling, it would no doubt strike others as the misguided politicization of the liturgy. But Cavanaugh's argument suggests that such polarization of the churches would simply reflect the apostle's own theology: "indeed, there have to be factions among you, for only so will it become clear who among you are genuine" (1 Cor 11:19 NRSV)!

The question of the Eucharist's relation and relevance to current realities of social injustice is not only theoretical. Direct actions by Christian communities against a wide array of restrictive, militaristic, and punitive social policies include Eucharistic assembly as a constitutive element.[18] Actual Eucharistic assemblies have proven "subversive," to use Metz's term, as they have challenged systematic oppression. As Cavanaugh reports, in Chile, Christians converged in street Eucharists to mark the buildings where political prisoners were being tortured by the Pinochet regime.[19] In Haiti, priests of *ti legliz*, the "little church," drew tens of thousands into the streets in open-air Masses that rendered Jean-Claude Duvalier's dictatorship untenable.[20] The Eucharist provided Archbishop Oscar Arnulfo Romero a platform to challenge U.S. military support for the murderous junta in El Salvador.[21] U.S. peace activists incorporated the Eucharist into their direct action campaigns.[22]

Such practices (and the list could be expanded) have of course been contested. Enthusiastic Eucharistic celebrations in Sandinista Nicaragua provoked censure by the adamantly anti-Communist Pope John Paul II. Visiting the country in 1983, the pope publicly scolded liberationist priest Ernesto Cardenal for serving in the Sandinista government; warned the Nicaraguan bishops against the ideological "infiltration" he perceived in terms like "iglesia popular"; and used the occasion of a public Eucharist sternly to admonish priests and the people themselves to relinquish any "doctrine or ideology" that set "earthly considerations," such as the preferential option for the poor, above "transcendent" values, which included "*obedience to the bishops and to the pope*"[23]—a value invoked by appeal to the pseudo-Pauline letter to the Ephesians.

18. Bill Wylie-Kellermann offers astute observations about the issues involved: *Seasons of Faith and Conscience*, ch. 5.

19. Cavanaugh, *Torture and Eucharist*.

20. Wilentz, *Rainy Season*.

21. Romero, *Voice of the Voiceless*.

22. Wylie-Kellermann, *Seasons of Faith and Conscience*; Dear, *Sacrament of Civil Disobedience*. Both authors place themselves in a larger *communio sanctorum* including Philip and Daniel Berrigan, William Stringfellow, Dorothy Day, and many others.

23. Pope John Paul II, "Unity of the Church" (emphasis in original). The pope did not explicitly repudiate the preferential option for the poor (a hallmark of the theology

Moreover, Eucharistic assemblies and ministers have been attacked by state apparatuses. Priests were tortured and murdered in Pinochet's Chile and in El Salvador, where Archbishop Romero was assassinated at the Eucharistic table. In Haiti, the Church of St. Jean Bosco was attacked by a death squad in police uniforms who killed thirteen people with pistols and machetes; liberationist priest Jean-Bertrand Aristide was spared only because a would-be assassin's pistol misfired.[24] Notoriously, the architects of these crimes have to date gone unpunished.

In our day, the Eucharist has become a site of ideological contestation, both in terms of theory and of praxis. Paul's voice is claimed on either side of these skirmishes; the interpretation of his words concerning the Lord's Supper in 1 Corinthians seems therefore particularly relevant.

THE SOCIAL-SCIENTIFIC INTERPRETATION OF 1 CORINTHIANS 11:17-34

By contrast, during this same period, when New Testament scholars have discussed 1 Cor 11:17–34, their tone has been calm and generally upbeat. Beginning in the 1980s, some scholars applying social-science concepts to the New Testament have found a case study in this passage. If previous interpretations of Paul's rebuke focused on religious or theological currents among the Corinthians (e.g., Judaism, Gnosticism, "crude sacramentalism," etc.), Gerd Theissen sought to understand the "divisions" and "factions" around the table (so Paul called them: σχίσματα, v. 17; αἱρέσεις, v. 19) not in terms of theological parties but as evidence of social stratification.

This was a degree of social stratification that distinguished the Pauline ἐκκλησίαι from more socially homogeneous Hellenistic associations (θίασοι). "The conflict over the Lord's Supper is a conflict between poor and rich Christians," Theissen proposed. The conflict was caused by "a particular habit of the rich" who had made the common meal possible, yet took part in it on their own, apart, without sharing with others. The fact that some went hungry (v. 21) meant in Paul's eyes that the rich had shown contempt for the poor, i.e., those who "have nothing" (as Theissen translated τοὺς μὴ ἔχοντας, v. 22).[25]

---

of liberation), but admonished his Nicaraguan audience not to imagine that anyone in the church "has a greater right to citizenship" in the church than anyone else: "neither Jews, nor Greeks, nor slaves, nor freed men, nor men, nor women, *nor the poor, nor the rich*" (330). My italics mark the pope's supplement to Paul's words in Gal 3:28.

24. The incident is recounted in Wilentz, *Rainy Season*.

25. Theissen, *Social Setting of Pauline Christianity*, 151.

In this way, Theissen argued, the wealthier members were reproducing patterns and expectations from the banquets of Hellenistic associations to which they were accustomed, where officers and members who had pro-vided long service to an association would be expected to receive larger portions of better food as a matter of course, if not indeed of bylaw. In those contexts, Theissen wrote, "nobody was in the least offended" by such dispar-ities in the recognition of status. Different shares in the meal were "in fact considered fair and proper."[26] But the socially more disparate Corinthian ἐκκλησία had no such regulations in place. When the wealthier members presumed that they were entitled to reserve more of the common food for themselves—food that they themselves might well have provided—as their "private meal" (ἴδιον δεῖπνον), and to eat it apart, before the common meal began, they gave to lower-status members a degree of offense that their ac-tion would never have occasioned in the social circles in which the wealthy more routinely traveled.[27]

Wayne A. Meeks largely followed Theissen's reconstruction of the episode. Meeks proposed that if someone like Gaius, who was a host of the whole ἐκκλησία in Corinth (Rom 16:23), had brought the customs and as-sumptions of his social class into the common meal—held, after all, in his own dining room—and had "made distinctions in the food he provided for those of his own social level and those who were of lower rank, that would not have been at all out of the ordinary." Meeks observed that just such prevalent practices (or at the least, their occasional abuse) had offended a few Roman moralists.[28] Paul, Meeks thought, objected to the Corinthian practice "on quite different grounds" than the moralists, however. Steeped in a characteristically Jewish "apocalyptic determinism," Paul regarded divi-sions in the community as an example of inevitable eschatological testing (11:19).[29]

Jerome Murphy-O'Connor agreed that the Corinthian ἐκκλησία prob-ably met in the home of a wealthier member. He went further, relying on archaeological excavations from Corinth and Pompeii to estimate how

26. Theissen, *Social Setting of Pauline Christianity*, 156, citing Carcopino, *Daily Life in Ancient Rome*, 270–71.

27. Theissen, *Social Setting of Pauline Christianity*, 153–55.

28. Meeks, *First Urban Christians*, 67–70. On this point, Meeks follows Theissen, *Social Setting of Pauline Christianity*, 156–58. Theissen cites Pliny, *Epistulae* 2.6; Martial, *Epigram* 3.60; 1.20; 4.85; 6.11; 10.49; Juvenal, *Satire* 5. Most of these are expressions of personal indignation at being slighted rather than protests against the principle or practice of social variability at banquets.

29. Meeks, *First Urban Christians*, loc. cit. Here, too, Meeks was persuaded by Theissen, *Social Setting of Pauline Christianity*, 164 ("the eschatological testing of the congregation").

many individuals might have gathered in the public space of a typical villa. His estimation was that no more than nine guests could have reclined comfortably on the couches in the triclinium, a room furnished for private dining, but that some thirty to forty people might have massed in the atrium (see Fig. 10.1). Murphy-O'Connor speculates that a host like Gaius would have invited "his closest friends, . . . who would have been of the same social class," into the triclinium with himself, while the rest were relegated to the "greatly inferior" space in the atrium. Discrimination via space was compounded by discrimination via time: Gaius and his peers would have gathered earlier to feast at leisure, then joined the poorer members upon their arrival later, after a hard day's work, to share whatever was left—perhaps only "the bread and wine of the Eucharist."[30] The "factions" to which Paul refers seemed vividly apparent.

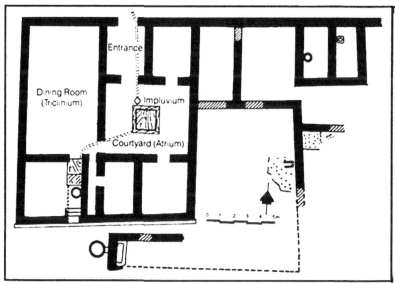

Fig. 10.1. Floor plan of the villa at Anaploga, Corinth, showing the dining room at left and the courtyard at left center; Murphy-O'Connor, St. Paul's Corinth, 154.

These three scholars have provided the components of what has become a widely accepted reconstruction of the situation in Corinth.[31] It bears note that this reconstruction is part of a larger understanding of the social status of members of Paul's assemblies, an understanding hailed already in

30. Murphy-O'Connor, St. Paul's Corinth, 153–61.

31. For example, Gordon D. Fee makes these judgments the basis for his exegesis of the passage: Fee, First Epistle to the Corinthians.

the late 1970s as a "new consensus."[32] According to that consensus, Paul's churches included a mix of persons holding different social statuses. They were mostly poor, but included "middle-class" artisans and even a few well-to-do members like Gaius, whom Paul could hail as the "host of the whole church."

Furthermore, Theissen regarded Paul's admonition in 1 Cor 11:17–34 as an expression of the "ethos of early Christian love-patriarchalism which arose in the Pauline communities."[33] Elsewhere he describes this love-patriarchalism as "a new pattern of integration" that would have been readily adopted by "the society of late antiquity":

> In it [love-patriarchalism] equality of status was extended to all—to women, foreigners, and slaves . . . At the same time, however, all of this was internalized: it was true "in Christ." In the political and social realm class-specific differences were essentially accepted, affirmed, even religiously legitimated. No longer was there a struggle for equal rights but instead a struggle to achieve a pattern of relationships among members of various strata which would be characterized by respect, concern, and a sense of responsibility.[34]

Paul intended just this strategy of community integration. Theissen grounded that judgment particularly in 1 Cor 11:34, which he read as a straightforward instruction: "In fact [Paul] recommends that they celebrate the 'private meal' at home."[35]

> Paul wants to settle the problem of the "private meal" by confining it to private homes. At home everybody may eat and drink in whatever way seems proper. The final result would be a lessening of the role conflict in which the wealthier Christians find themselves. Within their own four walls they are to behave according to the norms of their social class, while at the Lord's Supper the norms of the congregation have absolute priority. Clearly this is a compromise. It would be much more consistent with the idea of community to demand that this "private meal" be shared.[36]

Theissen regards this "compromise" of Paul's values as practically inevitable:

32. Malherbe, *Social Aspects of Early Christianity*, 31.
33. Theissen, *Social Setting of Pauline Christianity*, 164.
34. Theissen, *Social Setting of Pauline Christianity*, 109.
35. Theissen, *Social Setting of Pauline Christianity*, 155.
36. Theissen, *Social Setting of Pauline Christianity*, 163–64.

Paul's compromise, which simply acknowledges the class-specific differences within the community while maintaining their manifestations, corresponds to the realities of a socially stratified congregation which must yield a certain preeminence to the rich—even contrary to their own intentions. Within such a community the compromise suggested by Paul is realistic and practical.[37]

The result is an undeniable tension: Paul confronts a social conflict, but does not intend finally to resolve it. Rather, "the social tensions between rich and poor Christians have been transposed to a symbolic world transcending the everyday reality. They become part of an eschatological drama" in which divisions between rich and poor constitute an eschatological test as the whole community stands in judgment before the Lord.[38]

Depending in part on Theissen's discussion, Meeks argued that social status was a quite fluid phenomenon in Paul's world. It resulted from a number of factors, including sex, class, family, ethnicity, status as slave or free, etc., of which relative wealth or poverty was only one. Further, some factors—such as wealth—offered opportunity for "social mobility" to ambitious or enterprising individuals who might climb the social ladder, transcending the conditions of their birth. It followed, Meeks argued, that first-century individuals such as those who filled Paul's congregations shared a common experience of "status inconsistency" or "status dissonance." Meeks asked, at length, whether such inconsistency would have generated "not only anxiety but also loneliness, in a society in which social position was important and usually rigid?" He suggested that such alienated emotions might have made nascent Christianity all the more appealing. "Would, then, the intimacy of the Christian groups become a welcome refuge, the emotion-charged language of family and affection and the image of a caring, personal God powerful antidotes, while the master symbol of the crucified savior crystallized a believable picture of the way the world really seemed to work?"[39]

Meeks generally follows Theissen's interpretation of 1 Cor 11:17–34. In particular, he considers it Paul's advice that the "private suppers" practiced by the Corinthians "ought to be eaten 'at home' (22a, 34)."[40] Where Theissen describes a "compromise," Meeks perceives "some confusion" or inconsistency on the part of the apostle. "For Paul," he writes, "it was a matter of intense concern that *at least one* of the typical instances of reunification

---

37. Theissen, *Social Setting of Pauline Christianity*, 164.

38. Theissen, *Social Setting of Pauline Christianity*, 164.

39. Meeks, *First Urban Christians*, 22–23; 191.

40. Meeks, *First Urban Christians*, 67.

declared in the 'baptismal reunification formula' [i.e., Gal 3:28] should have concrete social consequences." That one instance involved the breaking down of distinction between Jew and Greek; Paul was less concerned, however, to insist on equality between male and female or slave and free—the other pairs named in Galatians 3. After all, Meeks observes, Paul "nowhere urges Philemon or other owners to free their slaves."[41] How much less was Paul concerned with the gap between rich(er) and poor(er). Paul's answer regarding private meals in Corinth was thus of a piece (on Meeks' view) with his broader *inconsistency* regarding the implication of baptism as a symbol of unity and of the Lord's Supper as a ritual of solidarity.

In the social-science-oriented reconstruction of the situation, then, our earliest discussion of the Lord's Supper, which is also the first text to relate the meal to the plight of the poor in the Christian assembly, represents something of an apostolic failure of nerve. Instead of a vital call to social justice, Paul's text constitutes a ready compromise of ideals.

CHALLENGING THE "NEW CONSENSUS"

The reading of 1 Cor 11:17–34 that I have just sketched has won wide acceptance from a range of scholars. Part of its power may lie in its apparent ability to offer a social-scientific explanation for what has long been perceived as Paul's "social conservatism."[42] There are reasons to question the allure of this reading, however.

1. We should note, first of all, that if seeking a social-scientific explanation for the Corinthian correspondence is a modern development, awareness of social disparities at the communal table is hardly a recent discovery.

Clement of Alexandria already recognized, on the basis of 1 Corinthians 11, that there were rich and poor side by side in the Corinthian assembly. As he read the passage, the wealthy person who "eats without restraint or is insatiable . . . disgraces himself," both by adding to the burden of those who do not have and by laying "his own intemperance bare in front of those who do have." The offense, for Clement, was in part an embarrassing breach of etiquette before one's elite peers.[43]

Later, John Chrysostom knew that "*of course* some were poor, but others rich" in the Corinthian assembly. The disparity was so great, he declared, that the Corinthians simply couldn't have managed the community of goods

---

41. Meeks, *First Urban Christians*, 161 (emphasis added). For a different reading of Philemon, see Petersen, *Rediscovering Paul*.

42. On Paul's social conservatism, see Elliott, *Liberating Paul*, 31–52.

43. Clement of Alexandria, *Christ the Educator* 2.13 (*Ante-Nicene Fathers*, vol. 2).

that had characterized the first assembly in Jerusalem, so they did only what they could. As Chrysostom imagines the scene, the Corinthians shared a ritual meal "on stated days," then went off to "a common entertainment, the rich bringing their provisions with them, and the poor and destitute being invited by them, and all feasting in common."[44] On this scenario, the Lord's Supper was not an actual meal, but a ritual one. The "feasting" that was the occasion of "schisms" came afterward, at some (apparently public) entertainment to which the poor had access only as they were "invited" by the rich. The offense was not, for Chrysostom, the deprivation of the poor, but first, the partisanship Paul named at the beginning of the letter (1:26), and second, the sin of immoderate desire. When Paul wrote that "one is hungry, and another is drunken," Chrysostom understood him to mean that the craving of one and the excess of another were equally failures of self-discipline. The poor were at fault, then, "even," he stipulated, "when the poor are hungry."[45] Economic disparity of itself was for Chrysostom inevitable; the point was for members of the upper class not to embarrass themselves or to shame the poor or treat them with contempt.[46] In the bishop's eyes, Paul chose to tread delicately here because he didn't wish to be dismissed by the prosperous in Corinth by appearing to side with the poor.[47]

Both Clement and Chrysostom already presumed that Paul's comments indicated economic stratification within the Corinthian community. Strikingly, without the benefit of sophisticated modern social-scientific analysis, they both managed to attribute to Paul a sort of benevolent paternalism appropriate to members of the upper strata. In contrast to modern social-scientific interpreters, however, for these ancient readers there was no cause to speak of Paul's "inconsistency" or of a "compromise" of his values, since Paul simply represented the values of his (and their) class.

44. John Chrysostom, *Homilies on First Corinthians* 27.1 (*Nicene and Post-Nicene Fathers*, vol. 12; emphasis in original).

45. John Chrysostom, *Homilies on First Corinthians* 27.1, 4 (*Nicene and Post-Nicene Fathers*, vol. 12).

46. Recall that Chrysostom took from the Epistle to Philemon the lesson that "we ought not to withdraw slaves from the service of their masters"; he was concerned that Christianity was getting a reputation for solicitude toward slaves, which was tantamount to "the subversion of everything" (John Chrysostom, *Homily on Philemon*, argument; *Nicene and Post-Nicene Fathers*, vol. 13).

47. "Further, that he might not seem to say these things on account of the poor only, he does not at once strike into the discourse concerning the tables, lest he render his rebuke such as they might easily come to think slightly of" (John Chrysostom, *Homilies on First Corinthians* 27.2; *Nicene and Post-Nicene Fathers*, vol. 12).

2. Despite the implication of objectivity in the phrase "social-scientific interpretation," however, it appears that modern exegesis is no less influenced by the political and ideological currents of our own age.

In an important essay, Steven Friesen has pointed out that the "new consensus" announced by Abraham Malherbe in the 1970s actually had older antecedents. Around the turn of the twentieth century, Adolf Deissmann already argued that the Pauline churches included "certain fairly well-to-do Christians," including Gaius, "who offered the hospitality of his house to the whole body of the church" in Corinth and, with Erastus (Rom 16:23), must have belonged "to the middle class."[48] Contrary to the later representation of Deissmann as favoring a "proletarian Christianity," Friesen shows that he had little sympathy for the masses. (Deissmann wrote that "the poor folk who made up his churches and who lived on obols and denarii, envious persons who even, as St. Paul once says, 'bite and devour one another,' and who by trooping before pagan judges in their miserable disputes over some mere bagatelle exposed the brotherhood to mockery—these people . . . were not inaccessible to vulgar suspicion and unworthy gossip about a great man," i.e. Paul.[49] Indeed, on Deissmann's account, Paul recognized among the Corinthians plenty who had formerly been "not too scrupulous" about private property: "'thieves' and 'extortioners,' says St. Paul in plain language." Deissmann is certain Paul is referring here to the unscrupulous poor, though he offers no explanation for that certainty;[50] in fact, to the ancients, avarice, πλεονεξία, was at least as likely to be a vice of the well-to-do.)[51]

It appears, then, that Deissmann, an early advocate of views later associated with the social-scientific "new consensus," was hardly a neutral, objective observer. Friesen shows that he was a partisan in the class struggle of his time, seeking to thwart the "dramatic advances" of the Marxist Social Democratic Party in Germany. At an important congress in 1908, Deissmann and Adolf von Harnack gave speeches in which, as Friesen summarizes,

> the social description of Paul's assemblies was intertwined with a determined effort to deny a need for structural change in German society . . . Most of [the speakers] maintained that the gospel could transform the lower classes without disrupting the status quo because the gospel brought inner enlightenment and peace to individuals . . . Social stratification was not a problem,

48. Deissmann, *St. Paul*, 216–17.
49. Deissmann, *St. Paul*, 71, citing Gal 5:15; 1 Cor 6:1–11.
50. Deissmann, *St. Paul*, 71, citing 1 Cor 6:10.
51. Delling, "πλεονέκτης, κτλ.," 266–74.

[dissenting voices] were told, and poverty was not important. The churches simply needed to do a better job of caring for the souls of individuals in order to win back the hearts and minds of the German working class.[52]

I raise the example of Deissmann to ask (as does Friesen) whether more recent exegetes have escaped the influence of capitalist assumptions and predispositions. In fact, Friesen shows that the celebration of a "new consensus" beginning in the 1970s simply perpetuated Deissmann's characterizations regarding socially mixed assemblies that represented a "cross-section" of society, even as heralds of this new consensus attributed to Deissmann himself a "proletarian" view of early Christianity that he never in fact held.[53] Elsewhere, Friesen reviews a series of twentieth-century U.S. textbooks on the New Testament that reveal that during the same period that social-science critics have been exploring status ambiguity, "poverty and economic inequality have not been important topics in Pauline studies."[54] As Friesen described the situation, "Instead of remembering the poor, *we prefer* to discuss upwardly mobile individuals and how they coped with the personal challenges of negotiating their ambivalent social status."

Friesen perceives an "unacknowledged bias" at work among New Testament scholars: "our preoccupation with 'social status' is the very mechanism by which we have ignored poverty and economic issues."[55] That preoccupation, and the tendency of textbook authors to "portray the Roman Empire with a booming economy" so that poverty has been marginalized as a topic,[56] fit well in the atmosphere of higher education in the industrial and post-industrial U.S., where "the primary function of the American professoriate" has been "to train members of the professional-managerial class." In short, Friesen declares, "higher education taught future professionals to accept and to overlook economic inequality, and Pauline studies did so as well."[57] Indeed, one prominent textbook on the Mediterranean culture of the New Testament goes so far as to deny any relevance at all to the terms "poverty" or "the poor."[58]

52. Friesen, "Poverty in Pauline Studies," 330–31.

53. On the mistaken attribution of a "proletarian" picture to Deissmann, see Friesen, "Poverty in Pauline Studies," 326.

54. Friesen, "Blessings of Hegemony," 121.

55. Friesen, "Poverty in Pauline Studies," 332–35.

56. Friesen, "Blessings of Hegemony," 123.

57. Friesen, "Blessings of Hegemony," 125–27.

58. "We simply cannot get any idea" what New Testament authors meant when they referred to "the poor," declares Bruce M. Malina (Malina, *New Testament World.* 99). See my critique, Elliott, "Diagnosing an Allergic Reaction" (Chapter 6 in this volume).

3. It is one thing, of course, to posit (as does Friesen) a correlation between the values of industrial capitalism and the sort of broad generalizations about the ancient world that appear in textbooks. It is another to revisit the sources on the basis of which those generalizations have been made.

In fact, an important stream of scholarship by classicists challenges the trend that Friesen has identified among New Testament interpreters. The former have focused attention precisely on the question of the poor and poverty in the Roman world. As Friesen points out, the measure of wealth "is, after all, the most important component of social status," even if it is "the one least likely to be addressed systematically by New Testament scholars."[59] In 1974—before the announcement of a "new consensus" in New Testament studies—classicist Ramsay MacMullen had described the Roman world in terms of a "steep social pyramid" with a few fantastically wealthy people at the top and the poorer masses at the bottom.[60] The breathtaking inequality and exploitive nature of the Roman economy was described, masterfully, by G. E. M. de Ste. Croix,[61] as well as by others.[62] Justin J. Meggitt criticizes the credulous acceptance on the part of New Testament scholars of the picture provided by elite sources from the Roman period, in which the poor play little role at all. These sources were the products of "a very tiny clique." The more appropriate approach should be to read such sources "against the grain."[63] Meggitt argues that in the preindustrial, agrarian Roman economy, "almost everyone lives near the level of subsistence," except for a tiny and extraordinarily powerful elite. Friesen agrees: "There is no economic middle class" in Roman society because there are no economic structures for amassing surplus wealth.[64]

4. Meggitt and Friesen have led the charge in particular against the "new consensus" regarding the members of Paul's churches.

Meggitt objects to the broad tendency to generalize about all Paul's churches from the particular circumstances and tensions in Corinth when,

---

59. Friesen, "Prospects," 362, 364. Similarly, classicist Greg Woolf observes that in the Roman world, access to wealth was "one of the most explicit and formal measures of an individual's social standing and a key component of his public identity" ("Writing Poverty in Rome," 92).

60. MacMullen, *Roman Social Relations*, 90.

61. De Ste. Croix, *Class Struggle in the Ancient Greek World*.

62. See, inter alia, Hopkins, *Conquerors and Slaves*; Garnsey and Saller, *Roman Empire*; Scheidel, *Cambridge Companion to the Roman Economy*.

63. Meggitt, *Paul, Poverty and Survival*, chs. 1–3.

64. Friesen, "Prospects," 364, citing MacMullen, *Roman Social Relations*; Meggitt, *Paul, Poverty and Survival*, 6–7 and passim.

in fact, "we have no reliable information about individuals from most of the churches [Paul] founded." The poor are therefore "doubly afflicted": by their own poverty, and by their neglect in Paul's letters, which—except for the passage under discussion here—generally leave them in silence.[65] The members of Paul's churches—and Paul himself—were poor, Meggitt argues at length, probably living just above subsistence level. They practiced a form of economic mutuality that was the principal strategy for survival among the urban poor who could not produce their own food.[66] Friesen has conducted a prosopographic study of all the people named in Paul's letters, concluding that the wealthiest members, like Phoebe (the leader in Cenchrae) and Erastus (the "city steward"), probably had only modest means, enjoying "moderate surplus resources"; others were, simply, indigent.[67] Bruce Longenecker points out that Paul "expected treasuries for the poor (or their equivalent) to be established within communities that he founded," evidence that the poor were present in those communities and that Paul was aware of their need.[68]

5. As to the interpretation of 1 Corinthians 11 in particular, several scholars have challenged the scenario advanced by Meeks, Theissen, and Murphy-O'Connor.

I limit my discussion to three challenges that cast doubt, from different angles, on the social-science reconstruction of social disparity in the context of a fairly luxurious context, as described above. These challenges also highlight how much remains uncertain about the situation in Corinth.

In her 1994 study of the apostle's rhetoric in 1 Corinthians, Antoinette Clark Wire argued that the assembly's meals were unlikely to have been on the order of formal cultic banquets in the Roman world but were more probably regular, even daily gatherings, at which lower-status women were more likely to have been responsible for providing food. Paul's reference to each eating their own meal suggests "that the food has been cooked in various homes and carried to a common place," a likely scenario "for a group meeting too regularly in one home to expect full hospitality."[69] Nor does the complaint that "one is hungry while another is drunk . . . prove an orgy," she declares with some hyperbole: it simply shows "that at least occasionally . . . food has run out before everyone arrives and this has caused conflict."[70]

---

65. Friesen, "Prospects," 358–61.

66. Meggitt, *Paul, Poverty and Survival,* ch. 5.

67. Friesen locates the two at level 4 or 5 on his Poverty Scale ("Prospects," 368); Meggitt, *Paul, Poverty and Survival,* 135–41, 148.

68. Longenecker, "Socio-economic Profiling," 41; Longenecker, *Remember the Poor.*

69. Wire, *Corinthian Women Prophets,* 106–7.

70. Wire, *Corinthian Women Prophets,* 108.

Since on Wire's view there is no householder/host "in charge" of the meal, Paul's "final solution," his "insistence that hunger be satisfied at home" (1 Cor 11:34), would have had the chief effect of depriving Spirit-filled women of their shared responsibility for providing the community's meal and sending them back to their homes to prepare household meals, "in traditional roles of female and/or servile subordination."[71] Wire does not address Paul's charge that the Corinthians are showing contempt for the "have-nots," τοὺς μὴ ἔχοντας, but her discussion implies that no one is being regularly deprived of food.

As part of his argument that the Pauline congregations were largely constituted of poor men and women, Justin J. Meggitt disputes that any of the references in 1 Corinthians 11 signal a disparity of rich and poor in the Corinthian assembly. That some were able to acquire ample amounts of food and drink, or "had homes," hardly requires that they were wealthy, he argues. Furthermore, the Greek phrase τοὺς μὴ ἔχοντας, often translated "the have-nots" (e.g., NRSV), requires an implied direct object, which Meggitt identifies as the bread and wine of the Eucharist; this was not, then, Paul's reference to destitute persons. Meggitt concludes that some Corinthians were approaching the Lord's Supper, which he identifies with the Eucharist, to satisfy their hunger, so that others were left unable to share in it. The problem appears, on this reading, to have been a case of bad manners among poor Corinthians in the absence of any wealthier members. Paul's "practical advice" was that, "in order to avoid the [Eucharistic] elements being treated as food, those that were tempted to do so should consume a real meal before coming together."[72]

David Horrell has challenged Murphy-O'Connor's reliance on the archaeological remains of a "sumptuous villa" at Anaploga. Horrell argues that we cannot be sure of the actual use of any particular room in that villa (as a "triclinium," for example); we cannot tell that even a "host of the whole church" like Gaius would have lived in such a villa; and, since other, less sumptuous residential spaces have been excavated in Corinth, we cannot say just where or how most of the members of the Corinthian ἐκκλησία lived. It is at least as possible that they would have gathered in much humbler residential spaces on the second or third floor of other buildings, *insulae* (such as those found east of the Corinthian theater), the first floors of which were used commercially. Horrell cites the story in Acts of a young man in Troas who fell from a third-story window as Paul waxed overlong in

---

71. Wire, *Corinthian Women Prophets*, 109–10.

72. Meggitt, *Paul, Poverty and Survival*, 118–22.

preaching (Acts 20:7–12) as indirect corroboration that such spaces might indeed have accommodated a Christian assembly.[73]

These arguments all dispute one key aspect of the now-prevalent reconstruction described above: namely, that the Lord's Supper was being eaten in the private house of a wealthy Christian in such a way that disparities between rich and poor were exacerbated to the point of the humiliation of the latter. In this regard, these scholars provide salutary reminders of how little we can say with certainty about the Corinthian situation.

On the other hand, Wire's and Meggitt's arguments effectively minimize any implication that men and women were regularly leaving the assembly hungry, or that this constituted an actual offense against the destitute (usually perceived in the phrase τοὺς μὴ ἔχοντας). For Wire, any hunger is merely "occasional." It follows that Paul's rhetoric is overheated; it might simply be that the Corinthian women responsible for preparing food simply "were not interested in enforcing more structured patterns of community life," as was Paul.[74] On Wire's reading, the apostle appears as an unreliable source regarding the situation in Corinth. For Meggitt, those who "do not have" are being deprived on occasion of the bread and wine of the Eucharist, but are not actually going hungry.

In this regard, these authors have allowed their larger arguments—concerning the different social experience of the Corinthian women prophets (Wire) or the general poverty of the Pauline congregations (Meggitt)—to eclipse the possibility of tensions caused by actual socioeconomic disparity in the assembly. We may readily concede that Paul's description of what happens at the common meal—"one goes hungry, and another becomes drunk" (v. 21)—may rely on exaggeration, but it is deliberate exaggeration, meant to drive home the accusation that some in Corinth have given offense to their disadvantaged neighbors. In Paul's heated language, they have shown contempt for the church by humiliating "those who have nothing" (καταισχύνετε τοὺς μὴ ἔχοντας). These accusations are not instrumental to some other, extrinsic purpose: they are made to achieve a reversal of the behavior that Paul finds offensive. It is not plausible that he means simply "those who do not have a share in the Eucharistic elements" (contra Meggitt); the meal being shared is evidently a substantial meal at which the satisfaction of hunger is an important expectation.[75] Indeed, Andrew McGowan has recently argued that there may not have been a "token" or "symbolic"

73. Horrell, "Domestic Space and Christian Meetings."

74. Wire, *Corinthian Women Prophets,* 108.

75. On the meal as a real supper, see Conzelmann, *1st Corinthians,* 194–95; Theissen, *Social Setting of Pauline Christianity,* 147–53; Wire, *Corinthian Women Prophets,* 102–10.

meal of bread and wine, distinct from a shared supper, at this point in history. Paul's invocation of Jesus' action at the last supper may be directed to describe the ethos that should infuse the common meal, not to provide an "institution narrative" for a ceremonial "Lord's supper."[76]

We should exercise appropriate caution regarding the precise scenario addressed in Corinth, or regarding the precise circumstances of the parties involved. But socioeconomic disparity—and the indifference of some in Corinth to the sensibilities of their social inferiors—are clearly the factors behind some incident (or incidents) of affront that have so provoked the apostle. As Richard A. Horsley judiciously frames the matter, "Judging from Paul's rhetoric, it is impossible to determine just what the schisms at the assembly meals were." Nevertheless, social disparities allowed a "few well-off members" to repeat at the common meal practices of recognizing hierarchy and rank that were abundant in the environment. "Paul insists that they break with those hierarchical patterns" as they gather for the common meal.[77]

ATTENDING TO PAUL'S IRONY

It is surprising, given Wire's focus on a rhetorical-critical reading of 1 Corinthians, that both Wire and Meggitt read parts of Paul's admonition as rhetorically neutral. They thus perpetuate a particular weakness of the reconstruction proposed by Theissen, Meeks, and Murphy-O'Connor. As we have seen, all these authors read v. 19 without a hint of irony. When Paul declares that "indeed, there have to be factions among you, for only so will it become clear who among you are genuine," he is (on their view) giving straightforward expression to his "eschatological" viewpoint. Again, all these scholars read v. 34, Paul's declaration that the Corinthians should "eat at home," as plainly practical advice, a simple "recommendation" or "suggestion" or "solution" that effectively removes the satisfaction of hunger from the sacred context of the assembly. The result of this flattened reading is that Paul has "privatized" the satisfaction of hunger in order to extend a superficial collegiality at what now becomes a purely ritual meal.

These are remarkable failures to recognize the texture of Paul's rhetoric. In contrast, other scholars have recognized that a tone of ironic censure permeates this passage, beginning with the *litotēs* in v. 17 ("I do not commend you" = "I rebuke you"), repeated in v. 22.[78] Margaret M. Mitchell holds that

---

76. McGowan, "Myth of the 'Lord's Supper.'"

77. Horsley, *1 Corinthians*, 164–65.

78. *Litotēs* is a figure of speech using an understated negative to express a positive,

Paul's declaration, "when you come together it is not for the better but for the worse" (v. 17; 18, 20), plays on the possible double meaning of συνέρχεσθε, an important term in Hellenistic political discourse. Paul means that they do not come together "in the good sense of the term," by being united, but merely assemble.[79] His "mock disbelief" that there are factions among the Corinthians (v. 18) is a rhetorical tactic: Mitchell shows that mock disbelief was used on occasions of grave censure when divisions had undermined the concord expected of a community.[80] His declaration that there "have to be [δεῖ] factions among you, for only so will it become clear who among you are genuine," drips with irony: Paul has already rejected the legitimacy of "divisions" and "quarrels" among them (σχίσματα, ἔριδες, 1:10–13). Further, the manifestation of the "genuine" among them would clearly *not* mean the recognition of those who consider themselves socially superior, whom Paul accuses of showing "contempt for the church of God and humiliat[ing] those who have nothing" (v. 22 NRSV). As Horsley summarizes the point, Paul's comment "should be taken as irony, even sarcasm."[81]

Whatever the specifics of the activity surrounding the meal—as we have seen, no single explanation compels universal acceptance—Paul is clearly concerned that some are being disadvantaged, and in a way that publicly humiliates them. It is possible that this is his overheated reaction to a slight that others in Corinth may not have perceived (so Wire), but (as Wire also recognizes) Paul's perception of a fundamental wrong in the Corinthian assembly permeates the whole letter. The "have-nots" in 11:22 echo the "nothings" (τὰ μὴ ὄντα) named at the beginning of the letter, in 1:28—a peculiar phrase but apparently meant to invoke the members of the Corinthian assembly who were not "wise . . . powerful . . . well-born" (1:26), but were "weak" or powerless (τὰ ἀσθενῆ, 1:27). Paul rebukes the distinctions made by some Corinthians with harsh rhetorical questions in 4:7 ("For who sees anything different in you?" etc.), then admonishes them with sarcastic praise: "Already you have all you want!" (lit. "are satiated," κεκορεσμένοι); "already you have become rich! Quite apart from us you have become kings!" (4:8). In contrast, the apostles are weak (or powerless), hungry and thirsty, and so on (4:9–13).[82]

---

favored for example by the author of Luke–Acts: Aune, *Westminster Dictionary of New Testament*, 280.

79. Mitchell, *Paul and the Rhetoric of Reconciliation*, 153–56.

80. Mitchell, *Paul and the Rhetoric of Reconciliation*, 151–52, with citations of ancient orators.

81. Horsley, *1 Corinthians*, 158–59.

82. Pseudo-Libanius's discussion of epistolary styles describes the ironic style, εἰρωνική, as "that in which we feign praise of someone at the beginning, but at the

Even if the details of the common meal at last elude our scrutiny, then, it is clear enough that differences in status have created tensions in Corinth, and that Paul seeks repeatedly to address the higher-status members by taking the side of the poor; indeed, by insisting that *God* has taken their side (1:27–31).[83] Whatever the slight to the poorer members, it constitutes, in Paul's eyes, "contempt for the church of God" (11:22).

In this light, we should read the rhetorical question in v. 22 as a stinging rebuke. The NRSV expresses this tone fittingly (if not precisely) by the addition of an exclamation: "What! Do you not have homes to eat and drink in?" The double negative μὴ γὰρ οἰκίας οὐκ ἔχετε expects an affirmative answer.[84] But the question is ironic. Of course Paul knows they have houses: he is not asking for information on which to predicate his solution ("oh, you *do* have houses? Then I suggest you simply eat at home"). His question is an example of the arch invective that Peter Lampe finds throughout 1 and 2 Corinthians, involving suggestive questions, indirect and direct accusations, irony, and "sarcastic shaming" of opponents.[85] The questions that follow continue the tone of rebuke.[86] Horsley neatly brings out the antagonistic force of these questions: "Those obsessed with their own dinner can banquet in their own houses some other time!"[87]

The point of Paul's declaration that when the Corinthians gather, it is "not to eat the Lord's supper," as well as of his extended discussion of divine judgment manifest in the meal (11:23–32), is that their practice has nullified the meal's very purpose. It would therefore be not simply a prudent "compromise" but an extraordinary capitulation for Paul to declare at last, in v. 34, that the very purpose of the assembly for the Lord's Supper should be abandoned.

That purpose was not (to use the anachronistic categories of later Christianity) primarily "sacramental." So, for example, we cannot accept Hans Conzelmann's judgment that Paul summons the Corinthians "to

---

end display our real aim." His example is a letter of censure: "I am greatly astonished at your sense of equity, that you have so quickly rushed from a well-ordered life to its opposite—for I hesitate to say wickedness . . ." Paul's ironic praise ("Already you have everything you want!") is similarly employed in censure. See Malherbe, "Ancient Epistolary Theorists."

83. As Fee notes, "The perspective is clearly 'from below,' taking the side of the 'have-nots'" (*First Epistle to the Corinthians*, 594).

84. Blass et al., *Greek Grammar of the New Testament*, 220–21.

85. Lampe, "Can Words Be Violent," 226–27.

86. The particle ἤ ("or") marks "a reproachful question": Conzelmann, *1 Corinthians*, 195.

87. Horsley, *1 Corinthians*, 195.

separate satisfaction of hunger and the community Supper . . . to separate the *sacrament* from satisfaction of hunger."[88] The purpose of the supper is best gleaned, rather, by restoring it to its first-century context. This requires examining the broader phenomenon of associations (θίασοι) in the Hellenistic world.

Relying on recent research into Hellenistic associations, the centrality of convivial meals for constituting those associations, and the space provided in those meals for "social experimentation" in subtle divergence from, and tension with, the values of Hellenistic and Roman imperial culture, Hal Taussig has argued that "early Christian congregations were almost certainly modeled on associations." Comparison with associations, about which we have a wealth of literary but, even more important, epigraphic information, suggests that early Christian gatherings, too, "were not an elite assembly but most likely included—perhaps even predominantly—many laborers with few resources, women of similar means, and slaves."[89] One important task of association meals was to embody a measure of equality across unequal classes in an atmosphere of liminality.[90] My point in invoking the analogy is not to argue that Paul's initial foundation of the Corinthian ἐκκλησία was an egalitarian paradise, but that *any* impulse in an egalitarian direction (which was constitutive of the association phenomenon in general) would immediately have been neutralized by the surrender of its chief medium, sharing food at a common meal. Just such surrender is what Theissen, Meeks, and others allege Paul to have proposed in 11:34. But this seems unlikely.

Luise Schottroff makes a similar point, but regarding early Christianity more broadly, by means of comparison with the Acts of the Apostles. "What is presumed in 1 Cor 11:17–34 is a law of possessions that we also find in Acts 2:42–45 and 4:32—5:11. The congregation is a community sanctified by God, with a common property consecrated to God (*koina*, Acts 2:44; 4:32)." Private property is the opposite of common property: it *becomes* common property as it is consecrated to the community's use. Thus, "the wealthy in Corinth could have eaten at home (1 Cor 11:22, 33), *but in doing so they would have withdrawn from the congregation and its holiness.*"[91]

These arguments suggest that we cannot take Paul's simple declaration in 11:34 at face value. The NRSV's paraphrase, "If you [pl.] are hungry, eat at home," is already a distortion of Paul's words in the direction of a general

<hr/>

88. Conzelmann, *1 Corinthians*, 195.

89. Taussig, *In the Beginning Was the Meal*, 98, 100. Taussig depends on the rich and important work of Harland, *Associations, Synagogues, and Congregations*.

90. Taussig, *In the Beginning Was the Meal*, 122–23.

91. Schottroff, "Holiness and Justice," 54; also Bieler and Schottroff, *Eucharist*, 120 (emphasis added).

rule for the congregation. The Greek uses the indefinite pronoun τις in service of a general conditional phrase: "if *anyone* is hungry, let that person
eat at home." In v. 22, the prospect of satisfying hunger at home was not a
matter of simple practicality for everyone, but was characterized as a gesture
of contempt for the church and scorn for the poor, shown by some in the
assembly. It is not possible, then, that εἴ τις πεινᾷ in v. 34 is meant generally,
for v. 22 clearly suggests that some Corinthians, the "have-nots," are not able
to satisfy hunger by simply "eating at home."

Neither is it possible, then, that v. 34 is advice directed to the same
"hunger" referred to in v. 21. Richard A. Horsley is no doubt closer to the
sense of Paul's words with his paraphrase, "if you are hungry (i.e., want a
more sumptuous dinner), eat at home."[92] Similarly Gordon Fee writes that
the phrase "almost certainly means, 'if anyone wants to gorge.'" "Those who
want to glut at the common meal are being told to do so at home, as it
were."[93] But this means that v. 34 is not a piece of prosaic advice; it continues
the sarcastic rhetoric of rebuke begun in v. 17. Or, as I suggested in an earlier
discussion, Paul's response in v. 34 "is a humiliating sarcasm for any who
would display their status in the quality of food they are served at the common meal: 'eat at home' (where no one can see what you eat)!"[94] The premise
behind both references to eating at home—the rebuking question of v. 22
and the mock command in v. 34—is that the people being addressed are
accustomed to a level of self-satisfaction in their dining "at home," among
their social peers, that is inappropriate and offensive in the assembly, where
they are gathered together out of (ἐκ-κλησία!) their homes. To bring those
attitudes and practices to the common meal is to "come together . . . for
your condemnation" (11:34). "Eat at home" is not, then, Paul's "advice" or
"solution" to what he regards as the abuse of the supper. That answer comes
rather in v. 33: "wait for one another" (or "receive one another," ἀλλήλους
ἐκδέχεσθε).[95]

It cannot be an accident that at this point Paul drops argument and
invective and seems to put the Corinthians on hold until his arrival: "about
the other things I will give instructions when I come" (11:34). We cannot
tell what "the other things" (τὰ δὲ λοιπὰ) might be; the fact that he proceeds

92. Horsley, *1 Corinthians*, 163.

93. Fee, *First Epistle to the Corinthians*, 629, 603.

94. Elliott, *Liberating Paul*, 208.

95. Just how we should understand what is happening in the Corinthian gatherings
depends in part on translating the verbs προλαμβάνει (v. 21) and ἐκδέχεσθε (v. 33).
Either verb might carry a temporal sense—some are "going ahead" and eating "before"
others, and are encouraged to "wait"—or a nontemporal sense: προλαμβάνει might
mean "devour," and ἐκδέχεσθε "accept each other" (in normal hospitality).

with other topics ("now concerning spiritual gifts," 12:1) might suggest that he has simply dropped a subject about which he is not convinced that further argument will be persuasive.

At last, the exact practices that so exercised the apostle may forever remain tantalizingly elusive. Their precise estimation depends on other judgments concerning the socioeconomic status of the Corinthians—which includes judging whether or not some of them were as impoverished as the common translation "the have-nots" (v. 22) would imply. The apparent goal of Paul's rhetoric is clearer, however: he wishes to safeguard in the Corinthian assembly a meal practice that embodies a shared mutuality among its participants. We have seen reason to doubt the prevalent view that Paul stood ready to compromise that goal when it became difficult: that is, when the pressure of social expectations in a socially stratified Roman colony became too great.

The tremendous energy that continues to be expended in the interpretation of this passage suggests that we continue look to it for some insight, some compass bearing in our own time, when socioeconomic disparity threatens not only the coherence of the church's witness, but the survival of millions, and the viability of countless communities. Our responsibility for those challenges persists.

11

Ephesians as the Quintessence of Pauline Deracination

IN HIS LANDMARK WORK *The Christian Imagination*, theologian Willie James Jennings developed the thesis that the modern toxins of racism and colonialism not only developed through history in intricate connection with the Christian heritage, but were made possible because of the legacy of ancient Christian supersessionism.[1] My purpose here is, after a brief review and evaluation of Jennings's argument, to amplify it by assessing one particular generative resource offered to the history of supersession: the Epistle to the Ephesians.

THE THEO-LOGIC OF CONQUEST

Jennings argues that, from early on, "Gentile Christians"—a peculiar, though common phrase, to which we will return, below—began to imagine themselves as the "people of God." That is, they began to see themselves as occupying a central place of privilege that had previously belonged to Israel, a place that Israel had forfeited through lack of faith in the messiah Jesus. Gentile Christians thus deracinated the biblical understanding of the people of God, severing any ties of that conception to land, history, or ethnicity. Unmoored, the now-abstract concept was open to Gentile-Christian appropriation.

1. Jennings, *Christian Imagination*.

That distinctively *Gentile*-Christian imagination allowed the representatives of later Christian empires in Europe to perceive the human peoples they encountered in the "New World," for example, as "pagans under the control of the devil," and themselves as the equivalent of ancient Israel—playing the central role in history, according to divine providence.

Jennings's argument is compelling overall, and impressive in the detail with which he explores particular historical episodes. He devotes a key chapter to an extraordinary example, the 16th-century Jesuit academic José de Acosta Porres, "arguably the most thoroughly trained, intellectually accomplished, and doctrinally prepared theologian to enter the New World" in that century. Indeed, for Jennings's purposes, Acosta, the "first Jesuit theologian in residence in Peru," is "paradigmatic of a theologian in the New World,"[2] an "embodiment" of the Christian theological tradition that had shaped him.[3]

As Jennings shows, Christianity was not a supplement to colonization; it was not a coincidental accompaniment of European conquest of the indigenous peoples of the hemisphere. Rather, "the reordering of Indian worlds was born of Christian formation itself," as the land, its resources, and the labor of the people who lived from it were presumed to be the rightful property of (one or another kingdom of) Christian Europe. He writes,

> What is crucial here is the new groundlessness within which Christian theology was presented to the indigenes. Detached from the land, oblivious to the ongoing decimation of native ecologies, deeply suspicious of native religious practices, and, most important, enclosed within Iberian whiteness, the performance of Christian theology would produce a new, deformed and deforming intellectual circuit.[4]

Christian theology was a "discourse of displacement," Jennings shows. What was never at issue for Acosta or his Iberian peers in their relationship with native peoples "was the rightness of conquest, the providential reality of Spanish imperial presence, and the viceroy's refashioning of the Andean world."[5] More important for Jennings's purpose (and my own), Acosta's writings "reveal the adjustments Christian theology will make in the New World, adjustments that will undermine theology's deepest materiality, its humanity, and its intimacy."[6]

2. Jennings, *Christian Imagination*, 82.
3. Jennings, *Christian Imagination*, 68–72.
4. Jennings, *Christian Imagination*, 81–82.
5. Jennings, *Christian Imagination*, 83.
6. Jennings, *Christian Imagination*, 83.

Acosta's theological writings, *Natural and Moral History of the Indies* and his *Procurement of Indian Salvation,* were "translated into multiple European languages, reprinted for centuries," and offered "a crucial resource in the development of Enlightenment science."[7] Because the discovery of the New World was *not safe* for traditional European Christian ways of knowing, Acosta's task in these writings was to *make* the New World and its peoples intelligible, safe, within a *biblical* and *European Christian* frame. His theology was thus "a manifestation of colonial power" that reveals "the future of theology in the New World"—as a "strongly traditioned Christian intellectual posture made to function wholly within a colonialist logic."[8]

Acosta "fashioned a theological vision for the New World that drew its life from Christian orthodoxy and its power from conquest."[9] As Jennings summarizes Acosta's achievement, although "he entered the New World, his central epistemological gesture was bringing the New World inside his theological vision, rendering it intelligible inside Christian theology."[10] Conquest itself became a moment of divine providence: the Creator had filled the New World with resources attractive to Christian empires, inciting their desire for the land as a means to achieve the evangelization and, thus, the salvation of its peoples.[11]

As for the native peoples? Their perception of themselves, their land, and their own culture and history were of negligible value to Acosta. He rendered the natives' religious practices—by the time of his arrival, surviving primarily in fragments—intelligible within a biblical frame. "Acosta reads the Indian as though he (Acosta) represented the Old Testament people of God," and "reads the religious practices of indigenes from the position of . . . Israel." That is, the indigenes are, like the biblical Canaanites, *idolaters,* worshippers of false gods. As Jennings observes, "Christian theology contains at its core a trajectory of reading 'as Israel,'" and this trajectory has predetermined the possibilities of how Acosta will perceive the peoples of Peru.[12]

The *supersessionism* at the heart of Acosta's reflection consists in the "evacuation" and "replacement" of Israel *by Christianity,* so that it does not occur to Acosta to "position himself with the Indians within a history of Gentile (that is, non-Jewish) existence." The Indians are fundamentally *not*

---

7. Jennings, *Christian Imagination,* 85–86. The first is available as *Historia Natural y Moral de las Indias*; ET *Natural and Moral History of the Indies.* The second is *De Procuranda Indorum Salute.*

8. Jennings, *Christian Imagination,* 83.

9. Jennings, *Christian Imagination,* 83.

10. Jennings, *Christian Imagination,* 87.

11. Jennings, *Christian Imagination,* 92, citing Acosta, *Historia* IV:2.

12. Jennings, *Christian Imagination,* 97.

like him. It does not occur to him to imagine them, and himself, equally as peoples outside of Israel, to whom scripture offered Israel's invitation. Acosta is, in Jennings's memorable phrasing, "cut off from a simple Gentile remembrance that would enable a far more richly imagined possibility of movement toward faith from within the cultural logics and spatial realities of Andean life. That is to say, he is cut off from active remembering that he and his people were also 'like the Indians,'" and responding to them with a corresponding "generosity of spirit."

Instead, "the demonic" is the category on which Acosta repeatedly depends in his perceptions of the peoples of the land.[13]

The encounter with New-World spatial, material, and social realities became, in the Christian imagination of the likes of Acosta, an opportunity not to learn, accept, and welcome others (and be welcomed by them!) so much as to dominate them. The logic of progress in Christian formation was deformed by realities of colonizing power into a logic of constant evaluation and racial ranking, in which other peoples were necessarily inferior. In Acosta's words, "it is the stupidity and the ignorance of the Barbarians that militates against us" in our civilizing, Christianizing mission.[14] Here, Jennings perceives, "the performance of theology . . . becomes the articulation of processes of colonialist evaluation." Theology existed, for Acosta, "in constant evaluative mode, exposing native deficiency." The work of "forming theological subjects" was merged into "the operation of forming productive workers for the mines, encomiendas, haciendas, the obrajes, and the reducciones"—the Spanish inventions for concentrating labor and exploiting land that replaced indigenous forms of community.[15]

As Jennings frames the matter, Acosta was not capable of encountering the Incas as equals, let alone of perceiving himself as a *guest* entering *their* land and *their* world, because he had been formed by a tradition—the Christian theological tradition—in which the guest, the Gentile, had decisively usurped the place of centrality, "with Israel evacuated and replaced."[16]

ANTECEDENTS IN ROMANS

I find this core aspect of Jennings's argument utterly compelling. Although (as we shall see) he does not develop the point in this way, I also find his

13. Jennings, *Christian Imagination*, 98.

14. Jennings, *Christian Imagination*, 104, citing *De Procuranda*, I:4.

15. Jennings, *Christian Imagination*, 107; on the mechanisms and effects of Spanish exploitation, Jennings, *Christian Imagination*, 72–82.

16. Jennings, *Christian Imagination*, 97.

argument evocative of the theological vision expressed in Paul's letter to the Romans—a point that will become relevant below. In Romans, Paul emphasizes Israel's "irrevocable" call and priority in God's purpose,[17] and solemnly warns non-Jews ("Gentiles," as the NRSV and other translations render τὰ ἔθνη) not to presume that they have in any way supplanted Israel.[18] Although the interpretation of these chapters of Romans and, indeed, of the whole letter remain hotly contested,[19] I endorse several important late twentieth- and early twenty-first-century developments in interpretation:

(a) Landmark twentieth-century works already undermined the tendency, driven by Christian theological interests, to read Paul's gospel, and Romans in particular, as fundamentally a "debate with Judaism," either conceived as a religion of "works-righteousness" or (in the so-called "New Perspective") of ethnocentric privilege. While earlier studies focusing attention on the integrity of ancient Jewish sources cast doubt on Paul's theological coherence,[20] more recent studies have invoked the standards of comparative religion in calling us to understand Paul *as an ancient Jew* and *within Judaism.*[21]

(b) Some late twentieth- and early twenty-first-century scholarship has focused on interpreting Romans as *rhetorically competent argumentation.* This has led to recognition that Paul addresses his readers *as non-Jewish believers in Christ*; that he addresses them with exhortation, as in all his letters; and that his argumentation reaches a climax in chapters 9–11 (seen already by F. C. Baur). Furthermore, attention to Paul's deployment of apostrophe and diatribe, the rhetorical questions Paul raises and the rhetorical answers he rejects, taken together point to an incipient *anti-Jewish* formation within at least some Roman

---

17. Rom 9:6; 11:1–2, 11–12, 26, 29.

18. Rom 11:13–27.

19. The most significant recent contribution to the discussion is Campbell, *Romans.*

20. So E. P. Sanders already regarded Paul as "thinking backwards" in Romans, "from solution to plight": Sanders, *Paul and Palestinian Judaism*; Heikki Räisänen attributed the apostle's theological incoherence to his status as a convert and salesman-cum-missionary: Räisänen, *Paul and the Law.*

21. The "Paul within Judaism" school is growing (now represented by a Group in the Society of Biblical Literature), with important representative works by Mark Nanos, Magnus Zetterholm, Pamela Eisenbaum, and Anders Runesson; I would include in this category the work of William S. Campbell and the more-or-less parallel "path not taken" of John Gager and Lloyd Gaston. See now the superb discussion by Paula Fredriksen, "What Does It Mean to See Paul 'within Judaism'?"

communities of non-Jewish Christ-followers—a formation Paul exerts himself to oppose.[22]

(c) The heart of that exhortation is to warn non-Jewish Christ-believers against "boasting" over Israel on the basis of their own having come to belong in Christ.[23] This argument has gone hand-in-hand with a fuller understanding of *the socio-historical environment,* and particularly of ethnicity in the Roman world. Too often, functionalist social-science studies of Paul and his letters have relied on essentialized understandings of ethnicity and social identity—posing "Jewish" against "Gentile" or "Greek" ethnicity as idealized alternatives, and often emphasizing Jewish "ethnocentrism" as a negative foil to the supposed universalism of the Pauline gospel.[24] A more nuanced understanding has recognized the decisive role played by Roman imperial ideology and its evaluative hierarchy of peoples—as "civilized" or "civilizable," or "barbaric" (and thus fit only for subjugation)—that shaped and distorted ancient understandings of ethnicity.[25]

It follows from the last point that Paul's admonition to his non-Jewish readers in Romans is not just a matter of asserting ethnic equality "in Christ." It also involves Paul's contestation of *imperial* construals of the worth of peoples. In contemporary terms, it is thus irreducibly political. This argument is, I think, congenial to Professor Jennings's interests in *The Christian Imagination,* and maps fairly precisely onto the theological vision

22. This position has been most consistently advanced over the years by William S. Campbell: see his essays collected in Campbell, *Paul's Gospel in an Intercultural Context.* I depended on some of these essays in my own dissertation, Elliott, *Rhetoric of Romans.* See also Stowers, *Rereading of Romans.*

23. I have argued this case at greater length in Elliott, *Rhetoric of Romans* and Elliott, *Arrogance of Nations.* In the latter work I argued more specifically that the "incipient anti-Judaism" Paul combatted in Rome had its origins, not in a perceived "failure" of Israel-in-general to believe in Jesus, but in elite Roman perceptions of Israel as an already-vanquished people.

24. Important critiques of this move are Buell and Hodge, "Politics of Interpretation"; see also Buell, *Why This New Race*; Hodge, "Apostle to the Gentiles"; and Eisenbaum, "Paul, Polemics."

25. The scholarship on these questions is vast and diverse. Suffice it to point to the exemplary work of Kahl, *Galatians Re-imagined,* on Galatians, and the larger-scope view of Lopez, *Apostle to the Conquered.* I have taken a comparable approach to Romans in Elliott, *Arrogance of Nations,* esp. in chs. 1, 4, and 5. On this view, the formation Paul opposes in Rom 11 is not derived either from Paul's own proclamation or from some purported Jewish or "Gentile" ethnocentrism, but reflects *Roman* perceptions of the Jews as a subjugated people—perceptions non-Jewish Christians were tempted to share *by virtue of living in Rome.*

he holds out as he poses "Gentiles" as the *guests* who have, to date, failed catastrophically to learn their respectful place in Israel's space.

TWO CHALLENGES

Here I pause to note two critiques, one historical and another theological, that have been raised against Jennings's argument.

The first, historical objection is readily dispatched. In a panel discussion of *The Christian Imagination* at the 2021 AAR/SBL Annual Meeting, organized by the Society for Post-Supersessionist Theology, theologian Gerald McDermott argued that Jennings had failed to make a historical case for the "origin of racism in supersessionism," which he dubbed the "ORS theory." McDermott argued that particular episodes of racism discussed in *The Christian Imagination* had not been immediately preceded by recorded outbreaks of supersessionist fervor, so the correlations Jennings sought to draw were illusory.[26]

McDermott's criticisms appear off the point. Jennings does not argue for what we might call a *hydraulic* explanation of colonialism or racism such as McDermott exerts himself to refute. That is to say, Jennings does not argue that one or another eruption in the history of racism or colonialism was caused by a sudden, prior swelling of Christian-supersessionist pressure at a particular place and time. Jennings's argument has to do with the necessary logical or rhetorical conditions, the intellectual framework provided by the supersessionist Christian legacy, that limited the individual and collective imaginations of Christians in the modern (colonial) period so that theological, racial, and colonial frames could converge and merge into coherent, destructive systems. Jennings's compelling discussion of José de Acosta Porres as "paradigmatic" of Western theology in the colonial reality is itself paradigmatic of the argument throughout *The Christian Imagination*. That McDermott failed entirely to mention the chapter on Acosta in his critique, as Jennings observes, suggests that he has misunderstood Jennings's argument overall.

A second, theological critique bears more weight, in my own judgment. In an online symposium on Jennings's book hosted by the Syndicate network, Cynthia R. Nielsen notes that some of Jennings's theological affirmations seem to express a "'mild' supersessionism." As Nielsen paraphrases Jennings, "Christ's body is the new place that unites *all* people." Nielsen asks,

---

26. Society for Post-Supersessionist Theology, "Supersessionism, Nations, and Race."

"since many Jewish believers would deny the role that Jennings claims for the Jewish Jesus, how is this not another form of supersessionism?"[27]

Nielsen identifies a genuine and troublesome tension in *The Christian Imagination*. Israel is, for Jennings, "the hermeneutic horizon" for Christian theology, an assertion that immediately poses the challenge, in his words, "whether Christian theology can explain *how* Israel is important to Christian existence."[28] One part of his answer to that question is that "Israel's story" (as narrated in Israel's scripture) "opens to all people not simply the very nature of humanity, but the drama of peoples in the presence of the living God. With breathtaking power, biblical Israel performs humanity."[29] So far, so good.

But this theological horizon *as Jennings describes it* is not simply a "theology of Israel's scriptures" as that might be developed, for example, *within Judaism.*[30] Jennings's theological approach to "biblical Israel" and "living Israel," by which he means contemporary Judaism,[31] is constrained by a distinctly *Christian* conviction that Jesus' life recapitulates Israel's history: it is a story of Israel *as told by Christians*. As Jennings puts it, "Jesus *is* Israel for the sake of Israel."[32]

Jennings acknowledges the "danger" of "collaps[ing] Israel's life into Jesus," but in my estimation, he nevertheless comes very near that danger in his final chapter, which depends in part on glosses on various Gospel texts, especially from John, unencumbered by critical questions of historicity.[33]

Jennings writes, for example, that "Jesus' Israel-centrism is bound to a power that will break it open . . . By calling Israel to receive the presence of their God *through his teachings,* he is also asking them to witness *to its absolute embodiment in him* . . . Jesus entered fully into the kinship

27. See *Syndicate* (website), Symposium on *The Christian Imagination*. Nielsen, "Rending New Life," also objects to Jennings's evocation of the biblical God as violent, a matter to which Jennings responds, but which I will not take up here.

28. Jennings, *Christian Imagination,* 251 (emphasis added).

29. Jennings, *Christian Imagination,* 252–53.

30. I think for example of Sweeney, *Tanak*; see also Kalimi, ed., *Jewish Bible Theology*; Sweeney, *Theology of the Hebrew Bible,* vol. 1, *Methodological Studies*; Rom-Shiloni, "Hebrew Bible Theology."

31. Jennings, *Christian Imagination,* 251. It is noteworthy—though Jennings does not dwell on the point—that his definition of Israel does not involve the modern nation-state.

32. Jennings, *Christian Imagination,* 260 (emphasis added).

33. Jennings, *Christian Imagination,* 261. Jennings intentionally "bypasses" critical issues in New Testament studies such as the historicity of various Gospel accounts; he thereby also fails to reckon with questions of the possible anti-Jewish tendencies in one or another Gospel account.

structure [of Israel] not to destroy it but to reorder it—around himself . . .
Jesus does not intend the destruction of Israel, only its rebirth in him."[34]
Such statements—all of which Jennings derives from one or another Gospel
text—show the contours of what we should at least call a *Jesus-centric* or
Christ-centric understanding of Israel, if not an understanding that *collapses*
Israel's life into Jesus.

For Jennings, it seems, the new "communion" that "is taking place in
the gathering of listeners to Jesus"—and, after his death and resurrection, in
the community of Jews and Gentiles gathered in his name, as described in
Acts—*is* the realization of Israel's destiny. "The disciples rightly understood
what the resurrected Jesus meant for Israel's fortunes—the reign of its God
was now visible in the world through his Son who had overcome death."[35]

That rings as a common enough Christian theological assertion, plausible in terms of an uncritical reading of the Gospels and Acts. But Jennings
has aspired to do more: he has set *Israel* as the "hermeneutic horizon" for
his account, and thus opened his project to evaluation according to that criterion. So, one must wonder how many *in Israel* would have perceived "the
reign of God . . . visible in the world" more tangibly the day after Easter, or
Pentecost, than the day before? Surely, the longed-for "reign of God" should
have involved more than participation in the post-Pentecost community, if
we may judge from the Prophets and the Psalms: peace and justice, *šalôm*
and *ṣedaqah*, established within Israel; peace and justice established through
the nations of the earth. Surely, the reign of God should *involve* more, if we
may judge from the petitions that *Christian communities* continue to pray
today as Jesus' own prayer, for the coming of God's kingdom and the realization of God's will "on earth as it is in heaven."

It is not clear, then, why the potentialities available in the post-Easter
community of Jesus' disciples should set the limits to "Israel's fortunes," or
to what Israel-as-hermeneutic-horizon is allowed to mean. Such limits seem
to be in force when Jennings implicitly dismisses clear biblical themes that
Israel had much more to hope for. I mean, for example, that he finds in
Acts the clear repudiation of dreams of "world dominance" by Israel, and
hails instead the "counterhegemonic reality" produced by the Spirit—the
ever-more-intimate sharing with others through mutual immersion in one
another's languages.[36] Not only does such language of "dominance" and "hegemony" implicitly caricature prevalent themes in Israel's scripture; it also
reduces the biblical vision of what *may* be hoped for to the horizon of *the*

---

34. Jennings, *Christian Imagination*, 263; emphases added.

35. Jennings, *Christian Imagination*, 264; 265–56.

36. Jennings, *Christian Imagination*, 266.

church—that "new reality of kinship" that "turns Israel's election outward" and simply *is* "the Creator reclaiming the world through communion," as Jennings describes it.[37]

My point can perhaps be best expressed by returning to Romans, but this time to contrast Jennings's last chapter with the theological vision expressed in that letter. In Romans—*written to a community of Christ believers, after* the putative events of Easter and Pentecost as Luke-Acts describes them—Paul is not content to describe the life of that community as the satisfaction of "Israel's fortunes." Rather, he pointedly evokes the fulfillment of Israel's hopes as *future events, beyond* the experience of the church. These events include the incoming of the full number of the nations (ἄχρις οὗ τὸ πλήρωμα τῶν ἐθνῶν εἰσέλθῃ, 11:25) and the salvation of all Israel (πᾶς Ἰσραὴλ σωθήσεται, 11:26), events that together constitute the glorious redemption of the children of God awaited by all creation—indeed, a redemption in which creation will also share (καὶ αὐτὴ ἡ κτίσις ἐλευθερωθήσεται, 8:21). These events, which the apostle evokes lyrically, movingly, are expectations well documented in Israel's scriptures. They are, one might say in Jennings's language, "Israel's fortunes," as seen within Israel's space *and Israel's time.*

To play again on Jennings's language, I argue that in Romans, Israel and Israel's hopes are the "hermeneutic horizon" for the apostle. It is from that horizon that Paul is able to recognize, and criticize, a tendency at work already among the non-Jewish Christ-followers that are his target in the letter. For that reason, I was surprised that Romans did not play a more significant role in Jennings's work.

In Jennings's last chapter, by contrast, the hermeneutic horizon seems to have closed inward on the establishment, after Easter and at Pentecost, of a multi-ethnic communion of Jews and Gentiles. That horizon, I contend, would not have been nearly enough from the apostle's vantage-point. Here, *the life of Jesus and the formation of the church of Jews and Gentiles,* as narrated in other parts of the New Testament, appear to have set the limits for what "Israel's fortunes," and the fortunes of "the nations," can mean.

Jennings has clearly avoided the danger of minimizing Jesus' connection to Israel, but has he avoided collapsing "Israel's life into Jesus" (and the church of Jews and Gentiles)? When he claims, at the beginning of his last chapter, that "Christianity itself offers hope of [the] joining [of space and peoples]," and that the "spatial and racial unmaking of modern peoples" is "the remaking that should be the constitution of Christian people,"[38] we

---

37. Jennings, *Christian Imagination*, 267.
38. Jennings, *Christian Imagination*, 250.

may wonder whether he has escaped the problematic he has so clearly put before our eyes.

The risk, I think, is that an idealized picture of Christianity is allowed to serve here as hermeneutic horizon for what Israel's story is allowed to mean. As Nielsen suggests in her critique, asserting that Israel's story is summed up, recapitulated, finds its full meaning in the life (and death and resurrection) of Jesus and the establishment of the church of Acts is a premature *foreshortening* of Israel's story. Indeed, it is an apocopation of time itself. It releases the tension present in Paul's fervent expectation in Romans. It constricts the limits of the possible to an indefinite extension of what has already appeared.

There is another way.

A *MARXIST*-THEOLOGICAL CHALLENGE

At one point, Jennings aptly calls us to address the *"racial unconscious* that continues to shape Christian readings of biblical Israel and Christian interaction with living Israel."[39] He plays here on the phrase *political unconscious* developed by Marxist theorist Fredric Jameson, though he prefers not to follow Jameson's project onto the landscape of class struggle, but to "draw it toward a different, uninterrupted narrative, of God with Israel."[40]

But this is not just to "draw" Jameson in a different direction. It is to flout Jameson's central argument, which is that "political interpretation" is "the absolute horizon of all reading and all interpretation." It follows inevitably for Jameson that "the convenient working distinction between cultural texts that are social and political and those that are not"—say, in this particular case, texts that are presumed to be primarily *theological*—"is something worse than an error." Such privileging of certain texts, Jameson writes, is symptomatic of the culture of late capitalism in its pervasive tendency to reduce the individual imagination to the sphere of the merely private (e.g., the "religious"). It "maims our existence as individual subjects and paralyzes our thinking about time and change just as surely as it alienates us from our speech itself."[41]

Seen from Jameson's Marxist standpoint, it would seem that the theological risk involved in Jennings's project is not simply one of "collapsing Israel into Jesus," but of collapsing *human history* into a neatly packaged Christian story of Israel, which has already found its fulfillment in the story

39. Jennings, *Christian Imagination*, 252 (emphasis added).
40. Jennings, *Christian Imagination*, 342 n. 14, citing Jameson, *Political Unconscious*.
41. Jameson, *Political Unconscious*, 17, 20.

of Jesus-and-the-church. Of course, this has proven to be a risk endemic in Christianity as such, not solely in Jennings's complex and nuanced work!

From Jameson's Marxist standpoint, however, history can only be rightly understood on the premise that "the human adventure is one." Only thus, Jameson writes,

> can we glimpse the vital claims upon us of . . . long-dead issues . . . These matters can recover their original urgency for us only if they are retold within the unity of a single great collective story; only if, in however disguised and symbolic a form, they are seen as sharing a single fundamental theme—for Marxism, the collective struggle to wrest a realm of Freedom from a realm of Necessity; only if they are grasped as vital episodes in a single vast unfinished plot.[42]

I invoke Jameson and Marxism to suggest a sweeping, programmatic generalization about Christian origins—with the possible exception of the apostle Paul. What has been forgotten, what has been suppressed into the "political unconscious" of the Christian imagination—almost from the beginning—is precisely *the failure of the messianic age to appear* in the lifetime of Jesus' contemporaries (or, of course, thereafter).[43] Of course, that memory has *not* been suppressed in Judaism—which is what makes Israel's story so dangerous to the Christian imagination, and the necessity of managing that story so urgent for it.

In her 1988 work *From Jesus to Christ*, Paula Fredriksen has done our discipline(s) a great good by describing, with admirable clarity and lucidity, the "dynamics of expectation and disappointment" that produced early Christianity and its literary expressions, the writings of the New Testament.[44] I will not attempt to summarize her superb work here, but presume it for my argument. Suffice it to observe with her that the accounts provided by the canonical Gospels, in particular, are determined, not so much by a simple impulse of reminiscence as by the need to explain (away) facts that seem to contravene faith *in Jesus*. Those facts include:

42. Jameson, *Political Unconscious*, 19–20.

43. I posit the apostle as a *possible* exception because his rhetoric in Romans, as invoked above, allows us to imagine that he sees "Israel-as-hermeneutic-horizon" to overlap with *human history and all of creation* as hermeneutic horizon. To play on Jameson's terms, I suggest that in the apostle Paul we are more in touch with the "political unconscious" of early Christianity than anywhere else in early Christian literature, a theme I have developed elsewhere. I pursue this suggestion in the epilogue to Elliott, *Arrogance of Nations*.

44. Fredriksen, *From Jesus to Christ*.

- the death of the presumptive Messiah;

- the destruction, by an aspiring world empire, of the presumptive Messiah's presumptive capital city and of its Temple;

- the continued subjugation by that empire of the Messiah's own people, among others;

- the demographic shift, through the earliest decades, in the company of the crucified Messiah's followers to include fewer of his own people and more and more ethnic outsiders; and

- the dismal continuation of history more or less as before.

As Fredriksen concisely put the last developments: "too many gentiles, too few Jews, and no end in sight."[45]

These observations, which Fredriksen elaborates, suggest that describing the supersessionism that quickly became normative in Christian tradition[46] as a merely *religious*, or *racial*, or *ethnic* dynamic is not enough. Christian supersessionism, from the beginning and no less as it has developed in the modern period (as Jennings so penetratingly shows!), must be understood as well—I would argue, *primarily*—in *material* terms. That is, the "erasure" and "displacement" of Israel that Jennings ably describes also involves the effacement of the temporal horizon of Israel's hopes—which, on Israel's telling, included the fulfillment of human history, including the satisfaction of hunger and want—in what many in the first century expected as the coming rule of the Messiah.[47]

Christian supersessionism today is also a supersession of the material. It overlaps with class power and presumption, with conquest and exploitation and colonization, because it has from the beginning been about minimizing material realities—from the beginning, the disconfirming facts named above; today, the staggering economic inequality that imperils the majority of the world's population—as negligible. Today, the dominant form of Christian supersessionism is not *racial* animosity alone, but a racialized logic of social expendability that tends to immunize the individual conscience from what Göran Therborn has called "the killing

---

45. Fredriksen, *From Jesus to Christ*, 169.

46. Jennings describes the array of contemporary explorations into the origins of Christian supersessionism: *Christian Imagination*, 341 n. 12.

47. Fredriksen summarizes the general atmosphere of Jewish expectation, "restoration eschatology," which could involve myriad variations in detail (Fredriksen, *From Jesus to Christ*, ch. 5 and passim), and describes the progressive relaxation of that expectation in the Christian movement(s).

fields of inequality."[48] This supersession of material reality understands history to reach its consummation in the appropriate disposition of power and privilege that discriminates worthy from unworthy. In the perspective of the self-satisfied, nothing is to be expected from the future, then, but the further unfolding of this centrifugal dynamic. Religion, race, and ethnicity are particularly effective channels of this supersessionism, but they do not exhaust its effects.[49]

"Actually existing" Christian eschatology, of the sort so prevalent in the United States (and elsewhere), fails to put a dent in this ideological formation. Rather, it normally sees the future as the intensification and confirmation of contemporary power relations (nationally, racially, culturally, and of course in material terms).[50]

My purpose here is not to contest Jennings's central argument but perhaps to draw an even more direct connection between early Christianity and the later patterns of racial, cultural, *and material* displacement that he describes. Early Christianity became a distinct social, intellectual, and cultural formation by suppressing awareness precisely of the *unfulfilled* nature of Israel's hopes—and caricaturing these as Judaism's misconceived and self-centered materialism (cf. Jennings's language of "world dominance," "hegemony"). That dynamic shaped the Gospels.

Jennings's own project would seem to require sustained critical attention to this distortion in the Christian imagination *of time,* the collapse of history itself into the self-confirming account that sees the first century as its climactic center. In my view, however, Jennings does not give this distortion sufficient attention. Instead, he writes at one point that one of the great challenges facing Christians today is "how to imagine their space. *It has been much easier for Christians to imagine their time and live in their time."* He continues,

> At a very basic level, the vast majority of Christians would agree that they live between the ascension of Jesus the Christ and his second coming, the *parousia.* Most Christians can grasp this Christ-shaped time, even if they never speak of it in formal

---

48. Therborn, *Killing Fields of Inequality.*

49. I am guided here by Ivan Petrella's *Beyond Liberation Theology.*

50. So, for example, Canadian journalist and activist Naomi Klein makes the trenchant observation about the extreme religious conservatism of the new U.S. Supreme Court: "They aren't worried about the world burning because they think we are in the End Times and that their faith will protect them (and failing that, that their wealth and their guns will, which is the way Republicans enact the Rapture without divine intervention)." Klein, "Supreme Court's Shock-and-Awe Judicial Coup."

language or understand the implications of such a vision of time for how they should live.[51]

This broad statement seems to me over-generous. Isn't the history that Jennings so powerfully evokes, of Christians failing to understand their *place* and to share *space* with their planetary neighbors, also a matter precisely of their failing to understand themselves as inhabiting *time* with others, in what Jameson calls the "vast unfinished plot" of human history? Isn't the very vagueness that Jennings describes—the indefinite and almost inarticulate affirmations Christians routinely make that oh, yes, there's *something* still to be awaited in history, isn't there?—evidence that Christianity as we know it *suppresses* awareness of our shared participation, with all other human beings, in that story?

More often—in the historical episodes that Jennings recounts, and in our own day—the affirmation that "Christ will come again" seems to serve emotionally, libidinally, to *foreshorten* that "vast unfinished plot," to suppress the urgency of its very indeterminateness, and to identify the affirmers as among the elect, who can continue to live as though history's conclusion—and their vindication—has been predetermined.

To a significant extent, the Christian supersession *of material reality* that I am describing maps well onto the ideological contours of neoliberal capitalism today.[52] What is the de facto theology of the West but the doxological exclamation that "by the grace of God, we won the Cold War"[53]—so that "there is no alternative" anymore to capitalism? What is that naïve neoliberal assertion of living "at the end of history" but what biblical scholars call "realized eschatology"?[54] When Marxists quip that "it is easier to imagine the end of the world than the end of capitalism," we may wonder to just what ideological service Christian eschatology has so effectively been put.[55]

THE COLONIZATION OF
THE MESSIANIC IMAGINATION IN EPHESIANS

My thesis—that a supersession of material reality was built into the rise of Christianity as a distinct religious formation, and thus was not a later

51. Jennings, *Christian Imagination*, 339 n. 1 (emphasis added).

52. So Kotsko, *Neoliberalism's Demons*. I explore these issues further in Elliott, *Bodies of Christ* (in preparation).

53. George H. W. Bush's State of the Union address, January 28, 1992.

54. Fukuyama, *End of History and the Last Man*.

55. Mark Fisher attributes the line to both Fredric Jameson and Slavoj Žižek: Fisher, *Capitalist Realism*, ch. 1.

mutation from it—is intended to amplify the force of Jennings's argument (and to sharpen the contrast with McDermott's misunderstanding of it). But to develop this point, I must take issue with one more aspect of Jennings's work.

He and I both propose to find a countervailing formation (if not the antidote) to the diseased, distorted, supersessionistic Gentile-Christian imagination in the theological vision of the apostle Paul. But while I have invoked that vision as Paul evokes it in Romans (see above), Jennings relies on the Epistle to the Ephesians, which he regards as genuine.[56] I think this is a mistake, and want here to explain why.

Jennings is aware of critical disputes of the Epistle's authorship, but declares that for his concerns, this is "not the crucial matter"; he is content that even when Paul's authorship is disputed, scholars often agree "that this letter reflects *the outgrowth of Paul's insights* and may even be, if indeed Pauline, written by a *mature* Paul *in whom these insights grew* through years of life in and between Jewish and Christian communities." What matters, for Jennings, is how Ephesians aptly "captures the Gentile situation."[57]

My concern here goes beyond quibbling over exegetical or historical-critical details regarding the authorship of Ephesians. It has to do with the general representation of the apostle Paul's theology.

An older, theologically driven appropriation of Paul persists, especially in Protestantism. Here, the apostle and his gospel of salvation for all who believe in Christ are posed over against a caricatured picture of Judaism as a bastion of ethnic privilege. It is a curiosity—as evangelical scholar Clinton E. Arnold puts it, "rather ironic"—that even as critical scholars have debated the authenticity of Ephesians, the Epistle is widely hailed as the "crown" of Pauline universalism, understood in this way.[58] Indeed, in his John Rylands lecture of 2016, Arthur S. Peake described the "quintessence of Paulinism" in just these terms. It was a "universal religion," Peake declared, achieved when, "with the abolition of the Law the great barrier between Jew and Gentile has been broken down."[59]

56. Jennings refers to it as "his letter addressed to the Gentile church at Ephesus" (*Christian Imagination,* 271).

57. Jennings, *Christian Imagination,* 350 n. 61; emphases added.

58. Arnold, "Ephesians," 240a.

59. Peake, "Quintessence of Paulinism," 310. F. F. Bruce later made the equation more explicit, referring to "that 'quintessence of Paulinism' which we call the Epistle to the Ephesians" ("Some Thoughts on Paul and Paulinism," 14). It is noteworthy in this respect that one session of the Disputed Paulines Group at the 2022 SBL Annual Meeting was dedicated to readings *of* Ephesians as "a word of hope for the climate of racial tensions today" (program session S19–121).

It bears emphasis that these putative achievements are named *in Ephesians, and nowhere else in the Pauline corpus.* Peake evidently accepted Ephesians as genuine, as does Arnold today. But, as Jennings suggests, the question of authenticity is rather moot for a significant sector of scholarship today (to say nothing of church life apart from scholarly circles), since *many scholars regard the theology of Ephesians as so congruent with Paul's own as to be an acceptable summary of it*—whether Paul himself wrote it, later in his life, when he was more "mature" (!), or another, faithful disciple had developed the "outgrowth" of Paul's "insights," to use Jennings's quite conventional phrases.

My arguments with this part of Jennings's presentation, built as it is in part on Ephesians, are as follows.

Christ's Impossible Achievements

The "achievements" named in Eph 2:14–15—that Christ has "broken down the dividing wall" separating Jews and non-Jews (NRSV: τὸ μεσότοιχον τοῦ φραγμοῦ λύσας, Eph 2:14), specifically, by "abolish[ing] the law with its commandments and ordinances" (τὸν νόμον τῶν ἐντολῶν ἐν δόγμασι καταργήσας, 2:15)—would have been impossible for Paul.

The declaration that the Torah had been *abolished* should certainly have surprised the author of Rom 3:31, who used the same verb in a contradictory assertion: "Do we then overthrow [καταργοῦμεν] the law by this faith? By no means! On the contrary, we uphold the law." Indeed, Paul could have been spared much of his effort in Romans if he had only realized that "Christ has abolished the law"! More conservative scholarship provides a thicket of exegetical or theological suggestions to soften the contradiction, but Arnold rightly rejects these. However, his equanimity is astonishing when he declares that the "Paul" of Ephesians really does mean that "the law in its entirety has been abolished insofar as it functions as the basis of the covenant relationship between God as his people."[60] Arnold is concerned to remind his readers (presumably conservative contemporary Christians) that the Torah continues to have some moral value, but the starkly supersessionist implications of that statement trouble his exposition not at all.

As for the "dividing wall" that Ephesians declares Christ has "broken down," the metaphor of the Torah serving as a protective "hedge" or "fence" around Israel was not unusual in Jewish sources (so m. Avot 1:1). The *Letter of Aristeas* describes this prophylactic function in terms of "unbroken

60. Arnold, *Ephesians,* 162b. I engage with Arnold's work in particular because it represents a thoughtful recent expression of traditional premises.

palisades and iron walls" *separating* Jews from non-Jews to keep them pure from "false beliefs" and idolatry (139–42).[61] The metaphor in Ephesians, however, is a dividing wall of separation, μεσότοιχον, that has been torn down, λύσας.

The most plausible reference of the term is to the *soreg*, the barricade separating the Court of (Jewish) Women from the Court of the Nations in the Temple precincts. Of course, the *soreg* had *not* been "torn down" in Paul's day, which one might think would make the metaphor difficult for those who consider Ephesians genuine. Here again, Arnold exemplifies the effort to undergird the conservative viewpoint with some semblance of historical argument. He thinks the apostle Paul would naturally have had this barrier in mind, since "he was falsely accused of taking a Gentile into the inner courts of the temple" (that is, in Acts 21:28–29, which Arnold accepts as historical), and since that accusation was the basis for his arrest and (on his reconstruction) current imprisonment, its function would have been fresh in his mind as he wrote Ephesians.[62] Arnold also suggests that Paul's non-Jewish readers in Asia Minor would have recognized his metaphor because they likely had heard of the *soreg* from their Jewish neighbors recounting their pilgrimages to Jerusalem.[63] The obvious problem—that declaring the *soreg* "torn down" by Christ might constitute an implicit retroactive admission of Paul's *guilt* to the charge of having breached a holy barrier, in opposition to the narrative of Acts (and in contrast to Paul's protest of respect for the Temple worship in Rom 9:4)—does not arise in Arnold's imaginative reconstruction.

I suggest it is far more likely that these declarations come from an author writing well after Paul's death, lacking Paul's Jewish sensibilities regarding the sanctity of the Temple (and unaware of the problems generated by the narrative in Acts 21), but happy enough to exploit the metaphor of the removal of the *soreg*—along with the destruction of most of the Temple's structures—in the recent war (66–70 CE), which *was* undoubtedly well known, indeed, was proclaimed as a Roman achievement, throughout the provinces.[64]

---

61. Arnold provides the citations (Arnold, *Ephesians*, 162b).

62. Arnold, *Ephesians*, 159–60.

63. Arnold, *Ephesians*, 162.

64. See Overman, *First Revolt and Flavian Politics*.

The Impossibility of Gentile Ethnicity

The alleged achievement of making "one entity" or "one humanity" (ἕνα καίνον ἄνθρωπον, 2:15 NRSV) out of two (ὁ ποιήσας τὰ ἀμφότερα ἕν, Eph 2:14a), meaning Jews and Gentiles, is inconsistent with Paul's thought and, in the ancient context, nonsensical.

Paul insisted in Romans on an eschatological scenario, which he grounded in scripture, in which Israel *and the many nations* would together turn to worship the true God. He does not envision Israel and the nations as "two," or imagine that they would become fused into a single ethnicity, or that the differences between them would be erased. Quite the contrary: the admonitions in Romans 14 make little sense if the laws of *kashrut* were abolished and Jews and non-Jews had become "one." Similarly, the argumentation in Galatians makes little sense if Paul does not wish his non-Jewish readers to continue their status in Christ precisely *as non-Jews*, distinct from Israel.[65]

The rhetoric of making "one humanity out of two" (2:14, 15) implies that there are two ethnicities in play, Jewish and "Gentile." Jennings presumes this, but takes the implication in a novel direction, arguing that Ephesians "radically undermined any distinction Gentiles held for themselves vis-à-vis other peoples. It is the ultimate deconstructive statement regarding Gentile ethnocentrism."[66] But however appealing this rhetoric may be to some today, it makes no sense historically.

There was no such ethnicity as "Gentile"; no one in Paul's world thought of themselves as "a Gentile." Paul consistently, reasonably, and alongside the Septuagint and other Hellenistic Jewish writings uses τὰ ἔθνη to mean "the nations," meaning "the nations *other than Israel.*" The NRSV does well to translate the word in that way at Rom 4:17–18. But the capitalized term *Gentile*—as with other ethnicities or nationalities—is an unfortunate and misleading convention, implying a proud people from a land called Gentilia. This usage is an "indefensible anachronism."[67] It follows that the category "Gentile ethnocentrism" is, strictly speaking, meaningless.

---

65. See, again, the arguments in Kahl, *Galatians Re-imagined.*

66. Jennings, *Christian Imagination,* 271.

67. So Esler, *Conflict and Identity in Romans,* 12; 75; 113. See also Stanley, "'Neither Jew nor Greek'"; LaGrand, "Proliferation of the 'Gentile'"; Elliott, *Arrogance of Nations,* 190 nn. 130, 131. This is not to deny that Paul's practice of referring to addressees as ἔθνη marked already a transition in the meaning of the term, a shift toward "privatiz[ing] this corporate body by using *ethnē* to denote individual *goyim*"—though still *in the plural*—as Ishay Rosen-Zvi and Adi Ophir observe ("Paul and the Invention of the Gentiles," 14). They note that Paul was completely uninterested in (so to speak) the *ethnicity(ies)* of the *ethnē* he addressed: "his generalized and privatized appeal to

To be sure, *in Romans, Paul* protested an incipient boast against Israel on the part of non-Jews. But this (as I and others have argued) was a matter of his non-Jewish readers being tempted to accept the *Roman imperial construal of ethnic worth* according to a hierarchy of peoples, and in particular the Roman estimation of *Jews* as a vanquished people, at or near the bottom of that hierarchy.[68] Nothing like *"Gentile* ethnocentrism" was in play in the context Paul addressed.

The Creation of "Gentile-Christian" Identity

That same Roman imperial construal of the worth of subject peoples is at work in Ephesians, I argue, but not in the way Paul engaged it. Rather, the author of Ephesians is doing what Paul could not have done—what Paul in fact *resisted*: forming a community on the basis of the erasure of Jewish distinctiveness.

Precisely what held Jewish identity together, God's gift of the Torah, has here been abrogated "by Christ." Note that the letter is addressed, consistently and throughout, to non-Jews; there is no indication that actual Jews are on the landscape of the letter at all. (Compare this fact to the warm greetings Paul sends to believers with Jewish names in Romans 16; compare it, too, with the report in Acts 18:9–10 that Paul began his months-long mission in Ephesus *in the synagogue*.) It seems that neither Paul nor any of his συγγενεῖς are available to object.

Interpreters wrestle with the alternation of pronouns, "we" and "you," in Ephesians. Are "we" Paul-and-his-companions; Paul-and-other-Jews; Paul-and-others-in-Christ, including the non-Jewish readers? The question is poorly framed if it is taken literally (as it must be when Ephesians is considered authentic). Rather, the pronouns inhere in a pseudepigraphic device: "we" are the *pseudonymous* Paul and his Jewish-Christian cohort—all long dead, in reality, and thus easily collapsed, in the artificial rhetoric of pseudonymity, into a cohesive, manageable Christian identity that retains no meaningful trace of Jewish distinctiveness *in the epistolary present.*

This singular Christian identity-without-distinction is the only "mystery" Ephesians recognizes (3:3–5). Again, the actual apostle would have

---

the *ethnē* erases ethnic distinction between the different groups that he is approaching" (15). They are, for him, all simply *other than Israel*: non-Jews. Still, Rosen-Zvi and Ophir note that Paul was forced to use a different term, like "the Greek," to designate an individual non-Jew, since the Greek ἔθνος simply could not serve that purpose—as the English "Gentile" readily does.

68. Elliott, *Arrogance of Nations.*

been spared time and anguish wrestling over what *he* considered a divine mystery, the inscrutable development that *Israel had been hardened,* however temporarily, even as non-Jews had become part of the Christ-honoring community (Rom 11:25). Ephesians doesn't worry about such matters, I believe, because there are no actual Jews within the rhetorical circle of its "church."

Through the device of the pseudepigraphic Paul, the author of Ephesians congratulates non-Jews for having been "brought near," and more: he assures them they are "no longer aliens or foreign visitors [ξένοι καὶ πάροικοι]; you are fellow-citizens [συμπολῖται] with the holy people of God and part of God's household" (Eph 2:19). Not guests, then (as Jennings repeatedly pleads), but full equals, part of the family. It is *as Gentiles* (τὰ ἔθνη)—here the translation "the nations" is no longer attractive, since it is only *non-Jewish members of the church* who are in view—that these have become full and equal co-inheritors, sharers in the same body, and co-recipients of the same promise (συγκληρονόμα καὶ σύσσωμα καὶ συμμέτοχα, Eph 2:6).

The Disappearance of Israel's World

Note that not a word is said *to Jewish members of the church* regarding their status in this new single humanity. Jews are referred to, obliquely, as "those who speak of themselves as the circumcised," who *in the past* referred to the Epistle's readers as "the uncircumcised" (Eph 2:11). But *Jews as such,* within or outside the church, do not appear as actual inhabitants of the rhetorical landscape; they cannot, in Jennings's terms, serve as "hosts" for Gentile guests. "Paul" and his Jewish cohort, of course, qualify as Jews—but within the pseudonymous world of the Epistle, as figures of the past, about which the readers "have surely heard" (Eph 3:2) and whose letters they surely know (3:3–4). Otherwise, the presence of living, breathing Jews in the readers' environment is not imagined.

Neither is any account of their actual absence provided. So—*where did the Jews go?* Did they—according to the logic of the Epistle—simply stop observing the Torah, did they stop thinking of themselves as Jewish? Did their number dwindle from the Ephesian church (or the churches of Asia Minor, on the postulate of a "circular" letter); did they withdraw, move away, over time? I am not asking a *historical* question here, but a question about the world projected by the Epistle's rhetoric. Considering that on the account in Acts, the Ephesian church began *in the synagogue,* we might expect *some* reference to Gentile-Jewish interaction: but we hear nothing of it in the Epistle.

The readers are invited, not to imagine themselves *in Israel's space* (as Jennings's language might suggest), but to understand themselves "brought near" (ἐγγὺς ἐγενήθητε, 2:13)—*to what* or *to whom* remaining unspecified. The space they inhabit is the church, a "holy temple in the Lord" (ναὸν ἅγιον ἐν Κυρίῳ, 2:21). The relationship of the community-as-temple to the Jerusalem Temple does not occur to the author as a topic; the replacement of the latter by the former would have been impossible, of course, for Paul, for whom Israel's λατρεία remained one of its sacred privileges (Rom 9:1–4).

The readers of Ephesians are also told that they occupy "the heavenly places" (ἐν τοῖς ἐπουρανίοις, 2:6), to which they have been "raised with [Christ]." This language, routinely contrasted with Paul's consistent use of the future tense (Rom 8:11; 1 Cor 6:14; etc.), is not just a marker of a shift in eschatological theory, as some wish to imagine on the part of a "mature" apostle. With W. G. Kümmel, I consider such a radical shift in theology "completely impossible."[69] But the over-realized eschatology (if it can still be called that) of the Epistle marks *a collapse of Israel's time as well.* The resurrection of the dead, or of the righteous, the vindication of God's long-suffering people before the nations—none of this remains outstanding for the author of Ephesians.

Ephesians as an Engine of Supersession

One implication of this collapse of eschatology is that there is nothing in particular to await from a climactic future (such as Israel clearly expected). On the terms set out in Ephesians, "we" Gentile Christians already experience all the benefits God has in store for us in Christ; indeed, this is all God has purposed for the human race "from the foundation of the world" (1:3). It follows that current social inequities are not problems awaiting the intervention of a just God—or, for that matter, agitating the Christian conscience.

The subordination of women, of children, of slaves is simply part of the "home economics" of the "household of God" (5:21—6:9). No change in social relationships is anticipated, so long as warm fellow-feeling and sexual modesty prevail in the church (ch. 4). Here Gerd Theissen's language of "love patriarchalism" in the Pauline communities is certainly apt, *for Ephesians.*[70] The climactic placement of the admonition to slaves to "obey your earthly masters with fear and trembling"—out of obedience to Christ,

69. Kümmel, *Introduction to the New Testament,* 360.

70. Theissen, *Social Setting of Pauline Christianity.* Whether the phrase applies elsewhere remains debated.

"doing the will of God from the heart" (6:5–8)—may not be incidental, but the goal of the whole passage. Indeed, Ann Holmes Redding has argued that the fulsome rhetoric of unity and reconciliation in the first part of the letter may have had as its only purpose providing a basis for putting slaves firmly in their place within the Christian household.[71]

It is not difficult to imagine a historical context for the invention of a device like Ephesians. The letters of Paul are already windows onto the flux of ethnic identities, inflected by imperial power and ideology, that pertained in the first century. Historian Greg Woolf has described the larger context under the Principate as one in which provincials could aspire to "becoming Roman, staying Greek"[72]—that is, retaining one's kinship network while navigating the cultural intricacies of the Roman colony. We know that Roman perceptions of the Jews were mixed, including genuine admiration (episodically, within the circles of Roman Senators' wives and the imperial household as well), tactical alliance and formal approval (under Augustus), as well as suspicion and antagonism (on the part of imperial advisors in the courts of Tiberius and, later, Nero).[73] We know that Jewish identity was prestigious enough in some circumstances that *non-Jews* imagined, and even tried to fabricate, Jewish heritage for themselves.[74] Concern by some anxious Galatians to find shelter in the relatively higher status of the Jewish community was part of the broader atmosphere in which Galatians was written.[75]

Various scholars have observed that Ephesians is well known to Christians in the late first and early second century (Ignatius, Polycarp, Marcion). For some, that is evidence that Ephesians belongs to that post-Pauline milieu; for others, only that a genuine Pauline letter impressed and "influenced" the theology and vocabulary of later Christians. I consider it especially relevant that for Ignatius and Marcion, the notion of *Jewish Christians* was oxymoronic: *Ioudaismos* and "Judaizing" were incompatible with receiving Christ's grace (Ignatius, *To the Magnesians* 8.1). For Ephesians, similarly, there is simply no place for belonging to the "new humanity" in Christ and still

71. Redding, "Together, Not Equal."

72. Woolf, "Becoming Roman, Staying Greek."

73. See the voluminous records collected in Stern, *Greek and Latin Authors on Jews and Judaism* (3 vols.).

74. L. L. Welborn discusses the example of a Roman magistrate who sought to establish a genealogical link of his family with that of Herod—including an imagined ancient connection between Judeans and Spartans, another prestigious ancestry—en route to ingratiating himself into Gaius's court: Welborn, *End to Enmity*, 288–335.

75. Again, as argued by Kahl, *Galatians Re-imagined.*

observing "the law with its commandments and ordinances"—which has been abolished precisely *by Christ.*

I do not mean to argue here for a particular date for Ephesians; only that it is later than Paul, and closer in social world to the figures and texts just named. I mean to draw attention to what seems the very clear, intentional, and thoroughly peculiar *fabrication* of a "Gentile-Christian" identity in Ephesians that was impossible for Paul himself. That Gentile-Christian identity is constructed as a full participation in the prestige and symbolic legacy of Israel, meaning the approval of Israel's God—without actual Israelites cluttering the scene. The *pseudepigraphic* Paul who writes here is no exception: his own Jewishness is a matter more of posthumous reputation ("you have heard of me") than of the apostle's own conviction. He serves as an honorary "good Jew," appearing on stage just long enough to hand off Israel's privileges to the new Torah-free community in Christ.

Historically, we can readily imagine circles of educated, aspiring, non-Jewish provincials intrigued, attracted, by the prestige of Judaism—and aware, after 70, that actually being Jewish was a liability in the Roman world.[76] That prestige, the symbolic treasure of the "household of God," was in the eyes of some—in the eyes of the author of Ephesians, I propose—a symbolic treasure ripe for the taking, so much unclaimed booty, like the actual empty houses of refugees, in Judea and throughout the Diaspora, standing ready in the wake of the Judean War to be occupied by others.

We are probably dealing with one of the "well-educated, formerly pagan intellectuals" whom Paula Fredriksen and Oded Irshai describe as the fountainheads of Gentile Christianity in the early second century. "In articulating their respective commitments to Christian revelation," they write, "these men necessarily had to make sense of the literary medium of that revelation—the Septuagint and the burgeoning body of specifically Christian writings (gospels, apocalypses, pseudepigraphic epistles)—in light of their shared rhetorical and philosophical culture, *paideia.*" In different ways, these intellectuals repudiated the *Jews'* use of their own scriptures as inappropriate, misguided, or malevolent, and thus "the momentous interpretive struggle between these Gentile contestants over the construction of Christianity created the context within which the rhetoric and ideology of classical Christian anti-Judaism took shape."[77] We may imagine the author of Ephe-

76. On the aftermath of the Roman War and the toll on Jewish populations throughout the Roman world, see Schürer, *History of the Jewish People in the Age of Jesus Christ,* 1:484–557.

77. Fredriksen and Irshai, "Christian Anti-Judaism," 978. Similarly, Maia Kotrosits compares Ephesians with the Gospel of Truth, Kotrosits, *Rethinking Early Christian Identity,* 188–89.

sians as one of these Gentile-Christian intellectuals—but at a slightly earlier point, logically and probably historically, when it was possible to *enter* the symbolic space of Israel's scriptures, to imagine *taking place alongside Israel, without having either to negotiate that imaginary occupation with actual Jewish partners, or (as the later *anti*-Jewish tradition did) to formulate a rationale for Israel's *dislocation.*

I conclude that Ephesians is precisely an instantiation of the process Jennings describes as beginning *later*: that is, of identity-in-Christ being formed precisely by the *evacuation* of Israel from the "people of God," and their *replacement* by "Gentile Christians." The new "one humanity" that Ephesians celebrates is inhabited precisely by "Gentiles," on principles drawn—anachronistically and in contradiction to his own purposes—from the language of Paul's letters, but now with the distinctives of Jewish identity calmly swept away. "Gentile Christianity" comes here to mean what it will mean for centuries: "full participation in the benefits of Israel's heritage, free of involvement with actual Jews."

I propose, then, that Ephesians is *not* the solution to the theological and moral catastrophe that Jennings so ably describes in *The Christian Imagination,* but a key moment in its development, something like a "patient zero" in the appearance of the epidemic of Christian supersessionism. The "hermeneutic horizon" of Israel has disappeared here. What remains of Israel's legacy in Ephesians is a repertoire of claims to prestige and divine approval (the fulsome language of chs. 1–3), but torn free from any connection to Jewish kinship or land. That prestige and divine approval are enjoyed in the here-and-now, without fear of any upheaval of social circumstances.

Ephesians offers a *material* as well as a *racial* supersession: it is one fountainhead, perhaps the earliest clear example, of the flood of displacement and subjugation that continues to flow through our world.[78] Resisting the currents of that flood requires a clear-eyed recognition of its origins, and toward that end I offer this friendly amendment to Professor Jennings's important work.

---

78. I acknowledge that I have written this essay while living on land first inhabited by the ancestral Pueblo, who have never ceded it—to Spanish, Mexican, or American conquerors, or even to the horde of retired Anglo migrants like myself.

Bibliography

Ábel, František, ed. *The Message of Paul the Apostle within Second Temple Judaism*. Lanham, MD: Lexington Books/Fortress Academic, 2019.

Achcar, Gilbert. *The Clash of Barbarisms: The Making of the New World Disorder*. New York: Routledge, 2006.

Ackerman, Spencer. "What the Rules Allow." Forever Wars. *Nation*, Dec. 11–18, 2023.

Acosta, José de. *De Procuranda Indorum Salute (Predicación del Evangélio en las Indias)*. Madrid: n.p., 1952.

———. *De procuranda Indorum salute*. Translated and edited by G. Stewart McIntosh. Tayport, Scotland: Mac Research, 1996.

———. *Natural and Moral History of the Indies*. Edited by Jane E. Mangan. With an introduction and commentary by Walter Mignolo. Translated by Frances López-Morillas. Chronicles of the New World Order. Durham: Duke University Press, 2002.

The Advocates for Human Rights. *Another Violence against Women: The Lack of Accountability in Haiti*. Minneapolis, Jan. 2, 1995. Executive summary online at https://www.theadvocatesforhumanrights.org/Publications/A/Index?id=49/.

Agamben, Giorgio. Homo Sacer: *Sovereign Power and Bare Life*. Translated by Daniel Heller-Roazen. Meridian: Crossing Aesthetics. Stanford: Stanford University Press, 1998.

———. *The Time That Remains: A Commentary on the Letter to the Romans*. Translated by Patricia Dailey. Meridian: Crossing Aesthetics. Stanford: Stanford University Press, 2005.

Ahmad, Aijaz. *In Theory, Classes: Nations, Literatures*. London: Verso, 1994.

Alcock, Susan E. *Graecia Capta: The Landscapes of Roman Greece*. Cambridge: Cambridge University Press, 1993.

Aristide, Jean-Bertrand. *Eyes of the Heart: Seeking a Path for the Poor in the Age of Globalization*. Edited by Laura Flynn. Monroe, ME: Common Courage Press, 2000.

Arnold, Clinton E. *Ephesians*. Zondervan Exegetical Commentary on the New Testament 10. Grand Rapids: Zondervan, 2010.

———. "Ephesians, Letter to the." In *Dictionary of Paul and His Letters*, edited by Gerald F. Hawthorne et al., 240–42. Downers Grove, IL: InterVarsity, 1993.

Asad, Talal. *Genealogies of Religion: Discipline and Reasons of Power in Christianity and Islam*. Baltimore: Johns Hopkins University Press, 1993.

Ashcroft, Bill, et al. *The Empire Writes Back: Theory and Practice in Post-colonial Literatures*. New Accents. London: Routledge, 1998; 2nd ed., 2002.

Ashtari, Shadee. "Former Counterterrorism Czar Richard Clarke: Bush, Cheney Committed War Crimes." *Huffington Post*, May 29, 2014. https://www.huffpost.com/entry/richard-clarke-george-bush-war-crimes_n_5410619/.

Augustus. *Res Gestae divi Augusti*. In *Velleius Paterculus, Compendium of Roman History; and Res Gestae Divi Augusti*. Translated by Frederick W. Shipley. LCL. Cambridge: Harvard University Press, 1998.

Aune, David E. *The New Testament in Its Literary Environment*. Library of Early Christianity 8. Philadelphia: Westminster, 1987.

———. *The Westminster Dictionary of New Testament and Early Christian Literature and Rhetoric*. Louisville: Westminster John Knox, 2003.

Awad, Sumaya, and Annie Levin. "Roots of the Nakba: Zionist Settler Colonialism." In *Palestine: A Socialist Introduction*, edited by Sumaya Awad & brian bean, 15–38. Chicago: Haymarket, 2020.

Badiou, Alain. "The Communist Hypothesis." *New Left Review* 49 (Jan/Feb 2008) 29–42.

———. *Saint Paul: The Foundation of Universalism*. Translated by Ray Brassier. Cultural Memory in the Present. Stanford: Stanford University Press, 2003.

Balakrishnan, Gopal. "Virgilian Visions." *New Left Review* 5 (2000) 142–48.

Baldwin, Neil. *Henry Ford and the Jews: The Mass Production of Hate*. New York: Public Affairs, 2001.

Bammel, Ernst. "Ein Beitrag zur paulinischen Staatsanschauung." *Theologische Literaturzeitung* 85 (1960) 837–40.

———. "Romans 13." In *Jesus and the Politics of His Day*, edited by Ernst Bammel and C. F. D. Moule, 366–75. Cambridge: Cambridge University Press, 1984.

Bammel, Ernst, and C. F. D. Moule, eds. *Jesus and the Politics of His Day*. Cambridge: Cambridge University Press, 1984.

Barclay, John M. G. "'Do We Undermine the Law?' A Study of Romans 14:1—15:6." In *Paul and the Mosaic Law*, edited by James D. G. Dunn, 287–308. WUNT 89. Tübingen: Mohr Siebeck, 1996.

———. *Jews in the Mediterranean Diaspora: From Alexander to Trajan (332 BCE—117 CE)*. Berkeley: University of California Press, 1996.

———. "'Neither Jew nor Greek': Multiculturalism and the New Perspective on Paul." In *Ethnicity and the Bible*, edited by Mark G. Brett, 197–214. BibInt 19. Leiden: Brill, 1996.

———. *Obeying the Truth: Paul's Ethics in Galatians*. Edited by John Riches. SNTW. Edinburgh: T. & T. Clark, 1988.

———. *Pauline Churches and Diaspora Jews*. WUNT 275. Tübingen: Mohr Siebeck, 2011.

———. "Why the Roman Empire Was Insignificant to Paul." Draft of a paper given at the Annual Meeting of the Society of Biblical Literature, San Diego, CA, November 2007. Subsequently published in revised form in Barclay, *Pauline Churches and Diaspora Jews*, 363–87. WUNT 275. Tübingen: Mohr Siebeck, 2011.

Barth, Karl. *The Epistle to the Romans*. Translated from the 6th German edited by Edwyn C. Hoskyns. 2nd English ed. London: Oxford University Press, 1933.

Bartov, Omer. "'From the River to the Sea': Omer Bartov on Contested Slogan & Why Two-State Solution Is Not Viable." Interview, *Democracy Now!* November 10, 2023. https://www.democracynow.org/2023/11/10/bartov_two_state/.

Baum, Gregory. *Man Becoming: God in Secular Language*. New York: Herder & Herder, 1970.

Baur, Ferdinand Christian. *Paul the Apostle of Jesus Christ: His Life and Works, His Epistles and Teachings*. Translated by Eduard Zeller. 2 vols. Theological Translation Fund Library. ATLA Monograph Preservation Program. ATLA Historical Monographs Collection, Series 1. London: Williams & Norgate, 1873, 1876.

———. *Paul, the Apostle of Jesus Christ*. Edited by Peter C. Hodgson. Translated by Robert F. Brown. Eugene, OR: Cascade Books, 2021.

Beker, J. Christiaan. "The Faithfulness of God and the Priority of Israel in Paul's Letter to the Romans." *Harvard Theological Review* 79 (1986) 10–16.

———. *Paul the Apostle: The Triumph of God in Life and Thought*. Philadelphia: Fortress, 1980.

———. *The Triumph of God: The Essence of Paul's Thought*. Translated by Loren T. Stuckenbruck. Minneapolis: Fortress, 1990.

Bell, Caleb K. "Poll: Americans love the Bible but don't read it much." Belief. *Religion News Service*, April 4, 2013. https://religionnews.com/2013/04/04/poll-americans-love-the-bible-but-dont-read-it-much/.

Bell, Daniel M., Jr. "Badiou's Faith and Paul's Gospel." *Angelaki: Journal of the Theoretical Humanities* 12.1 (2007) 97–111.

Bellah, Robert N. *The Broken Covenant: American Civil Religion in Time of Trial*. 2nd ed. Chicago: University of Chicago Press, 1992.

Bieler, Andrea, and Luise Schottroff. *The Eucharist: Bodies, Bread, & Resurrection*. Minneapolis: Fortress, 2007.

Blanton, Ward. "Disturbing Politics: Neo-Paulinism and the Scrambling of Religious and Secular Identities." *Dialog* 46.1 (2007) 3–13.

———. "Mad with the Love of Undead Life: Understanding Paul and Žižek." In *Paul in the Grip of the Philosophers: The Apostle and Contemporary Continental Philosophy*, edited by Peter Frick, 193–216. Paul in Critical Contexts. Minneapolis: Fortress, 2013.

———. *A Materialism for the Masses: Saint Paul and the Philosophy of Undying Life*. Insurrections: Critical Studies in Religion, Politics, and Culture. New York: Columbia University Press, 2014.

Blanton, Ward, and Hent de Vries, eds. *Paul and the Philosophers*. New York: Fordham University Press, 2013.

Blass, Friedrich, et al. *A Greek Grammar of the New Testament and Other Early Christian Literature*. Chicago: University of Chicago Press, 1961.

Blumenfeld, Bruno. *The Political Paul: Justice, Democracy, and Kingship in a Hellenistic Framework*. JSNTSup 210. Shef-field: Sheffield Academic, 2001.

Boer, Roland. "Marx, Postcolonialism, and the Bible." In *Postcolonial Biblical Criticism: Interdisciplinary Intersections*, edited by Stephen D. Moore and Fernando F. Segovia, 166–83. The Bible and Postcolonialism. London: T. & T. Clark, 2005.

———. *Marxist Criticism of the Bible*. London: T. & T. Clark, 2003.

———. *Marxist Criticism of the Hebrew Bible*. 2nd ed. London: T. & T. Clark, 2015.

———, ed. *Tracking the Tribes of Yahweh: On the Trail of a Classic*. Journal for the Study of the Old Testament Supplement Series 351. London: Sheffield Academic, 2002.

———. "Twenty-Five Years of Marxist Biblical Criticism." *Currents in Biblical Research* 5 (2007) 298–321.

———. *Rescuing the Bible*. Blackwell Manifestos. Malden, MA: Blackwell, 2007.

————. "Western Marxism and the interpretation of the Hebrew Bible." *Journal for the Study of the Old Testament* 23/78 (1998) 3–21.

————. "The Zeal of G. E. M. De Ste. Croix." In *Criticism of Theology: On Marxism and Theology III*, 103–58. Historical Materialism Book Series 27. Leiden: Brill, 2011.

Boer, Roland, and Christina Petterson. *Idols of Nations: Biblical Myth at the Origins of Capitalism*. Minneapolis: Fortress, 2014.

Boers, Hendrikus. "The Problem of Jews and Gentiles in the Macrostructure of Romans." *Svensk exegetisk årsbok* 47 (1982) 184–96.

Bornkamm, Günther. *Paul*. Translated by D. M. G. Stalker. New York: Harper & Row, 1971.

Borón, Atilio A. *Empire and Imperialism: A Critical Reading of Michael Hardt and Antonio Negri*. Translated by Jessica Casiro. London: Zed Books, distributed in the USA exclusively by Palgrave Macmillan, 2005.

Boyarin, Daniel. *A Radical Jew: Paul and the Politics of Identity*. Contraversions. Berkeley: University of California Press, 1994.

Breton, Stanislas. *Saint Paul*. Philosophies 18. Paris: Presses universitaires de France, 1988.

Bruce, F. F. "Some Thoughts on Paul and Paulinism." *Vox Evangelica* 7 (1971) 5–16.

Buell, Denise Kimber, and Caroline Johnson Hodge. "The Politics of Interpretation: The Rhetoric of Race and Ethnicity in Paul." *JBL* 123 (2004) 235–51.

Bultmann, Rudolf. *Theology of the New Testament*. 2 vols. Translated by Kendrick Grobel. New York: Scribner, 1951–1955.

Bush, George H. W. State of the Union Address, January 28, 1992. Transcript at the University of Virginia Miller Center. https://millercenter.org/the-presidency/presidential-speeches/january-28-1992-state-union-address/.

Câmara, Dom Hélder. *Spiral of Violence*. London: Sheed & Ward, 1971.

Campbell, William S. *Paul's Gospel in an Intercultural Context: Jew and Gentile in the Letter to the Romans*. Studies in the Intercultural History of Christianity 69. Frankfurt: Lang, 1992.

————. "Revisiting Romans." *Scripture Bulletin* 12 (1981) 2–10.

————. *Romans: A Social Identity Commentary*. T. & T. Clark Social Identity Commentaries on the New Testament London: T. & T. Clark, 2023.

————. "The Rule of Faith in Romans 12:1—15:13: The Obligation of Humble Obedience to Christ as the Only Adequate Response to the Mercies of God." In *Pauline Theology*, Vol. 3, *Romans*, edited by David M. Hay and E. Elizabeth Johnson, 59–86. Minneapolis: Fortress, 1993.

————. "Why Did Paul Write Romans?" *Expository Times* 85 (1973/74) 264–69.

Caputo, John D., and Linda Martin Alcoff, eds. *St. Paul among the Philosophers*. Indiana Series in the Philosophy of Religion. Bloomington: Indiana University Press, 2009.

Carcopino, Jérôme. *Daily Life in Ancient Rome: The People and the City at the Height of the Empire*. Edited with bibliography and notes by Henry T. Rowell. Translated from the French by E. O. Lorimer. New Haven: Yale University Press, 1968.

Carnegie, Andrew. "The Gospel of Wealth." In *The Gospel of Wealth, and Other Timely Essays*, 1–46. New York: Century, 1901.

Carson, D. A., and Douglas J. Moo. *An Introduction to the New Testament*. 2nd ed. Grand Rapids: Zondervan, 2005.

Carter, T. L. "The Irony of Romans 13." *Novum Testamentum* 46 (2004) 209–28.

Castillo, José María. "Donde no hay justicia, no hay eucaristía." *Estudios Eclesiásticos. Revista de investigación e información teológica y canónica* 52 (1977) 555–90.

Cavanaugh, William T. *Torture and Eucharist*. Challenges in Contemporary Theology. Oxford: Blackwell, 1998.

Chakrabarty, Dipesh. "Postcoloniality and the Artifice of History: Who Speaks for 'Indian' Pasts?" *Representations* 37 (1992) 1–26.

Champlin, Edward. *Nero*. Cambridge: Belknap, 2003.

Chancey, Mark. Foreword to *Paul and Palestinian Judaism*, by E. P. Sanders, xi–xxvi. 40th anniversary ed. Minneapolis: Fortress, 2017.

Chancey, Mark, et al., eds. *The Bible in the Public Square: Its Enduring Influence in American Life*. Biblical scholarship in North America 27. Atlanta: SBL Press, 2014.

Charles, Ronald. "A Bhabhaian Reading of Paul as a Diasporic Subject of the Roman Empire." Paper presented at the Annual Meeting of the Society of Biblical Literature, New Orleans, LA, November 2009.

Chomsky, Noam. *Deterring Democracy*. Paperback ed. New York: Hill & Wang, 1994.

———. *Hegemony or Survival: America's Quest for Global Dominance*. New York: Holt, 2003; with a new afterword by the author, 2004.

Chow, John K. *Patronage and Power: A Study of Social Networks in Corinth*. JSNTSup 75. Sheffield: JSOT Press, 1992.

Clarkson, Frederick. "The Battle for the Mainline Churches." *The Public Eye Magazine*, Spring 2006, published by Political Research Associates. http://www.publiceye.org/magazine/v20n1/clarkson_battle.html/.

Codina, Víctor. "Sacraments" In Mysterium Liberationis: *Fundamental Concepts of Liberation Theology*, edited by Ignacio Ellacuría and Jon Sobrino, 653–76. Maryknoll, NY: Orbis, 1993.

Cohen, Shaye. *The Beginnings of Jewishness: Boundaries, Varieties, Uncertainties*. Berkeley: University of California Press, 1999.

Collum, Danny Duncan. "Should Christians Be Socialists?" *Sojourners*, February 2016. https://sojo.net/magazine/february-2016/economic-democracy-and-common-good/.

Commission on Faith and Order. *Baptism, Eucharist and Ministry*. Faith and Order Paper no. 111. Geneva: World Council of Churches, 1982.

———. *Baptism, Eucharist and Ministry 1982—1990: Report on the Process and Responses*. Faith and Order Paper no. 149. Geneva: World Council of Churches, 1990.

Conzelmann, Hans. *1 Corinthians: A Commentary on the First Epistle to the Corinthians*. Edited by George W. MacRae. Translated by James W. Leitch. Bibliography and references by James W. Dunkly. Hermeneia. Philadelphia: Fortress, 1975.

Correa, Luis Fernando Jaramillo. "Globalization and the World Trade Organization: Latin America at a Crossroads." In *Latin America: Its Future in the Global Economy*, edited by Patricia Gray Rich, 1–24. London: Palgrave Macmillan, 2002.

Cort, John C. *Christian Socialism: An Informal History*. Maryknoll, NY: Orbis, 1988.

Crockett, William R. *Eucharist, Symbol of Transformation*. New York: Pueblo, 1989.

Crossan, John Dominic. *The Historical Jesus: The Life of a Mediterranean Jewish Peasant*. San Francisco: HarperSanFrancisco, 1991.

Crossley James G. "Jesus the Jew since 1967." In *Jesus Beyond Nationalism*, edited by Halvor Moxnes et al., 119–37. London: Equinox, 2009.

———. *Why Christianity Happened: A Sociohistorical Account of Christian Origins (26–50 CE)*. Louisville: Westminster John Knox, 2006.

Cullmann, Oscar. *Jesus and the Revolutionaries*. Translated from the German by Gareth Putnam. New York: Harper & Row, 1970.

Danker, Frederick W. *Benefactor: Epigraphic Study of a Graeco-Roman and New Testament Semantic Field*. St. Louis: Clayton, 1992.

Danker, Frederick W., et al. *Greek-English Lexicon of the New Testament and Other Early Christian Literature*. 3rd ed. Chicago: University of Chicago Press, 2000.

Danner, Mark. *The Massacre at El Mozote: A Parable of the Cold War*. New York: Vintage, 1994.

———. *Torture and Truth: America, Abu Ghraib, and the War on Terror*. New York: New York Review Books, 2004.

Davies, W. D. *Paul and Rabbinic Judaism*. 4th ed. Philadelphia: Fortress, 1980.

Davies, W. D., and Dale C. Allison. *A Critical and Exegetical Commentary on the Gospel according to Saint Matthew*. 3 vols. International Critical Commentary. Edinburgh: T. & T. Clark, 1988–1997.

Davis, Creston. Introduction. In *Paul's New Moment: Continental Philosophy and the Future of Christian Theology*, by John Milbank et al., 1–20. Grand Rapids: Brazos, 2010.

———. "Subtractive Liturgy." In *Paul's New Moment: Continental Philosophy and the Future of Christian Theology*, by John Milbank et al., 146–68. Grand Rapids: Brazos, 2010.

Davis, Mike. *Late Victorian Holocausts: El Niño Famines and the Making of the Third World*. London: Verso, 2002.

———. *Planet of Slums*. Paperback ed. London: Verso, 2007.

Day, Richard J. F. *Gramsci Is Dead: Anarchist Currents in the Newest Social Movements*. London: Pluto, 2005.

de Ste. Croix, G. E. M. *Class Struggle in the Ancient Greek World: From the Archaic Age to the Arab Conquests*. Ithaca: Cornell University Press, 1981.

Dear, John, SJ. *The Sacrament of Civil Disobedience*. Baltimore: Fortkamp, 1994.

Deidun, Thomas. "James Dunn and John Ziesler on Romans in New Perspective." *Heythrop Journal* 33 (1992) 79–94.

Deissmann, Adolf. *Licht vom Osten: Das neuen Testament und die neuentdeckten Texte der römischen-hellenistischen Welt*. Tübingen: Mohr, 1908. 4th ed., 1923.

———. *Light from the Ancient East*. Translated by Lionel M. R. Strachan. 1910. Reprint, Eugene, OR: Wipaf & Stock, 2004.

———. *St. Paul: A Study in Social and Religious History*. Translated by Lionel R. M. Strachan. ATLA Monograph Preservation Program. ATLA Historical Monographs Collection. Series 2. New York: Hodder & Stoughton, 1912.

———. *Das Urchristentum und die unteren Schichten*. Göttingen: Vandenhoeck und Ruprecht, 1908.

Delling, Gerhard. "πλεονέκτης, κτλ." In *TDNT* 6 (1965) 266–74.

Diamond, Sara. *Roads to Dominion: Right-Wing Movements and Political Power in the United States*. Critical Perspectives. New York: Guilford, 1995.

———. *Spiritual Warfare: The Politics of the Christian Right*. Boston: South End, 1989.

Dirlik, Arif. "The Postcolonial Aura: Third World Criticism in the Age of Global Capitalism." *Critical Inquiry* 20 (1994) 328–56.

Donfried, Karl P., ed. *The Romans Debate*. Rev. and exp. ed. Peabody: Hendrickson, 1991.

Donfried, Karl P., and Peter Richardson, eds. *Judaism and Christianity in First-Century Rome*. Grand Rapids: Eerdmans, 1998.

Dorrien, Gary. *Soul in Society: The Making and Renewal of Social Christianity*. Minneapolis: Fortress, 1995.

Douglas, Mary. *Natural Symbols: Explorations in Cosmology*. London: Routledge, 1970; 2nd ed., 1998.

Dube, Musa W. *Postcolonial Feminist Interpretation of the Bible*. St. Louis: Chalice, 2000.

Duff, J. Wight, and Arnold M. Duff, trans. *Minor Latin Poets*, vol. 1. 2 vols. LCL. Cambridge: Harvard University Press, 1934.

Duff, Paul B. "Metaphor, Motif, and Meaning: The Rhetorical Strategy behind the image 'Led in Triumph' in 2 Corinthians 2:14." *CBQ* 53 (1991) 79–92.

Dunn, James D. G. *Jesus, Paul, and the Law*. London: SPCK, 1990.

———. "The New Perspective on Paul." *Bulletin of the John Rylands Library* 65 (1983) 95–122.

———, ed. *Paul and the Mosaic Law*. WUNT 89. Tübingen: Mohr Siebeck, 1996.

———. *Romans*. 2 vols. Word Biblical Commentary 38A, 38B. Dallas: Word, 1988.

———. "Romans 13:1–7: A Charter for Political Quietism?" *Ex Auditu* 2 (1986) 55–68.

———. *The Theology of Paul the Apostle*. Grand Rapids: Eerdmans, 1998.

Dupuy, Alex. *Haiti in the New World Order: The Limits of the Democratic Revolution*. Boulder, CO: Westview, 1997.

DuToit, Philip La Grange. "The Radical New Perspective on Paul, Messianic Judaism, and Their Connection to Christian Zionism." *HTS Teologiese Studies/Theological Studies* 73.3 (2017) 1–8.

Dyson, Stephen L. "Native Revolts in the Roman Empire." *Historia: Zeitschrift für alte Geschichte* 20.2/3 (1971) 239–74.

Eagleton, Terry. *After Theory*. New York: Basic Books, 2003.

———. *Ideology: An Introduction*. London: Verso, 1991.

———. *Literary Theory*. London: Blackwell, 1983.

———. *Marxism and Literary Criticism*. Berkeley: University of California Press, 1976.

Eisenbaum, Pamela. "Paul, Polemics, and the Problem of Esssentialism." *BibInt* 13 (2005) 224–38.

———. *Paul Was Not a Christian: The Original Message of a Misunderstood Apostle*. New York: HarperOne, 2009.

Ellacuría, Ignacio, SJ. "The Crucified People." In Mysterium Liberationis: *Fundamental Concepts of Liberation Theology*, edited by Ignacio Ellacuría and Jon Sobrino, 580–603. Maryknoll, NY: Orbis, 1993.

Elliott, Neil. "The Apostle Paul's Self-Presentation as Anti-Imperial Performance." In *Paul and the Roman Imperial Order*, edited by Richard A. Horsley, 67–88. Harrisburg, PA: Trinity, 2004.

———. *The Arrogance of Nations: Reading Romans in the Shadow of Empire*. Paul in Critical Contexts. Minneapolis: Fortress, 2008.

———. "'Blasphemed among the Nations': Pursuing an Anti-Imperial 'Intertextuality' in Romans." In *As it is Written: Studying Paul's Use of Scripture*, edited by Stanley E. Porter and Christopher D. Stanley, 212–33. Society of Biblical Literature Symposium Series 50. Atlanta: Society of Biblical Literature, 2008. Reprinted in Elliott, *Paul against the Nations*, 171-90. Eugene, OR: Cascade Books, 2023.

————. *Bodies of Christ: A Materialist Theology of the New Testament.* N.p.: forthcoming.

————. "Creation, Cosmos, and Conflict in Romans 8–9." In *Apocalyptic Paul: Cosmos and Anthropos in Romans 5–8*, edited by Beverly Roberts Gaventa, 131–56. Waco, TX: Baylor University Press, 2013. Reprinted in Elliott, *Paul against the Nations<*, 219-44. Eugene, OR: Cascade, 2023.

————. "Diagnosing an Allergic Reaction: The Avoidance of Marx in Pauline Scholarship." *Bible & Critical Theory* 8.2 (2012): 3–15 (Chapter 6 in this volume).

————. "Figure and Ground in the Interpretation of Romans 9–11." In *The Theological Interpretation of Scripture: Classic and Contemporary Readings*, editing Stephen E. Fowl, 371–89. Blackwell Readings in Modern Theology. Oxford: Blackwell, 1997. Reprinted in Elliott, *Paul against the Nations*, 245-63. Eugene, OR: Cascade, 2023.

————. "Ideological Closure in the Christ-Event: A Marxist Response to Alain Badiou's Paul." In *Paul, Philosophy, and the Theopolitical Vision: Critical Engagements with Agamben, Badiou, Žižek and Others*, edited by Douglas Harink, 135–54. Theopolitical Visions 7. Eugene, OR: Cascade Books, 2010 (chapter 7 in this volume).

————. "Liberating Paul." Lecture presented at the International Seminar on St. Paul. Society of St. Paul. Ariccia, Italy, 2009.

————. *Liberating Paul: The Justice of God and the Politics of the Apostle.* The Bible & Liberation. Maryknoll: Orbis, 1994. Reprint, Minneapolis: Fortress, 2005.

————. *Paul against the Nations: Soundings in Romans.* Eugene, OR: Cascade Books, 2023.

————. "Paul and the Politics of Empire: Problems and Prospects." In *Paul and Politics: Ekklesia, Israel, Imperium, Interpretation; Essays in Honor of Krister Stendahl*, edited by Richard A. Horsley, 17–39. Harrisburg, PA: Trinity, 2000.

————. "Paul between Jerusalem and Rome." Lecture presented at the International Seminar on St. Paul. Society of St. Paul. Ariccia, Italy, 2009.

————. *Paul the Jew under Roman Rule.* Eugene, OR: Cascade Books, forthcoming.

————. *The Rhetoric of Romans: Argumentative Constraint and Strategy and Paul's Dialogue with Judaism.* JSNTSup 45. Sheffield: JSOT Press, 1990. Reprint, Minneapolis: Fortress, 2006.

————. "Romans 13:1–7 in the Context of Neronian Propaganda." In *Paul and Empire: Religion and Power in Roman Imperial Society*, edited by Richard A. Horsley, 184–204. Harrisburg, PA: Trinity, 1997. Reprinted in *Paul against the Nations: Soundings in Romans*, 264–84. Eugene, OR: Cascade Books, 2023.

Elliott, Neil, and Mark Reasoner. *Documents and Images for the Study of Paul.* Minneapolis: Fortress, 2010.

Elliott, Neil, and other staff members of the Lambi Fund of Haiti. "Successful Strategies among Peasant Organizations in Haiti." Presented to the Annual Meeting of the Haitian Studies Association, Miami, FL, 2000.

Elwell, Walter A. "Belief and the Bible: A Crisis of Authority?" *Christianity Today* 24 (March 21, 1980) 21–23.

Engels, Frederick. "On the History of Early Christianity." German original published in *Die neue Zeit*, 1894. ET by the Institute of Marxism-Leninism, 1954. https://www.marxists.org/archive/marx/works/1894/early-christianity/index.htm/.

Episcopal Church. *The Book of Common Prayer and Administration of the Sacraments and Other Rites and Ceremonies of the Church: Together with the Psalter or Psalms of David according to the Use of the Episcopal Church.* New York: Church Hymnal, 1979.

Esler, Philip F. *Conflict and Identity in Romans: The Social Setting of Paul's Letter.* Minneapolis: Fortress, 2003.

———. *Galatians.* New Testament Readings. London: Routledge, 1998.

Evans, Craig A. *Matthew.* New Cambridge Bible Commentary. New York: Cambridge University Press, 2012.

Fanon, Frantz. *The Wretched of the Earth.* (French original 1961; first English translation by Constance Harrington, 1963.) Translated by Richard Philcox, with 1961 preface by Jean-Paul Sartre and 2004 foreword by Homi K. Bhabha. New York: Grove, 2004.

Farmer, W. R., et al., eds. *Christian History and Interpretation: Studies Presented to John Knox.* Cambridge: Cambridge University Press, 1967.

Fee, Gordon D. *The First Epistle to the Corinthians.* Rev. ed. New International Commentary on the New Testament. Grand Rapids: Eerdmans, 2014.

Feldman, Louis H., and Meyer Reinhold, eds. *Jewish Life and Thought among Greeks and Romans: Primary Readings.* Minneapolis: Fortress, 1996.

Finkelstein, Norman G. *Gaza: An Inquest into Its Martyrdom.* Oakland: University of California Press, 2018.

———. *Method and Madness: The Hidden Story of Israel's Assaults on Gaza.* New York: OR Books, 2014.

Fisher, Mark. *Capitalist Realism: Is There No Alternative?* Winchester, UK: Zero Books, 2009.

Fitzgerald, Timothy. *The Ideology of Religious Studies.* New York: Oxford University Press, 2000.

Food and Agriculture Organization of the United Nations. *The State of Food Security in the World, 2001.* Rome: United Nations, 2001.

Fowl, Stephen E., ed. *The Theological Interpretation of Scripture: Classic and Contemporary Readings.* Blackwell Readings in Modern Theology. Oxford: Blackwell, 1997.

———. "A Very Particular Universalism: Badiou and Paul." In *Paul, Philosophy, and the Theopolitical Vision: Critical Engagements with Agamben, Badiou, Žižek and Others,* edited by Douglas Harink, 119–34. Theopolitical Visions 7. Eugene, OR: Cascade Books, 2010.

Fox News. "'Glenn Beck': State of Religion in America." Transcript. *Fox News,* July 2, 2010. https://www.foxnews.com/story/glenn-beck-state-of-religion-in-america/.

Fredriksen, Paula. *From Jesus to Christ: The Origins of the New Testament Images of Jesus.* New Haven: Yale University Press, 1988; 2nd ed. Yale Nota Bene. New Haven: Yale University Press, 2000.

———. "Judaism, the Circumcision of Gentiles, and Apocalyptic Hope: Another Look at Galatians 1 and 2." *Journal of Theological Studies* 42 (1991) 533–64.

———. "What Does It Mean to See Paul 'within Judaism'?" *JBL* 141 (2022) 359–80.

Fredriksen, Paula, and Oded Irshai. "Christian Anti-Judaism: Polemics and Policies." In *The Cambridge History of Judaism,* edited by W. D. Davies and Louis Finkelstein, 4:977–1034. Cambridge: Cambridge University Press, 2006.

Frick, Peter. "Paul in the Grip of Continental Philosophers: What Is at Stake?" In *Paul in the Grip of the Philosophers: The Apostle and Contemporary Continental Philosophy,* edited by Peter Frick, 1–13. Paul in Critical Contexts. Minneapolis: Fortress, 2013.

————, ed. *Paul in the Grip of the Philosophers: The Apostle and Contemporary Continental Philosophy*. Paul in Critical Contexts. Minneapolis: Fortress, 2013.

Friesen, Steven J. "The Blessings of Hegemony: Poverty, Paul's Assemblies, and the Class Interests of the Professoriate." In *The Bible in the Public Square: Reading the Signs of the Times*, edited by Cynthia Briggs Kittredge et al., 117–28. Minneapolis: Fortress, 2008.

————. "Poverty in Pauline Studies: Beyond the So Called New Consensus." *JSNT* 26 (2004) 323–61.

————. "Prospects for a Demography of the Pauline Mission: Corinth among the Churches." In *Urban Religion in Roman Corinth: Interdisciplinary Approaches*, edited by Daniel N. Schowalter and Steven J. Friesen, 351–70. Harvard Theological Studies 53. Cambridge: Harvard Theological Studies, Harvard Divinity School, distributed by Harvard University Press, 2005.

Fukuyama, Francis. *The End of History and the Last Man*. New York: Free Press, 1992.

Furnish, Victor Paul. *The Moral Teaching of Paul*. Nashville: Abingdon, 1979.

————. *Theology and Ethics in Paul*. Nashville: Abingdon, 1968.

Gager, John G. *The Origins of Anti-Semitism: Attitudes toward Judaism in Pagan and Christian Antiquity*. New York: Oxford University Press, 1983.

————. *Reinventing Paul*. New York: Oxford University Press, 2000.

Galinsky, Karl. *Augustan Culture*. 1st paperback ed. Princeton: Princeton University Press, 1998.

Gandhi, Leela. *Postcolonial Theory: A Critical Introduction*. Australia: Allen & Unwin, 1998; 2nd ed. New York: Columbia University Press, 2019.

Garnsey Peter D. A. *Famine and Food Supply in the Graeco-Roman World*. Cambridge: Cambridge University Press, 1988.

————. "Grain for Rome." In *Trade in the Ancient Economy*, edited by Peter Garnsey et al., 118–30. Berkeley: University of California Press, 1983.

————. "Mass Diet and Nutrition in the City of Rome." In *Cities, Peasants, and Food in Classical Antiquity: Essays in Social and Economic History*, 226–52. Edited with addenda by Walter Scheidel. Cambridge: Cambridge University Press, 1998.

Garnsey, Peter D. A., and Richard Saller. *The Roman Empire: Economy, Society, and Culture*. Berkeley: University of California Press, 1987. 2nd ed., 2015.

Garnsey, Peter D. A., and C. R. Whittaker. *Imperialism in the Ancient World: The Cambridge University Research Seminar in Ancient History*. Cambridge Classical Studies. Cambridge: Cambridge University Press, 1978.

Gaston, Lloyd. *Paul and the Torah*. Vancouver: University of British Columbia Press, 1987.

Georgi, Dieter. *Die Geschichte der Kollekte des Paulus für Jerusalem*. Hamburg-Bergstet: Reich, 1965.

————. "Gott auf den Kopf stellen." In *Theokratie*, edited by Jacob Taubes. Paderborn: Schöning, 1987.

————. *Remembering the Poor: The History of Paul's Collection for Jerusalem*. Nashville: Abingdon, 1992.

————. *Theocracy in Paul's Praxis and Theology*. Translated by David Green. Minneapolis: Fortress, 1991.

Gessen, Masha. "In the Shadow of the Holocaust." The Weekend Essay. *New Yorker*, December 9, 2023. https://www.newyorker.com/news/the-weekend-essay/in-the-shadow-of-the-holocaust/.

Gignac, Alain. "Taubes, Badou, Agamben: Contemporary Reception of Paul by Non-Christian Philosophers." In *Reading Romans with Contemporary Philosophers and Theologians*, edited by David W. Odell-Scott, 155–211. Romans through History and Culture Series. New York: T. & T. Clark, 2007.

Gilbert, Martin. *The Holocaust: A History of the Jews of Europe during the Second World War*. First Owl Book ed. New York: Holt, 1987.

Girard, René. *The Scapegoat*. Translated by Yvonne Freccero. Baltimore: Johns Hopkins University Press, 1986.

———. *Things Hidden since the Foundation of the World*. In collaboration with Jean-Michel Oughourlian and Guy Lefort. Translated by Stephen Bann and Michael Metteer. Stanford: Stanford University Press, 1987.

———. *Violence and the Sacred*. Translated by Patrick Gregory. 1977. Reprint, Bloomsbury Revelations. London: Bloomsbury Academic, 2017.

Goldberg, Michelle. "The GOP's Poverty Denialism." *Nation*, November 6, 2013. https://www.thenation.com/article/archive/gops-poverty-denialism/.

Goodenough, Erwin R. *An Introduction to Philo Judaeus*. 2nd ed. Oxford: Blackwell, 1962.

Goodman, Amy. "Another Nakba? Israeli Intel Ministry Proposes Expelling Every Palestinian in Gaza to Egypt." Interview with journalist Yuval Abraham. *Democracy Now!* November 3, 2023. https://www.democracynow.org/2023/11/3/israel_leak_gaza_expulsion_egypt#:~:text=One%20Israeli%20government%20office%2C%20the,residents%20to%20Egypt's%20Sinai%20Peninsula/.

———. "State Department Official Resigns, Says Israel Is Using U.S. Arms to Massacre Civilians in Gaza." *Democracy Now!* November 3, 2023. https://www.democracynow.org/2023/11/23/dissenters_2/.

Goodman, Martin. *The Ruling Class of Judaea: The Origins of the Jewish Revolt against Rome, A.D. 66–70*. Cambridge: Cambridge University Press, 1987.

Gordon, Richard. "From Republic to Principate: Priesthood, Religion and Ideology." In *Pagan Priests: Religion and Power in the Ancient World*, edited by Mary Beard and John North, 179–98. Ithaca: Cornell University Press, 1990.

Gottwald, Norman K. *The Politics of Ancient Israel*. Library of Ancient Israel. Louisville: Westminster John Knox, 2001.

———. *The Hebrew Bible: A Socio-Literary Introduction*. Philadelphia: Fortress, 1985.

———. *The Tribes of Yahweh: A Sociology of the Religion of Liberated Israel, 1250–1050 B.C.E.* Maryknoll, NY: Orbis, 1979.

Gouldner, Alvin W. *The Coming Crisis of Western Sociology*. Studies in the Series on the Social Origins of Social Theory. New York: Basic Books, 1970.

Graeber, David. "Can Debt Spark a Revolution?" *Nation*, September 5, 2012. https://www.thenation.com/article/archive/can-debt-spark-revolution/.

———. *Debt: The First 5,000 Years*. Updated and expanded ed. Brooklyn, NY: Melville House, 2014.

Gramsci, Antonio. *Selections from the Prison Notebooks*. Edited and translated by Quintin Hoare and Geoffrey Nowell Smith. London: Lawrence & Wishart, 1971.

Grassi, Joseph A. *Broken Bread and Broken Bodies: The Lord's Supper and World Hunger*. Rev. ed. Maryknoll, NY: Orbis, 2004.

Griffiths, Paul J. "Christ and Critical Theory." *First Things* 145 (August/September 2004) 46–55.

———. The Cross as the Fulcrum of Politics: Expropriating Agamben on Paul." In *Paul, Philosophy, and the Theopolitical Vision: Critical Engagements with Agamben, Badiou, Žižek and Others,* edited by Douglas Harink, 179–97. Theopolitical Visions 7. Cascade Books, 2010.

Gruen, Erich S. *Diaspora: Jews amidst Greeks and Romans.* Cambridge: Cambridge University Press, 2002.

Ha'aretz. "'100–200,000, not One Million': Israel's Finance Minister Envisions Depopulated Gaza." *Ha'aretz,* December 31, 2023. https://www.haaretz.com/israel-news/2023-12-31/ty-article/100-200-000-not-two-million-israels-finance-minister-envisions-depopulated-gaza/0000018c-bfe8-d6c4-ab8d-fffcob910000/.

Hafemann, S. J. "Paul and His Interpreters." In *Dictionary of Paul and His Letters,* edited by Gerald F. Hawthorne et al., 666–89 Grand Rapids: Eerdmans, 1993.

Hallward, Peter. *Badiou: A Subject to Truth.* Minneapolis: University of Minnesota Press, 2003.

———. *Damming the Flood: Haiti, Aristide, and the Politics of Containment.* London: Verso, 2007.

Hamerton-Kelly, Robert G. *Sacred Violence: Paul's Hermeneutic of the Cross.* Minneapolis: Fortress, 1992.

———, ed. *Violent Origins: Walter Burkert, René Girard & Jonathan Z. Smith on Ritual Killing and Cultural Formation,* by Walter Burkert et al. With an introduction by Burton L. Mack and a commentary by Renato Rosaldo. Stanford: Stanford University Press, 1987.

Hamerton-Kelly, Robert G., and Robin Scroggs, eds. *Jews, Greeks, and Christians: Religious Cultures in Late Antiquity; Essays in Honor of William David Davies.* Studies in Judaism in Late Antiquity 21. Leiden: Brill, 1976.

Hanson, K. C., and Douglas E. Oakman. *Palestine in the Time of Jesus: Social Structures and Social Conflicts.* 2nd ed. Minneapolis: Fortress, 2008.

Hardt, Michael, and Antonio Negri. *Empire.* Cambridge: Harvard University Press, 2000.

———. *Multitude: War and Democracy in the Age of Empire.* New York: Penguin, 2005.

Hare, Douglas R. A. *The Theme of Jewish Persecution of Christians in the Gospel according to St. Matthew.* Society for New Testament Study Monograph Series 6. Cambridge: Cambridge University Press, 1967.

Harink, Douglas, ed. *Paul, Philosophy, and the Theopolitical Vision: Critical Engagements with Agamben, Badiou, Žižek, and Others.* Theopolitical Visions 7. Eugene, OR: Cascade Books, 2010.

Harvey, David. *A Brief History of Neoliberalism.* Oxford: Oxford University Press, 2005.

Hauck, Friedrich. "κοινος." In *TDNT* 3 (1965) 797–809.

———. "μαμωνος." In *TDNT* 4 (1967) 388–99.

Hellwig, Monika K. *The Eucharist and the Hunger of the World.* 2nd ed., rev. and exp. Kansas City, MO: Sheed & Ward, 1992.

Hengel, Martin. *Was Jesus a Revolutionist?* Translated by William Klassen. Facet. Philadelphia: Fortress, 1971.

Hennelly, Alfred T., ed. *Liberation Theology: A Documentary History.* Maryknoll, NY: Orbis, 1990.

Herman, Edward S., and Noam Chomsky. *Manufacturing Consent: The Political Economy of the Mass Media.* Updated ed. With a new introduction by the authors. New York: Pantheon, 2002.

Hersh, Seymour M. *Chain of Command: The Road from 9/11 to Abu Ghraib*. New York: HarperCollins, 2004.

Herzog, William R., II. *Parables as Subversive Speech: Jesus as Pedagogue of the Oppressed*. Louisville: Westminster John Knox, 1994.

Heschel, Susannah. "Anti-Judaism in Christian Feminist Theology." *Tikkun* 5.3 (1990) 25–28.

Hodge, Caroline Johnson. "Apostle to the Gentiles: Constructions of Paul's Identity." *BibInt* 13 (2005) 270–88.

———. *Why This New Race: Ethnic Reasoning in Early Christianity*. New York: Columbia University Press, 2005.

Hogg, Alec. "As Inequality Soars, the Nervous Super Rich Are Already Planning Their Escapes." Analysis. *Guardian*, January 23, 2015. https://www.theguardian.com/public-leaders-network/2015/jan/23/nervous-super-rich-planning-escapes-davos-2015/.

Hopkins, Keith. *Conquerors and Slaves*. Sociological Studies in Roman History 1. Cambridge University Press, 1978.

Horace. *Satires*. Translated by H. R. Fairclough. LCL. London: Heinemann, 1929.

Horrell, David G. "Domestic Space and Christian Meetings at Corinth: Imagining New Contexts and the Buildings East of the Theatre." *NTS* 50 (2004) 349–69.

Horsley, Richard A. "Ancient Jewish Banditry and the Revolt against Rome, A.D. 66-70." *CBQ* 43 (1981) 409–32. Republished in Horsley, *Politics, Conflict, and Movements in First-Century Palestine*, edited by K. C. Hanson, 58–81. Eugene, OR: Cascade Books, 2013.

———, ed. *Christian Origins*. The People's History of Christianity 1. Minneapolis: Fortress, 2005.

———. *1 Corinthians*. Abingdon New Testament Commentaries. Nashville: Abingdon, 1998.

———. "1 Corinthians: A Case Study of Paul's Assembly as an Alternative Society." In *Paul and Empire: Religion and Power in Roman Imperial Society*, edited by Richard A. Horsley, 242–52. Harrisburg, PA: Trinity, 1997.

———. *Galileans under Jerusalem and Roman Rule*. Edited by K. C. Hanson. Eugene, OR: Cascade Books, 2024.

———. *Galilee: History, Politics, People*. Valley Forge, PA: Trinity, 1995.

———, ed. *Hidden Transcripts and the Arts of Resistance: Applying the Work of James C. Scott to Jesus and Paul*. Semeia Studies 48. Atlanta: Society of Biblical Literature, 2004.

———, ed. *In the Shadow of Empire: Reclaiming the Bible as a History of Faithful Resistance*. Louisville: Westminster John Knox, 2008.

———. *Jesus and the Politics of Roman Palestine*. 2nd ed., with a revised preface. Eugene: Cascade Books, 2013.

———. *Jesus and the Powers: Conflict, Covenant, and the Hope of the Poor*. Minneapolis: Fortress, 2011.

———. *Jesus and the Spiral of Violence: Popular Jewish Resistance in Roman Palestine*. 1987. Reprint, Minneapolis: Fortress, 1993.

———. *Jesus in Context: Power, People, & Performance*. Minneapolis: Fortress, 2008.

———. "Josephus and the Bandits." *Journal of Jewish Studies* 10 (1979) 37-63. Republished in Horsley, *Politics, Conflict, and Movements in First-Century Palestine*, edited by K. C. Hanson, 33–57. Eugene, OR: Cascade Books, 2023.

————, ed. *Paul and Empire: Religion and Power in Roman Imperial Society*. Harrisburg, PA: Trinity, 1997.

————, ed. *Paul and Politics: Ekklesia, Israel, Imperium, Interpretation; Essays in Honor of Krister Stendahl*. Harrisburg, PA: Trinity, 2000.

————, ed. *Paul and the Roman Imperial Order*. Harrisburg, PA: Trinity., 2004.

————. *Politics, Conflict, and Movements in First-Century Palestine*. Edited by K. C. Hanson. Eugene, OR: Cascade Books, 2023.

————. "Popular Messianic Movements around the Time of Jesus." *CBQ* 46 (1984) 471-95. Republished in Horsley, *Politics, Conflict, and Movements in First-Century Palestine*, edited by K. C. Hanson, 85–109. Eugene, OR: Cascade Books, 2023.

————. "Rhetoric and Empire—and 1 Corinthians." In *Paul and Politics: Ekklesia, Israel, Imperium, Interpretation; Essays in Honor of Krister Stendahl*, 72–102. Harrisburg, PA: Trinity, 2000.

————. *Revolt of the Scribes: Resistance and Apocalyptic Origins*. Minneapolis: Fortress, 2010.

————. "The Sicarii: Ancient Jewish Terrorists." *JR* 59 (1979) 435-58. Republished in Horsley, *Politics, Conflict, and Movements in First-Century Palestine*, edited by K. C. Hanson, 167–91. Eugene, OR: Cascade Books, 2023.

————. *Sociology and the Jesus Movement*. 2nd ed. New York: Continuum, 1994.

————. "Submerged Biblical Histories and Imperial Biblical Studies." In *The Postcolonial Bible*, edited by R. S. Sugirtharajah, 152–73. The Bible and Postcolonialism 1. Sheffield: Sheffield Academic, 1998

Horsley, Richard A., with John S. Hanson. *Bandits, Prophets & Messiahs: Popular Movements in the Time of Jesus*. Harrisburg, PA: Trinity, 1999.

Hubbard, Ben. "While Gazans Suffer, Hamas Reaps the Benefits." *New York Times*, December 9, 2023. https://www.nytimes.com/2023/12/09/world/middleeast/hamas-gaza-israel.html/.

Hughes, Richard T. *Myths America Lives By: White Supremacy and the Stories That Give Us Meaning*. 2nd ed. Urbana: University of Illinois Press, 2018.

Hunsinger, George, ed. *Karl Barth and Radical Politics*. 2nd ed. Eugene, OR: Cascade Books, 2017.

Huntington, Samuel P. "The Clash of Civilizations." *Foreign Affairs* 72.3 (1993) 22–49.

————. *The Clash of Civilizations and the Remaking of World Order*. New York: Simon & Schuster, 1996.

Hurtado, Larry W. "Fashions, Fallacies, and Future Prospects in New Testament Studies." *JSNT* 36 (2014) 299–324.

————. "New Testament Studies at the Turn of the Millennium: Questions for the Discipline." *Scottish Journal of Theology* 52 (1999) 158–78.

Isserman, Maurice. "Why I Just Quit DSA." *Nation*, October 23, 2023. https://www.thenation.com/article/activism/quit-dsa-gaza-israel/.

James, C. L. R. *The Black Jacobins: Toussaint L'Ouverture and the San Domingo Revolution*. 2nd ed., rev. New York, Vintage, 1963.

Jameson, Fredric. "On Interpretation: Literature as a Socially Symbolic Act." In *The Political Unconscious: Narrative as a Socially Symbolic Act*, 17–102. Ithaca, NY: Cornell University Press, 1981.

————. *The Political Unconscious: Narrative as a Socially Symbolic Act*. Ithaca, NY: Cornell University Press, 1981.

———. *Postmodernism, or, The Cultural Logic of Late Capitalism*. Post-Contemporary Interventions. Durham: Duke University Press, 1991.

Japanese Broadcasting Corporation, ed. *Unforgettable Fire: Pictures Drawn by Atomic Bomb Survivors*. New York: Pantheon, 1977.

Jeffers, James S. *The Greco-Roman World of the New Testament Era: Exploring the Background of Early Christianity*. Downers Grove, IL: InterVarsity, 1999.

Jennings, Theodore W., Jr. "Paul and (Post-modern) Political Thought." Paper presented to the Paul and Politics Section of the Annual Meeting of the Society of Biblical Literature, Atlanta, GA, November 2003.

———. *Reading Derrida/Thinking Paul: On Justice*. Cultural Memory in the Present. Stanford: Stanford University Press, 2006.

Jennings, Willie James. *The Christian Imagination: Theology and the Origins of Race*. New Haven: Yale University Press, 2010.

Jervell, Jacob. *The Unknown Paul: Essays on Luke-Acts and Early Christian History*. Minneapolis: Augsburg, 1984.

Jobling, David. "'Very Limited Ideological Options': Marxism and Biblical Studies in Postcolonial Scenes." In *Postcolonial Biblical Criticism: Interdisciplinary Intersections*, edited by Stephen D. Moore and Fernando F. Segovia, 184–201. The Bible and Postcolonialism. London: T. & T. Clark, 2005.

Jobling, David, and Tina Pippin, eds. *Ideological Criticism of Biblical Texts*. Semeia 59. Atlanta: Society of Biblical Literature, 1992.

Jobling, David, et al., eds. *The Bible and the Politics of Exegesis: Essays in Honor of Norman K. Gottwald on His Sixty-Fifth Birthday*. Cleveland: Pilgrim, 1991.

John Paul II, Pope. "Unity of the Church." *The Pope Speaks* 28 (Fall 1983) 206–10. Reprinted in *Liberation Theology: A Documentary History*, edited by Alfred T. Hennelly, 329–33. Maryknoll, NY: Orbis, 1990.

Johnson-DeBaufre, Melanie, and Laura Salah Nasrallah. "Beyond the Heroic Paul: Toward a Feminist and Decolonizing Approach to the Letters of Paul." In *The Colonized Apostle: Paul through Postcolonial Eyes*, edited by Christopher Stanley, 161–74. Paul in Critical Contexts. Minneapolis: Fortress, 2011.

Juvenal. *Satires*. Translated by G. G. Ramsay in *Juvenal and Persius*. LCL. Cambridge: Harvard University Press, 1957.

Kahl, Brigitte. *Galatians Re-Imagined: Reading with the Eyes of the Vanquished*. Paul in Critical Contexts. Minneapolis: Fortress, 2010.

———. "Toward a Materialist-Feminist Reading." In *Searching the Scriptures*. Vol. 1, *A Feminist Introduction*, edited by Elisabeth Schüssler Fiorenza with the assistance of Shelly Matthews, 225–40. 2 vols. New York: Crossroad, 1993–1994.

Kalimi, Isaac, ed. *Jewish Bible Theology: Perspectives and Case Studies*. Winona Lake, IN: Eisenbrauns, 2012.

Käsemann, Ernst. *Commentary on Romans*. Translated by Geoffrey W. Bromiley. Grand Rapids: Eerdmans, 1980.

———. *New Testament Questions of Today*. Translated by W. J. Montague. Philadelphia: Fortress, 1969.

———. "Principles of the Interpretation of Romans 13." In *New Testament Questions of Today*, 196–216. Translated by W. J. Montague. Philadelphia: Fortress, 1969.

Kaufman, Gordon. *An Essay on Theological Method*, 3rd ed. AAR Reflection and Theory in the Study of Religion 5. Atlanta: Scholars, 1995; first ed. 1975.

————. *In Face of Mystery: A Constructive Theology.* Cambridge: Harvard University Press, 1993.

Kautsky, Karl. *Foundations of Christianity.* German original 1908. Translated by Henry F. Mins. London: Russell & Russell, 1953.

Kee, Alistair. *Marx and the Failure of Liberation Theology.* London: SCM, 1990.

Keller, Catherine. *Cloud of the Impossible: Negative Theology and Planetary Entanglement.* Insurrections: Critical Studies in Religion, Politics, and Culture. New York: Columbia University Press, 2015.

————. *God and Power: Counter-Apocalyptic Journeys.* Minneapolis: Fortress, 2005.

Kelley, Shawn. *Racializing Jesus: Race, Ideology, and the Formation of Modern Biblical Scholarship.* Biblical Limits. London: Routledge, 2002.

Khalidi, Rashid. "It's Time to Confront Israel's Version of 'From the River to the Sea.'" *Nation,* Nov. 22, 2023. https://www.thenation.com/article/world/its-time-to-confront-israels-version-of-from-the-river-to-the-sea/.

Kittredge, Cynthia Briggs. *Community and Authority: The Rhetoric of Obedience in Pauline Tradition.* Harvard Theological Studies 45. Cambridge, MA: Harvard University Press, 1998.

————. "Reconstructing 'Resistance' or Reading to Resist: James C. Scott and the Politics of Interpretation." In *Hidden Transcripts and the Arts of Resistance: Applying the Work of James C. Scott to Jesus and Paul,* edited by Richard A. Horsley, 145–55. Semeia Studies 48. Atlanta: Society of Biblical Literature, 2004.

Klein, Naomi. *No Is Not Enough: Resisting Trump's Shock Politics and Winning the World We Need.* Chicago: Haymarket, 2017.

————. *The Shock Doctrine: The Rise of Disaster Capitalism.* New York: Metropolitan, 2007.

————. "The Supreme Court's Shock-and-Awe Judicial Coup." *Intercept,* June 30, 2022. https://theintercept.com/2022/06/30/supreme-court-climate-epa-coup/

Koester, Helmut. "Imperial Ideology and Paul's Eschatology in 1 Thessalonians." In *Paul and Empire: Religion and Power in Roman Imperial Society,* edited by Richard A. Horsley, 158–66. Harrisburg, PA: Trinity, 1997.

————. *Introduction to the New Testament,* 2nd ed. 2 vols. New York: de Gruyter, 2000.

Kołakowski, Leszek. *Main Currents of Marxism: The Founders, the Golden Age, the Breakdown.* Translated from the Polish by P. S. Falla. New York: Norton, 2005.

Kotrosits, Maia. *Rethinking Early Christian Identity: Affect, Violence, and Belonging.* Minneapolis: Fortress, 2015.

Kotsko, Adam. *Neoliberalism's Demons: On the Political Theology of Late Capital.* Stanford: Stanford University Press, 2018.

————. *Žižek and Theology.* Philosophy and Theology. London: T. & T. Clark, 2008.

Kowalinski, P. "The Genesis of Christianity in the Views of Contemporary Marxist Specialists in Religion." *Antonianum* 47 (1972) 541–75.

Kümmel, Werner Georg. *Introduction to the New Testament.* Rev. ed. Translated by Howard Clark Kee, Nashville: Abingdon, 1975.

————. *Römer 7 und die Bekehrung des Paulus.* Untersuchungen zum Neuen Testament 17. Leipzig: Hinrichs, 1929.

Kwok, Pui-lan. *Postcolonial Imagination and Feminist Theology.* Louisville: Westminster John Knox, 2005.

LaGrand, James. "Proliferation of the 'Gentile' in the New Revised Standard Version." *Biblical Research* 41 (1996) 77–87.

Lampe, Peter. "Can Words Be Violent or Do They Only Sound That Way? Second Corinthians: Verbal Warfare from Afar as a Complement to a Placid Personal Presence." In *Paul and Rhetoric*, edited by J. Paul Sampley and Peter Lampe, 223–39. T. & T. Clark Biblical Studies New York: T. & T Clark, 2010.

———. *From Paul to Valentinus: Christians in Rome in the First Two Centuries*. Translated by Michael Steinhauser. Edited by Marshall Johnson. Foreword by Robert Jewett. Minneapolis: Fortress, 2003.

Lee, Carol E., and Courtney Kube. "Biden Officials Voice New Concerns and Warnings over Israel's War with Hamas." *NBCNews.com*, November 2, 2023. https://www.nbcnews.com/politics/white-house/biden-officials-voice-new-concerns-warnings-israels-war-hamas-rcna123445/.

Lee, Matthew. "Blinken Will Return to Israel as the US Hopes to See Further Extensions of the Gaza Cease-fire." Associated Press release posted on NBC New York website on November 27, 2023. https://www.nbcnewyork.com/news/national-international/blinken-will-return-to-israel-as-the-us-hopes-to-see-further-extensions-of-the-gaza-cease-fire/4899324/.

Lee, Micah. "Anti-Defamation League Maps Jewish Peace Rallies with Anti-Semitic Attacks." *TheIntercept.com*, November 11, 2023. https://theintercept.com/2023/11/11/palestine-israel-protests-ceasefire-antisemitic/

Lenin, V. I. "On the Famine: A Letter to the Workers of Petrograd," *Pravda* 101, May 22, 1918.

Lenski, Gerhard E. *Power and Privilege: A Theory of Social Stratification*. New York: McGraw-Hill, 1966.

Leon, Harry J. *The Jews of Ancient Rome*. Updated ed. Peabody, MA: Hendrickson, 1995.

Leuchter, Mark. "Leveraging the Academy against Itself: Misogyny, Method and Social Media in Public Scholarship." Presented at the Annual Meeting of the Society of Biblical Literature, San Antonio, TX, November 18, 2023.

Levine, Amy-Jill. "The Disease of Postcolonial New Testament Studies and the Hermeneutics of Healing." *Journal of Feminist Studies in Religion* 20.1 (2004) 91–99.

Liew, Tat-siong Benny. "Margins and (Cutting-) Edges: On the (Il) Legitimacy and Intersections of Race, Ethnicity, and (Post) Colonialism." *Postcolonial Biblical Criticism: Interdisciplinary Intersections*, edited by Stephen D. Moore and Fernando F. Segovia, 114–65. The Bible and Postcolonialism. The Bible and Postcolonialism. London: T. & T. Clark, 2005.

Liptak, Kevin, et al. "US Warns Israel amid Gaza Carnage It Doesn't Have Long before Support Erodes." *CNN.com*, November 3, 2023. https://www.cnn.com/2023/11/02/politics/biden-administration-warning-israel-gaza-civilians/index.html/.

Longenecker, Bruce W. *Eschatology and the Covenant: A Comparison of 4 Ezra and Romans 1–11*. JSNTSup 57. Sheffield: JSOT Press, 1991.

———. *Remember the Poor: Paul, Poverty, and the Greco-Roman World*. Grand Rapids, MI: Eerdmans, 2010.

———. "Socio-economic Profiling of the First Urban Christians." In *After the First Urban Christians: The Social-Scientific Study of Pauline Christianity Twenty-Five Years Later*, edited by Todd D. Still and David G. Horrell, 36–59. London: Continuum, 2009.

López, Davina A. *Apostle to the Conquered: Reimagining Paul's Mission.* Paul in Critical Contexts. Minneapolis: Fortress, 2008.

———. "Visual Perspectives." In *Studying Paul's Letters: Contemporary Perspectives and Methods,* edited by Joseph A. Marchal, 93–116. Minneapolis: Fortress, 2012.

López, Davina A., and Todd Penner. "Paul and Politics." In *The Oxford Handbook of Pauline Studies,* edited by R. Barry Matlock, 580–97. Oxford Handbooks Online. New York: Oxford University Press, 2017.

———. "Rhetorical Approaches: Introducing the Art of Persuasion in Paul and Pauline Studies." Approaches: Introducing the Art of Persuasion in Paul and Pauline Studies." In *Studying Paul's Letters: Contemporary Perspectives and Methods,* edited by Joseph A. Marchal, 33–52. Minneapolis: Fortress, 2012.

Luz, Ulrich. *Matthew 8–20: A Commentary.* Edited by Helmut Koester. Translated by James E. Crouch. Hermeneia. Minneapolis: Fortress, 2001.

Mack, Burton L. "The Innocent Transgressor: Jesus in Early Christian History." In *René Girard in Biblical Studies,* edited by Andrew J. McKenna, 135–65. *Semeia* 33. Decatur, GA: Scholars, 1985.

———. *A Myth of Innocence: Mark and Christian Origins.* Philadelphia: Fortress, 1988.

MacMullen, Ramsay. *Paganism in the Roman Empire.* New Haven: Yale University Press, 1981.

———. *Roman Social Relations 50 B.C. to A.D. 284.* New Haven: Yale University Press, 1974.

Malherbe, Abraham. "Ancient Epistolary Theorists." *Ohio Journal of Religious Studies* 5 (1977) 3–77.

———. *Social Aspects of Early Christianity.* 2nd ed. 1983. Reprint, Eugene, OR: Wipf & Stock, 2003.

Malik, Nesrene. "The War in Gaza Has Been an Intense Lesson in Western Hypocrisy." Opinion. *Guardian,* November 27, 2023. https://www.theguardian.com/commentisfree/2023/nov/27/war-gaza-lesson-western-hypocrisy-international-community/.

Malina, Bruce J. *The New Testament World: Insights from Cultural Anthropology.* 3rd ed. Louisville: Westminster John Knox, 2001.

Malina, Bruce J., and John J. Pilch. *Social-Science Commentary on the Letters of Paul.* Minneapolis: Fortress, 2006.

Malina, Bruce J., and Richard L. Rohrbaugh. *Social-Science Commentary on the Synoptic Gospels.* 2nd ed. Minneapolis: Fortress, 2003.

Marchal, Joseph A. *Appalling Bodies: Queer Figures before and after Paul's Letters.* New York: Oxford University Press, 2020.

———. *The Politics of Heaven: Women, Gender, and Empire in the Study of Paul.* Paul in Critical Contexts. Minneapolis: Fortress, 2008.

———, ed. *Studying Paul's Letters: Contemporary Perspectives and Methods.* Minneapolis: Fortress, 2012.

Markwell, Bernard Kent. *The Anglican Left: Radical Social Reformers in the Church of England and the Protestant Episcopal Church, 1846–1954.* With a preface by Martin E. Marty. Chicago Studies in the History of American Religion 13. Brooklyn: Carlson, 1991.

Marshall, John W. "Hybridity and Reading Romans 13." *JSNT* 31 (2008) 157–78.

Marshall, Peter. *Enmity in Corinth: Social Conventions in Paul's Relations with the Corinthians.* WUNT 2/23. Tübingen: Mohr Siebeck, 1987.

Martin, Dale B. "Heterosexism and the Interpretation of Romans 1:18–32." *BibInt* 3 (1995) 332–55. Reprinted in *Sex and the Single Savior*, 51–64. Louisville: Westminster John Knox, 2006.

———. "Paul and the Judaism/Hellenism Dichotomy: Toward a Social History of the Question." In *Paul beyond the Judaism/Hellenism Divide*, edited by Troels Engberg-Pedersen, 29–62. Louisville: Westminster John Knox, 2001.

———. "Review Essay: Justin J. Meggitt: *Paul, Poverty and Survival*." *JSNT*, 24.2 (2001) 51–64.

Marty, Martin. "America's Iconic Book." In *Humanizing America's Iconic Book: Society of Biblical Literature Centennial Addresses 1980*, edited by Gene M. Tucker and Douglas A. Knight, 1–23. Biblical Scholarship in North America 6. Chico, CA: Scholars, 1982.

Mayer, Jane. *Dark Money: The Hidden History of the Billionaires behind the Rise of the Radical Right*. New York: Doubleday, 2016.

McDaniel, Charles. "Financialization and the Changing Face of Poverty: Christian and Muslim Perspectives." In *The Bible, the Economy, and the Poor*, edited by Ronald A. Simkins and Thomas M. Kelly, 190–216. Journal of Religion & Society Supplement, 10 2014.

———. "Financialization and the Emerging Monopoly on Public Discourse: A Biblical Perspective." Paper presented at the Annual Meeting of the Society of Biblical Literature, San Diego, CA, November 2014.

———. *God & Money: The Moral Challenge of Capitalism*. Lanham, MD: Rowman & Littlefield, 2007.

———. "Theology of the 'Real Economy': Christian Economic Ethics in an Age of 'Financialization.'" *Journal of Religion and Business Ethics* 2.2 (2011) 1–29.

McGinn, Sheila E., and Megan T. Wilson-Reitz. "2 Thessalonians vs. the Ataktoi: A Pauline Critique of 'White-Collar Welfare.'" In *By Bread Alone: The Bible through the Eyes of the Hungry*, edited by Sheila E. McGinn et al., 195–208. Minneapolis Fortress, 2014.

McGowan, Andrew. "The Myth of the 'Lord's Supper': Paul's Eucharistic Meal Terminology and Its Ancient Reception." *CBQ* (2015) 503–21.

Meeks, Wayne A. *The First Urban Christians: The Social World of the Apostle Paul*. 2nd ed. New Haven: Yale University Press, 2003.

———. "Judgment and the Brother: Romans 14.1—15.13." In *Tradition and Interpretation in the New Testament: Essays in Honor of E. Earle Ellis*, edited by Gerald F. Hawthorne and Otto Betz, 293–300. Grand Rapids: Eerdmans, 1987.

Meggitt, Justin J. *Paul, Poverty and Survival*. SNTW. Edinburgh: T. & T. Clark, 1998.

———. "Response to Martin and Theissen." *JSNT* 24.2 (2001) 85–94.

Menand, Louis. *The Marketplace of Ideas: Reform and Resistance in the American University*. Issues of Our Time. New York: Norton, 2010.

Metz, Johann Baptist. *Faith in History and Society: Toward a Practical Fundamental Theology*. New York: Crossroad, 1979.

———. "The Future in the Memory of Suffering." In *New Questions on God*, 9–25. Concilium: Religion in the Seventies. Church and World 76. New York: Herder & Herder, 1972.

Milbank, John, et al. *Paul's New Moment: Continental Philosophy and the Future of Christian Theology*. Grand Rapids, MI: Brazos, 2010.

Miller, William Lee. *Piety along the Potomac: Notes on Politics and Morals in the Fifties.* Boston, Houghton Mifflin, 1964.

Miranda, José Porfírio. *Marx and the Bible: A Critique of the Philosophy of Oppression.* Translated by John Eagleson. 1974. Reprint, Eugene, OR: Wipf & Stock, 2004.

Mitchell, Margaret M. *Paul and the Rhetoric of Reconciliation: An Exegetical Investigation of the Language and Composition of 1 Corinthians.* Hermeneutische Untersuchungen zur Theologie 28. Tübingen: Mohr Siebeck, 1991.

Mofokeng, Takatso. "Black Christians, the Bible and Liberation." *Journal of Black Theology* 2 (1988) 34–42.

Mohanty, Chandra Talpade. *Feminism without borders: Decolonizing Theory, Practicing Solidarity.* Durham: Duke University Press, 2003.

Montefiore, C. G. *Judaism and St. Paul.* London: Goschen, 1914.

Moore, G. F. "Christian Writers on Judaism." *Harvard Theological Review* 14 (1921) 197–254.

———. *Judaism in the First Centuries of the Christian Era: The Age of the Tannaim.* 3 vols. Cambridge, MA: Harvard University Press, 1927–1930.

Moore, Stephen D. "Paul and Empire." In *The Colonized Apostle: Paul through Postcolonial Eyes*, edited by Christopher Stanley, 9–23. Paul in Critical Contexts. Minneapolis: Fortress, 2011.

Moore, Stephen D., and Yvonne Sherwood. *The Invention of the Biblical Scholar: A Critical Manifesto.* Minneapolis: Fortress, 2011.

Morton, Russell. "Parable and Proverb." In *Encyclopedia of the Historical Jesus*, edited by Craig A. Evans, 435–38. New York: Routledge, 2008.

Moxnes, Halvor. "Honor and Righteousness in Romans." *JSNT* 32 (1988) 66–68.

———. "The Quest for Honor and the Unity of the Community in Romans 12 and in the Orations of Dio Chrysostom." In *Paul in His Hellenistic Context*, edited by Troels Engberg-Pedersen, 203–30. Minneapolis: Fortress, 1995

Munck, Johannes. *Christ and Israel: An Interpretation of Romans 9–11.* Translated by Ingeborg Nixon. Philadelphia: Fortress, 1967.

———. *Paul and the Salvation of Mankind.* Translated by Frank Clarke. Richmond, VA: John Knox, 1959.

Murphy-O'Connor, Jerome. *St. Paul's Corinth: Texts and Archaeology.* Good News Studies 6. Wilmington, DE: Glazier, 1983.

Nanos, Mark D. *The Irony of Galatians: Paul's Letter in First-Century Context.* Minneapolis: Fortress, 2002.

———. *The Mystery of Romans: The Jewish Context of Paul's Letter.* Minneapolis: Fortress, 1996.

———. "Paul and Judaism." Paper delivered at the Central States Meeting of the Society of Biblical Literature, St. Louis, MO, March 28, 2004. https://marknanos.com/wp-content/uploads/2019/11/CodexPauli-Nanos-PJ.pdf/.

Nanos, Mark D., and Magnus Zetterholm, eds. *Paul within Judaism: Restoring the First-Century Context to the Apostle.* Minneapolis: Fortress, 2015.

Nielson, Cynthia R. "Rending New Life from These Mangled Places." Response as part of the *Syndicate* Symposium on *The Christian Imagination: Theology and the Origins of Race*, by Willie James Jennings. July 23, 2014. https://syndicate.network/symposia/theology/the-christian-imagination/.

Noack, B. "Current and Backwater in the Epistle to the Romans." *Studia Theologica* 19 (1965) 155–66.

Oakes, Peter. *Reading Romans in Pompeii: Paul's Letter at Ground Level.* Minneapolis: Fortress, 2009.

Oakman, Douglas E. "The Ancient Economy." In *The Social Sciences and New Testament Interpretation,* edited by Richard L. Rorbaugh, 126–43. Peabody, MA: Hendrickson, 1996.

————. "The Buying Power of Two Dinarii." In *Jesus and the Peasants,* 40–45. Matrix: The Bible in Mediterranean Context 4. Eugene, OR: Cascade Books, 2008.

Odell-Scott, David, ed. *Reading Romans with Contemporary Philosophers and Theologians.* New York: T. & T. Clark, 2007.

Ohmann, Richard. *Politics of Knowledge: The Commercialization of the University, the Professions, and Print Culture.* Middletown, CT: Wesleyan University Press, 2003.

O'Loughlin, Thomas. *The Eucharist: Origins and Contemporary Understandings.* London: Bloomsbury T. & T. Clark, 2015.

Overman, J. Andrew. "The First Revolt and Flavian Politics." In *The First Jewish Revolt: Archaeology, History, and Ideology,* edited by Andrea M. Berlin and J. Andrew Overman, 213–20. London: Routledge, 2002.

Pagels, Elaine H. "Paul and Women: A Response to Recent Discussion." *Journal of the American Academy of Religion* 42 (1974) 538–49.

Pappé, Ilan. *A History of Modern Palestine: One Land, Two Peoples.* Cambridge: Cambridge University Press, 2004.

Parenti, Michael. *The Assassination of Julius Caesar: A People's History of Ancient Rome.* New York: New Press, 2003.

Park, Eung Chun. *Either Jew or Gentile: Paul's Unfolding Theology of Inclusivity.* Louisville: Westminster John Knox 2003.

Peake, Arthur S. "The Quintessence of Paulinism." *Bulletin of the John Rylands Library* 4.2 (1918) 285–311.

Pearson, Birger A. "1 Thessalonians 2:13–16: A Deutero-Pauline Interpolation." *Harvard Theological Review* 64 (1971) 79–94.

————. "1 Thessalonians 2:13–16: A Deutero-Pauline Interpolation." In *The Emergence of the Christian Religion: Essays on Early Christianity,* 58–74. Harrisburg, PA: Trinity, 1997.

Perelman, Ch., and L. Olbrechts-Tyteca. *The New Rhetoric: A Treatise on Argumentation.* Translated by John Wilkinson and Purcell Weaver. Notre Dame: University of Notre Dame Press, 1965.

Peterson, Norman R. *Rediscovering Paul: Philemon and the Sociology of Paul's Narrative World.* 1985. Reprint, Eugene, OR: Wipf & Stock, 2008.

Petrella, Ivan. *Beyond Liberation Theology: A Polemic.* London: SCM, 2008.

Pew Research Center. "'Nones' on the Rise." October 9, 2012. https://www.pewresearch. org/religion/2012/10/09/nones-on-the-rise/.

Philo. *On Dreams.* Translated by F. H. Colson and G. H. Whitaker. In *The Works of Philo* 5:285–579. LCL. Cambridge: Harvard University Press, 1934.

————. *On the Embassy to Gaius.* Translated by F. H. Colson and J. W. Earp. In *Philo* 10:2–187. LCL. Cambridge: Harvard University Press, 1962.

————. *On the Special Laws.* Translated by F. H. Colson. In *Philo* 7:98–609. LCL. Cambridge: Harvard University Press, 1937.

————. *Philo.* Translated by F. H. Colson et al. 10 vols. LCL. Cambridge: Harvard University Press, 1927–1962.

Piketty, Thomas. *Capital in the Twenty-First Century*. Translated by Arthur Goldhammer. Cambridge: Belknap, 2014.

Pilkington, Ed. "Top UN Official in New York Steps Down Citing 'Genocide' of Palestinian Civilians." *Guardian,* October 31, 2023. https://www.theguardian.com/world/2023/oct/31/un-official-resigns-israel-hamas-war-palestine-new-york/.

Plaskow, Judith. "Anti-Judaism in Feminist Christian Interpretation." In *Searching the Scriptures*. Vol. 1: *A Feminist Introduction*, edited by Elisabeth Schüssler Fiorenza with the assistance of Shelly Matthews, 117–29. 2 vols. New York: Crossroad, 1993–1994.

Premawardhana, Shanta. "Greed as Violence: Methodological Challenges in Interreligious Dialogue on the Ethics of the Global Financial Crisis." *Journal of Religious Ethics* 39 (2011) 223–45.

Price, S. R. F. *Rituals and Power: The Roman Imperial Cult in Asia Minor*. Cambridge: Cambridge University Press, 1984.

Räisänen, Heikki. *Paul and the Law*. Philadelphia: Fortress, 1983.

Rasgon, Adam, and David D. Kirkpatrick. "What Was Hamas Thinking?" News Desk. *New Yorker*, October 13, 2023. https://www.newyorker.com/news/news-desk/what-was-hamas-thinking/.

Rasmussen, Larry. "Was Reinhold Niebuhr Wrong about Socialism?" *Political Theology* 6 (2005) 429–57.

Reasoner, Mark. *Romans in Full Circle: A History of Interpretation*. Louisville: Westminster John Knox, 2005.

———. *The "Strong" and the "Weak": Romans 14.1—15.13 in Context*. Society of New Testament Studies Monograph Series 103. Cambridge: Cambridge University Press, 1999.

Redding, Ann Holmes. "Together, Not Equal: The Rhetoric of Unity and Headship in the Letter to Ephesians." PhD diss., Union Theological Seminary, 1999.

Rehmann, Jan. *Einführung in die Ideologietheorie*. Hamburg: Argument, 2008.

———. "Ideology Theory." *Historical Materialism* 15 (2007) 211–39.

Rieger, Joerg. *No Rising Tide: Theology, Economics, and the Future*. Minneapolis: Fortress, 2009.

Robbins, Jeffrey W. "The Politics of Paul." *Journal for Cultural and Religious Theory* 6.2 (2005) 89–94.

———. *Radical Theology: A Vision for Change*. Indiana Series in the Philosophy of Religion. Bloomington: Indiana University Press, 2016.

Roberts, Alexander and James Donaldson, eds. *Ante-Nicene Fathers*. Vol. 2, *Fathers of the Second Century: Hermas, Tatian, Athenagoras, Theophilus, Clement of Alexandria*. 25 vols. Edinburgh: T. & T. Clark, 1875–1877.

Robinson, Randall. *An Unbroken Agony: Haiti, from Revolution to the Kidnapping of a President*. New York: Basic Books, 2007.

Romero, Oscar Arnulfo. *Voice of the Voiceless: The Four Pastoral Letters and Other Statements*. Translated by Michael J. Walsh. Maryknoll, NY: Orbis, 1985.

Rom-Shiloni, Dalit. "Hebrew Bible Theology: A Jewish Descriptive Approach." *Journal of Religion* 96 (2016) 165–84.

Rosen-Zvi, Ishay, and Adi Ophir. "Paul and the Invention of the Gentiles." *Jewish Quarterly Review* 105 (2015) 1–41.

Ruether, Rosemary Radford. *Faith and Fratricide: The Christian Roots of Anti-Semitism*. New York: Seabury, 1974.

Rutgers, Leonard Victor. "Roman Policy toward the Jews: Expulsions from the City of Rome during the First Century C.E." In *Judaism and Christianity in First-Century Rome*, edited by Karl P. Donfried and Peter Richardson, 93–116. Grand Rapids: Eerdmans, 1998.

Said, Edward. *Culture and Imperialism*. New York: Vintage, 1993.

Sanders, E. P. "Jewish Association with Gentiles and Galatians 2:11–14." In *The Conversation Continues: Studies in Paul & John in Honor of J. Louis Martyn*, edited by Robert Fortna and Beverly R. Gaventa, 170–88. Nashville: Abingdon, 1990.

———. *Jewish Law from Jesus to the Mishnah*. London: SCM, 1990.

———. *Paul and Palestinian Judaism: A Comparison of Patterns of Religion*. Philadelphia: Fortress, 1977.

———. *Paul, the Law, and the Jewish People*. Philadelphia: Fortress, 1983.

Schäfer, Peter. *Judeophobia: Attitudes toward the Jews in the Ancient World*. Cambridge: Harvard University Press, 1997.

Schaff, Philip, et al., eds. *Nicene and Post-Nicene Fathers*. Vol. 12, *Homilies on the Epistles of Paul to the Corinthians*, by John Chrysostom. Edited by Philip Schaff et al. Translated by Talbot W. Chambers. 14 vols. Edinburgh: T. & T. Clark, 1889.

———, eds. *Nicene and Post-Nicene Fathers*. Vol. 13, *Homilies on Galatians, Ephesians, Philippians, Colossians, Thessalonians, Timothy, Titus, and Philemon*, by John Chrysostom. Edited and translated by Philip Schaff. 14 vols. Edinburgh: T. & T. Clark, 1889.

Schmemann, Alexander. *For the Life of the World: Sacraments and Orthodoxy*. 2nd rev. and exp. ed. Crestwood, NY: St. Vladimir's Seminary Press, 1973.

Schmithals, W. *Der Römerbrief als historisches Problem. Studien zum Neuen Testament 8*. Gütersloh: Gütersloher, 1975.

Schneider, Tal. "For Years, Netanyahu Propped up Hamas: Now It's Blown up in Our Faces." *Times of Israel*, October 8, 2023. https://www.timesofisrael.com/for-years-netanyahu-propped-up-hamas-now-its-blown-up-in-our-faces/.

Schottroff, Luise. "'Give to Caesar What Belongs to Caesar and to God What Belongs to God': A Theological Response of the Early Christian Church to Its Social and Political Environment." In *The Love of Enemy and Nonretaliation in the New Testament*, edited by Willard M. Swartley, 223–57. Studies in Peace and Scripture 3. Louisville: Westminster John Knox, 1992.

———. "Holiness and Justice: Exegetical Comments on 1 Corinthians 11.17–34." Trans-lated by Brian McNeil. *JSNT* 23.79 (2001) 51–60.

———. "Human Solidarity and the Goodness of God: The Parable of the Workers in the Vineyard." In *God of the Lowly: Socio-historical Interpretations of the Bible*, edited by Willy Schottroff and Wolfgang Stegemann, 129–47 Translated by Matthew J. O'Connell. Maryknoll, NY: Orbis, 1984.

———. "'Not Many Powerful': Approaches to a Sociology of Early Christianity." In *Social-Scientific Approaches to New Testament Interpretation*, edited by David G. Horrell, 275–87. Edinburgh: T. & T. Clark, 1999.

———. *The Parables of Jesus*. Translated by Linda M. Maloney. Minneapolis: Fortress, 2006.

Schottroff, Luise, et al. *Feminist Interpretation: The Bible in Women's Perspective*. Translated by Martin and Barbara Rumscheidt. Minneapolis: Fortress, 1998.

Schürer, Emil. *The History of the Jewish People in the Age of Jesus Christ.* New English ed. by Geza Vermes, Fergus Millar, and Martin Goodman. 3 vols. Edinburgh: T. & T. Clark, 1973—1987.

Schüssler Fiorenza, Elisabeth. *But She Said: Feminist Practices of Biblical Interpretation.* Boston: Beacon, 1992.

———. *Democratizing Biblical Studies: Toward an Emancipatory Educational Space.* Louisville: Westminster John Knox, 2009.

———. "The Ethics of Biblical Interpretation." *JBL* 107 (1988) 3–17.

———. *In Memory of Her: A Feminist Theological Reconstruction of Christian Origins.* New York: Crossroad, 1983.

———. "Paul and the Politics of Interpretation." In *Paul and Politics: Ekklesia, Israel, Imperium, Interpretation,* edited by Richard A. Horsley, 40–57. Harrisburg, PA: Trinity, 2000.

———. *The Power of the Word: Scripture and the Rhetoric of Empire.* Minneapolis: Fortress, 2007.

———. *Rhetoric and Ethic: The Politics of Biblical Studies.* Minneapolis: Fortress, 1999.

———. "Rhetorical Situation and Historical Reconstruction in 1 Corinthians." *NTS* 33 (1987) 386–403.

Schweitzer, Albert. *The Mysticism of Paul the Apostle.* Translated by William Montgomery. London: Black, 1931.

Scott, James C. *Domination and the Arts of Resistance: Hidden Transcripts.* New Haven: Yale University Press, 1990.

———. "Protest and Profanation: Agrarian Revolt and the Little Tradition, Part I." *Theory and Society* 4.1 (1977) 1–38.

———. *Weapons of the Weak: Everyday Forms of Peasant Resistance.* New Haven: Yale University Press, 1985.

Sedgwick, Timothy F., and Philip Turner, eds. *The Crisis in Moral Teaching in the Episcopal Church.* Harrisburg, PA: Morehouse, 1992.

Segal, Alan F. *Paul the Convert: The Apostolate and Apostasy of Saul the Pharisee.* New Haven: Yale University Press, 1990.

———. "Universalism in Judaism and Christianity." In *Paul in His Hellenistic Context,* edited by Troels Engberg-Pedersen, 1–29. Minneapolis: Fortress, 1995.

Segovia, Fernando F. "Biblical Criticism and Postcolonial Studies: Toward a Postcolonial Optic." In *The Postcolonial Bible,* edited by R. S. Sugirtharajah, 49–65. The Bible and Postcolonialism. Sheffield: Sheffield Academic, 1998.

———. "Criticism in Critical Times: Reflections on Vision and Task." *JBL* 134 (2015) 6–29.

Segovia, Fernando F., and R. S. Sugirtharajah, eds. *A Postcolonial Commentary on the New Testament Writings.* The Bible and Postcolonialism. London: T. & T. Clark, 2007.

Segundo, Juan Luis. *The Humanist Christology of Paul.* Translated by John Drury. 1986. Reprint, Eugene, OR: Wipf & Stock, 2007.

———. *The Sacraments Today.* In collaboration with the staff of the Peter Faber Center in Montevideo, Uruguay. Translated by John Drury. 1974. Reprint, Eugene, OR: Wipf & Stock, 2005.

Seneca. *Moral Essays,* vol. 1. 3 vols. Translated by John W. Basore. LCL. Cambridge, MA: Harvard University Press, 1928.

Shedinger, Robert F. *Was Jesus a Muslim? Questioning Categories in the Study of Religion.* Minneapolis: Fortress, 2009.

Sirota, Dave. "Naomi Klein and Omar Baddar on the Gaza Onslaught." *TheLever.com*, October 18, 2023. https://www.levernews.com/live-event-tonight-naomi-klein-omar-baddar-on-the-gaza-onslaught/. Recording on YouTube: https://www.youtube.com/watch?v=2kNDOLX66oM/.

Slingerland, H. Dixon. *Claudian Policymaking and the Early Imperial Repression of Judaism at Rome.* South Florida Studies in the History of Judaism 160. Atlanta: Scholars, 1997.

Sobrino, Jon. *No Salvation outside the Poor: Prophetic-Utopian Essays.* Maryknoll, NY: Orbis, 2008.

Society for Post-Supersessionist Theology. "Supersessionism, Nations, and Race: Society for Post-Supersessionist Theology 2021 Annual Meeting." Panel discussion on Zoom, moderated by Holly Taylor Coolman and featuring Willie James Jennings, Daniel D. Lee, and Gerald R. McDermott. November 19, 2021. Recording on Youtube: https://www.youtube.com/watch?v=BDlFvKAGGTo/.

Spivak, Gayatri Chakravorty. *Outside in the Teaching Machine.* London: Routledge, 1993; Routledge Classics ed. 2009.

Spivey, Robert A., et al. *Anatomy of the New Testament: A Guide to Its Structure and Meaning.* 7th ed. Minneapolis: Fortress, 2013.

Stanley, Christopher, ed. *The Colonized Apostle: Paul through Postcolonial Eyes.* Paul in Critical Contexts. Minneapolis: Fortress, 2011.

———. "'Neither Jew Nor Greek': Ethnic Conflict in Graeco-Roman Society." *JSNT* 64 (1996) 101–24.

———, ed. *Paul and Scripture: Extending the Conversation.* Early Christianity and Its Literature 9. Atlanta: Society of Biblical Literature, 2012.

Stegemann, Ekkehard W. "Coexistence and Transformation: Reading the Politics of Identity in Romans in an Imperial Context." In *Reading Paul in Context*, edited by Kathy Ehrensperger and J. Brian Tucker, 3–23. Library of New Testament Studies 428. London: T. & T. Clark, 2010.

Stendahl, Krister. *A Final Account: Paul's Letter to the Romans.* With a foreword by Jaroslav Pelikan. 1st Fortress Press ed. Minneapolis: Fortress, 1995.

———. *Paul among Jews and Gentiles, and Other Essays.* Philadelphia: Fortress, 1976.

Stern, Menahem, ed. and trans. *Greek and Latin Authors on Jews and Judaism.* 3 vols. Jerusalem: Israel Academy of Sciences and Humanities, 1976–1984.

Still, Todd D., and David G. Horrell, eds. *After the First Urban Christians: The Social-Scientific Study of Pauline Christianity Twenty-Five Years Later.* London: Continuum, 2009.

Stowers, Stanley K. *The Diatribe and Paul's Letter to the Romans.* Society of Biblical Literature Dissertation Series 57. Chico, CA: Scholars, 1981.

———. *Letter-Writing in Greco-Roman Antiquity.* Library of Early Christianity 5. Philadelphia: Westminster, 1986.

———. *A Rereading of Romans: Gentiles, Jews, Justice.* New Haven: Yale University Press, 1994.

Stringfellow, William. *Conscience & Obedience: The Politics of Romans 13 and Revelation 13 in Light of the Second Coming.* Waco, TX: Word, 1977.

Strauss, David Friedrich. *The Life of Jesus Critically Examined.* 4th ed. Trans. George Eliot. London: Swan Sonnenschein, 1902.

Stubbs, Monya A. "Subjection, Reflection, Resistance: A Three-Dimensional Process of Empowerment in Romans 13 and the Free-Market Economy." *Society of Biblical Literature Seminar Papers* 135 (1999) 375–404.

Sutton, Matthew Avery. *American Apocalypse: A History of Modern Evangelicalism.* Cambridge: Belknap, 2014.

Sweeney, Marvin A. *Tanak: A Theological and Critical Introduction to the Jewish Bible.* Minneapolis: Fortress, 2012.

———, ed. *Theology of the Hebrew Bible.* Vol. 1, *Methodological Studies.* Atlanta: SBL Press, 2018.

Syndicate (website). Symposium on *The Christian Imagination: Theology and the Origins of Race,* by Willie James Jennings. July 2014. https://syndicate.network/symposia/theology/the-christian-imagination/.

Támez, Elsa. *The Amnesty of Grace: Justification by Faith from a Latin American Perspective.* Translated by Sharon H. Ringe. Nashville: Abingdon, 1991.

———. *Toda Condena: La Justificación por la Fe desde los Excluidos.* San José: Departmento Ecuménico de Investigaciones, Seminario Biblico Latinoamericano, 1991.

Taubes, Jacob. *The Politische Theologie des Paulus: Vorträge gehalten an der Forschungsstätte der evangelischen Studiengemeinschaft in Heidelberg, 23–27 Februar 1987.* Edited by A. Assman et al. Munich: Fink, 1995.

———. *The Political Theology of Paul.* Translated by Dana Hollander. Cultural Memory in the Present. Stanford: Stanford University Press, 2004.

Taussig, Hal. *In the Beginning Was the Meal: Social Experimentation and Early Christian Identity.* Minneapolis: Fortress, 2009.

Taylor, Mark Lewis. *The Theological and the Political: On the Weight of the World.* Minneapolis: Fortress, 2011.

Tharoor, Ishaan. "The Israeli Right Hopes not Just for Victory in Gaza, but for Conquest." Today's Worldview. *Washington Post,* November 17, 2023. https://www.washingtonpost.com/world/2023/11/17/israel-government-right-gaza-endgame-conquest/.

Theissen, Gerd. *Social Reality and the Early Christians: Theology, Ethics, and the World of the New Testament.* Translated by Margaret Kohl. Minneapolis: Fortress, 1992.

———. *The Social Setting of Pauline Christianity: Essays on Corinth.* Translated by John Schütz. Philadelphia: Fortress, 1982.

———. "The Social Structure of Pauline Communities: Some Critical Remarks on J. J. Meggitt, *Paul, Poverty and Survival.*" *JSNT* 24.2 (2001) 65–84.

Theoharis, Liz. "Reading the Bible with the Poor." *Kairos Center for Religion, Rights & Social Justice* (website), February 23, 2015. https://kairoscenter.org/reading-the-bible-with-the-poor/.

Therborn, Göran. *From Marxism to Post-Marxism?* London: Verso, 2008.

———. *The Killing Fields of Inequality.* Cambridge: Polity, 2013.

Theron, Daniel Johannes. *Evidence of Tradition.* Grand Rapids: Baker, 1958.

Tomson, Peter. *Paul and the Jewish Law: Halakha in the Letters of the Apostle to the Gentiles.* Compendia rerum Iudaicarum ad Novum Testamentum. Section 3, Jewish Traditions in Early Christian Literature 1. Minneapolis: Fortress, 1990.

Troeltsch, Ernst. *The Social Teaching of the Christian Churches.* German original 1912. Translated by Olive Wyon. London: Allen & Unwin, 1931.

Trouillot, Michel-Rolph. *Haiti, State against Nation: The Origins and Legacy of Duvalier-ism.* New York: Monthly Review Press, 1990.

United Nations, Human Rights Council. *Human Rights in Palestine and Other Occupied Arab Territories: Report of the United Nations Fact-Finding Mission on the Gaza Conflict.* New York: United Nations, 2009. Ebook.

Virgil. *Aeneid.* Translated by H. Rushton Fairclough and revised by G. Goold. LCL. London: Heinemann, 1918.

Wainwright, Geoffrey. *Eucharist and Eschatology.* London: Epworth, 1971.

Walker, Corey D. B. "Theology and Democratic Futures." *Political Theology* 10 (2009) 199–208.

Wallace-Hadrill, Andrew. "Patronage in Roman Society: From Republic to Empire." In *Patronage in Ancient Society,* edited by Andrew Wallace-Hadrill, 63–87. Leicester-Nottingham Studies in Ancient Society 1. London: Routledge, 1989.

Wallerstein, Immanuel. "New Revolts against the System." *New Left Review* 18 (Nov/Dec 2002) 29–39.

———. *Modern World-System IV: Centrist Liberalism Triumphant, 1789–1914.* Berkeley: University of California Press, 2011.

Walters, James C. *Ethnic Issues in Paul's Letter to the Romans.* Valley Forge, PA: Trinity, 1993.

———. "Romans, Jews, and Christians: The Impact of the Romans on Jewish/Christian Relations." In *Judaism and Christianity in First-Century Rome,* edited by Karl P. Donfried and Peter Richardson, 175–95. Grand Rapids: Eerdmans, 1998.

Wan, Sze-Kar. "Collection for the Saints as Anti-colonial Act." In *Paul and Politics: Ekklesia, Israel, Imperium, Interpretation,* edited by Richard A. Horsley, 191–215. Harrisburg, PA: Trinity, 2000.

Welborn, Larry L. *An End to Enmity: Paul and the "Wrongdoer" of Second Corinthians.* Beihefte zur Zeitschrift für die neutestamentliche Wissenschaft und die Kunde der älteren Kirche 185. Berlin: de Gruyter, 2011.

———. "Jacob Taubes—Paulinist, Messianist." In *Paul in the Grip of the Philosophers: The Apostle and Contemporary Continental Philosophy,* edited by Peter Frick, 69–90. Minneapolis: Fortress, 2013.

———. *Paul's Summons to Messianic Life: Political Theology and the Coming Awakening.* Insurrections: Critical Studies in Religion, Politics, and Culture. New York: Columbia University Press, 2015.

———. *That There May Be Equality: Paul's Appeal for Partnership in the Collection.* Paul in Critical Contexts. Lanham, MD: Lexington Books/Fortress Academic, 2023.

West, Gerald O. *The Academy of the Poor: Towards a Dialogical Reading of the Bible.* Interventions 2. Sheffield: Sheffield Academic, 1999.

———. "Disguising Defiance in Ritualisms of Subordination: Literary and Community-Based Resources for Recovering Resistance Discourse within the Dominant Discourses of the Bible." In *Reading Communities, Reading Scripture: Essays in Honor of Daniel Patte,* edited by Gary A. Phillips and Nicole Wilkinson Duran, 194–217. Harrisburg, PA: Trinity, 2002.

Wilcox, Max. "Mammon." In *The Anchor Bible Dictionary,* edited by David Noel Freedman, 4:490. 6 vols. New York: Doubleday, 1992.

Wilentz, Amy. *The Rainy Season: Haiti since Duvalier.* New York: Simon & Schuster, 1989.

Williams, James G. *The Bible, Violence, and the Sacred: Liberation from the Myth of Sanctioned Violence.* With a foreword by René Girard. Valley Forge, PA: Trinity, 1995.

Williamson, Lucy. "Israel, Gaza: Hamas Raped and Mutilated Women on 7 October, BBC Hears." *BBC.com,* December 5, 2023. https://www.bbc.com/news/world-middle-east-67629181/.

Wintour, Patrick. "Jared Kushner says 'Gaza waterfront property could be very valuable.'" *Guardian,* March 19, 2024. https://www.theguardian.com/us-news/2024/mar/19/jared-kushner-gaza-waterfront-property-israel-negev/.

Wire, Antoinette Clark. *The Corinthian Women Prophets: A Reconstruction through Paul's Rhetoric.* 1990. Reprint, Eugene, OR: Wipf & Stock, 2003.

———. "Performance, Politics, and Power: A Response." *Semeia* 65 (1994) 129.

Witherington, Ben, III. Review of *The Arrogance of Nations,* by Neil Elliott. *Review of Biblical Literature* 3 (2009). https://www.sblcentral.org/API/Reviews/6481_7367.pdf/.

Witherington, Ben, III, with Darlene Hyatt. *Paul's Letter to the Romans: A Sociorhetorical. Commentary.* Grand Rapids: Eerdmans, 2004.

Woolf, Greg. "Becoming Roman, Staying Greek: Culture, Identity and the Civilizing Process in the Roman East." *Cambridge Classical Journal* 40 (1994) 116–43.

———. "Beyond Romans and Natives." *World Archaeology* 28 (1997) 339–50.

———. "Writing Poverty in Rome." In *Poverty in the Roman World*, edited by Margaret Atkins and Robin Osborne, 83–99. Cambridge: Cambridge University Press, 2006.

Wrede, William. *Paul.* Translated by Edward Lummis. 1908. Reprint, Eugene, OR: Wipf & Stock, 2001.

Wright, N. T. *Paul and His Recent Interpreters.* Minneapolis: Fortress, 2015.

———. *Paul and the Faithfulness of God,* Parts I and II. Christian Origins and the Question of God 4. Minneapolis: Fortress, 2013.

———. *Paul in Fresh Perspective.* Minneapolis: Fortress, 2005.

———. "Paul's Gospel and Caesar's Empire." In *Paul and Politics: Ekklesia, Israel, Imperium, Interpretation*, edited by Richard A. Horsley, 160–83. Harrisburg, PA: Trinity, 2000.

———. "Romans in the Theology of Paul." In *Pauline Theology III: Romans*, edited by David M. Hay and E. Elizabeth Johnson 62–75. Minneapolis: Fortress, 1993.

Wylie-Kellermann, Bill. *Seasons of Faith and Conscience: Kairos, Confession, Liturgy.* Maryknoll, NY: Orbis, 1991.

Yee, Gale A. "Ideological Criticism: Judges 17–21 and the Dismembered Body." In *Judges and Method: New Approaches in Biblical Studies*, edited by Gale A. Yee, 146–70. Minneapolis: Fortress, 1995.

———. *Poor Banished Children of Eve: Woman as Evil in the Hebrew Bible.* Minneapolis: Fortress, 2003.

Zanker, Paul. *The Power of Images in the Age of Augustus.* Translated by Alan Shapiro. Ann Arbor: University of Michigan Press, 1988.

Zetterholm, Magnus. *Approaches to Paul: A Student's Guide to Contemporary Scholarship.* Minneapolis: Fortress, 2009.

Zimmerman, Jens. "Hermeneutics of Unbelief: Philosophical Readings of Paul." In *Paul, Philosophy, and the Theopolitical Vision*, edited by Douglas Harink, 227–53. Theopolitical Visions 7. Eugene, OR: Cascade Books, 2010.

Zinn, Howard. *A People's History of the United States*. 35th ann. ed. Harper Perennial Modern Classics New York: Harper Perennial, 2015.

Žižek, Slavoj. *The Fragile Absolute, Or, Why Is the Christian Legacy Worth Fighting For?* Wo Es War. London: Verso, 2000.

———. "How to Begin from the Beginning." In *The Idea of Communism*, edited by Costas Douzinas and Slavoj Žižek, 209–26. London: Verso, 2010.

———. *In Defense of Lost Causes*. London: Verso, 2008.

———. *Living in the End Times*. London: Verso, 2010.

———. "Meditation on Michelangelo's *Christ on the Cross*." *SPECS Journal of Art and Culture* 1.1 (2008) article 42, 122–33.

———. *The Puppet and the Dwarf: The Perverse Core of Christianity*. Short Circuits. Cambridge: MIT Press, 2003.

———. *The Year of Dreaming Dangerously*. London: Verso, 2012.

Žižek, Slavoj, and John Milbank. *The Monstrosity of Christ: Paradox or Dialectic?* Edited by Creston Davis. Short Circuits. Cambridge: MIT Press, 2009.

Zizioulas, John D. *The Eucharistic Communion and the World*. Edited by Luke Ben Tallon. London: T. & T. Clark, 2011.

Ancient Document Index

Author Index

Printed in Great Britain
by Amazon

48765099R00169